'This updated edition of *The State* explores ⟨
on the idea of the state, the state apparatus, tl.
social bases, whilst also critically engaging with its fundamental features like
sovereignty, security, business, territory, nationhood, and populism. The result
is a comprehensive and nuanced review of historical, theoretical and empirical
themes on state power, relevant to key issues past and present.'

Bob Jessop, Professor Emeritus, Lancaster University, UK

'Recent events like the Covid-19 pandemic underline the importance of the state
in contemporary politics. This text, drawing on the expertise of leading scholars,
is an authoritative and indispensable source for understanding the theoretical
debates and key issues in the study of the modern state.'

Andrew Gamble, Professor of Politics, University of Sheffield, UK

'A revised edition of this classic text has been long overdue and the editors and
authors have not let us down. *The State* sheds new and penetrating light on a
concept we all use, but struggle to pin down. It will be a welcome resource for
students and scholars alike.'

Jack Corbett, Professor of Politics, University of Southampton, UK

'Any political scientist cannot help but reflect on the concept of the state. This
volume does an excellent job of introducing the major perspectives on, and
discussions of, the state with the help of chapters written by leading political
scientists. I strongly recommend it.'

Marco Verweij, Professor of Political Science, Jacobs University
Bremen, Germany

Political Analysis

The *Political Analysis* series provides a showcase for political science in all its variety and a channel for political scientists in different specialisms and different parts of the world to talk to each other and to new generations of students. Written in an accessible style, books in the series provide introductions to, and exemplars of, the best work in the discipline and its various subareas.

Published

Jon Pierre and B. Guy Peters
Governance, Politics and the State (2nd edition)

Johanna Kantola and Emanuela Lombardo
Gender and Political Analysis

Vivien Lowndes, David Marsh and Gerry Stoker (eds)
Theory and Methods in Political Science (4th edition)

Dimiter Toshkov
Research Design in Political Science

Keith Dowding
The Philosophy and Methods of Political Science

Andrew Hindmoor and Brad Taylor
Rational Choice (2nd edition)

Gerry Stoker, B. Guy Peters and Jon Pierre (eds)
The Relevance of Political Science

Jean Grugel and Matthew Louis Bishop
Democratization: A Critical Introduction (2nd edition)

David Beetham
The Legitimation of Power (2nd edition)

B. Guy Peters
Strategies for Comparative Research in Political Science

Ioannis Papadopoulos
Democracy in Crisis? Politics, Governance and Policy

Vivien Lowndes and Mark Roberts
Why Institutions Matter: The New Institutionalism in Political Science

Lina Eriksson
Rational Choice Theory: Potential and Limits

Heather Savigny and Lee Marsden
Doing Political Science and International Relations: Theories in Action

Rudra Sil and Peter J. Katzenstein
Beyond Paradigms: Analytic Eclecticism in the Study of World Politics

Cees van der Eijk and Mark Franklin
Elections and Voters

Martin J. Smith
Power and the State

Peter Burnham, Karin Gilland Lutz, Wyn Grant and Zig Layton-Henry
Research Methods in Politics (2nd edition)

Colin Hay
Political Analysis: A Critical Introduction

The State

Theories and Issues

Second Edition

**Edited by
Colin Hay
Michael Lister
David Marsh**

BLOOMSBURY ACADEMIC
LONDON • NEW YORK • OXFORD • NEW DELHI • SYDNEY

BLOOMSBURY ACADEMIC
Bloomsbury Publishing Plc
50 Bedford Square, London, WC1B 3DP, UK
1385 Broadway, New York, NY 10018, USA
29 Earlsfort Terrace, Dublin 2, Ireland

BLOOMSBURY, BLOOMSBURY ACADEMIC and the Diana logo are
trademarks of Bloomsbury Publishing Plc

First published in Great Britain 2005
This edition published 2022

A catalogue record for this book is available from the British Library.

Library of Congress Cataloging-in-Publication Data
Names: Hay, Colin, editor. | Lister, Michael, editor. | Marsh, David, editor.
Title: The state: theories and issues / edited by Colin Hay,
Michael Lister, David Marsh.
Description: 2nd Edition. | New York: Bloomsbury Publishing Plc, 2022. |
Series: The Political Analysis series|
| Includes bibliographical references and index. |
Identifiers: LCCN 2022002196 | ISBN 9781350328303 (Hardback) | ISBN
9781350328310 (Paperback) | ISBN 9781350328297 (pdf) | ISBN
9781350328327 (epub) | ISBN 9781350328334 (XML)
Subjects: LCSH: State, The. | State, The–History–20th century.
Classification: LCC JC131.S82 2022 | DDC 320.1–dc23/eng/20220419
LC record available at https://lccn.loc.gov/2022002196

ISBN: HB: 978-1-3503-2830-3
        PB: 978-1-3503-2831-0
        ePDF: 978-1-3503-2829-7
        eBook: 978-1-3503-2832-7

Political Analysis Series

Typeset by Integra Software Services Pvt. Ltd.
Printed and bound in Great Britain

To find out more about our authors and books visit www.bloomsbury.com
and sign up for our newsletters.

For Florence, Ailsa and Ian,
Jessica and Thomas

Table of Contents

List of Figures and Tables

Figures

Tables

Acknowledgements

The first edition of *The State* was conceived whilst we were all at the University of Birmingham. Since that time, we have flown to pastures and/or continents new. This second edition, which builds upon, updates and extends the first edition therefore owes a wider debt of gratitude. To former colleagues at the University of Birmingham, we must add colleagues at Sciences Po, the University of Sheffield, Oxford Brookes University, the Australian National University and the University of Canberra – for support, inspiration, good humour and encouragement, all of which have helped the completion of this volume.

The book also has a wide range of editorial staff to thank. From Steven Kennedy who first suggested the idea of a second edition, through to Stephen Wenham, Lloyd Langman, Milly Weaver and Becky Mutton who helped us bring it ever closer to fruition. Each has shown enthusiasm and patience (the latter in particular demand as we struggled to complete the volume in the midst of the pandemic). We are also immensely grateful to Liz Holmes, Joanne Rippin and Virginia Rounding for their diligence and skill in and through the production process. We would also like to thank series editors Vivien Lowndes and Gerry Stoker, and the anonymous reviewers who provided insight and helpful suggestions. As always, any shortcomings remain our own.

List of Contributors

Pinar Bilgin is a Professor of International Relations and Head of Department of Political Science and Public Administration at Bilkent University. She is the author of *Regional Security in the Middle East: A Critical Perspective* (2005, 2019, 2nd edn), *The International in Security, Security in the International* (2016), and co-editor of the *Routledge Handbook of International Political Sociology* (with Xavier Guillaume, 2017), *Asia in International Relations: Unthinking Imperial Power Relations* (with L.H.M. Ling, 2017). She specializes in critical approaches to security.

William Bosworth is a Lecturer in the School of Politics and International Relations at the Australian National University. His research covers the field of Philosophy, Politics, and Economics (PPE), broadly construed. He has published in journals such as *Journal of Politics, Journal of Theoretical Politics, European Journal of Political Theory* and the *Review of Politics*. He was previously the LSE Fellow in Political Theory at the London School of Economics.

Chris Brown is Emeritus Professor of International Relations at the LSE, and the author of *International Society, Global Politics* (2015), *Practical Judgement in International Political Theory* (2010), *Sovereignty, Rights and Justice* (2002) and co-editor (with Terry Nardin and N.J. Rengger) of *International Relations in Political Thought* (2002) and (with Robyn Eckersley) of *The Oxford Handbook of International Political Theory* (2018). His textbook *Understanding International Relations* (2019) is now in its 5th edition. *The Politics of International Political Theory: Reflections on the Work of Chris Brown* (2018) edited by Mathias Albert and Anthony F. Lang Jr examines his work.

Daniel Cetrà is a Beatriu de Pinós postdoctoral researcher at the Institutions and Political Economy Research Group (IPERG), University of Barcelona. He specializes in the study of nationalism, the politics of language and comparative territorial politics. He is the author of *Nationalism, Liberalism* *and Language in Catalonia and Flanders* (2019). He has also published extensively in journals, including the *Journal of Common Market Studies* and *Territory, Politics, Governance*.

Mark Evans is Deputy Vice Chancellor (Research) at Charles Sturt University. He has played an international role in changing governance practices, acted as a senior policy advisor, and managed research and evaluation projects for the European Union, United Nations and the World Bank. His latest book with Gerry Stoker is *Saving Democracy* (Bloomsbury, 2022).

Alan Finlayson is Professor of Political and Social Theory at the University of East Anglia. His research combines contributions to the development of democratic political and cultural theory with the theoretical and historical analysis and interpretation of political ideologies and political rhetoric. His research has been funded by the Leverhulme Trust, and the AHRC. Publications include *Rhetoric in British Politics and Society* (edited with J. Atkins, J. Martin and N. Turnbull), *Democracy and Pluralism: The Political Thought of William E. Connolly* (ed.); *Contemporary Political Theory: A Reader and Guide; Making Sense of New Labour*, and articles in a wide range of journals.

Colin Hay is Professor and Director of Doctoral Studies in Political Sciences at Sciences Po, Paris and founding Director of the Sheffield Political Economy Research Institute (SPERI) at the University of Sheffield. He is lead editor of *New Political Economy* and founding co-editor of *Comparative European Politics* and *British Politics*. He is a Fellow of the UK Academy of Social Science and, until recently, President of the European University Institute's Research Council.

Roger Hildingsson is a Senior Researcher in Political Science at Lund University, Sweden, holding a PhD on the role of the state in the new politics of climate change (2014). His research focuses on environmental politics, climate governance and urban sustainability, with a particular interest in green state theory and the capacities of the (environmental) state to govern post-fossil transitions and industrial decarbonization, which he has published in numerous books and articles.

Rhys Jones is Professor of Political Geography and a former Head of Department of Geography and Earth Sciences at Aberystwyth University.

His research focuses on geographies of the state and nationalism in historic and contemporary contexts. More recently, his research has examined the growing public policy engagement with behavioural insights and well-being in many states across the world.

Johanna Kantola is Professor of Gender Studies in the Faculty of Social Sciences at the University of Tampere. She is the director of the ERC Consolidator Grant (2018–2023) funded research project *Gender, Party Politics and Democracy in Europe: A Study of European Parliament's Party Groups* (EUGenDem). Her books include *Gender and Political Analysis* (with Emanuela Lombardo, 2017), *Gender and the European Union* (2010) and *Feminists Theorize the State* (2006). She is the editor of Palgrave Macmillan's Gender and Politics Book Series with Sarah Childs.

Annica Kronsell, Professor and Chair of Environmental Social Science at the School of Global Studies, Gothenburg University, is interested in how public state institutions can govern climate and environmental issues, as in the edited book *Rethinking the Green State: Environmental Governance towards Environmental and Sustainability Transitions*, co-authored with Karin Bäckstrand (2015). She also applies feminist theory to study power, inequities and inequalities in climate governance and institutions, approached in the edited *Gender, Intersectionality and Climate Institutions in Industrialized States*, co-authored with Magnusdottír (2021).

Mikko Kuisma is a Lecturer in Comparative Public Policy at the University of Tübingen. His research interests lie in comparative welfare states, especially the role of ideas and discourses in social policy, populist radical right parties and welfare chauvinism, and the future of European social democracy. His work has appeared in, amongst others, *West European Politics*, *New Political Economy*, *Public Administration*, *Policy and Society*, *Critical Social Policy* and *Critical Policy Studies*.

Michael Lister is Reader in Politics at Oxford Brookes University. His research focuses on the nature and significance of citizen attitudes and behaviours, with particular relevance to security and counter-terrorism policy. He is author of *Public Opinion and Counter Terrorism* (forthcoming), co-author of *Anti-Terrorism, Citizenship and Security* (with Lee Jarvis, 2015) and has published articles in a wide range of journals.

Nicola McEwen is Professor of Territorial Politics at the University of Edinburgh and Senior Research Fellow with the ESRC UK in a Changing Europe. She was founding Co-Director of the Centre on Constitutional Change. Nicola specializes in nationalism, devolution and intergovernmental relations, with a focus on Scotland and the UK in comparative perspective. Her current research examines the impact of Brexit on UK devolution, intergovernmental relations and the Union. She is actively involved in informing the policy process and public debate, through media work, public engagement, and advice and support to parliamentarians and governments.

David Marsh is Emeritus Professor in the Institute of Governance and Policy Analysis at the University of Canberra, Australia. He is the author or editor of 10 books and over 100 articles. For his sins he is a Bristol Rovers supporter.

James Martin is Professor of Politics at Goldsmiths, University of London. He has published work on figures such as Gramsci, Poulantzas, Marx, and Post-Marxist political theory, and explored approaches to ideology, discourse and rhetoric in political analysis. He has been a co-editor of the journal *Contemporary Political Theory*. His most recent book is *Hegemony* (2022).

Vivien A. Schmidt is Jean Monnet Professor of European Integration in the Pardee School at Boston University and Honorary Professor at LUISS University. Her latest book *Europe's Crisis of Legitimacy: Governing by Rules and Ruling by Numbers in the Eurozone* (2020) received the Best Book Award (2021) of the Ideas, Knowledge and Politics section of the American Political Science Association and Honorable Mention for the Best Book Award (2022) of the European Union Studies Association. She was recently named a *Chevalier* in the French Legion of Honour, received the European Union Studies Association's Lifetime Achievement Award, and was granted a Guggenheim Foundation Fellowship for her current project on the 'rhetoric of discontent,' a transatlantic investigation of populism.

Martin J. Smith is Anniversary Professor of Politics at the University of York where he has served as Head of Department and Pro-Vice Chancellor. He was previously Professor of Politics and Head of Department at the University of Sheffield. He has published widely on British politics, party politics, public policy and the changing nature of state power. His recent research has focused on the fragmented nature of governance and local level and he is currently co-investigator on a project funded by The Nuffield Foundation examining the effectiveness of Treasury control in a fragmented governance system.

Brad R. Taylor is Senior Lecturer in Economics and Political Economy at the University of Southern Queensland. He works in the areas of public choice theory, analytic political theory and political epistemology. His work has been published in journals such as *Journal of Politics*, *New Political Economy* and *Constitutional Political Economy*.

Introduction

Colin Hay and Michael Lister

No concept is more central to political discourse and political analysis than that of the state. Yet, while we all tend to think we know what we're talking about when we refer to the state, it is a notoriously difficult concept to define. Since the seventeenth century, when the term was first widely deployed, the concept of the state has been heavily contested (Skinner 1989; Viroli 1992). It remains so today. The state has meant, and continues to mean, a great variety of different things to a great variety of authors from a great variety of perspectives. Part of the aim of this volume is to look at family resemblances in those understandings of the state, in the hope that we might begin to piece together a more coherent picture of *what this state is* and, indeed, *how it is developing.* Yet that is no easy task, for whatever family resemblances we might discern are unlikely to hide the very considerable variations between contending accounts both of what the state is and of the trajectory of its development. We should then, from the outset, expect diversity.

Yet whether depicted as an overbearing apparatus of patriarchal oppression or as the very condition of social and political freedom, as an 'ideal collective capitalist' or a fetter on the self-regulating capacity of the market, few commentators would disagree that the concept of the state is fundamental to social, political and economic analysis. The state, for better or worse: offers to vaccinate us against Covid-19; mobilizes populations in defence of its realm; regulates, monitors and polices conduct within civil society; intervenes (whether we think we like it or not) within the economy; and regulates (and in some instances controls) the flow of information within the public sphere, to detail merely some of its more obvious activities. Few then would deny the ubiquity or pervasiveness of the influence of the state within modern societies.

Or so we might imagine. For in recent years the very relevance of the concept of the state has been increasingly questioned. In an era of globalization and of complex interdependence among nations it is often argued that the influence of the state (certainly in its incarnation as a nation-state) is waning, its very form and function under challenge. A second aim of the present volume is to review this influential if arguably rather blunt and premature proposition. Indeed, stated most simply, our ambition is to survey the range and diversity of theoretical and conceptual resources within the pantheon of state theory for the analysis of the developmental paths and trajectories of the contemporary state. It is important, before so doing, however, that we put to one side a few contagious myths and popular fictions.

Though the state almost certainly accounts for a higher aggregate share of global GDP than ever before in its history, it attracts considerably less attention than twenty or even 40 years ago when that share was considerably smaller. It is frequently suggested that the share of GDP devoted to state-like activities in OECD countries has fallen somewhat since the early 1990s. But, as Figure 0.1 shows clearly: (a) that fall proved far less pronounced than many commentators suggested; (b) it pre-dates the global financial crisis and the Covid pandemic; and (c) both those events have taken state expenditure as a share of GDP, even in the OECD, to previously unprecedented levels.

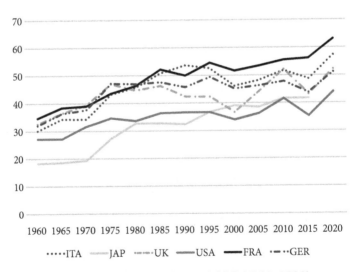

Figure 0.1 State expenditure as a share of GDP (1960–2020)
Source: Eurostat and OECD *Economic Outlook* (various years)

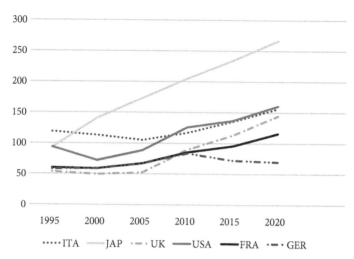

Figure 0.2 General government debt as a share of GDP (1995–2020)
Source: OECD *Economic Outlook* (various years)

Rather more accurate, it would seem then, is that the rate of increase of state expenditure lessened during the 1990s and has accelerated since. But arguably even that tells only part of the story. For this is not just about state spending per se. As Figure 0.2 shows very clearly, government debt has been expanding at the same time. In crisis, it seems, we have turned back to the state, with substantial increases in the level of public debt in the wake of the global financial crisis and during the Covid crisis.

We might well be more sceptical and less trusting of the state than ever; but, if anything, the early twenty-first century has reinforced and consolidated the role of the state as the public good provider of last resort. In the context of contagion on a potentially planetary scale, whether financial or viral, the only entity capable of bailing out the economy and of securing the continued supply of public goods, it turns out, is the very state we have come to distrust so much.

As this suggests, while intellectual interest in the state may have waxed and waned, the state is a constant – and, if anything, growing – presence at the heart of contemporary politics. This makes its seeming disappearance from the political analyst's radar since the 1990s somewhat difficult to explain. The result is that the theory of the state, once a raging torrent, is now little more than a trickle, an intellectual backwater traversed only by hardened theorists. A 'return to the state', by no means the first (see, for instance, Evans et al. 1985), is now long overdue; and, as many of the chapters in this volume make clear, the beginnings of such a return may just about be discerned in a number of contemporary developments from a diverse range of theoretical perspectives. Indeed, as the following chapters attest, the intellectual resources to sustain and animate such a 'bringing back in' of the state are today rather greater than they were when the first edition was published nearly two decades ago.

It would be presumptuous to think that a volume such as this might contribute in all but the most meagre of ways to such a 'return to the state'. What it can hope to offer, however, is something of a stock-taking exercise. If the continued centrality of the state to contemporary political life is to be acknowledged and reflected in the accounts of political dynamics offered by contemporary political analysts (as we think it should), then it is crucial that we deploy the range and diversity of theoretical resources at our disposal to interrogate the state, particularly at a moment when our reliance upon it seems greater than ever. That is the more modest aim of this volume.

In this relatively brief introductory chapter we examine first the emergence and development of the distinctive concept of the modern state in European political thought. We then turn to the still considerable influence of the Weberian approach to, and definition of, the state in more contemporary state theory. We show how the Weberian understanding of the state continues to exert a powerful influence on the traditional triumvirate of state theories – pluralism, elite theory and Marxism. We turn next to the challenge posed to the ascendancy of this mainstream conception of the state presented by Foucauldian, discourse-analytical and, above all, feminist perspectives. We conclude by considering the prospects for the state, and for the theory of the state, that in an era of globalization and neoliberal retrenchment have been called into question by the crises in and through which we now acknowledge ourselves to be living.

Defining the state

Introductions to the state tend, unremarkably, to begin by addressing the question of definition. All too frequently, however, they fall short of providing an answer. The importance of defining the state is all the greater given that, as Dunleavy and O'Leary note, the state is not a material object but a conceptual abstraction (1987: 1; see also Hay 2014). As such, its utility as a concept cannot and should not be taken for granted since it does not have a self-evident material object of reference. Its utility must be demonstrated; and in order to demonstrate that utility we must first be clear about what we are referring to.

That may sound fine in principle, yet the question of definition raises particular problems for a theoretically pluralistic volume such as this. Indeed, it is sorely tempting in a volume which makes something of a virtue of the diversity of theoretical resources we have on offer to interrogate the role of the state today to suggest that this is a question for each distinct approach to the state – and to leave it at that. And as already indicated and at the risk of sounding trite, the state does indeed mean a variety of different things from a variety of different perspectives.

Yet we cannot quite leave it at that. For while the state may, and indeed does, mean different things to different authors, the commonality between seemingly diverse definitions should not be overlooked – and cannot be allowed to provide an excuse for a failure to consider the ontology of the state – what the state *is*. In order to help us achieve this, and to offer some historical context for the chapters which follow, we consider first the genealogy of the concept of the state before turning to by far the most influential definition of the modern state – that offered by Weber.

Before doing so, however, it is first important to say something about the development of the modern state itself – or, at least, the development of the political institutions now generally held to characterize the modern state (for a far more extensive treatment see Gill 2003). For, unremarkably, our conception of the state has not developed in isolation from the development of the institutions we associate with the state. We cannot consider one without the other.

The development of the modern state

As John A. Hall and G. John Ikenberry note in their useful introduction to the term, 'most of human history has not been graced by the presence of states' (1989: 16). This is undoubtedly the case. Moreover, while the term has been used retrospectively to refer to mechanisms and processes of political governance arising in Mesopotamia as early as 3000 BCE, it is only since the seventeenth century that human history has been graced by the concept of the state. According to most conventional accounts, the origins of the state lie in the transition from the nomadic subsistence of hunter-gatherers to more agrarian societies characterized, increasingly, by organized agriculture (Hall 1986; Mann 1988; Sahlins 1974). Indeed, it was the relative geographical immobility of agricultural production that led to the development of the institutions and infrastructure capable of governing and projecting power, albeit at first in a rather diffuse way, over a specific and delineated territory. As Hall and Ikenberry again note, 'irrigation works – and date and olive trees – tie agricultural producers very firmly to the land, and thus make them better fodder for the state' (1989: 18). In this way the institutional capacity to project power over a territory which we now associate with the state owes its origins to the historical accident of the replacement, first in Mesopotamia, Meso-America, the Indus river valley, China and Peru and then more generally, of hunter-gathering by agriculture *in situ*.

In these initial stages of its development, the state was largely despotic and coercive in the manner in which it exercised power over a population. And it is in this context that a second key factor becomes important – religion. Hunter-gatherer communities tended to be tribal – with forms of association based on kinship ties. The agrarian states which replaced them were not. This made them both rather more reliant upon coercion and, in the absence of strong kinship relations amongst their members, rather more fragile politically when that coercion was challenged. In this context, as Patricia Crone (1989) demonstrates, it was the capacity of religion to lend legitimacy to the organized and increasingly centralized use of coercive power (through the appeal to divine authority) that made possible, where otherwise it might not have been, the consolidation of state power. This, in turn, facilitated the further development of the institutional capacity to govern and regulate a geographical territory and, with it, the capacity to mobilize militarily. The association between the state and military might was, then, established early on and arguably persists to the present day. Conquest rapidly became the primary mechanism through which the institutional form of the state became diffused, since the organizational capacity which the state developed conferred upon it a competitive advantage when it confronted pre-state-like societies.

If the origins of the state itself lie in Mesopotamia, then it is to Western Europe that we must turn if we are to establish the origins of the modern state. What is invariably taken to characterize the modern state is the simultaneous combination of, on the one hand, its claim to act as a public power responsible for the governance of a tightly delineated geographical territory and, on the other, its separation from those in whose name it claims to govern. The modern state is, then, an institutional complex claiming sovereignty for itself as the supreme political authority within a defined territory whose governance it claims and for which it is held responsible.

The factors that made possible the development of such an institutional form in Western Europe were, again, both complex and bound up with the role of religious authority. And once again the process was a highly contingent one. It was the church, in particular, that challenged the authority of imperial Rome. The result was a previously unprecedented degree of cultural homogeneity, as an initially unlikely synthesis of Christian doctrine, on the one hand, and the strong legal residue which carried over from the Roman Empire, on the other, which facilitated both the development of consensual trading relations throughout the European economy and the diffusion of the institutional template of the modern state. This in turn resulted in the birth of the so-called absolutist state in the sixteenth and seventeenth centuries in Bourbon France, Habsburg Spain and Tudor England. These were the precursors for the institutional complex we now recognize as the state. It in turn came to be characterized by a centralized bureaucracy and tax-raising capacity, a standing army, a system of diplomatic relations with other states and, for the most part, clearly delineated and commonly accepted territorial borders.

It is, once again, to Western Europe that the origins of the most recent phase of significant state restructuring and expansion can be traced. This bout of institutional dynamism, largely confined to the most developed economies and occurring in many cases in the immediate wake of the Second World War, is associated with the rise of the welfare state. It has seen the creation of the most extensive state regimes that the world has ever seen. As we saw in Figure 0.1 these welfare states account, in many cases, for in excess of 50 per cent of GDP; and they typically employ 10–20 per cent of the total workforce (Hay 2021). They represent, at least to date, the highest point in the development of the institutional capacity of the state. Whether they are increasingly anachronistic and a burden on economic growth and prosperity in an ever more closed integrated world economy is a source of very significant debate and a key theme of this volume. Suffice it for now to say that, despite the now customary hyperbole, there would seem to be little evidence to date of their ongoing or imminent demise. Sub-optimal as institutions of governance in an era of global interconnectedness though they may well be, thus far they have proved remarkably resilient. Though it might not be difficult to imagine more effective means of governing ourselves, given the typically planetary character of challenges we now face, rumours of the demise of the state appear, to date at least, ill-founded.

The genealogy of the concept of the state

Having considered the institutional origins and development of the state, we are now better placed to consider and contextualize the development of the concept of the state. Etymologically, the notion of the state is derived from the Latin *status*, meaning literally social status, stature or standing, specifically of an individual within a community. By the fourteenth century the use of the term to refer to the standing or status (indeed to the 'stateliness') of rulers, distinguishing and setting them apart from those subject to their rule, was commonplace. In the idea that the state resides in the body of the ruler, indeed that the state and the 'sovereign' are synonymous, this was a characteristically pre-modern formulation (Shennan 1974; Skinner 1989).

The development of a distinctively modern conception of the state would take a further three centuries – and its development would parallel the emergence of the institutional complex described above as the absolutist state. A first step was taken by the authors of the so-called 'mirror-for-princes' writings, most famously Machiavelli in his *Il Principe* (The Prince). In this literature, the state (*lo stato*) now became synonymous not only with the prince himself, but with the character of the political regime, the geographical area over which sovereign authority was claimed and maintained, and the very institutions of government required to preserve such authority (1988).

A second development came with the republican political theory of the Renaissance (see Skinner 1978; Viroli 1992). This movement championed the cause of a self-governing republican regime that might inaugurate a 'state' or condition of civic liberty — in Dante's terms *lo stato franco*. Here, at last, we see the emergence of a conception of an autonomous civil and political authority regulating the public affairs of an independent community or 'commonwealth'. The state is here presented as claiming and enjoying a monopoly over the legitimate use of violence, and as deriving the authority for this claim not from the power or stature of its ruler(s), but from the people themselves. The state is here referred to for the first time as a distinct apparatus of government which rulers have a duty to maintain and which will outlast their rule, as opposed to an extension of the ruler's innate authority.

The final step came with the rise of the absolutist state in Europe in the seventeenth century. Here, in particular in the writings of Bodin and Hobbes, the state is eventually conceptualized as truly separate from the powers of the ruler and the ruled. Three aspects of this formulation set it apart as a distinctively modern conception of the state: (i) individuals within society are presented as subjects of the state, owing duties and their allegiance not to the person of a ruler but to the state itself; (ii) the authority of the state is singular and absolute; and (iii) the state is regarded as the highest form of authority in all matters of civil government (Skinner 1989: 90). Hobbes's *Leviathan* (1968), and the rise of the absolutist state which this work reflects, marks the end of the pre-modern conception of the state in which political power is understood in personal and charismatic terms. The state now comes to be seen as a distinct form of authority, independent of those who give effect to its power.

The Weberian definition of the modern state

It is this modern conception of the state that still dominates contemporary state theory. Indeed, the definition of the state most often accorded the status of *the* definition – the Weberian one – displays considerable similarities with that of Hobbes. Weber, as is often noted, defined the state not in terms of its function but in terms of its *modus operandi*. More specifically, he saw the state in terms of its organization and deployment of the means of coercion and physical force. As he explained, 'a compulsory political organization with continuous operations will be called a "state" insofar as its administrative staff successfully upholds the claim to the monopoly of the legitimate use of physical force in the enforcement of its order' (Weber 1978: 54).

Two aspects of this definition are particularly noteworthy, providing as they do the basis, and/or point of departure, for much contemporary reflection on the state. First, the state for Weber is a set of institutions with a dedicated personnel. This observation has been taken up and developed by a diverse group of neo-Weberians, neo-statists and institutionalists working in particular in the United States (see Chapter 5). They argue that the differentiation of the state from civil society allows state managers to develop an array of distinct interests, preferences and capacities which cannot be explained by reference merely to societal factors.

In their efforts to 'bring the state back in' as both an actor and an independent force in social causation, the neo-statists have emphasized both the autonomy of the state from society and the power of 'state-centred' explanations of political outcomes. More specifically, they have concentrated on: the ability of state managers to exercise power independently and autonomously of non-state forces; the 'infrastructural power' of the state to infiltrate, control, supervise, police and regulate modern societies; and the ways in which the specific institutional structures of particular states at particular moments in time may enhance or undermine such general capacities. Such an idea has also proved increasingly influential in neo-Marxist state theory (see, for instance, Block (1990) and, more generally, the discussion in Chapter 3), in neo-pluralism (see Chapter 1) and, albeit in a rather different form, in public choice theory (see Chapter 4).

Second, Weber regards the modern state as wielding a monopoly of authoritative rule-making within a bounded territory. This is in turn backed by a monopoly of the means of physical violence within this same territorial space. Institutionalists and neo-statists, whose indebtedness to Weber is perhaps clearest, have concentrated on the mechanisms by which the state preserves (or at least seeks to preserve) its monopoly of authoritative rule-making. They have focused in particular on the question of political legitimacy, on the often democratic and/or nationalist strategies and mechanisms through which it is constructed and sustained, on the processes leading to its withdrawal, on the consequences for the always fragile balance between coercion and consent in modern societies, and on the mechanisms through which legitimacy might be re-established (through changes of regime and, in some instances, revolution). Yet, these too have increasingly become concerns for neo-Marxists (particularly those keen to develop the insights of Gramsci) and neo-pluralists. Other neo-statists, the so-called war-centred state theorists, but also realists and neo-realists in international relations theory (most famously, Waltz 1959), have focused on the state's supposed monopoly of the means of violence and in particular on the military dimension of state power. Stimulated perhaps by the intuitive appeal of Charles Tilly's remark that 'wars make states and states make war' (1975), war-centred state theorists in particular have considered the war-making capacity of the state, the extent to which the internal organization of the state apparatus reflects military imperatives, and the consequences of war-making and of mobilization for war on the evolution and transformation of the state itself — in short, on the relationship between war-making and state-shaping.

Such themes have also been taken up by feminist scholars, most notably perhaps Cynthia Enloe (1990), in interrogating the complex relationship between the state, organized violence, militarism and masculinity (see Chapter 6).

As the above discussion would seem to indicate, a substantial and rather disparate literature can trace some lineage from the Weberian conception of the state. Yet despite this seeming diversity, neo-Weberian perspectives do tend to display certain shared characteristics — and indeed weaknesses. First, such theories have tended to concentrate rather one-sidedly on political factors internal to the state. As a consequence, they have often relegated political forces outside and beyond the state, such as social movements and pressure groups, to a marginal role. Second, much neo-Weberian theory rests on the rather tenuous distinction between state and societal variables and an explanatory emphasis on the former at the expense of the latter. In the context of the attempt to 'bring the state back into' American social science in the 1970s and 1980s this tilting of the stick towards the side of the state was entirely appropriate. Yet now that 'state-centred' approaches have become as, if not more, dominant than their 'society-centred' counterparts ever were, it is crucial that we acknowledge that the casualty of both perspectives has been the attempt to develop an understanding of the complex and ever-changing relationship *between* the state and society, the public and the private. This is the challenge to which contemporary theories of the state must now respond (see Chapters 1, 6 and 9, in particular).

The concept of the state

It is all very well to have a clear and consistently articulated conception of the state and all the better if that is framed in a clearly articulated definition of the state. Yet, given that the state is not an immediately transparent or self-evident material object, this is merely one step in defending a view of politics which places the state at centre stage.

To develop a concept (and, by extension, a theory) of the state is to look at politics in a particular way. It is a choice which can and should be defended. This is an important point with clear implications. Political analysis can – and often does – proceed in the absence of a concept of the state (see, for instance, Easton 1967; Allen 1990). If we are, then, to justify a 'return to the state', we must first provide an answer to the question: what conceptual work does this concept (or theoretical abstraction) do? Stated more starkly still: what analytical purchase does the concept of the state offer the political analyst? What, in short, does it bring to the analytic feast that we might otherwise be missing? And what is the value of that additional insight?

However good, and however obvious, a series of questions this might seem, state theory has not been quick to provide ready answers. Even Dunleavy and O'Leary, who as we have seen perhaps get closest to tabling this as the relevant question, fail really to provide an answer, contenting themselves with noting that the state is an analytical abstraction and then pointing to certain family resemblances in the definitions of the state offered by theorists of the state (1987: 1–6). In so doing they identify the kinds of theoretical abstraction that state theorists are appealing to in invoking the state as a category, differentiating between organization and functional definitions. Yet what they do not do is assess and defend the analytical purchase on political reality offered by such abstractions. To be fair, some of this is implicit in what they say. But, for present purposes, it is important that we are perhaps a little more explicit. Two elements, in particular, of the analytical utility offered by the concept of the state might usefully be identified. Both are concerned with the ability to contextualize political behaviour: the first relates to the structural and/or institutional contextualization of political actors, the second to the historical contextualization of political behaviour and dynamics. We consider each in turn.

The state as institutional contextualization

As later chapters will testify, theories of the state vary significantly in terms of the assumptions about the state on which they are predicated and from which they build. Yet, almost without exception the state is seen, by those who deploy it as a concept, in structural and/or institutional terms. Thus, whether the state is seen organizationally or functionally – as a set of functions necessitating (in so far as they are performed) a certain institutional ensemble, or as an institutional ensemble itself – it provides a context within which political actors are seen to be embedded, with respect to which they must be situated analytically and which helps us to make sense of their behaviour. The state, in such a conception, provides (a significant part of) the institutional landscape which political actors must negotiate and the key to making sense of the things they do.

This landscape, in Bob Jessop's terms, is 'strategically selective' – in that it is more conducive to certain strategies, and by extension, the realization of the interests and/or preferences of certain actors, than others (1990: 9–10; see also Hay 2002: 127–131). It provides the unevenly contoured backdrop to political conflict, contestation and change – a strategic terrain with respect to which actors must orient themselves if they are to realize their intentions.

As this perhaps serves to suggest, the appeal to the concept of the state tends to draw the political analyst's attention to – and in the process, it might be hoped, to sharpen the analyst's purchase on – the opportunities and (more often than not) the *constraints* that political actors face in realizing their intentions, their preferences and their interests. A political analysis informed by a theory of the state is less likely to see political actors in voluntarist terms – as free-willed subjects in almost complete control of their destiny, able to shape political realities in the image of their preferences and volitions. For, in contrast to voluntarism and more agent-centred accounts, theorists of the state tend to see the ability of actors to realize their intentions as conditional upon often complex strategic choices made in densely structured institutional contexts which impose their own strategic selectivity (the pattern of opportunities and constraints they present).

Such considerations are important and have the potential to provide a valuable and much-needed corrective to the tendency of an at times behaviouralist-dominated political science mainstream to see actors' preferences alone as the key to explaining political outcomes. State theory reminds us that the access to political power associated with a landslide electoral triumph does not necessarily bring with it the institutional and/or strategic capacity to translate such a mandate into lasting social, political and economic change. If political will and the access to positions of power and influence were all that were required (as, for instance, in some pluralist and elitist conceptions), wholesale political change would be endemic. That this is not the case suggests the value of institutionally contextualizing abstractions like the state. And that, in turn, encourages a rather more sanguine and realistic assessment of 'political opportunity structures' (Tarrow 1998).

Yet such valuable insights do not come without their own dangers. State theory, as many of the chapters in this volume demonstrate, has at times been characterized by a tendency to structuralism. Indeed, this would seem to be the pathology to which it is most prone. In at least some of their many variants, Marxism, institutionalism, green theory, feminism and even public choice theory, have all legitimately been accused of structuralism. For each has, at times and in certain forms, appealed to essential and non-negotiable characteristics of the state (its capitalism, its patriarchy, its complicity in the destruction of the natural environment, and so forth) reproduced independently of the will, volition or agency of political actors. Such essentialism is both fatalistic and apolitical; it does nothing to enhance the analyst's purchase on political reality. Indeed, in a sense it denies that there is a *political* reality to be interrogated (on politics as the antithesis of fate, see Gamble 2000; Hay 2007). Yet while structuralism has proved an almost perennial target for critics of state theory, contemporary theories of the state would seem more acutely aware of its dangers today than at any point in the past. Indeed, the recent development of state theory can at least in part be read as a retreat from structuralism and an attempt to 'bring state *actors* back in'.

The state as historical contextualization

If the appeal to the concept or abstraction of the state serves to sensitize political analysts to the need to *contextualize political agency and agents institutionally*, then no less significant is its role in sensitizing political analysts to the need to *contextualize the present historically*. Indeed, the two are intimately connected.

The characteristic concern of the political scientist with government and the holders of high office tends to be associated with an analytical focus on the present. Within this conventional framework, the determinants of political outcomes are invariably seen to lie in factors specific to a particular context at a particular point in time – typically, the motivations and intentions of the actors immediately involved and their access to positions of power and influence. This somewhat ahistorical approach is immediately problematized by appeal to the concept of the state. For while governments come and go, the state, as an institutional ensemble, persists – even while it evolves over time. That evolution is shaped by the intended and unintended consequences of governing strategies and policies. Yet this is a reciprocal relationship. For, at any given point in time, the strategic context in which governments find themselves is in turn a reflection of the strategic capacities and competences of the institutions of the state and the constraints and opportunities these impose. To understand the capacity for governmental autonomy is, then, to assess the extent of the institutional, structural and strategic *legacy* inherited from the past (on which, see Farrall, Gray and Hay 2020). It is, in short, to understand the dynamic relationship between state and governmental power over time.

A hypothetical example may serve to reinforce the point. If the institutions of the state at a given point in time look very different from those, say, two decades earlier, after a systematic process of reform (led perhaps by a radical and ideologically driven administration), then this is likely to exert a significant influence on the autonomy of any new incoming administration, regardless of the size of its majority. Yet, as this example perhaps already serves to indicate, there is a certain danger of structuralism here too. The newly incumbent administration certainly has to grapple with the institutional, political and cultural legacy of the reforms enacted over the previous two decades. Yet, in our desire to contextualize historically we may come to overemphasize the burden the past places on the present. In so doing we may inadvertently absolve the newly incumbent administration of responsibility for the consequences of its own conduct in office – attributing, say, the lack of radicalism of the new administration to the legacy of its predecessor when it might more plausibly be attributed to its own lack of an animating political conviction.

State theory, especially in its neo-institutionalist form (see Chapter 5), is perhaps rather too predisposed to see continuity, inertia and, at best, incremental evolution over time. It sometimes tends to downplay political agency as a consequence. States, like governments, change and, under certain conditions, despite their path-dependent nature, they may change surprisingly rapidly. It is important, then, that the historical contextualization of the present that the abstraction of the state encourages does not lead us to a historically undifferentiated account of the endless reproduction of the *status quo ante*. As this suggests, while the appeal to the concept of the state can certainly heighten our sensitivity to historical dynamics, it need not necessarily do so.

An overly structuralist and overly historicized account may in fact dull rather than sharpen our analytical purchase on questions of change over time. Yet, as already noted, contemporary theories of the state are perhaps rather more acutely aware of this danger than their predecessors. Recent developments in the theory of the state are characterized, as much as anything else, by their emphasis upon the uneven pace of the state's development over time – and of the significant role played by political agency as an accelerant or decelerant.

Recent developments in state theory

In recent years the ascendancy of the neo-Weberian perspective that came to dominate the revival of interest in the state since the 1970s has been challenged. Two theoretical currents are here particularly noteworthy: the development of a distinctly feminist theory of the state, and the rejection of the very notion of the state by poststructuralists (in particular Foucauldians and discourse-analysts).

Feminism, or so it is often argued, lacks a theory of the state. Yet where once Judith Allen's comment that 'where feminists have been interested in the state their ideas on its nature and form have often been imported from outside' (1990: 21) was certainly warranted, things are now somewhat more complicated. Some argue that feminism has no (independent) theory of the state and needs one urgently; others, that feminism has no theory of the state and has no need for one; while yet others suggest that feminism not only needs but has at last begun to develop precisely such a theory (see, for instance, Chappell 2003; Cooper 2019; Haney 2000; Kantola 2006).

The evidence of recent scholarship would seem to support this latter view: that in recent years feminists have indeed begun to establish the basis for very adequate and distinctively feminist *theories* of the state (see Chapter 6). Indeed, many of the most exciting and original developments in contemporary state theory have come from feminist scholars. Such insights include a number of key observations: (i) if the state can in some instances be seen to act as if an 'ideal collective capitalist' it may also be seen as a 'patriarch general', a key site in the reproduction of relations of patriarchal domination within society; (ii) with the growing feminization of poverty, ever-increasing numbers of women are becoming dependent upon the state for their very survival, giving the state a historically unparalleled prominence in the lives of women; (iii) paradoxically, at the same time the state is ever more dependent upon the unpaid domestic labour of women in an era of welfare retrenchment; (iv) as this demonstrates, the reproduction of capitalist social relations is integrally bound up with the reproduction of patriarchal relations — an adequate theory of either must deal with their mutual articulation.

If in recent years feminists have increasingly turned to a theory of the state then the rise of Foucauldian and discourse-analytical perspectives marks something of a counter move – a move *from* the state (see Chapter 8). Such approaches present a fundamental challenge to conventional theorists of the state, suggesting as they do that the notion of the state is itself something of a mystifying illusion. Following the work of Michel Foucault, they argue that the concept and discourse of the state is but one part of a broader process governing and shaping our very conduct and bringing it in line with various 'governing strategies'. From this perspective, state effects exist precisely because people act as if the state existed, orienting themselves to the image constructed of it. Thus in so far as the state exists, it exists in the ideas we hold about it. This has led many theorists to reject the notion of the state altogether (see, for instance, Abrams 1988). Yet the idea that discourses of the state are partly constitutive of its power, authority and essence is hardly as devastating for the theory of the state as some might contend. It does, however, demonstrate that, if theorists of the state are not to reproduce its mythology, they must give rather more attention to the processes through which the state is conceived of on the one hand, and the relationship between such conceptions and the institutions, processes and practices of the state on the other.

Beyond the state?

A final challenge to the theory of the state has come from a rather unexpected source – the challenge to the state itself. In recent years, the value of state theory has come under attack from those who reject neither its sophistication nor the significance of the insights it has generated. What they do reject, however, is its contemporary relevance. The state, they argue, in an era of globalization and internationalization, financial integration and capital mobility is rapidly becoming obsolete. It is becoming (if it has not already become) an anachronism. To paraphrase Daniel Bell (1987), it is too small to deal with the big problems which are now increasingly projected on an international or global stage and too clumsy to deal with the small problems which are increasingly displaced to the local level. It is difficult to deny the appeal of such an argument. Yet it is important to treat some of the often heroic claims made about the contemporary crisis of the nation-state with a degree of caution and some scepticism. First, globalization is not a particularly novel phenomenon. Indeed, it can be traced at least as far back as the imperial age. The mode of globalization has certainly changed with time, but the mere presence of globalizing forces need not herald the demise of the state form.

It is certainly true that financial integration, heightened capital mobility, the emergence of regional trading blocs and the proliferation of supra-national regulatory bodies, to say nothing of planetary contagions of a variety of kinds, significantly alter the context (economic, political, social and cultural) within which states operate, and may indeed be reflected in the changing form and function of the state. Yet this is in no sense to pronounce the death of the state. In all likelihood people will continue to live, as they do now, in territorially bounded communities governed primarily by state institutions on which they continue to confer legitimacy, and which they continue to regard as responsible in the first instance for the social and economic context in which they find themselves. As this suggests, globalization may well pose a challenge to the nation-state, but it is a challenge that has so far reinforced at least as much as it has undermined the state-based organization of politics.

The state may struggle to deal with problems which are planetary in their reach, scope and scale; but that those are the kinds of challenges it increasingly faces has not as yet been associated with any significant scaling back or retrenchment of its activities. Indeed, the tension between the proliferation of planetary problems on the one hand and the non-proliferation of planetary solutions arguably now defines the contemporary agenda for state theorists. On all the available evidence, then, rumours of the death of the state and of the demise of state theory would seem, for good or ill, greatly exaggerated.

Structure of the book

The volume begins with reappraisals of the classical triumvirate of pluralism, elitism and Marxism. All three chapters note that these approaches are not uniform bodies of thought and each pieces together strands of thought to highlight key ideas, concepts and thinkers. In his chapter on pluralism, Martin Smith begins by noting the paradox at the heart of pluralist thought: that concentration of power in a body such as the state is seen to be problematic and undesirable, yet the state is also seen to be the arena of democratic politics, where the different interests in society are represented. Pluralism struggles to reconcile this paradox, yet coheres around a view of politics and the state which rejects centralized theories and focuses on the importance of groups to political outcomes. Yet Smith argues that pluralism consistently struggles to adequately conceptualize the unequal power of such interests and groups, particularly with regard to economic and business elites, despite the attempts of neo-pluralism to better account for such criticisms. Nonetheless, as Smith details, the influence of pluralism and its attention to complexity, diversity and multiplicity continues to offer a vibrant and influential way of thinking about the state.

Providing an overview of the development of elitism, Mark Evans points to the ways in which various scholars have identified the concentration of power within and without the state. He examines the key propositions for elite theory originally stated: that rulers form a cohesive group, selected on the basis of their access to economic, political or ideological resources, are based within a territory, and are closed off from those who are ruled. More recent contributions to elite theory extend the focus to transnational or global elites, where power and influence are diffused, sometimes in subtle and nuanced ways, raising issues for democratic governance. In addition, Evans argues that the recent populist turn represents perhaps less the rise of 'the people' against elites, than an example of elite circulation, of competition between older and newer elites over authentic representation of 'the people'. The chapter ends by considering the potential impact of AI and technology on current and future elites.

Hay's account of Marxist state theory begins by exploring two questions: what is Marxist state theory, and why does Marxism need a theory of the state? In terms of the latter, Hay argues that the state plays a crucial role in the regulation and reproduction of capital and that, therefore, the state is of central interest to Marxism. In terms of the first question, there is a wide array of accounts and responses. Key issues which Marxist state theory has sought to grapple with include whether and how the state contributes to the construction of consent for capitalist reproduction and whether the state is inherently capitalist or capitalist by virtue of existing within a capitalist system. More recent work seeks to move beyond such dualisms. Hay points to Jessop's strategic-relational approach, emphasizing strategic selectivity where past struggles shape, but do not determine, future outcomes, as an approach which has much to offer analyses and understandings of the contemporary state.

Moving on from the classic theories of the state, Chapter 4 considers the ways in which public choice theory has conceived of, and critiqued, the state. Taylor and Bosworth begin by specifying the foundational assumptions of public choice theory, derived from economics, as a commitment to methodological individualism, and the view that individuals seek to maximize their self-interest. From this, a view of the state emerges which is sceptical of its ability to efficiently and effectively correct for market failures, whether due to the unequal nature of interest-group politics or through inefficient public bureaucracies. Taylor and Bosworth note that public choice theory does not assume that markets do not fail, but rather that states and governments fail too. Thus, public choice theory has been heavily associated with neoliberal government reforms which seek to limit the state and its interventions.

In contrast to this perspective, new institutionalism, a reaction to the assumptions of public choice theory and the behaviouralist revolution of the 1960s, sought to rehabilitate the state. New institutionalism, as Vivien Schmidt argues, rather than reducing political action to its individual parts, sought to analyse the collective element of political action. There is a range of new institutionalisms to which the chapter attends: rational choice institutionalism, historical institutionalism, sociological institutionalism and discursive institutionalism, which vary in quite how they approach this insight, but all share a concern with how institutions, broadly understood, modify individual action; be that through incentive structures, historical legacies, or cultural and/or discursive norms. The overall effect of this diversity is, Schmidt argues, that the new institutionalist approaches constitute ways of studying and thinking about the state rather than a substantive theory of the state.

In chapter 6, Johanna Kantola argues that feminism has long been marked by an uneasiness about the state. States have increased equality in some ways for some women, while at the same time entrenching other types of inequality. The chapter explores liberal feminist views of the state as neutral and benign, before moving on to consider critiques of this position – that the state is patriarchal. Addressing the frequent Western-centric nature of much work on the state, Kantola points to the feminist work around the postcolonial state and the ways in which diverse state practices and contexts impact upon women. Poststructuralist feminists have rejected totalizing narratives on the state and seek instead to point to its differentiated nature. Through analysis of a range of issues such as neoliberalism and populism, Kantola points to the ways in which feminist theorizing about the state seeks to explore the ways in which power relations within and across the state are complex and co-constitutive.

In a similar vein to Kantola and feminism, Annica Kronsell and Roger Hildingsson point to an ambivalence around the state within green political thought, with the state seen as responsible for the (re)production of structures which contribute to environmental degradation, while at the same time state action and intervention are seen as important for addressing the environmental crisis. After reviewing the features of the green state both as a normative ideal and by comparing the performance of different states in environmental governance, the chapter assesses the arguments that the development of the welfare state offers potential avenues for greening of the state. Kronsell and Hildingsson conclude the chapter by considering three challenges for the green state: reconciling economic and environmental imperatives, processes of change and transition, and whether new political and democratic forms are needed to address environmental challenges.

The final chapter in the theories section of the book turns to poststructuralism. James Martin and Alan Finlayson begin by characterizing poststructuralism as an interest in rationalities and how certain rationalities become dominant, and how these might be contested. They argue that many important institutions, systems of meaning and identities are open, flexible and unstable, achieving a sense of permanence through discursive frameworks. The chapter points to the ways in which poststructuralism seeks to destabilize and decentre the state and its associated practices, to see the state as a complex ensemble of contingent rationalities rather than a fixed, singular actor or entity; both site and outcome of a struggle to articulate particular meanings. The state is therefore an outcome of politics rather than something with which to explain politics. The work of Foucault on governmentality and his analysis of how power is dispersed throughout society highlights the complexity and plurality of state practices.

The second section of the book moves from state theory to critical engagement with key concepts and ideas raised or implied by debates about the state. An orthodox view of the state would see it as a body which exercises sovereignty over a given territory to secure 'the people' and protect private property. In the chapters which comprise the second section, each of these terms is subject to further interrogation, to develop our understanding of the state. The choice of chapters also speaks to some of the major ways in which politics and international relations have changed and developed in the years since the first edition of the book. The global financial crisis raised a series of questions around the (in)ability of the nation-state to regulate international financial systems and the power of business vis-à-vis the state. Issues like terrorism have also led to a renewed emphasis on security politics, and Brexit and the election of Donald Trump, as well as the gains of nationalist/populist political parties across Europe, have given renewed attention to sovereignty, nationalism and populism. Each of these developments prompts questions and debate about the state, which the subsequent chapters seek to explore.

Brown's analysis of the relationship between the state and sovereignty begins by noting the concentration of power and authority which emerged in the person of the sovereign in mid-seventeenth-century Europe. Reviewing different regimes and understandings of sovereignty, from that established under the Westphalian treaties, through debates around sovereignty and (non) intervention in the UN system, a key aim of the chapter is to emphasize that sovereignty, understood as dominium, the ability to dispose entirely as one wishes, has never been widely accepted. From cooperation around economic management issues, to human rights regimes, the international system has been one which envisages and allows for constraints and limits on sovereignty. Yet in many contemporary Western states, populist campaigns have fixed onto the idea of sovereignty as a means of articulating opposition to international governance regimes. While these understandings of sovereignty may be analytically thin and partial, Brown argues the idea of sovereignty remains a symbolically potent force.

Pinar Bilgin, in Chapter 10, explores the state-security relationship. As Bilgin notes, the study of security has been almost completely bound up with a focus on the state. Within a Hobbesian framework, it is only the state that can provide security; security is unthinkable absent the state. This focus on the state has tended to work with a notion of the state as fixed and prior to security, as well as the thing, or referent, to be secured. The latter of these, including the idea that states provide security 'inside' and seek to defend their citizens from 'outside' remains a persistent limitation. Bilgin points to the myriad ways in which states are implicated in practices of insecurity, including for those 'inside', often in the name of states providing (national) security. The chapter concludes by considering the ways in which conceptions of the state have informed, sometimes implicitly, thinking about global, and postcolonial, security and calls for greater attention to the historical complexity of these relations.

The relationship between the state and territory comes into focus in Rhys Jones's chapter. It is, Jones notes, almost impossible to think of the state without a territorial dimension – states claim sovereignty (see above) over a particular territory. The measurement and control of such territory, as well as the embodied experiences of people, are crucial. Space becomes territory through processes of measurement and calculation, such that we might think of territory in terms of political technology, Jones argues. Yet these are contested and incomplete, such that state territories are not 'flat' but fractured, uneven and incomplete. The chapter goes on to consider ideas about networks and flows, which suggest a lesser, declining significance of territory and whether they necessitate the rethinking of state territory as porous, unstable and, often, aspirational. These dynamics, Jones illustrates, are created and challenged by people and material infrastructures, leading to a conception of state territories (and therefore states themselves) as fractured and incomplete works in progress.

David Marsh analyses the relationship between the state and capital. Beginning with an overview of two of the key theories on this relationship, Marxism and pluralism, Marsh notes a convergence of views: that business is an important, but not undifferentiated or uncontested, actor within the state. Marsh goes on to argue that the global financial crisis has given renewed impetus and focus to accounts of the role and position of capital within the state. Drawing on structure/agency and the faces of power debates, the chapter considers a range of authors and arguments with differing positions on the relationship between the state and capital – from positions which argue that business has a dominant relation to the state through to arguments that business power fluctuates and is subject to countervailing pressures. In doing so, Marsh gives an account of the strategies and techniques which capital deploys to further its interests.

In their chapter considering the relationship between the state and nationalism, Nicola McEwen and Daniel Cetrà suggest an equivalence is frequently assumed between the nation and the state; that the state is the appropriate repository for the nation, giving the former the legitimacy and affective attachment of the latter. This view is underpinned by dominant approaches to nationalism which argue that nations are phenomena intimately related to the emergence of states. The chapter notes that there are different forms of nationalism, which draw the boundary of the people – the ultimate source of political authority and sovereignty for modern states – in different ways. Yet, McEwen and Cetrà argue, a simple equivalence between nation and state is not always present. The state can be both agent of nationalism, fostering national identity, and also the object of nationalism, where subnational groups and entities seek greater recognition for their national identity. Nationalism, the chapter argues, establishes a central source of legitimacy – the people. But who are the people? Different forms of nationalism draw the boundaries of belonging in different ways, including civic identity, ethnicity, language and gender.

Mikko Kuisma's chapter on populism brings together a number of different themes which have featured throughout the book. He notes that, while populism is subject to a significant degree of definitional ambiguity, its core features include a concern with inequality in the state and concerns around the dominance of elites and business. Populism also, Kuisma argues, seeks to place popular sovereignty, understood as national sovereignty, at the heart of politics, against the power of elites and global capitalism. The chapter argues that, rather than being seen as a challenge to the state per se, populism, in either its left- or right-wing forms, represents a series of fundamental questions about the relationship between people and the state.

Further Reading

Evans, P.B. et al. (eds) (1985), *Bringing the State Back In*, Cambridge: Cambridge University Press.

Hay, C. (1996), *Re-Stating Social and Political Change*, Buckingham: Open University Press.

Hay, C. (2014), 'Neither real nor fictitious but "as if real"? A political ontology of the state', *The British Journal of Sociology*, 65(3), 459–480.

Mann, M. (1988), *States, War and Capitalism*, Oxford: Blackwell.

Pierson, C. (1996), *The Modern State*, London: Routledge.

Skinner, Q. (1989), 'The State', in T. Ball et al. (eds), *Political Innovation and Conceptual Change*, 90–131, Cambridge: Cambridge University Press.

Part I

Theories

1

Pluralism

Martin J. Smith

Introduction

The problem of discussing pluralism and state theory is that, whilst pluralism developed as a critique of the state, it rarely, if ever, explicitly discusses the nature of the state. Pluralism is difficult to define in relation to a conception of the state because, by its very nature, it is pluralistic, rejecting monistic definitions and conceptions of politics or the state. Indeed, there is no clear and definitive body of literature that sets out a pluralist theory of the state or of politics. For Jordan (1990) there is, unlike for Marxism (see Chapter 3) or elitism (see Chapter 2), no pluralist canon or consistent pluralist theory. Underpinning pluralism is a paradox. In principle, pluralists see the state as a malign organization that concentrates power and needs pluralistic forms of social organization to limit and constrain the threat of absolute power. Yet, whilst seeing the state as a threat to civil society, pluralists fail to problematize the state and, in failing to do so, tend to treat it as a benign, or at least neutral, set of institutional arrangements either reflecting varying interests, as in the democratic pluralist tradition, or as a fragmented institution, in the more recent debates around network governance. On one side, the state is a 'monopoly of legitimate violence' (Weber 1946) and therefore needs to be constrained because otherwise it is a threat to a free and open society. On the other hand, the state is an arena in which democratic politics operates: the state is the guarantor of pluralism that reflects the demands of various interests in society. This paradox is never reconciled because it is a consequence of the way pluralism has developed; not as a consistent school of theory but as a collection of a whole range of different theories, approaches and methods.

Pluralism has long been characterized as providing a simplistic understanding of power by focusing on group interactions in the context of what is portrayed as a relatively benign state or government that mediates between conflicting interests in order to make decisions in the broad national interest. Certainly, a range of Marxist approaches from Lenin (1917) through to Miliband (1969) and Jessop (1978) have highlighted the way in which notions of pluralistic democracy are ideological mechanisms for justifying the political interest of capital in the context of a bourgeois state (see Chapter 3). It is certainly the case that much of US pluralism, which became highly influential in the post-war era, took a relatively benign view particularly of the US political process where writers such as Dahl (1973) and Truman (1951) were keen to emphasize the differentiated nature of politics and the ways in which a range of groups could draw on different resources in order to influence political outcomes.

In the words of Galbraith (1952), liberal democratic systems operate through a range of countervailing powers that prevent the dominance of a single interest. The result of these constraints is the major distinguishing feature of pluralism: the dispersal of power in modern industrial society. The very complexity and interdependence of society, combined with a political system open to many interests, lead to pluralism. Furthermore, although resources are not shared equally, those who lack one resource, like money, often have an alternative resource; for example, votes. For the pluralist there is a wide dispersal of power between various leaders, constraints on leadership from non-elites and competing elites and uncertainty about who benefits from a policy. Consequently, there is no single elite making and benefiting from all decisions. For pluralists, liberal democracy provides a frame for a complex and multidimensional polity that allows for many voices to influence outcomes.

In order to understand the pluralist conception of the state it is necessary to see how pluralists define groups and their role in the generation of political interests. This chapter will highlight how pluralist group theory has changed from its initial development in the nineteenth century and how this has been reflected in pluralist conceptions of government. The chapter will suggest that few of the writers who focus on government and the state in pluralist forms explicitly think of themselves as pluralists. They implicitly accept many of the pluralist assumptions about politics and the state and, in doing so, they often disempower state institutions in their analysis. The chapter will begin by highlighting that, despite the complex and diverse nature of pluralism, there are some shared themes that provide a core to a range of different pluralist approaches.

The core of pluralism

Pluralism, or more accurately pluralists, have drifted between analytical, normative and prescriptive approaches and, as we will see, pluralism in many ways became integrated into legitimizing and defending Western democratic systems. What unites pluralism is a rejection of monistic approaches to knowledge or politics and a belief that groups have interests that need to be respected and represented. It rejects elite and Marxist approaches which see power and resources concentrated within the state (see Chapters 2 and 3). The key theme is that: 'The social order of many contemporary states seems marked by vertical cleavages that separate the society into structurally distinct compartments on a cultural, social and/ or racial basis' (Leon and Léons 1977: 5). Whilst it is difficult to define a single pluralist theory and the term pluralism or pluralist is applied to many different theories and theorists, it is still the case that there is a broad set of ideas or understandings that link different pluralist approaches. There is, within the broad field of pluralist thinking, some common principles in relation to the state, power and groups.

The state

There are two competing conceptions of the state with pluralism. The original nineteenth- and early twentieth-century pluralists saw the state as a malign force and were strongly opposed to any mechanisms that concentrated or monopolized power within governmental institutions. For early English pluralists, groups were a mechanism for limiting the growing power of the developing modern state as it was going through a process of nationalizing local associations into the nascent welfare state. There was a strong anarchical streak within early pluralism that saw groups and guilds as self-organizing mechanisms for limiting state power and linking decision-making to communities. The fundamental issue for pluralists, contra Hobbes, is that sovereignty does not reside with the state (see Chapter 9) but the state should reflect the range of interests in society. Nevertheless, even the early pluralists who were wary of the state were not strongly critical. Laborde (2000: 177) illustrates how, for English pluralism, the distinction between state and civil society is one of the fundamental principles of pluralism but points out that: 'such a distinction was hardly couched in antagonistic terms. The state was seen as an unproblematic instrumental requirement and the border between public and private was confused in pluralist writings.'

Classical American pluralism developed an even more benign view of the state. Rather than groups being a counterweight to the state, the state was the mechanism for realizing group interests. Classical American pluralists accepted the constitutional position: government is an open and democratic process concerned with the public interest. In the case of the US system of government there was a fragmented political process, a constrained executive and representation which ensured that many interests could influence political outcomes. Indeed, much pluralist writing on policymaking is concerned with outlining the mechanisms of the policy process, seeing it as a process built on establishing rational knowledge and aggregating interests rather than focused on power. As Dunleavy and O'Leary (1987) suggest, pluralism saw the state as either a vector carrying interests to government or a ring within which various interests could battle it out. The assumption is that in some way the state is neutral. However, many pluralists would suggest that they were trying to develop more realistic and empirically verifiable models of policymaking which recognize the imperfections, complexity and incremental nature of the policy process (Lindblom 1959, 1965). Pluralists do not reject the idea that, at least at the policy sector level, policymaking is susceptible to capture by particular interests (notable examples being health and agriculture) but they suggest that alternative power centres, such as the media, legislators and campaign groups, can challenge the dominance of particular interests over a long period. This conception of group politics builds on a market analogy. Should one group develop a monopoly of power, other groups will enter the market to undercut and challenge the predominance. The point Dahl (1973) makes with his notion of polyarchy is that, whilst democratic political systems may be imperfect, different interests have a voice and are able to influence political outcomes.

Groups

A principle feature of all pluralist thought is the focus on groups rather than individuals. Individual identity exists through groups and groups are the main constitutive element of society. In the words of Bentley (1908: 208),

'When the groups are adequately stated, everything is stated.' For the early English pluralists, groups were seen as 'persons' with agency (Nicols 1974: 5). Groups play a key role in pluralist thought. First, groups, rather than individuals, are the basis of identity. This is a key principle of the early pluralists who saw groups as a fundamental basis of social organization, through to the American pluralists who saw pressure groups in particular as central to politics. Anthropological pluralists saw societies as being made up of a range of different value groups – a view developed by multiculturalists later on. Consequently, Kuper (1969) highlights the contrast between the consensus model of society as proposed by American pluralists, which sees groups bound by cross-cutting values, and a balance of power and conflict model which sees societies being made up of divisions and inherent conflicts. Second, the role of groups is to act as a limit on the state or, in some approaches, as an alternative to the state – a conception that is picked up to some degree by the work of Putnam on social capital (as discussed later) or even in ideas around the big society in the UK. There is a strong tradition within pluralism going back to the nineteenth century of the idea of free association and that self-organized groups or communities could be responsible for the delivery of public goods and ensuring a more democratic policy process by seeing decisions reflecting the wishes of local communities.

Power

Many twentieth-century pluralists were seen as having a limited and naive view of power. The point made by critics such as Lukes (1974) is that pluralists adopt a behaviouralist position and see power as something that is direct and observable; by seeing who succeeds in winning resources it is possible to see who has power. For pluralists, power works through visible forces and not through unseen structures or elites. For Dahl (1957), power is defined when 'A has power over B to the extent that he can get B to do something that B would otherwise not. In the decision-making process power exists when A gets B to choose policy X when B would have chosen policy Y.' This view of power determines the pluralist methodology: actual behaviour is observed or reconstructed from documents, witnesses and so on. Consequently, it is possible to determine empirically whether or not the same group achieves success in two or more issue areas.

For Hewitt (1974), by observing the way political decisions are made and the particular outcomes, it is apparent that different interests succeed in different policy areas. Nevertheless, some pluralist approaches are more sophisticated in their analysis of power than some of the caricatures allow. For instance, even the classical American pluralists recognized that institutionalized relations existed with groups which prevented access for some groups (Truman 1951), and Kelso (1978) highlighted what he called corporate pluralism where certain interests captured government. Both Dahl (1961) and Truman (1951) suggested that business had privileges, with business having a 'favored position in the conventional myth pattern' and, like Lindblom (1977), he recognizes that the favoured position of 'business' groups is furthered by the existence of an economic system under which businessmen's confidence and expectations of profit are of crucial importance to the health of the economy.

The development of pluralism

The origins and development of pluralism can be found in the reaction both to the monistic approaches of Hobbesian political thought and the individualism of liberalism. Hobbes saw a strong sovereign as a mechanism for order in a society of conflicting interests. Liberals such as Locke and Mill saw a Hobbesian state as a threat to the rights of individuals and tried to define the legitimate limits of the state. The early pluralists wanted to avoid the development of an over-powerful state but also to save communities or society from what they saw as the potential impact of market individualism. Hence the early English pluralists developed a socialist and collectivist approach. In Britain the development of pluralism in the early twentieth century reflected concerns about an increasingly strong state and was built on the notion of a strong civil society – through voluntary organizations and trade unions – delivering public goods. However, the period between 1914 and 1945 effectively destroyed the liberal state form that existed in Britain. The British state nationalized the pluralistic delivery of public goods so that the services delivered by the voluntary sector, private business and local government were taken over by the central government (for example, supplies of gas or the creation of the National Health Service). In addition, the primacy of parliamentary sovereignty and the Haldane conception of the civil service – which saw decisions being made within a symbiotic relationship between ministers and officials – meant that power was monopolized within a closed and elitist state. Whilst Middlemas (1979) emphasizes a corporate bias in the British state, the role of groups was always mediated through a sovereign core executive and was highly limited in its influence on policy. Whilst pluralist conceptions existed within British political discourse, particularly in the high Toryism of people like Quentin Hogg and Harold Macmillan, the reality of British government was an increasingly centralized, sovereign state. The British state is based on the notion of indirect, individual representation, a decision-making elite isolated from civil society and unresponsive to group interests, combined with an indivisible notion of internal and external sovereignty. The epitome of anti-pluralism was the Thatcherite conception of the state with its suspicion of groups and intermediate institutions and emphasizing the direct relationship between a sovereign government and the individual (Smith 2015). As a consequence of these developments, pluralism had little purchase in Britain and the work of Cole, Figgis and Laski effectively disappeared from both political and academic debate until the 1980s. In the United States the state form was not so suffocating of pluralist thought. There, despite the very considerable expansion of state activity during the New Deal in the 1930s, the state never sought or developed the capabilities to draw all areas of activity into its domain. A comprehensive welfare state failed to develop, local and federal state level government retained considerable autonomy, the private sector remained strong – there was no attempt beyond specific sectors in planning or nationalization – and the central state was institutionally fragmented as a consequence of the separation of powers entrenched within the constitution. Consequently, there was sufficient plurality in the political system to ensure that pluralism continued to reflect some elements of the reality of American politics. The period between the First World War and the end of the 1960s saw pluralism becoming the dominant conception of the American state.

In the post-war period, pluralism (what some call interest-group pluralism) became the dominant paradigm in US political science and had a considerable impact on the analysis of politics in the rest of the world. (It was even used to study the Soviet Union (see Solomon 1983).) It developed as both an empirical and normative political theory; a mechanism for understanding US politics and a framework of what politics should be. There is an assumption in the literature on pluralism of a break between the pluralism of the early twentieth-century theorists and the post-war empirical political pluralism. In fact, many of the concerns and conceptions of post-war pluralism are indebted to the more radical pluralism of the early twentieth century. And through the founder of modern American pluralism, Arthur Bentley, there is a direct link to John Dewey (Ratner and Altman 1964). From Bentley, modern pluralists have adapted the classical pluralist emphasis on the role of groups in politics and the need to contain the power and competence of the state. The themes of Bentley's work were developed by David Truman (1951) and empirically in the analysis by the work of Dahl, Lindblom and 'the Yale school' (see Merelman 2003). As pluralist theory developed, however, it transformed from a normative theory – this is how things should be – to an empirical theory – analysing how power is distributed. It then became, in the words of Merelman (2003: 18), a legitimizing discourse: 'That is, they support the claims American political leaders typically make to justify their power.' Pluralist theorists in post-war America confused normative claims with empirical reality. Pluralists desired a state limited by multiple power centres and the influence of groups and this was their perception of politics in post-war America. Consequently, the US pluralist theory of the state was actually a model of how they believed American politics operated and, in a manner similar to the way in which the works of Walter Bagehot and Sir Ivor Jennings legitimized executive sovereignty in Britain, the pluralists legitimized the US political system. As writers such as C. W. Mills recognized, it became part of the Cold War armoury in the sense that pluralists reinforced the idea that the US political system was morally superior to other forms of government and gave representation to the range of interests in US society.

Critics of pluralism

The positioning of pluralism as legitimizing the democratic nature of Western regimes coincided with it becoming the dominant paradigm in political science. However, the irony was that the moment of its apotheosis was also the moment when significant theoretical and empirical criticisms were being raised about the concept of pluralism. As Merelman (2003) points out: whilst the ink was still drying on Dahl's claim (1967: 24) that 'The theory and practice of American pluralism tend to assume that the existence of multiple centres of power, none of which is wholly sovereign will help (may indeed be necessary) to tame power, to secure the consent of all, and to settle conflicts peacefully', blacks in the South were being killed for demanding their political and civil rights. The point where the Yale school thought pluralism was firmly established in the United States was the point when its limitations were becoming apparent. During the 1960s and 1970s pluralism was subject to both an empirical and academic critique. Empirically, many of the assumptions concerning pluralism were challenged by the civil rights movement and the anti-Vietnam War movements of the 1960s. The civil rights movement illustrated that a group with a forceful grievance was excluded from the political process. Despite the apparent pluralism of the American system, there were considerable barriers to political participation. Robert Putnam's response to the assassination of Martin Luther King, and the riots that followed, captures the pluralist impasse: 'What that glow in the sky on that evening of the Martin Luther King assassination conveyed was a sense that there was something happening in American politics that was not encompassed by the conceptual framework that we were all working with' (Merelman 2003: 211–212). In many ways the Vietnam War was a greater challenge to pluralism. It undermined any claim that American politics was based on consensus. The anti-war protests refuted the idea of a shared sense of US politics and society-wide agreement over the form of the political system. The collapse of the consensus fed into a number of academic critiques of pluralism. First, rather than there being a consensus, what pluralism was presenting was a Cold War-inspired view of the American system. The picture of a perfect functioning democracy, differentiating power and open to all interests, was hiding a process of manipulation, exclusion and elite dominance. This was Merelman's legitimizing discourse, intent on demonstrating the superiority of the American system. Second, the Vietnam War and civil rights movement, and the more radical women's and gay movements that followed, undermined the notion that there was a general acceptance of values in society (see Lockwood 1964). Indeed, the period since the 1960s has seen a considerable bifurcation of beliefs in the United States between, say, those who support the notion of gay marriage and the fundamentalist Christian Right. Bachrach and Baratz (1962) and Lukes (1974) highlighted the way in which the notion of consensus can be manipulated in the political process. Moreover, elitist and Marxist scholars like C.W. Mills (1956) (see Chapter 2), Domhoff (1967) and Miliband (1969) (see Chapter 3) empirically demonstrated the concentration of power and the ways in which outcomes favoured elites in the government policy. Pluralism was based on observable power, not on the way hidden structures and ideas shape the political agenda (Polsby 1963: 4; Polsby 1960: 477). The work of Lukes highlighted the structural mechanisms that meant that consensus often covered forms of coercion. As Merelman (2003: 99) boldly states, a combination of social change and theoretical critique meant that: 'By the early 1970s, pluralism had been dethroned at Yale.'

The reinvigoration of pluralism

Pluralist theorists did respond to the events of the 1960s and 1970s and there was some considerable rethinking of its key propositions. The reformulation took different forms in the United States and in Britain. In the United States there was the development of a distinct notion of neo-pluralism which grew out of some critiques of American democracy in the work of Lowi (1969) and McConnell (1953, 1966) and the rethinking of the nature of pluralism in the work of Dahl and Lindblom. Neo-pluralism continued the pluralist concern with the role of groups in the policy process but accepted that particular groups, especially business, will often come to dominate within policy areas and are at a clear advantage compared to groups like consumers (Dunleavy and O'Leary 1987; Kelso 1978). McConnell (1966) saw business as exercising great power in the US polity and, for Lowi (1969), interest groups did not result in pluralism but in structures of privilege that excluded the public from policymaking arenas. Lindblom was firmly in the Yale school of pluralists but recognized that business enjoyed extra resources in the political sphere. First, government is dependent on economic growth for its own success and therefore it is likely to meet business demands for favourable tax and economic policies. As a consequence, business is in 'a privileged position in government' (see also Chapter 12). Second, in a market system many decisions that have a major impact on the lives of people are taken without any democratic control (Lindblom 1977: 175). Businesses can close factories or pollute environments without any accountability. Lindblom saw business as not just having power through its lobbying ability but as having structural power. His volte-face placed him closer to Marxists such as Claus Offe (1984) and David Coates (1980) than to the classical pluralists of post-war America (see McLennan 1995 on convergence). However, unlike Marxists, Lindblom maintained the pluralist focus on groups and paid little attention to the nature of the state. He continued to see the state as a fragmented institution but then argued that business has a privileged position in that fragmented state. The state was not inherently capitalist but business was in an inherently strong position within a capitalist system (see Chapter 12). Lindblom (1982) recognized the many flaws in the conventional pluralist conception of the state and argued for the mainstream to at least consider the hypothesis of radical and Marxist conceptions of the state. For instance, Lindblom examined the notion of socialization, which in US social science was used in a benign sense of transmitting social values and rules, and asked whether the Marxist notion that it is a form of indoctrination allowing the advantaged to retain control should at least be tested (1982: 19–20). In what is a strong critique of pluralism Lindblom (1982: 19) argued:

> We fall into a bad habit of simply taking for granted that people in society will think alike, as though agreement was a natural phenomenon that requires no explanation. Even natural phenomena require explanation ... Agreement on political fundamentals cries for an explanation.

Lindblom questioned the fundamental pluralist notion that consensus is necessarily an indication of political contentment. He concluded by calling for conventional theory to bring in radical thought 'from the cold' (Lindblom 1982: 20). Neo-pluralists escape from the pluralist position of seeing policymaking as *a priori* pluralistic and the Marxist position as seeing it as *a priori* dominated by a ruling class (see Marsh in Chapter 12 of this book for further discussion).

In the UK notions of pluralism were revived through the concept of policy networks and policy communities, particularly in the work of Richardson and Jordan (1979). They focused on using empirically rich case studies to highlight the complexity of the policy process and implicitly critique the generalized assumptions of Marxist and elitist approaches. Richardson and Jordan used empirical analysis of British politics to emphasize the complex and fragmented nature of policymaking in the UK. They again emphasized the role of groups in policymaking and highlighted the consultative and consensual nature of the policy process. For Richardson and Jordan there was a strong imperative in the British political system for government to consult with groups and more particularly for different groups to be represented in different policy areas, thus ensuring no single group dominated (see Richardson and Jordan 1979; Jordan and Richardson 1987a; Jordan and Richardson 1987b; Jordan 1981). Their work drew explicitly on the work of American political scientists in the pluralist tradition such as Bentley. They argued that 'the interplay of interest groups is the dominating feature of the policy process in Western Europe' (Richardson and Jordan 1979: 3) and that the adoption of policies is 'the reflection of the strength of particular groups at any one time' (Richardson and Jordan 1979: 6). Both of these were hyperbolic claims considering the strength of state traditions in many West European countries, including Britain. However, Richardson and Jordan did try to develop the pluralist tradition by drawing on the work of later American group theorists, such as Heclo (1978), Ripley and Franklin (1987) and Gais, Peterson and Walker (1984), who saw the political system as fragmented into distinct policy domains. Within some of these domains it was possible that there were barriers to entry and that particular groups dominated. Richardson and Jordan maintained most of the presumptions of the pluralist position. First, they saw groups as crucial to the policy process and in fact saw state–group relations as undermining the parliamentary system. Second, they maintained that power was dispersed and fragmented across a range of policy areas with no single interest dominating across a range of policy communities. Third, they presented the dominant policy style in Britain (if there can be such a thing) as one of negotiation. They suggested that civil servants were driven by the imperative of consensus to consult widely and to take account of the views of different groups. Policymaking was characterized by cooperation and consensus (Jordan and Richardson 1987b). Fourth, they believed that access to policymaking was relatively open, with most reasonable groups being able to gain access to the consultation lists of Whitehall departments. Richardson and Jordan's framework was undermined by the fact that the Thatcher government was anything but consensual in terms of most pressure groups (Smith 2015) and by their failure to recognize that many groups were excluded from the policy domains that they saw as relatively open. They made three fundamental errors. One was the common error of pluralists: to mistake, as Marsh (2002) argues, plurality for pluralism. The existence of many groups and policy domains does not mean that power is dispersed and that access is open. Second, they assumed that the existence of groups on consultation lists and involved in discussion with officials meant they had influence. Third, they saw networks as essentially agency-based, in other words dependent on personal relationships, and so, like other pluralists, they ignored the structural basis of power.

Developments in contemporary pluralism

Despite almost a century of empirical and theoretical critiques of pluralism, the pluralist tradition remains strong. It has reinvigorated itself over the past decade in a range of fields, each drawing on different parts of the pluralist tradition. Pluralism's strength derives from its normative appeal and the fact that much of it accords with our intuitive sense of liberal democracy.

In addition, the critics of pluralism, in particular Marxism and elitism, have in the case of the former been discredited, or in the case of the latter have either not developed or become incorporated into different elements of pluralist thought (see Chapters 2 and 3). There are four main ways that pluralism has developed in contemporary political science. Notions of governance have developed out of post-war American pluralism. Interests in social capital and civil society have drawn on themes highlighted by the early American pluralists. Similarly, notions of associational democracy and radical democracy have explicitly borrowed from the early English pluralists and the anarchist strands found in French pluralism (Laborde 2000). Finally, the development of multiculturalism can be linked back to what Nichols (1974) calls the plural society literature. We will now examine each of these developments.

Governance

Governance, developing out of the policy network approach, is a term used to describe the making of public policy and the delivery of public goods in modern states following the rise of the New Right, the development of new public management, public-sector reform and globalization. For the theorists of governance, it is a way of understanding the state and its relationship with civil society in the context of an increasingly complex society. However, much of what comes within the framework of governance could be derived from mainstream American pluralism. The term governance, like pluralism, covers a wide spectrum of views and a range of different sub-disciplines within political science. The fundamental premise of the governance position is that the central state is no longer the dominant force in determining public policy. For some, such as Rosenau (1990), we now live in a centreless society. There is not a single centre of government but, like Dahl's polycentrism, many that include a variety of actors. Consequently, the policy process is highly fragmented. The key point from this perspective is that, in a world with multiple interests, it is more realistic to see the policy process as one that is complex and multi-centred. As Cairney, Heikkila and Wood (2019: 2) suggest:

> Many theories embrace the notion of complex, polycentric or multi-level governance. They recognise that a focus on a single central government, consisting of a core group of actors making policy in a series of linear stages, provides a misleading description of the policy process. Instead,

policymaking occurs through multiple, overlapping and interacting centres of decision-making containing many policymakers and influencers. An image of kaleidoscopic activity should replace the misleading image of a single circle associated with the policy cycle.

What is interesting about this approach is that it effectively reproduces a pluralist conception of policymaking by recognizing the complex, fragmented and multi-centred idea of the policy process. In the context of an increasingly complex world, it is difficult, if not impossible, for a single authority to control the policy process.

Like the work of classic US pluralists such as Lindblom, governance is presented as reflecting a 'realistic' view of policymaking. In doing so, it makes some of the same errors as traditional pluralism. There is a failure to problematize the state, there is a lack of recognition of asymmetries of power and an assumption that complexity equals plurality. In addition, like the policy network approach, it focuses on the multiple actors that can be involved in policy areas and the ways in which membership of networks is functionally differentiated. However, it fails to pay sufficient attention to the groups that are excluded from the policy process. In many ways, increased complexity highlights the difficulties of democratic representation as citizens find it difficult to negotiate the complex processes involved in policymaking. It is also worth noting that many radical/Marxist approaches to the state seem to accept some element of the governance approach in their recent conceptualizations of the state. No longer is the state a simple instrument of a class or of capital but a 'multidimensional institution' which has to deal with a range of interests and conflicts over multiple sites (Glasberg, Willis and Shannon 2017: 137 and see Jessop 2007), with policy outcomes reflecting power conflicts between groups rather than the dominance of a single interest. Davies (2011) provides a Marxist-influenced critique of governance, pointing out that notions of governance are linked to neoliberal approaches to governing and the reality is that governance processes continue to be in the shadow of hierarchy (Jessop 2007) and so are effectively an alternative means for reproducing government control that favours business interests. In addition, the notion of depoliticization demonstrates how the fragmentation of decision-making into quasi-governmental organizations is a mechanism for excluding citizens from political debates rather than pluralizing decision-making (Fawcett et al. 2017). For example, the creation of the National Institute of Clinical Excellence as a body that licenses drug use is a way of limiting public debate about the use of certain drugs through making decisions technocratic (Wood 2015).

Civil society and social capital

One of the themes of early pluralists in both the United States and Britain is that a strong civil society, community organization and citizen activism are important both as bulwarks against the state and as mechanisms for delivering public goods. The early American pluralists, Dewey and Follet, emphasized that individual identity did not exist outside of groups and that group identity was essential both to protect individual freedom and to limit the power of the state. For Follet (1918) the group was the building block of a healthy and democratic polity. In a sense, groups provided an alternative mode of collective organization to the state and also, then, a mechanism for delivering public goods and political interaction. Follet believed that groups were a mechanism for self-government. For authoritarian and social democratic thinkers, the resolution to collective action problems lies in the state. For pluralists, the dependence on the state for collective provision of goods results in an overbearing state and the loss of individual liberty. Consequently, many pluralists looked to the community or the group for collective provision. This is precisely the sort of argument that Putnam is making in his work on social capital. Putnam sees the decline in membership of local associations of whatever type as a major cause of social and economic ills in the United States and elsewhere. For Putnam, membership of associations builds trust and this social capital is essential for economic development: 'Social capital is coming to be seen as a crucial ingredient in economic development around the world' (Putnam 1993: 37). Putnam, like the early English and American pluralists, sees membership of associations as essential for both personal and community development. For Putnam, the strengthening of civil society is a necessary mechanism for restoring democracy and economic development throughout the world. Putnam is a graduate of Yale and locates himself firmly within the tradition of American pluralism (Merelman 2003: 196). He makes errors similar to those of traditional and American pluralism. The poor of the inner cities are not poor because of structured inequality, but because of their failure to build social capital (see DeFilippis 2001). Putnam examines Tuscany and Sicily and suggests that Sicily's lack of economic development and democracy is because of the absence of social capital, not because of patterns of land ownership or its position on the periphery of Europe. He is insistent on the causal relation being one of lack of social capital leading to the absence of economic development rather than the other way around. Like other pluralists he sees a simple, voluntarist solution to deep-seated structural problems and ignores the constraints that may exist on group organization. What this perspective leads to is a limited role for the state. The state has to develop social linkages rather than develop large-scale welfare and economic programmes to tackle social inequality and economic development.

Radical democracy and associationalism

Modernized notions of pluralism, which have resonance with social capital, are the concepts of radical democracy and associationalism. Ironically, whilst pluralism appears foundationalist in its epistemology and positivist in its methodology, pluralist concerns can be discerned in postmodernist writings. Like pluralists, postmodernists reject monism and in particular the Marxist belief in a single truth and explanation. Postmodernists and radical democrats pick up on many of the traditional concerns of pluralism. According to McClure (1992: 15), they have been articulated in crucial opposition to unitary, monolithic or totalizing conceptions of the political domain, particularly in so far as these presume some singularly sovereign or unique agency overseeing or determining political processes and/or social relations This leads to a pluralist conception of knowledge. No organization can have a monopoly of knowledge. Wainwright (1994) highlights knowledge as socially constructed; it is impossible for a single person, group or party to know everything. Ideally, knowledge should be demystified into a range of social movements. Thus, central to radical democrats, like Putnam, is a strong belief in the richness of civil society and the importance of social movements as a mechanism for controlling and circumventing the monopolizing tendencies of the state. Like traditional pluralists, radical democrats see social movements as crucial elements in society. Civil society is complex and pluralist, with individuals belonging to an array of social groups. These groups do not have a preordained existence or identity but develop as a consequence of struggle and social interaction (McClure 1992: 115). Radical democrats offer their pluralism as a critique, rather than legitimization, of liberal democracy and in their extreme relativism take a very different epistemology to classical pluralism. Nevertheless, some of the criticisms of traditional pluralism can also be made of radical democracy. Like most of the forms of pluralism discussed in this chapter they fail to develop a convincing theory of the state. State power is almost bracketed off into a separate sphere from the world of social movements and self-organization.

Where radical democrats do conceptualize the relationship between the state and civil society, they tend to offer an almost benign notion of the state (see Dryzek 1996). Consequently, they do not offer effective strategies for overcoming state power. Similarly to traditional pluralists and Putnam, hope for political transformation is vested in social groups. However, the relativism of postmodernists means that they can make no moral claims regarding the status of various groups and thus cannot deal with groups that do not subscribe to the goals of radical democracy. Their approach is to politicize the whole of society (which is very different from traditional pluralism). The problem then arises of how the interests of minorities are protected if the state is weak and political interests are highly salient?

Multiculturalism and the plural society

Multiculturalism attempts to deal with some of the problems radical pluralism raises in a more grounded and normative approach. Multiculturalism can be rooted in pluralist thought because it is based on the idea that no single set of norms or values should dominate a society and that the role of the state should be about reconciling different interests rather than ensuring the dominance of a particular group. It can be traced back to the notions of the plural society which developed as a way of analysing colonial societies where different groups were forced together. Consequently, within a colonial system there could be a number of ethnic groups living side by side with little interaction and each maintaining their traditional patterns of social life, norms and values (see Nichols 1974). However, unlike notions of multiculturalism which is seen as normatively good, plural societies were held together merely by the existence of a shared economic system and force. Multiculturalism has become one of the central debates in political theory. Whilst in many ways it differs from the sorts of pressure-group pluralism we have discussed earlier in the chapter, and unlike the notion of a plural society, it does not see a multicultural society as being based on force but as being normatively good. It reflects some of the themes that recur in plural society. First, multiculturalism is based on the notion of group identities. What is important for multiculturalists is group rights. Second, multiculturalists are opposed to the notion that a single pluralism (particularly the majority group) can dominate other groups. The basis of multiculturalism is the equal treatment of groups and so the role of the state is to balance conflicting group interests. There is a presumption amongst some multiculturalists, such as Walzer (2002: 151), that the state 'stands above all the various ethnic and nationalist groups in the country' (Kymlicka 2001: 16). Walzer in particular, like the mainstream American pluralists, takes a benign view of the US state, seeing it as 'neutral among the various thick cultures sustained by different groups of immigrants' (Walzer 2002: 151). However, the multiculturalist debate has been moved on to examine how the state should adopt a positive role in developing and protecting the rights of minority groups. This view is based again on a benign view that the state is the force able, and possibly willing, to protect the rights of minorities. Of course, whilst in some liberal states policy will make rhetorical concessions to minority rights, the impact on groups in terms of employment, housing and education may be limited. Other liberal states, such as France, are still concerned with protecting the rights of majorities from a multiculturalist frame. Multiculturalists also draw on the pluralist tradition of seeing rights as group-based rather than individually based. It may be a good thing to protect the rights of Muslims to sustain their culture and religion in Britain. However, there may be some Muslim women who want to have their rights protected as individuals rather than as Muslims. Why should our rights be linked to groups that are essentially arbitrary? This, of course, is the dilemma of multiculturalism: how do group rights impact on individual rights and is there a tension between the two?

Pluralism in an unequal world

Many of the classic and recent pluralist approaches see liberal democracy as providing a framework for the representation of diverse views and argue for political equality being a constraint on the unequal distribution of wealth. It is relatively easy to point to examples of identity politics, for instance, having considerable impact on the rights of a range of excluded groups and a shift to a much stronger rights-based approach that sees different groups having their interests protected or even enshrined in legislation. However, at the same time, the twenty-first century has seen growing economic inequality that has had a significant impact on the distribution of both power and public goods (Dorling 2019). As Machin (2013) highlights, the super rich provide a direct challenge to the notion of political equality as the scale of inequality distorts the processes of democratic representation. It is estimated that the richest 1 per cent controls 44 per cent of the world's wealth (Credit Suisse

2019). In the United States, the early twenty-first century has seen a return to the level of inequality of the early twentieth century. This inequality has direct and indirect impacts on power. Directly, the super rich have very close relationships with the political elite and provide a considerable amount of the funding of political parties and individual politicians. In addition, corporate lobbyists spend considerable amounts of money attempting to influence government policy (Culpepper 2010). The last twenty years have seen the rich benefit disproportionately from fiscal policy (Blyth 2013) and the poorest sections of society paying for the 2008 financial crash through austerity policies (Mendoza 2015). The indirect consequences of rising inequality are dramatic, with the poorest sectors of society seeing the worst outcomes in terms of education, life chances and, in particular, health (Wilkinson and Pickett 2010; Dorling 2019). The Covid-19 crisis clearly illustrates the impact of inequality, with the poorest suffering most in terms of both the economic impact and health outcomes (see also Conclusion). Inequality has managed to prevent the political system operating in the interest of the less well off; a point recognized by the growth of populism in the United States and Europe (see Chapter 14). Pluralists failed to see how economic inequalities shaped political outcomes. At the same time there have been attempts to defend pluralism against the populist surge (Galston 2017).

Conclusion

Pluralism is a remarkable theory because, despite the many criticisms of the approach – and not a small number of empirical refutations – it continues to have influence on how politics is conceived and studied. In a sense, this is a consequence of its not being a single, coherent theory but more an approach that focuses on the role of groups in the policy process and its rejection of monistic ways of thinking. Pluralism has been effective in helping the development of more realistic and complex models of policymaking. However, it has been able to do this by insufficiently attending to the nature of state and economic power. What nearly all pluralists fail to recognize in any systematic way are the asymmetries of power as a consequence of the concentrations of economic power and the social concentration of economic power embedded in inequality. Pluralists undoubtedly complexify our understanding of policy processes by highlighting the complex and fragmented nature of policymaking and the fact that policy outcomes are often the result of compromise as governments and policymakers attempt to build coalitions of support. However, they assume that there are many different forms of power that can limit and contradict economic power. From a pluralist perspective, political systems, decision-making and successful policy outcomes rely on some degree of wider social cooperation and therefore the imposition of policies without consent is problematic. However, pluralists fail to confront the ways in which outcomes tend to favour particular groups (Marsh 2002). Yet the period since 2008 has seen a realization that both the economic power of business and the political power of the wealthy affect political outcomes in ways that make access to the political system difficult for the ordinary citizen. The consequence of the 2008 financial crisis was that governments across Europe imposed austerity as a mechanism for reinforcing the banking system.

Further Reading

Cairney, P., T. Heikkila and M. Wood (2019), *Making Policy in a Complex World*, Cambridge: Cambridge University Press.

Dahl, R.A. (1961), *Who Governs?*, New Haven, CT: Yale University Press.

Galston, W.A. (2017), *Anti-Pluralism: The Populist Threat to Liberal Democracy*, New Haven, CT: Yale University Press.

Laborde, C. (2000), *Pluralist Thought and the State in Britain and France, 1900–25*, Basingstoke: Palgrave Macmillan.

Lindblom, C.E. (1982), 'Another state of mind', *American Political Science Review*, 76(1), 9–21.

Lukes, S. (1974), *Power: A Radical View*, Basingstoke: Macmillan.

Merelman, R.M. (2003), *Pluralism at Yale: The Culture of Political Science in America*, Madison: University of Wisconsin Press.

2

Elitism

Mark Evans

Introduction

This chapter presents a critical review of the nature of elite theory and assesses its contribution to our understanding of contemporary state theory. It traces its classical origins in the thought of Robert Michels ([1911] 1962), Vilfredo Pareto (1935) and Gaetano Mosca ([1896] 1939) and their critique of Marxism and pluralism to the views of the modern elitists and contested perspectives on the character of governing elites in advanced industrial societies. The chapter then turns to the contemporary elitists, the study of statecraft and the rediscovery of populist leadership democracy in response to economic crisis and declining trust in the established political order.

The chapter examines the core propositions associated with elite theory, such as the inevitability of elite domination, circulation and renewal. It places a particular emphasis on how and why new elite projects emerge in critique of the established political order driven by charismatic leaders. It observes that in recent times successful leadership projects have been founded on anti-globalist rhetoric in critique of the neoliberal competition state. However, it ultimately questions whether such projects and the underpinning notion of 'strong man' leadership will bridge the trust divide between the liberal democratic state and civil society.

The discussion is organized into four parts. Part one investigates the emergence of classical elitism and its core propositions. In part two we examine the contribution of a select range of modern elitist perspectives, which seek to understand the operational bases of governing elites. Part three focuses on the contemporary study of three types of elite reflecting old and new power – political elites governing through traditional forms of statecraft, populist elites challenging traditional statecraft, and transnational policy elites. Part four assesses the potential of artificial intelligence (AI) in displacing traditional nation-state elites in future democratic governance. The study of these different types of elite provides important insights into the form and function of governing elites at global and national levels of governance.

Foundations

Elitism as a theory of social power is most associated with the work of Michels ([1911] 1962), Pareto (1935) and Mosca ([1896] 1939). Their common thesis was that the concentration of social power in a small set of controlling elites was inevitable in all societies and they disagreed with Karl Marx's vision of evolutionary change towards a classless society. As Gaetano Mosca ([1896] 1939: 50), puts it, the history of politics has been characterized by elite domination:

> In all societies – from societies that are very meagrely developed and have barely attained the dawning of civilization, down to the most advanced and powerful societies – two classes of people appear – a class that rules and a class that is ruled. The first class, always the less numerous, performs all political functions, monopolizes power and enjoys the advantages that power brings, whereas the second, the more numerous class, is directed and controlled by the first.

Each of these thinkers engaged in a critique of Marxism and pluralism and particularly the concepts of class domination and the diffusion of power on pluralist lines. Three important concepts can be derived from their work – the iron law of oligarchy, elite circulation and the political formula.

The iron law of oligarchy

Robert Michels ([1911] 1962: 364) argued that the practical ideal of democracy consisted in the self-government of the masses in conformity with the decision-making of popular assemblies. However, while this system placed limits upon the extension of the principle of delegation, it fails 'to provide any guarantee against the formation of an oligarchic camarilla'. In short, direct government by the masses was impossible. Michels applied a similar argument to political parties. In his view, the technical and administrative functions of political parties make first bureaucracy and then oligarchy inevitable. Hence, for Michels ([1911] 1962: 364), '[w]ho says organization, says oligarchy'. This maxim clearly determined his conception of the nature of elites. The notorious notion of the 'iron law of oligarchy' provides the key to Michels's theorization of the nature of elite structures, for it ensures the dominance of the leadership over the rank and file membership. Elite circulation is maintained by the inability of the masses to mobilize against the leadership view. This ensures their subjugation to the whim of the elite. In essence, it is the very existence of this system of leadership which is incompatible with the tenets of liberal democracy and pluralism.

Elite circulation

Pareto argued that historical experience provides testimony to the perpetual circulation of elites and oligarchy and that every field of human enterprise has its own elite. Pareto borrowed two categories of elites from Machiavelli, 'Foxes' and 'Lions' (1935: 99, 110), to illustrate the nature of governing elite structures. The two categories stand at opposite ends of a continuum of government. 'Foxes' govern by attempting to gain consent and are not prepared to use force; they are intelligent and cunning, enterprising, artistic and innovative. However, in times of crisis, their misplaced humanitarianism leads them towards compromise and pacifism. Hence, for Pareto, when final attempts to reach a political solution have failed the regime is fatally weakened. 'Lions' are situated at the opposite end of the continuum. They are depicted as men of strength, stability and integrity. Cold and unimaginative, they are self-serving and are prepared to use force to achieve or maintain their position. 'Lions' are defenders of the status quo in both the state and civil society and they are likely to be committed to public order, religion and political orthodoxy. For Pareto, the qualities of 'Fox' and 'Lion' are generally mutually exclusive and history is featured by a process of circulation between these two types of elites.

Pareto's identification of the concentration of power in the hands of a narrow political elite represented a rejection of the Marxist conception of the state as a mere tool of the ruling class and the notion of class conflict (see Chapter 3). At the same time, Pareto's elitist perspective is at odds with the claims of political liberalism that the state acts as a coordinator of the national interest in a plural society.

The political formula

In a similar vein, Mosca argued that elites were inevitable as all societies are characterized by the dictatorship of the majority by the minority. He identified the existence of a ruling, but not necessarily economically dominant, class from which key office holders were drawn. Within Mosca's formulation each ruling class develops a political formula, which maintains and legitimates its rule to the rest of the population. Elite circulation will usually occur through inheritance but, from time to time, power will pass into the hands of another class, due to the failure and collapse of the political formula.

Mosca's conceptualization of the political formula has much in common with the concept of hegemony, which springs from the views of Marx and Engels ([1845] 1987) in *The German Ideology*: that the ideas of the ruling class are in every historical stage the ruling ideas. However, unlike his Marxist contemporary, Antonio Gramsci, Mosca failed to develop the concept of the political formula in any systematic way. Nevertheless, the centrality of the ideological dimension to an understanding of the dialectic of power domination and control is an important consideration which Mosca clearly overlooked.

In sum, classical elite theory challenged the key premises of most Western liberal assumptions about politics, the organization of government and the relationship between the state and civil society. For elitists, the nature of any society – whether it is consensual or authoritarian, pacifist or totalitarian – is determined by the nature of its elite. Hence, in its classical formulation, elite theory had a clear set of propositions about the distribution of power in society: the rulers of society constitute a socially cohesive group; this group is territorially based within a nation-state; the ruling elite is 'closed-off' from the ruled; and its members are selected by virtue of their economic, political or ideological resources.

Michels, Pareto and Mosca generally assume the integration of elites without any rigorous empirical investigation. Michels argued that Western European political parties were characterized by elite domination but his fondness for selecting convenient empirical evidence to support his arguments is vulnerable to counter critique. Moreover, Pareto failed to demonstrate a theory of elite domination in his native Italy, given the advent of fascism and the overthrow of the social order by Benito Mussolini (1922–44). Moreover, while Mosca showed that governments in the past were often characterized by a self-serving elite, he did not establish that this was always the case. Perhaps not surprisingly then, given this classical legacy, subsequent elite theorists have strongly disagreed about the nature, causes and consequences of elite rule in Western industrialized societies.

The modern elitists

This section presents a selective review of modern elitist perspectives on who rules industrial societies. It concentrates on two key areas of consideration within the history of modern elitist thought: national elite power studies and state-centred 'governing elite' perspectives.

National elite power studies

The study of national elite power networks has long been a focus of study in the United States and Britain. The key concern of this literature has been to identify the degree to which national elite structures are unified or diversified. The origins of these studies lie in the pluralist-radical elitist debates of the 1940s and 1950s in the United States led by the radical elitist C. Wright Mills (1956). His theory involved a three-level gradation of the distribution of power. At the top level were those in command of the major institutional hierarchies of modern society – the executive branch of the national government, the large business corporations and the military establishment. According to Mills (1956: 292):

> The conception of the power elite and of its unity rests upon the corresponding developments and the coincidence of interests among economic, political, and military organizations. It also rests upon the similarity of origins and outlook, and the social and personal intermingling of the top circles from each of these dominant hierarchies.

The existence of a broad, inclusive network of powerful persons with similar social origins, in different institutions, is an important feature of this view of the power structure. However, the power elite literature identifies three key dimensions of political elite integration: social homogeneity which emphasizes shared class and status origins; value consensus which focuses on agreement among elites on the 'rules of the game'; and personal interaction among elites, both informally through social and personal interaction and formally through membership of common organizations. This third dimension is reflected in the interlocking directorates of major US corporations. These ties are seen to foster integration, cohesiveness and consensus within the business community. Many social scientists, particularly in the United States, have also examined these sociometric ties among elites in individual professional communities (see Burnham 1943 and Laumann 1976).

In the UK a number of historians have considered the fate of the English aristocracy (Perrott 1968 and Winchester 1981), dwelling on the changing nature of the relationship between landed and mercantile interests or the declining role of the landed aristocracy in the government of rural England. From 1977 to 1979 Heather Clemenson (1982) conducted a sample survey of landowners listed in John Bateman's compilation of the *Return of the Owners Land* ([1883] 2014). Clemenson showed that, more than 100 years after the Local Government Board published the Second Domesday census and despite their claims of near-extinction, half of her stratified sample of 500 'great English landowners' continued to own their original estates and mansions.

Roger Pierce revisited Clemenson's survey in 2004 and, indeed, reinforced the sample with data gathered from a case study of 'Derwent' in eastern Yorkshire in which narratives were obtained from a cross-section of residents of 'closed', 'intermediate' and 'open' villages in moorland, vale and wold villages, including local landowners and other leading members of rural society. His findings reveal that nearly all of the landowners identified by Clemenson continue to own the surviving estates and, indeed, more than 40 per cent of the original sample of estates remain in the ownership of the same families identified by Bateman in 1873. Moreover, while the number of 'great English landowners' halved between 1873 and 1980, the area of land retained has only been reduced by a third.

In contrast, Anthony Sampson (1962, 1982) in his exhaustive accounts of the anatomy of Britain has argued that the aristocracy no longer rules and, indeed, that there is no longer a real social elite at all. Further, Sampson contends that the various hierarchies of British society have become gradually more open in their recruitment and the diversity of these hierarchies is such that there is no single centre of power. However, Sampson's analyses fail to place political power in its broader economic and social context.

In contrast, John Scott (1991: 1), working within the power elite tradition argues that:

> The view is widely held that in Britain there is a small minority, which holds a ruling position in its economy, society, and political system. This minority has been described in numerous varying ways: 'The establishment', 'the powers that be', 'the ruling few', the 'elite', or more prosaically, 'them'.

Scott's (1991: 4–5) analysis epitomizes the convergence between elitist and Marxist theories of the state, drawing on the work of both Weber and Marx; '[s]pecifically, I use Weber's analytical distinctions between class, status, and party as ways of clarifying the Marxian concepts of the capitalist state and the ruling class'. His work gives much attention to the question of social status:

> The hierarchy of status is seen as an important element in the legitimation of power structures, and the dynamics of status group relations are seen as integral elements in class reproduction and in the formation of power blocs. (Ibid.)

Thus, for Scott, the concepts of 'capitalist class', 'upper circle' and 'state elite' are interchangeable terms for describing privileged groups, which exercise power deriving from class, status and politics (see Chapter 12). His conclusion (Scott 1991: 151– 152) reflects the balance of these concerns:

> The question 'Who Rules Britain?' can now be answered. Britain is ruled by a capitalist class whose economic dominance is sustained by the operations of the state and whose members are disproportionately represented in the power elite which rules the state apparatus. That is to say, Britain does have a ruling class.

The statists and the governing elite

By the mid-1980s virtually every significant current of theoretical work in political science was united in a renewed interest in the state itself as the fundamental unit of analysis. As Peter Evans, Dietrich Rueschemeyer and Theda Skocpol (1985: 3) acknowledge, 'the state as an actor or institution has been highlighted' (see also Chapter 5). The two leading exponents of the statist position were Theda Skocpol (1985) and Michael Mann (1988).

Skocpol (1979: 26) argues that fundamental conflicts of interest can arise between the existing dominant class or set of groups, on the one hand, and state rulers on the other. She developed six key propositions which characterize the statist position:

1 The class upheavals and socioeconomic transformations which have characterized social revolutions have been closely intertwined with the collapse of the state organizations of the old regimes and with the consolidation and functioning of the state organizations of the new regimes, hence, we can make sense of socio-revolutionary transformations only if we take the state seriously as a macrostructure.

2 The administrative (public services) and coercive (police, intelligence and military services) organizations are the basis of state power.

3 These organizations are potentially autonomous from direct-dominant class control.

4 State organizations necessarily compete to some extent with the dominant class(es) in appropriating resources from economy and society.

5 Although the state functions to preserve existing economic and class structures it nonetheless has its own distinct interests vis-à-vis the dominant class(es).

6 States will join geopolitical entities that share common economic and class interests (e.g. the institutions of global governance) as long as its activities do not threaten the interests of its ruling elite.

This formulation is significant in the sense that it stresses both the role of a powerful governing elite and the importance of treating the question of the legitimacy of governing elites as a key explanatory concept.

Mann's (1988: 4) principal interest lies in what he terms 'the centralized institutional ensembles called states and the powers of the personnel who staff them'; hence, the 'governing or state elite'. His work confronts the question: what is the nature of the power possessed by states and state elites? He contrasts the power of state elites with power groupings in civil society, such as ideological movements, economic classes and military elites. Mann emphasizes two meanings of state power, which correspond to the rise in the size and complexity of the state and the decision-making process in advanced industrial societies. These he recognizes as two analytically distinct and autonomous dimensions of power. The first, 'despotic power', relates to the range of actions which the elite is empowered to take without traditional negotiation with civil society while the second, 'infrastructural power', refers to the capacity of the state to actually penetrate civil society and to implement political decisions. Mann (1988: 5) observes that '[t]he state penetrates everyday life more than did any historical state. Its infrastructural power has increased enormously.'

It would be wrong to exaggerate the novelty of the revival of interest in the state, for as Bob Jessop (1990: 283) has observed, 'the statists have simply rediscovered themes well known to traditional state theorists and not unknown in more recent pluralist, neo-Marxist and structural-functionalist work'. This common observation stimulated considerable disagreement amongst commentators as to whether there is a distinctive elitist approach (see, for example, Birch 1993: ch. 11; Dunleavy and O'Leary 1987: ch. 4). Certainly there has been a great deal of convergence with the distinction between the pluralist, Marxist and elitist positions becoming more blurred as the capitalist state has matured. However, elitism has always been a broad church. Indeed, many theorists have treated Marxist theory as an elitist theory due to its emphasis upon the state as an instrument for securing ruling-class domination (see Birch 1993: 186; see also Chapter 3). Secondly, while most authors agree on the roots of classical elitism, there is little consensus on which modern theorists can be considered under the elitist banner. The conceptual ambiguity surrounding the elitist position means that, despite the challenge which elitist thought poses to the main premises of the liberal democratic model, there exists no adequate elitist theory which demonstrates satisfactorily that the distribution of political power can be described as elitist. As such, elite theory provides only a partial understanding of the relationship between the state and civil society.

Contemporary elitist approaches

This section of the chapter focuses on the contemporary study of three types of elite, reflecting old and new power (Tims and Heimans 2018) – political elites governing through traditional forms of statecraft, populist elites challenging traditional statecraft, and transnational policy elites.

Old power is based on *controlling* structures, specialism and oversight, while new power is driven by greater connectivity and *enabling* activity characterized by open sharing and conditional affiliation and more overall participation. Old power is not dissolved but it is being challenged. New power involves reforms that promise citizens not control but more power to get things done, to find their own solutions, individually and collectively. New power focuses on collaboration and rapid feedback loops and participation. Here participation is less about moving towards control and more about influence and creativity. Above all, we live in a more polarized world of 'us' and 'them'. In most liberal democracies the sense of belonging to a successful 'national' project is being questioned as income inequality widens. In between there are increasing numbers of distrusting citizens who are either economically marginalized, or feeling economically insecure, fearful for their jobs in an age of continual restructuring, cost containment and casualization.

Statecraft and the governing elite

Although the statecraft approach in certain aspects lacks conceptual clarity, it does provide a useful conceptual framework for understanding the approach of governing elites to contemporary policymaking. So what does the statecraft approach involve? The approach was originally developed by the British political scientist Jim Bulpitt in 1986 and has subsequently been applied to the study of prime ministerial leadership in the United Kingdom (Buller and James 2011) and Australia (Evans 2010; Evans and McCaffrie 2014, 2016), to European Union decision-making (Buller 2000) and to electoral statecraft (James 2012). It emerged in response to a number of authors who stressed the importance of the New Right ideological project as an understanding of the emergence and development of Thatcherism in the UK (see Hall and Jacques 1983). Bulpitt disagreed with writers such as Stuart Hall and Martin Jacques that the New Right project provided the grand design of the Thatcher project and shaped the nature of the policy agenda. He argued that ideas themselves were never that important. Instead, he emphasized the importance of what he termed statecraft or the 'politics of governing'.

Statecraft crystallizes around the study of a core political elite, which Bulpitt (1986) refers to as 'the Centre' or 'the Court', composed of party leaders and senior public servants and policy advisers. Bulpitt argues that this group has its own interests, which are distinct from those of the rest of society, and can often successfully pursue these interests, even in the face of opposition from other actors. In other words, the statecraft approach is an elite theory of public policymaking.

According to Bulpitt, there are three conditions of successful statecraft. First, the Centre/Court needs to establish a set of governing objectives with the aim of winning elections and retaining office by achieving an image of governing competence. Secondly, in order to achieve these objectives it has to develop a governing code (similar to Mosca's political formula) – a set of principles, beliefs and practices. This involves the preservation and promotion of domestic autonomy over what Bulpitt calls 'High Politics' and the devolution of delivery responsibility to 'Low Politics'. In practical terms, High Politics refers to all those policy issues which the Centre considers to be vital to its chances of winning elections and achieving an image of governing competence. Autonomy over High Politics is crucial to the achievement of governing competence. Low Politics is a residual category. It refers to all the other matters perceived by the Centre to be too mundane, difficult or time-consuming to handle. Thirdly, in trying to win elections and achieve some semblance of governing competence, the Centre/Court will employ a set of 'political support mechanisms' to assist the governing code. These mechanisms refer to the functions of party management and the achievement of political argument hegemony. As Bulpitt (1986: 22) puts it, this refers to 'a winning rhetoric in a variety of locations, winning because either the framework of the party's arguments becomes generally acceptable, or because its solutions to a particularly important political problem seem more plausible than its opponents'.

In short, then, statecraft is about the politics of governing. It involves short-term tactical manoeuvring – qualities which are essential to every successful electoral strategy. It is also concerned with longer-term strategic calculation and action to ensure governing elite circulation. For Bulpitt, governing elites can think strategically and alter institutions and structures to help them achieve their political goals more easily.

Empirically, there have been examples of sustained successful statecraft in Westminster-style democracies. In the United Kingdom, for example, we could refer to the governments of Margaret Thatcher (1979–90) and Tony Blair (1997–2007) and, in Australia, John Howard (1996–2007). The three projects achieved dominance in High Politics, combined with a necessary degree of governing competence and, with it, electoral dominance. Remarkably, each project was largely driven by pragmatism, owing more to the need to maintain electoral success than appeal to a particular ideology.

Governing across borders – the rise of transnational policy elites

As Timothy Legrand (2019: 200) observes, 'Global policy pathologies are transforming the processes, patterns, and outcomes of domestic policy.' This has been reflected in the emergence of new transnational administrative venues of policy praxis rooted in international organizations and networks that are addressing a broad range of cross-border issues resistant to nation-state action such as cyber security, climate change, intergenerational justice, migration and international terrorism (Stone and Ladi 2015). Diane Stone and Kim Maloney (2019: 3) argue that global policy networks and transnational administration 'are becoming key elements towards understanding the diversity of global governance' but, most significantly, they provide us with important insights into the emergence of an increasingly powerful and unaccountable transnational technocratic governing elite.

Diane Stone's (2004, 2012) research on transnational policy elites observes that in contrast to the nation-state domain, international organizations and non-state actors play a key role in facilitating 'soft' forms of policy transfer – such as the spread of norms – as a necessary complement to the hard transfer of policy tools. Indeed, transnational networks themselves are identified as the key strategic instrument for the spread of policy and practice not only cross-nationally but throughout the institutions of global governance. Stone (2012: 494) observes that 'the "soft" transfer of ideas and information via networks whether they be personal, professional or electronic is rapid and frequent'. As examples she refers to the role of the Inter-American Development Bank and the World Bank in facilitating the development of conditional cash transfer programmes through closed transnational policy networks with 'borrower governments' (Teichman 2007) and IMF training institutes providing courses for developing country policy elites, mostly economists. Other international organizations like the OECD use a comparative evidence base to diffuse common policy responses in specific fields to its membership. This encompasses critical governance issues from anti-corruption and public-sector productivity to public trust and gender equality and best practice guides to inform policy innovation, better governance and regulation.

The influence of this transnational policy elite will differ depending on the cultural styles of learning present at different spatialities of governance, dominant norms and values, the role that they have been asked to play and the resources that they bring to the process of policy learning (e.g. knowledge, social, economic and political capital). For example, André Broome (2010) evaluates the influence of the Joint Vienna Institute (JVI), an international training organization, in diffusing economic policy ideas (e.g. global policy norms) through the architecture of global governance. He argues that the Institute plays an important role in socializing national officials to accept new norms of national economic governance through the development of an interactive learning environment that facilitates three micro processes of socialization: mimicking, social influence and persuasion.

The JVI has played an important intermediate role in influencing the policy practices of the 23,000 policymakers and officials who have participated in policy-oriented economic training since the early 1990s and by helping to foster a transnational policy network among participants. More generally, international organizations operate as transnational administrative venues for both the socialization of national policy elites (Greenhill 2010) and for stronger forms of policy transfer to occur. Bulmer and colleagues (2007), in their groundbreaking study of policy transfer in the European Union, for example, find evidence to support the general hypothesis that stronger forms of policy transfer occur in highly institutionalized governance regimes. The evidence also points to *micro* institutional variables shaping transfer outcomes: the powers accruing to supra-national institutions; decision rules; and the density of exchange between national actors (see Evans 2019).

In sum, the scope and intensity of the activities of transnational policy elites in shaping domestic policy formation through transnational administration have increased at breathtaking speed over the past two decades. This has presented a significant dilemma for representative democracy at the national state level as this transnational policy elite has a limited legitimate basis for its exercise of political power (Skogstad 2019).

Political distrust, the governing elite and the rediscovery of populism

Jack Hayward writing in 1996 observed:

> The conflict between representative and direct democracy over which is the more authentic reflection of public opinion poses the tension between competing political leaders and a purported will of the people. The discredit of mediated party politics has led to increased recourse to referendums and to the emergence of social protest movements, notably extremists of left and right. The closed politics of the European Union, combined with the limited

democratic legitimacy of its decision taking, have promoted a tendency towards demagogic unreality expressed through anti-elitist populism.

Anti-elitist populism, if it ever went away, has moved back to the centre stage in contemporary democracies, providing an importance space for studying elite circulation. As Mikko Kuisma argues in Chapter 14, populist parties and movements are considered to represent an anti-establishment approach to politics, characterized by values that also stand in opposition to those of the liberal democratic state. But the latest populisms are not necessarily opposed to the state as such but to particular national elites that represent and protect the established political order. Hence, there is an important link here between elitism and populism in that the state itself becomes a site of struggle between old and new power, between traditional elites and populist elites that purport to represent an authentic expression of 'we the people'.

The substance of Hayward's commentary above remains as prescient today in explaining, for example, the 2016 Brexit vote in the UK, but there are some discernible differences to contemporary populism. In the past, populism has been associated with oppressive and intolerant political ideologies or creeds such as Nazism that were blatantly anti-democratic. But populism today finds its most common expression inside democracies and has in most cases forged an accommodation with democratic institutions. These contemporary forms of populism do not propose to abolish free elections or install dictatorships: on the contrary, their demand is for a democracy that 'delivers what the people want'. As Cas Mudde (2015) explains:

> Populism can be found on both the left and the right. This is not exactly the same as saying that populism is like a 'chameleon,' as it is not necessarily the same populist actor who changes colors. Populism rarely exists in a pure form, in the sense that most populist actors combine it with another ideology. This so-called host ideology, which tends to be very stable, is either left or right. Generally, left populists will combine populism with some interpretation of socialism, while right populists will combine it with some form of nationalism.

In Europe, much of the impact of populism has been through parties that have been set up to challenge the established political order with right-wing oriented populism doing better in northern Europe and left-leaning populism finding expression in southern Europe. By 2015 a populist party had gained at least 10 per cent of the popular vote in twenty European countries. In five they had become the largest party: Greece, Hungary, Italy, Slovakia and Switzerland. And in several countries populist parties have become the government or formed government coalitions (Mudde 2015). The 2016 Brexit vote in the UK was partly driven by populist politics (Stoker and Hay 2016) and Brexit Party leader Nigel Farage is widely seen as a populist politician. Even Jeremy Corbyn's unsuccessful but much better than predicted campaign for the Labour party in the 2017 UK general election is attributed by some to his populist framing of the election issues (Flinders 2017).

Beyond Europe, there is plenty of evidence of the impact of both old and new populisms on politics, such as the election of the authoritarian populist Rodrigo Duterte, the current president of the Philippines. Pauline Hanson in Australia, founder of the One Nation party, carries the flag of populism and, of course, the successful election campaign in 2016 for the US presidential office by Donald Trump has the hallmarks of a populist tilt at mainstream politics. Indeed, there are few contemporary democracies that remain untouched by the dynamics of populism (Rooduijn 2013, 2014; Rovira Kaltwasser and Taggart 2016).

There are also, of course, examples of elite circulation in recent times where populist movements have overthrown the established political order. For example, in Turkey beginning in 2003, Recep Tayyip Erdoğan embarked on a project 'to find a modus vivendi between democracy and Islam without altering the Republican structure' and raise 'pious generations' (Tol and Alemdaroglu 2020). Since Erdoğan's narrow success in the November 2002 general election with only 37 per cent of the vote, the Justice and Development Party (AKP) has passed a raft of constitutional amendments that have fundamentally changed the way Turkey is governed. This has included the replacement of a parliamentary system with a 'Turkish-style presidency', which will potentially keep Erdoğan in power until 2026. The armed forces have been neutralized and no longer have the power to oppose or evict Erdoğan and the AKP from the new office of the presidency. And he has used education reform as a force of Islamization by pouring billions of dollars into religious education. He dramatically increased the number of imam hatip secondary schools, which were originally founded by the state as vocational institutions to train young men to become imams and preachers, and extended this system to lower age groups. At state schools, he has increased the number of hours dedicated to religious education and banned the teaching of evolution from the curriculum. Islam is now predominant in Turkey's political arena and secularism is in decline. In 2007, the AKP obtained 46 per cent of the vote, whereas in 2011 this figure touched 50 per cent. Turkey under Erdoğan has been a classic example of elite circulation (Cagaptay 2017).

In contrast, on 3 September 2020 Sudan's transitional government agreed to separate religion from the state, ending thirty years of Islamic rule in the country (Reuters 2020). The leader of the Sudan People's Liberation Movement-North rebel group Abdel-Aziz al-Hilu and Sudanese prime minister Abdalla Hamdok signed the declaration in Addis Ababa:

> For Sudan to become a democratic country where the rights of all citizens are enshrined, the constitution should be based on the principle of 'separation of religion and state', in the absence of which the right to self-determination must be respected. (CGTN 2020)

Sudan is emerging from a period of international isolation that began when the former president Omar al-Bashir seized power in 1989 and implemented a hard-line interpretation of Islamic law that sought to make the nation the 'vanguard of the Islamic world'.

Most contemporary commentators agree that, at its core, populism is an anti-phenomenon that rests on exploiting the lack of political trust in governing elites; a relational concept that is about 'keeping promises and agreements' (Hetherington 2005: 1). And given that citizens in 80 per cent of the world's democracies distrust their governments this is a fertile period for anti-elitist populisms and elite circulation (Edelman 2019). Marc Hooghe and colleagues (2017: 214) observe that 'political trust, almost by definition, remains an elusive concept because of the complexity of the role it plays in a democratic society'. Citizen distrust of government provides an essential rationale for democratic oversight but a comprehensive lack of trust on the part of citizens in government might be considered disabling to state capacity to get things done.

David Easton (1965) makes a well-known distinction between specific and diffuse support for political systems. The former refers to support for the government of the day, its leaders and its policies. The latter refers to support for the basic political arrangements of democracy. If support fails on the first front, there is no issue in a democracy; lack of trust is doing its work if some citizens become sceptical of the government of the day. Elections are fought over that judgement. Rather, concern about lack of trust reflects worries about the diffuse support for democracy. Stoker and Evans (2014) argue that citizens might still be positive about the idea of democracy and its inalienable political rights yet diffuse support could be draining from the system because citizens are losing faith in the general operation of the polity and the current practice of politics. Hence, concern about political trust can be focused on whether citizens have lost faith in how their political system works. Loss of faith on a large scale can lead to fatalism and disengagement or, as we have seen, to openness to populism.

It also relies on the distinction between a pure and sovereign people, on the one hand, and a corrupt and unresponsive political elite on the other – and, of course, the (moral) primacy of the former over the latter (Mudde 2004). Populism flows from a sense of resentment about the way that politics is working and relies on an attractive leader to exploit the situation and create a dynamic of engagement and support among the public.

But political distrust could also open the way to support for democratic innovation – for doing democracy differently. The recent rise of populism is in part a product of the inability of mainstream political institutions and actors to reach out and empower disaffected citizens. Hence, a new politics that places communication at the heart of political practice, moves beyond the zero-sum road to renewal and sees participatory modes of democracy as a methodology for reinforcing the quality of representative democracy appears a sensible way forward. By implication, populism provides an obvious means for integrating representative and participatory modes of governance through the populist politician fuelled not by the desire to manipulate distrust via Führer démocratie but by the aspiration to solve societal problems through participatory decision-making.

In summary, then, it is worth drawing a further distinction between populism as a zeitgeist, a way of thinking about contemporary politics, and populism as a political movement or form of political mobilization (whether right or left). Populism is both a tool used by many politicians and campaigners and a base from which new political movements, parties or elites can spring in opposition to the established political order. Both aspects of populism are important to understanding the dynamics of contemporary democracies and the rise and fall of governing elites.

Artificial intelligence and future elite governance

As a parting shot, it is important to note an emerging literature on the role of artificial intelligence (AI) in either securing or eroding the role of national elites. Some observers, such as Konstantin Rovinskiy (2019), argue that AI can be used to replace traditional nation-state elites:

> To those who can read between the lines a complex contemporary trend of the AI-based social reformation is clear: traditional nation-state elites

are doomed to be replaced by smart machines all over the world. The state bureaucracy does not cope with governing people efficiently enough anymore ... bureaucratic national elites consume too much resources depriving supranational globocracy of a significant part of profit collected from the human flock. The old capitalism based on the Nation State is getting obsolete just because the State bureaucracy is getting more and more unfeasible in fleecing of the flock.

Although the management of Covid-19 has emphasized the importance of the regulatory role of the nation-state and effective governance in containing the spread of infection, Rovinskiy's vision could play a role in future governance. Tesla and SpaceX CEO Elon Musk further argues that artificial intelligence 'doesn't have to be evil to destroy humanity'. In the documentary *Do You Trust This Computer?*, Musk warns that the creation of superintelligence could lead to an 'immortal dictator' (Browne 2018). Musk therefore believes that humans should merge with AI to avoid the risk of becoming irrelevant. The choice of who governs? therefore becomes one between tech giants (a technocratic 'Skynet'-type elite) establishing a new global order through digital governance, traditional nation-state elites merging with AI to avoid the risk of becoming irrelevant or the 'immortal dictatorship' of machine over humankind.

Conclusion: Understanding the rise and fall of governing elites

At least four main conclusions can be drawn from this review of elite theory. First, elitism still provides an important focus for the work of social scientists and political philosophers and continues to draw attention to the vulnerabilities of the liberal democratic model, highlighting areas requiring urgent renewal and/or innovation.

Secondly, contemporary elite theory tends to be preoccupied with the nature and role of privileged governing elites in decision-making centres at different domains of governance and pays less attention to developing a broader theory of the relationship between the state and civil society. This is because, as Birch (1993: 202) reminds us, 'there is no adequate and convincing theory showing that democratic systems must always be elitist in practice'.

Thirdly, the credibility of the elitist approach increased in response to the dramatic rise in the size and complexity of the state, and, as we have seen, its future development should be concerned with the emergence of unaccountable transnational technocratic elites. How this development impacts on our understanding of the efficacy of the liberal democratic model should be a key concern for contemporary elite theorists.

And fourthly, given that OECD countries are experiencing the highest levels of income inequality for the past half-century – the average income of the richest 10 per cent of the population is about nine times that of the poorest across the OECD (OECD 2019) – anti-elitist populism is likely to remain a central focus of democratic politics in post-Covid-19 recovery processes. This will provide a living laboratory for social scientists to craft a more systematic understanding of the rise and fall of governing elites and counter the criticism that elite theory offers an insufficient conceptualization of elite circulation in the context of social, economic and political crisis.

Further Reading

Best, H. and J. Higley (eds) (2010), *Democratic Elitism:*
   New Theoretical and Comparative Perspectives, Leiden/Boston: Brill.
Dahl, R. (1966), 'Further reflections on "the elitist theory of democracy"',
   American Political Science Review, 60(2), 296–305.
Diamond, L. (2020), *Ill Winds,* New York: Penguin Books.
Domhoff, G. W. (1967), *Who Rules America?*, Englewood Cliffs, NJ:
   Prentice-Hall.
Gilens, M. and B. Page (2014), 'Testing theories of American politics: Elites,
   interest groups, and average citizens', *Perspectives on Politics*, 12(3), 564–581.
Michels, R. ([1911] 1962), *Political Parties*, New York: Free Press.
Mills, C.W. (1956), *The Power Elite*, New York: Oxford University Press.
See Chapter 14 for the key literature on populism.

3

Marxism

Colin Hay

Introduction

Seen, like feminism, as an 'engaged theory' (Bryson 1992: 1), not content merely to interpret the world but motivated by an overriding ambition to change it, the Marxist theory of the state cannot be judged a complete success. Indeed, three decades after the collapse of 'actually existing socialism', it is surely tempting to dismiss the Marxist theory of the state as of purely historical interest. Yet the argument of this chapter is that, partly by virtue of its attempts to explain capitalism's (for its) surprising longevity, Marxist theories of the state offer a series of powerful and probing insights into the complex and dynamic relationship between state, economy and society in capitalist democracies, from which other theorists of the state still can learn much.

In what follows I seek to provide an assessment of the contribution of Marxism to our understanding of the state while charting, albeit in a stylized way, the development of Marxist and neo-Marxist approaches to the study and analysis of the state from Marx and Engels, via Lenin and Gramsci, Miliband and Poulantzas to a range of contemporary authors, notably Block and Jessop. The argument unfolds in three sections. In the first we consider why it is that Marxists require a theory of the state and how Marxists have conceptualized this focus of their attention. The second section traces the development of the Marxist theory of the state through the work of the founding fathers, its reformulation by Lenin and Gramsci, and the revival of interest in Marxist state theory in the post-war period. The final section considers the contemporary development of Marxist/neo-Marxist state theory asking whether such theories have become ever more sophisticated by becoming ever less Marxist and asking whether we need a Marxist theory of the state today. It concludes by examining the theoretical resources that Marxist state theory provides to make sense of a world of globalization and of crisis-prone globalization.

Marxism and the state

As Philippe Schmitter suggests, 'The modern state is ... an amorphous complex of agencies with ill-defined boundaries performing a variety of not very distinctive functions' (1985: 33). It might seem somewhat strange, if not downright defeatist, to begin a chapter on the Marxist theory of the state with this comment. Yet in one sense it provides a particularly appropriate starting point. For, as I have remarked elsewhere, 'there is no more arduous task in the theory of the state than defining this notoriously elusive and rapidly moving target' (Hay 1996a: 2; see also Hay 2014). We begin then with perhaps the second most neglected question in the study of the state – what is it? – before moving on to the first – why do we need a theory of it anyway? In fact, as we shall see, although the definitions offered by Marxists are often implicit rather than explicit, and although their justifications for a concern with the state are often somewhat cryptic, it is to their credit that theorists within this tradition have not been short of answers.

What is the state?

Any more than the most fleeting of forays into the now substantial annals of Marxist state theory will reveal that, while Marxists may well rely *implicitly* upon certain conceptions and understandings of the state, they are notoriously bad at consigning these to the page. This makes it somewhat difficult to identify any analytically precise Marxist definition of the state as an object of inquiry, let alone one that is commonly agreed upon. Family resemblances in the assumptions which inform Marxist conceptions of the state can nonetheless be identified – indeed, these can be crystallized into four rather different conceptions of the state.

The state as the *repressive arm of the bourgeoisie*

According to Martin Carnoy: 'it is the notion of the [capitalist] state as the repressive apparatus of the bourgeoisie that is the distinctly Marxist characteristic of the state' (Carnoy 1984: 50). This is a somewhat crude and one-dimensional conception of state power. It views the capitalist state as the expression of the repressive might of the ruling class and is most closely associated with Lenin's *The State and Revolution* ([1917] 1968). Yet it has its origins in the work of Engels (see for instance [1844] 1975: 205–207; [1884] 1978: 340; cf. van den Berg 1988: 30–1). Its functionalism – the attempt to explain something by appeal to its consequences – is well captured by Hal Draper:

> The state ... comes into existence insofar as the institutions needed to carry out the common functions of society require, for their continued maintenance, the separation of the power of forcible coercion from the general body of society. (Draper 1977: 50)

The state as an *instrument of the ruling class*

The 'instrumentalist' position, as it has become known (see below), provides perhaps the most prevalent conception of the state within Marxist theory. It is most often accorded the status of *the* Marxist theory of the state, despite the fact that instrumentalism itself spans a wide diversity of positions expressing rather divergent *theories* of the state. In its most crudely stated form, it implies that the state is 'an instrument in the hands of the ruling class for enforcing and guaranteeing the stability of the class structure itself' (Sweezy 1942: 243). Within this distinctive school, 'the functioning of the state is ... understood in terms of the instrumental exercise of power by people in strategic positions, either directly through the manipulation of state policies or indirectly through the exercise of pressure on the state' (Gold et al. 1975a: 34). Instrumentalists or 'influence theorists', as Claus Offe terms them (1974: 32), have concerned themselves with the analyses of: (i) the patterns and networks of personal and social ties between individuals occupying positions of economic power in so-called 'power structure research' studies (Domhoff 1967, 1970, 1980, 2014; Mintz and Schwartz 1985; for a review see Barrow 1993: 13–24); (ii) the social connections between those holding positions of economic power and the state elite (Domhoff 1979, 1990; Miliband 1969; for a review see Barrow 1993: 24–41); and (iii) the social processes moulding the ideological commitments of the state and social elite (Miliband 1969). The election of Donald Trump as US president and the role played by corporate

America in both his candidacy and in office have, perhaps unsurprisingly, sparked fresh interest in this approach (see, for instance, Campbell 2018; Domhoff 2017; Pierson 2017).

The state as an *ideal collective capitalist*

The conception of the state as an ideal collective capitalist has its origins in Engels' frequently cited (though incidental) remark in *Anti-Dühring*, that 'the modern state, no matter what its form, is essentially a capitalist machine, the state of the capitalists, the ideal personification of the total national capital' ([1878] 1947: 338). Advocates of this conception of the state point to the fact that capital is neither self-reproducing nor capable on its own of securing the conditions of its own reproduction. For the very continuity of the capitalist social formation is dependent upon certain interventions being made which, though in the general interest of capital collectively, are not in the individual interest of any particular capital (Hirsch 1978: 66). In rational choice theoretical terms, this is a 'collective action problem' (see, for instance, Dunleavy 1991: 30–36). An external, and at least *relatively* autonomous, body or institutional ensemble is thus called upon to intervene on behalf of capital in its long-term general interests (as opposed to the conflicting short-term interests of individual capitals). This body is the state – the 'ideal collective capitalist' (Altvater 1973). As Offe explains,

> it is not without good reason that Engels … calls the state the 'ideal' collective capitalist; for the state as a 'real' collective capitalist would clearly be a logical impossibility … firstly because the state apparatus is not itself a capitalist … and secondly because the concept of the collective capitalist is itself nonsensical in that competition … is essential for the movement of capital. (1974: 31)

The state as a *factor of cohesion* within the social formation

Though most clearly associated with the work of Nicos Poulantzas, whose phrase it is, the notion of the state as a 'factor of cohesion' can be traced (as indeed it is by Poulantzas) to another incidental and (characteristically) underdeveloped comment by Engels in *The Origin of the Family, Private Property and the State*:

> In order that … classes with conflicting economic interests, shall not consume themselves and society in fruitless struggle, it became necessary to have a power seemingly standing above society that would moderate the conflict

and keep it within the bounds of 'order'; and this power, arisen out of society but placing itself above it and alienating itself more and more from it, is the state. (Engels [1884] 1978: 205–206; see also Bukharin [1921] 1926)

Within this conception, the state is understood in terms of its effects and is defined in terms of its role in maintaining 'the unity and cohesion of a social formation by concentrating and sanctioning class domination' (Poulantzas 1975: 24–25; see also 1973: 44–56, esp. 44, 304; Gramsci 1971: 244; Jessop 1985: 61, 177). We return to the problems of this conception below.

As the above discussion demonstrates, the state has meant (and continues to mean) many things to many Marxists.

Why do Marxists need a theory of the state?

Alan Wolfe suggests that,

> Like Henry Higgins who, through his work changed the object of his studies into something other than what it was, the purpose of the Marxist theory of the state is not just to understand the capitalist state but to aid in its destruction (Wolfe 1974: 131).

Given this comment, it would not seem unreasonable to expect of those who advance such a theory an answer to the question: 'How precisely does a Marxist theory of the state advance the cause of progressive social transformation?' Yet, unlike, say, their feminist counterparts (Brown 1992; Connell 1990; MacKinnon 1982, 1983, 1985; see also Chapter 6), Marxists have rarely been called upon to offer any such justification for their theoretical endeavours and choices. Explicit answers to the question 'why do Marxists need a theory of the state?' (far less, 'why might anyone else need a *Marxist* theory of the state?') are difficult to find. Yet answers are not, perhaps, so difficult to infer from what Marxist theorists have said about the state's form and function.

Here we can usefully follow the so-called German 'state derivationists'. For although their work is in many respects highly problematic (see Barrow 1993: 94–95; Jessop 1982: 78–101), it certainly served to highlight the centrality of the state to the process of capitalist reproduction. The derivationists, as the label would imply, sought to *derive* the form and function of the capitalist state from the requirements of the capitalist mode of production. For our purposes, we are not concerned to demonstrate, as were they, that the state must by some inexorable inner logic necessarily satisfy such functional requirements, but merely that it is indeed implicated in processes crucial to the reproduction of capitalist relations. Thus, although their perspective can never *explain* the form and/or (dys)function of the capitalist state, as its advocates believed, it can nonetheless provide us with an exceedingly useful heuristic. For in so far as capitalist social relations *are* reproduced (and it does not take much insight to see that in the societies we inhabit they are), such functions must indeed be performed by some institution, apparatus, or combination thereof. It is not a particularly large step to suggest that many (if not all) of these institutions are either state apparatuses themselves or are heavily regulated by the state. The state thus emerges as a nodal point in the network of power relations that characterizes contemporary capitalist societies and, hence, a key focus of Marxist attention. It is not surprising then that Ralph Miliband is led to conclude that: 'in the politics of Marxism there is no institution which is nearly as important as the state' (1977: 66).

So how, precisely, is the capitalist state implicated in the expanded reproduction of capital? Or, to put it another way, what are the functions that must be performed by the state *if* capitalist social relations are to be reproduced? Numerous aspects of this role can be identified. Taken together they provide ample justification for a distinctively Marxist theory of the state within Marxist theory more generally.

First, we might point to the fact that capital is fragmented into a large number of competitive units, yet crucially relies on certain generic conditions being satisfied if surplus value is to be extracted from labour and profit secured (Altvater 1973). The state is, in short, a response to capitalism's collective action problem. Picture a hypothetical capitalist economy unregulated by the state (the archetypal free market) and comprised inevitably of a multitude of competing capitals. Such an economy is inherently crisis-prone. For no individual capital competing for its very survival will sacrifice its own interest in the general interest. Contradictions or 'steering problems' inevitably arise within such an unregulated economy yet can never be resolved. Accordingly, left unchecked, they will tend to accumulate over time until they eventually threaten the very stability of capitalism itself – precipitating a fully fledged crisis of the mode of production. A capitalist economy without regulation, despite the now pervasive rhetoric of the free marketeers, is inherently unstable (Aglietta 1979; Habermas 1975: 24–31; Jänicke 1990: 8; Offe 1975; cf. the discussion of 'market failure' in Chapter 4).

Enter the state – as a more or less 'ideal collective capitalist'. Altvater argues that this state must necessarily intervene within the capitalist economy to secure conditions conducive to continuing capitalist accumulation, thereby performing what he calls a 'general maintenance function' (1973; Jessop 1982: 90–91). At minimum this entails: (i) the provision of general infrastructure

– 'the material conditions that are necessary to all business activities but that cannot be produced directly [*and profitably*] by individual private businesses' (Barrow 1993: 80); (ii) the defence (in the last resort, militarily) of a national economic space regulated by the state and the preservation, in the process, of an administrative boundary within which the state is sovereign; (iii) the provision of a legal system that establishes and enforces the right to possession of private property and which outlaws practices (such as insider dealing) potentially damaging to the stable accumulation of capital within the national economy; (iv) the intervention of the state to regulate and/or ameliorate class struggle and the inevitable conflict between capital and labour; and (v) crisis management in the face of endogenous (internally generated) or exogenous (externally generated) shocks, contagions and pathologies.

Such interventions establish what Jürgen Habermas (1975) terms the 'logic of crisis displacement'. By this he means that fundamental crises originating (as 'steering problems') within the economy (and which might otherwise have rung the death-knell of capitalism itself) now become the responsibility of the state as the supreme regulator of the economy. Crises are thus *displaced* from the economy (which does *not* have the internal capacity to resolve them) to the state (which *may*, or *may not*). If the state as currently constituted cannot resolve such a crisis, then in the first instance it is the particular form of the capitalist state that is called into question, not the very stability of the capitalist mode of production itself. Consider, for instance, the widely identified crisis of the late 1970s in the advanced capitalist economies. Though precipitated by a series of economic factors (such as the exhaustion of the post-war 'Fordist' mode of economic growth), as the subsequent neoliberal restructuring demonstrates, this was a crisis of a particular form of the state, not of capitalism per se (Hay 1996; Jessop 2016; Streeck 2014). A similar argument might be made about the more recent global financial crisis and the challenge to the deregulatory disposition of neoliberalism (rather than to capitalism per se) that it has led to.

The implications of this for a Marxist theory of the state are profound. For the state is revealed, once again, as playing a crucial role in safeguarding the circuit of capital. If we want to understand the operation of the capitalist mode of production, we cannot afford to dispense with a theory of the state. Moreover, Habermas's argument suggests that, if we wish to develop a theory of capitalist crisis (an understandably high priority within Marxist theory), then it is to the state that we must turn initially. For economic crises, at least within contemporary capitalism, are likely to become manifest as crises of economic regulation and hence crises of the state (for an account of the global financial crisis in such terms see Hay 2013). In summary, if we wish to develop insights into the 'normal' functioning of the capitalist mode of production, and into the transformation of capitalism in and through moments of crisis, we require a dynamic theory of the capitalist state. It is to the resources we have at our disposal in developing such a theory that we turn in the next section.

A genealogy of the state in Marxist theory

In 1977, in the first (and probably still the best) systematic and comprehensive review of Marxist theories of the state, Bob Jessop noted that it was a 'truism' that Marx and Engels developed no consistent, single or unified theory of the state (1977: 353). By 1982 (in his book *The Capitalist State*) this truism had become a 'commonplace' and it is now so oft-remarked upon that it is perhaps one of the few truly undisputed 'social scientific facts' (see for instance van den Berg 1988: 14; Bertramsen et al. 1991: 38; Carnoy 1984: 45; Dunleavy and O'Leary 1987: 203; Finegold and Skocpol 1995: 175; Miliband 1965; Poulantzas 1978: 20; Wolfe 1974: 131; cf. Draper 1977). *There is no (single) Marxian, far less Marxist, theory of the state.* This might be considered something of a devastating blow for a chapter on the Marxist theory of the state. Indeed, reviewing Marxist state theory might be considered not merely an exercise in flogging a dead horse, but one that first required the altogether more macabre practice of exhuming and assembling a dismembered corpse limb by limb. Moreover, given the great variety of concerns that animated Marx and Engels' work (to say nothing of Marxism more generally), it is not at all clear that all the limbs belong to the same corpse. For, as Jessop notes, 'Marx and Engels adopted different approaches and arguments according to the problems with which they were concerned' (1982: 28). Nonetheless, a clear development of Marx and Engels' ideas on the state can be traced.

The early Marx

The *Critique of Hegel's Doctrine of the State* ([1843a] 1975) contains Marx's first extended reflections on the state. Though a sustained and at times polemical critique of Hegel, it is still couched within a fundamentally Hegelian framework. In Hegel's almost mystical idealism the separation between the state and civil society – between the universal and the particular – finds its resolution in the state. The latter is understood, not as an ideal collective capitalist but as an *ideal collective citizen* capable of expressing the general and communal interest of all its subjects. Marx regards this as pure mystification. Thus, although he accepts Hegel's distinction between state and civil society, sharing his understanding of the latter as 'the sphere of economic life in which the individual's relations with others are governed by selfish needs and individual interests' (59), Marx denies that the state can indeed act in the universal interest. For in so far as state power is thoroughly implicated in the protection of property rights, the state actually functions to reproduce 'the war of each against all' in civil society.

The solution lies in what Marx terms 'true democracy', 'the first true unity of the particular and the universal' (88). The interpretation of this concept in the early Marx is highly contentious. The Althusserian structuralists wish to dismiss these early formulations as irredeemably Hegelian, and as separated by a radical 'epistemological break' from his 'mature' and 'scientific' later writings (Althusser 1969: 32–34, 62–64, 249). In complete contrast, Shlomo Avineri detects in the concept of 'true democracy' what would later be termed 'communism'. Accordingly, he argues:

> the decisive transition in Marx's intellectual development was not from radical democracy to communism, any more than it was from idealism to materialism ... The *Critique* contains ample material to show that Marx envisages in 1843 a society based on the abolition of private property and on the disappearance of the state. Briefly, the *Communist Manifesto* is immanent in the *Critique*. (1968: 34; see also Colletti 1975: 41–42)

This latter reading is perhaps reinforced by Marx's essay 'On the Jewish Question' ([1843b] 1975). Here he distinguishes between political emancipation – associated with formal (and constitutionally codified) democracy – and real human emancipation (or 'true democracy'). While the former represents a significant advance, it is but one step on the road to full human emancipation. The latter can only be realized by the transcending of bourgeois society to usher in a qualitatively new social order (Miliband 1965: 281–282). In his 'Introduction' ([1844] 1975) to the *Critique*, Marx eventually identifies the proletariat as the agents of this transformation, laying the basis for a class theory of the state in his later writings.

Marx mark two: The 'mature' works

In *The German Ideology*, Marx and Engels come closest to formulating a systematic theory of the state as a class state. They assert famously that the state is 'nothing more than the form of organisation which the bourgeoisie necessarily adopt both for internal and external purposes, for the mutual guarantee of their property and interest' ([1845/6] 1964: 59), a conception echoed in the *Communist Manifesto* ([1848] 1975: 82). This broadly instrumentalist framework (which conceives of the state as an instrument in the hands of the ruling class) is identified by Miliband as Marx and Engels' 'primary' view of the state (1965: 283; see also Sanderson 1963). Yet it is not their only formulation, nor does it remain unqualified. Indeed, as Marx notes in *The Class Struggles in France* ([1850] 1978) and *The Eighteenth Brumaire of Louis Bonaparte* ([1852] 1979) it is often not the ruling class so much as fractions of the ruling class which control the state apparatus. This is particularly so in the case of the most advanced capitalist societies of the time, England and France. Furthermore, the personnel of the state often belong to an entirely different class to that of the ruling class. Such comments are a reflection of a modified and qualified, but nonetheless still essentially instrumentalist, conception of the state. The state is granted a certain degree of autonomy from the ruling class, but it remains *their* instrument – ultimately those who pay the piper call the tune.

At times, however, and particularly in their more historical writings, Marx and Engels' qualified instrumentalism gives way to a more structuralist position. Thus in *The Eighteenth Brumaire* and again in *The Civil War in France* ([1871] 1986), Marx grants the state a far more independent role than that previously assigned to it in, say, *The German Ideology*. This 'secondary' view of the state, as Miliband describes it (1977: 284–285), is restated by Engels in *The Origin of the Family*. Thus, although Louis Bonaparte is seen by Marx as 'representing' (or at least claiming to represent) the smallholding peasants, neither he nor the state is a genuine expression of their interests. As Miliband explains, 'for Marx, the Bonapartist State, however independent it may have been *politically* from any given class remains, and cannot in a class society but remain, the protector of an economically and socially dominant class' (ibid.: 285, original emphasis). The very structure and function of the (capitalist) state would appear to guarantee (or at least powerfully select for) the reproduction of capitalist social relations. This impression is confirmed in *The Civil War in France*. Here Marx categorically states that the apparatus of the capitalist state cannot be appropriated for progressive ends and that the revolutionary project of the proletariat must be to smash this repressive bourgeois institution. In so doing:

> Marx implies that the state is a system of political domination whose effectiveness is to be found in its institutional structure as much as in the

social categories, fractions or classes that control it ... [T]he analysis of the inherent bias of the system of political representation and state intervention is logically prior to an examination of the social forces that manage to wield state power. (Jessop 1978: 62; see also 1982: 27)

Given the sheer scope and diversity of the positions briefly outlined above, it is not surprising that Alan Wolfe is led to conclude that 'to study the state from a Marxist perspective means not the application of an already developed theory to existing circumstances, but the creation of that very theory, based on some all too cryptic beginnings in Marx himself. Hence the excitement of the project, but hence also its ambiguity' (1974: 131). In the next section we embark on a roller-coaster ride through this exciting yet ambiguous world.

'The ambiguity and the excitement': Marxism and the state after Marx

Lenin and Gramsci

Lenin's writings on the state can trace a strong lineage to the Marx of *The Civil War in France*. In *The State and Revolution* ([1917] 1968), regarded by Lucio Colletti as 'by far and away his greatest contribution to political theory' (1972: 224), Lenin draws out the implications of Marx's writings on the Paris Commune for revolutionary strategy. The state, he argues, is 'an organ of class *rule*, an organ for the *oppression* of one class by another'. Since the state is simply and unequivocally the repressive apparatus of the bourgeoisie, it cannot be used to advance the cause of socialist transformation. Moreover, as a coercive institution it must be confronted by force. Hence, 'the liberation of the oppressed class is impossible not only without a violent revolution, but also without the destruction of the apparatus of state power' ([1917] 1968: 266, original emphasis.). As Colletti again observes:

> The basic theme of *The State and Revolution* – the one that indelibly inscribes itself on the memory, and immediately comes to mind when one thinks of the work – is the theme of revolution as a *destructive* and *violent* act ... The essential point of the revolution, the *destruction* it cannot forgo is ... the destruction of the bourgeois state as a power *separate* from and *counterposed* to the masses, and its replacement by a power of a new type. (1972: 219–220, original emphasis)

Lenin's narrow definition of the state as an essentially coercive apparatus is reflected in his vision of revolution as a violent act in which the repressive might of the state is pitched against the massed ranks of the proletariat. Its consequences, of historical proportions, are all too apparent. Thankfully, they may now be viewed with the benefit of some degree of hindsight. In contrast, Gramsci's more inclusive definition of the state leads him in a somewhat different direction.

Gramsci's distinctiveness and enduring significance lies in his attempt to incorporate human subjectivity as a dynamic agent within the Marxist philosophy of history (Femia 1981: 1). His work thus marks a clear break with the economism and crude reductionism that had come to characterize the Marxist tradition since the death of Marx. The central question that he poses, and with which contemporary Marxist theorists continue to grapple, is this – what gives capital the capacity to reproduce and reassert its dominance over time, despite its inherent contradictions? His search for an answer leads him to define a new concept (or, more accurately, to redefine an old concept) – that of *hegemony*; and to extend the Marxist definition of the state to include all those institutions and practices through which the ruling class succeeds in maintaining the consensual subordination of those over whom it rules (Gramsci 1971: 244, 262). The key to Gramsci's theoretical toolbox is the concept of hegemony. With this he demonstrated that a dominant class, in order to maintain its supremacy, must succeed in presenting its own moral, political and cultural values as societal norms; thereby constructing an ideologically engendered *common sense*. Yet, as Miliband observes, hegemony is not merely about instilling the values of the ruling class within civil society. Increasingly,

> it must also be taken to mean the capacity of the ruling classes to persuade subordinate ones that, whatever they may think of the social order, and however much they may be alienated from it, there is no alternative to it. Hegemony depends not so much on consent as on resignation. (1994: 11)

For Gramsci, then, the obstacles to class consciousness are far greater than Lenin envisaged (and, it might well be argued, have become far greater since the time of Gramsci). While there is football on TV, the revolution is likely to be postponed indefinitely. As Gramsci's biographer, Gioseppe Fiori, comments:

> the [capitalist] system's real strength does not lie in the violence of the ruling class or the coercive power of its state, but in the acceptance by the ruled of

a 'conception of the world' which belongs to the rulers. The philosophy of the ruling class passes through a whole tissue of complex vulgarisations to emerge as 'common sense': that is, the philosophy of the masses, who accept the morality, the customs, the institutionalised behaviour of the society they live in. (1970: 238)

Gramsci's central contribution is to insist that the power of the capitalist class resides not so much in the repressive apparatus of the state as an instrument of the bourgeoisie – however ruthless and efficient that might be – but in its ability to influence and shape the perceptions of the subordinate classes, convincing them either of the legitimacy of the system itself or of the futility of resistance. Given that Gramsci was, at the time, languishing in a cell in one of Mussolini's prisons and thus, presumably, only too well aware of the ruthless efficiency of the state's coercive arm, this insight was all the more impressive. It led him to a highly significant observation and one for which he is rightly famous:

In the East the state was everything, civil society was primordial and gelatinous; in the West, there was a proper relation between state and civil society, and when the state trembled a sturdy structure of civil society was at once revealed. The state was only an outer ditch, behind which there stood a powerful system of fortresses and earthworks. (1971: 238)

The implications of this for socialist strategy are highly significant, and Gramsci was not slow to point them out. Whereas in the East (Russia) where civil society was 'primordial and gelatinous' a *war of manoeuvre* – a 'frontal assault' on the state – was indeed appropriate, in the West such a strategy was doomed to failure. For in societies like his own the strength of the bourgeoisie lay not in the coercive resources that it could muster, but in its ability to legitimate its domination within civil society, thereby securing passive acquiescence. Thus, before the proletariat could challenge the state, it would first have to wage a successful *war of position* – a 'battle for the hearts and minds' within civil society. As Carnoy notes: '*consciousness itself* becomes the source of power for the proletariat in laying siege to the state and the means of production, just as lack of proletarian consciousness is the principal reason that the bourgeoisie remains in the dominant position' (1984: 88). Gramsci had indeed succeeded in reinserting human subjectivity as a dynamic agent within the Marxist philosophy of history.

Structuralism versus instrumentalism in the 'Miliband–Poulantzas debate'

If the historical significance (however unfortunate) of Lenin's writings on the state, and the theoretical and strategic prescience of Gramsci's work, should guarantee them both a place in any discussion of the Marxist theory of the state, then the same cannot be said of the (in)famous Miliband–Poulantzas debate (Poulantzas 1969, 1976; Miliband 1969, 1970, 1973; Laclau 1975). Its importance lies neither in the quality of the theoretical exchange, nor in its historical significance, but rather in the problems it reveals in Marxist conceptions of the state and in its symbolic status as a point of departure for many more contemporary developments. The debate sees neither protagonist at his brilliant theoretical best. Yet it does well display the extremes to which Marxist state theorists seem, on occasions, inexorably drawn.

It takes the form of a dense theoretical exchange, initially polite but increasingly ill-tempered, about the source of power within contemporary capitalist societies and the relationship between the ruling class and the state apparatus in the determination of the content of state policy. Is the modern state a state in capitalist society or a capitalist state – and what difference does it make anyway?

Poulantzas's opening salvo (1969) takes the form of a detailed textual critique of Miliband's path-breaking *The State in Capitalist Society* (1969). Poulantzas notes the absence (excepting the work of Gramsci) of a systematic attempt to formulate a Marxist theory of the state and praises Miliband for his attempts to fill this theoretical vacuum as well as his devastating critique of the bourgeois mythology of the state. However, after the spoonful of sugar comes the medicine. In seeking to expose the dominant bourgeois ideology of the neutrality and independence of the state, Miliband is unwittingly drawn onto the terrain of his adversaries (1969: 241–242). His reflections remains tarnished by the residue of bourgeois assumptions about the state – principally, that power resides not in the state apparatus itself but in the *personnel* of the state. He thereby fails to grasp what Poulantzas sees as the objective structural reality of social classes and the state. Instead, Miliband entertains the bourgeois mythology of the free-willed active agent. Accordingly, he focuses on *class* in terms of intersubjective relationships instead of objective structural locations within the relations of production, and on the *state* in terms of the interpersonal alliances, connections and networks of the state 'elite' (242) instead of the structure, form and function of this (capitalist) institution.

This point lies at the heart of the debate. Yet from here on, it degenerates into a somewhat crude and polarized struggle between *instrumentalism* (Poulantzas's caricature of Miliband's position) and *structuralism* (Miliband's caricature of Poulantzas's position). Ironically, in the debate itself (though not in their more thoughtful work), both protagonists come close to living up to the crude parodies they present of one another.

Instrumentalism, as we have seen, tends to view the state as a neutral instrument to be manipulated and steered in the interests of the dominant class or ruling 'elite' (the term Miliband deploys). Its basic thesis is that the modern state serves the interests of the bourgeoisie in a capitalist society because it is dominated by that class. Such a perspective asserts the causal primacy of *agency* (the conscious actions of individuals or social forces) over *structure*. In the determination of state policy, the personnel of the state are thus accorded primacy over the state's form and function (as a capitalist apparatus). As Kenneth Finegold and Theda Skocpol note:

> An instrument has no will of its own and thus is capable of action only as the extension of the will of some conscious actor. To understand the state as an instrument of the capitalist class is to say that state action originates in the conscious and purposive efforts of capitalists as a class. (Finegold and Skocpol 1995: 176)

Instrumentalism (as expressed in the work of Domhoff and the early Miliband) may thus be regarded as *agency*- or *personnel*-centred, and as expressing a simple view of the relationship between the state apparatus and the ruling class – the latter is an instrument of the former (see Table 3.1). The instrumentalist thesis can be summarized in terms of its answers to three questions (see also Gold et al. 1975a: 32; Barrow 1993: 16):

Q: *What is the nature of the class that rules?*
A: The capitalist class rules and is defined by its ownership and control of the means of production.
Q: *What are the mechanisms that tie this class to the state?*
A: Socialization, inter-personal connections, and networks. The capitalist class uses the state as an instrument to dominate the rest of society.
Q: *What is the concrete relationship between state policies and ruling class interests?*
A: State policies further the general interests of the capitalist class in maintaining their domination of society.

An instrumentalist theory of the state is thus a theory of *the state in capitalist society* (the title of Miliband's book) as opposed to a theory of the capitalist state. For if the state in a capitalist society is indeed capitalist it is only contingently so. That the state is engaged in the reproduction of capitalist social and economic relations is not in any sense guaranteed. Rather, such a situation can arise only by virtue of the dominance of a capitalist 'ruling elite' within capitalist society and its personal ties to the members of the state apparatus.

In marked contrast, a structuralist position (such as that outlined by the state derivationists and by the Poulantzas of 'the debate') asserts the causal priority of structures over agents and their intentions. Agents are conceived of as the 'bearers' (or *träger*) of objective structures over which they can exercise minimal influence. Within such a framework, the capitalist state is viewed as a structural system with form and function determined largely independently of the aspirations, motivations and intentions of political actors or members of the dominant class. It is a theory of the *capitalist state*. A structuralist account, as the term would imply, is *structure-* or *state-*centred. It also expresses a simple view of the relationship between the state apparatus and the ruling class – the former acts in the long-term collective interest of the latter (see Table 3.1).

The Miliband–Poulantzas debate did not advance the cause of Marxist theory very far. However, in pointing to the limitations of both structure-centred and agency-centred accounts, it has provided a point of departure for many recent developments in state theory. It is to the two most fruitful attempts to exorcise the ghost of the Miliband–Poulantzas debate that we now briefly turn.

Table 3.1 Beyond Structuralism vs. Instrumentalism

	Personnel-Centred (Agency-Centred)	State-Centred (Structure-Centred)
Simple view of the relationship between the state apparatus and the ruling class	*Instrumentalism* (Domhoff, early Miliband)	*Structuralism* (early Poulantzas, state derivationists)
Dialectical view of the relationship between the state apparatus and the ruling class	*The state as custodian of capital* (later Miliband, Block)	*Strategic-relational approach* (Jessop, later Poulantzas)

Beyond structuralism versus instrumentalism: Block and Jessop

Before considering the 'state of the art' in the Marxist theory of the state, it is important first to note that Miliband and Poulantzas were not to remain resolute and intractable in defence of the positions to which they were drawn in the heat of the theoretical exchange. Both moved towards more complex ('dialectical') conceptions of the relationship between structure and agency in their later work, locating political actors as strategic subjects within complex and densely structured state apparatuses. Thus Miliband, in an exercise of apparent contrition, concedes, 'the notion of the state as an "instrument" ... tends to obscure what has come to be seen as a crucial property of the state, namely its *relative autonomy* from the "ruling class" and from civil society at large' (1977: 74). He emphasizes the need for a consideration of 'the character of [the state's] leading personnel, the pressures exercised by the economically dominant-class, *and* the structural constraints imposed by the mode of production' (73–4; see also 1994: 17–18). Such observations are more systematically developed in the work of Fred Block (1987).

Block's concern is to demonstrate how, despite the division of labour between 'state managers' and the capitalist class, the state tends to act in the long-term collective interest of capital. He begins by noting that the capitalist class, far from actively sponsoring major reforms in its long-term interest, often provides the most vociferous opposition to such measures. The capitalist class must then be regarded as simply incapable of acting in its own long-term collective interest. Yet at the same time,

> ruling class members who devote substantial energy to policy formation become atypical of their class, since they are forced to look at the world from the perspective of state-managers. They are quite likely to diverge ideologically from politically unengaged ruling-class opinion. (1987a: 57)

This provides the basis for an answer to Block's conundrum. State managers may in fact have interests far closer to the long-term collective interest of capital than capital itself (see also Marsh 1995: 275). Here Block points to the relationship of 'dependency' between state managers on the one hand, and the performance of the capitalist economy on the other. As Carnoy explains, such dependency exists since:

> economic activity produces state revenues and because public support for a regime will decline unless accumulation continues to take place. State managers willingly do what they know they must to facilitate capital

accumulation. Given that the level of economic activity is largely determined by private investment decisions, such managers are particularly sensitive to overall 'business confidence'. (1984: 218)

The state becomes the *custodian* of the general interest of capital. Block manages to reconcile within a single account a sensitivity to the intentions, interests and strategies of state personnel (and their relative independence from the ruling class) with an analysis of the structural context within which these strategies are operationalized and played out. His work displays a complex and *dialectical* view of the relationship between the state apparatus and the ruling class which escapes both the intentionalism and indeterminacy of instrumentalist accounts and the functionalism and determinism of structuralist formulations. In its overarching concern with state managers as utility-maximizing rational subjects, it is nonetheless *personnel-* or *agency*-centred (see Table 3.1).

Though it represents a considerable advance on its more instrumentalist forebears, Block's work is still ultimately somewhat frustrating. For, as Finegold and Skocpol point out (1995: 198), he remains ambiguous as to whether capitalist reforms initiated by state managers – and the subject of political pressure from both working and ruling classes alike – will *always* prove functional for capital in the last instance (for evidence of this ambiguity, compare Block 1987: 62 with 1987: 66). If so, then Block's gestural nod to the independent interests of state managers in promoting economic growth is scarcely sufficient to account for such an exact (and convenient) functional fit. If not, then how precisely is it that dysfunctional outcomes that might prove threatening to capitalist stability are avoided while those less damaging to the system (and, one might have thought, easier to avoid) are allowed to develop? Either way, Block seems to fall back on a residual functionalism which is not so very different from that associated with the notion of the state as an 'ideal collective capitalist'. His achievement should not, however, be underemphasized. Yet it surely lies more in his *recognition* of the need to specify the mechanisms ensuring that the actions of state personnel do not, by and large, jeopardize continued capital accumulation, than in the particular mechanisms that he proceeds to specify.

If Block's conception of the state as *custodian of capital* is the dialectical heir to the legacy of instrumentalism, then Bob Jessop's *strategic-relational approach* is the dialectical heir to the structuralist inheritance (see in particular Jessop 1990, 2002, 2007; for commentaries see Barrow 1993: 153–156; Bonefeld 1993; Hay 1994, 2004; Mahon 1991). More convincingly than any other Marxist theorist, past or present, he succeeds in transcending the artificial dualism of structure and agency by moving towards a truly dialectical understanding of their interrelationship. Structure and agency logically entail one another; hence, there can be no analysis of action which is not itself also an analysis of structure. All social and political change occurs through strategic interaction, as strategies collide with and impinge upon the structured terrain of the strategic context within which they are formulated. Their effects (however unintentional, however unanticipated) are to transform (however partially) the context within which future strategies are formulated and deployed.

Such a formulation has highly significant implications for the theory of the (capitalist) state. Jessop follows the later Poulantzas in conceiving of the state as a strategic site traversed by class struggles and as 'a specific institutional ensemble with multiple boundaries, no institutional fixity and no pre-given formal or substantive unity' (Jessop 1990: 267; Poulantzas 1978). The state is a dynamic and constantly unfolding system (an institutional complex). Its specific form at a given moment in time in a particular national setting represents a 'crystallisation of past strategies' which privileges certain strategies and actors over others. As such, 'the state is located within a complex *dialectic of structures and strategies*' (129, emphasis added). This introduces the important notion that the state, and the institutions which comprise it, are *strategically selective*. The structures and modus operandi of the state 'are more open to some types of political strategy than others' (260). The state presents an uneven playing field whose complex contours favour certain strategies (and hence certain actors) over others.

Within such a perspective, there can be no guarantee that the state (and governments wielding state power) will act in the general interest of capital (whatever that might be). Indeed, in so far as the function of the capitalist state can be regarded as the expanded reproduction of capital, the specific form of the capitalist state at a particular stage in its historical development is always likely to problematize and eventually compromise this function (think, perhaps, of the inadequate regulation of financial markets in the period before the global financial crisis). The state thus evolves through a series of political and economic crises as the pre-existing mode of intervention of the state within civil society and the economy proves increasingly dysfunctional. The outcome of such crises, however, and the struggles that they engender cannot be predicted in advance. For if we are to apply the strategic-relational approach, they are contingent upon the balance of class (and other) forces, the nature of the crisis itself, and (we might add) popular *perceptions* of the nature of the crisis (Hay 1996b) – in short, on the strategically selective context and the strategies mobilized within this context.

Jessop's approach, then, despite its concern with state structures and their strategic selectivity (see Table 3.1), and despite its structuralist pedigree, eschews all forms of functionalism, reductionism and determinism. The strategic-relational approach offers no guarantees – either of the ongoing reproduction of the capitalist system or of its impending demise (though, given the strategic selectivity of the current context, the odds on the latter would appear remote). It is, in short, a statement of the contingency and indeterminacy of social and political change (1990: 12–13; 2007). The casualty in all of this is the *definitive* (and very elusive) Marxist theory of the state. As Jessop himself notes, there can be no general or fully determinate theory of the capitalist state, only theoretically informed accounts of capitalist states in their institutional, historical and strategic specificity (1982: 211–213, 258–259; 1990: 44; though cf. 2002, 2007).

We would appear to have come full circle. We end where we began, with a paradox – there is no Marxist theory of the state – there couldn't be.

Conclusions

Why do *we* need a *Marxist* approach to the state *today*? For in a world which is seemingly either globalized or globalizing and in which Marxism as a political project is defunct, it is tempting to dismiss Marxist attempts to theorize the state as anachronistic and of purely historical interest – if that. With the nation-state on the wane, do we really need a theory of the state anyway? And even if we think we do, with Marxism in retreat why a *Marxist* theory of the state?

The first objection can be dealt with fairly swiftly. Yes, the current phase of capitalist accumulation is qualitatively different from all previous stages – in terms of the international mobility of capital and in the truly global nature of the social, political and environmental crises with which it is associated. Yet it would be dangerous to conclude either: (i) that this threatens to precipitate the end of the nation-state; or (ii) that even if it did we could afford to dispense with the theory of the state. For while national communities, states and governments still provide the primary focus of political socialization, mobilization, identification and representation, the nation-state is firmly here to stay. Arguably, the rise of populist nationalism since the global financial crisis merely reinforces the point.

Moreover, while this remains so, the sort of concerted inter-state response necessary to deal with global ecological crisis is likely to be thwarted and hi-jacked by more parochial national interests and considerations. Again, the parallels with contemporary politics – particularly since the election of Donald Trump – hardly need to be underscored. For Marxists, the very form of the state itself (its national character) may militate against a genuinely global response to a genuinely global crisis. The *national* form of the state, in other words, may problematize any *global* function it might be seen to have. Environmentalism may concern itself with global problems, but environmentalists require a theory of the state (see Chapter 7). Furthermore, as Jessop notes, the internationalization of capital has rendered (more) porous the boundaries of formerly closed national economies, but it has not lessened the significance of national differences or indeed national *states* in the regulation of capitalist accumulation. The form of the state may have changed, and it may have been subject to a 'tendential hollowing-out' as many of its previous functions and responsibilities have been displaced upwards, downwards and outwards, but its distinctively national character remains (Jessop 2002, 2007, 2016). Thus the process of globalization (more accurately, the processes that may *interact* to sustain any tendency to globalization) merely demonstrate the continuing centrality of the state to the dynamics of capitalist accumulation.

It is one thing to demonstrate the continuing need for a theory of the state; it is another thing altogether to claim this as justification for a distinctively *Marxist* approach to the state. The proof of any pudding must be in the eating and it should be remembered that this particular pudding comes in a great variety of different flavours. Nonetheless, two general arguments for a sophisticated Marxist conception of the state (such as that formulated by Jessop) can be offered: one substantive, the other analytical.

For the first we can return to the above example. Environmental crisis has its origins in an industrial (and now perhaps also post-industrial) growth imperative. This might suggest the relevance of a theory of *the state in industrial* (and/or post-industrial) *society* to the political economy of ecology. Yet a moment's further reflection reveals that the growth imperative that characterizes contemporary societies – and is thus responsible for the environmental degradation we witness – is a *capitalist* growth imperative, sustained and regulated by the capitalist state. Environmentalists then need not merely a theory of the state, but a theory of the *capitalist* state. As such a theory, Marxism clearly has much to offer.

The second reason is somewhat more esoteric, and relates to the analytical sophistication of contemporary Marxist approaches to the state. Though characterized for much of its history by the seemingly intractable dispute between structural functionalism on the one hand and instrumentalism on the other, considerable analytical advances have been made in Marxist state theory in recent years. In this respect contemporary Marxist state theory has much to offer to Marxists and non-Marxists alike. For as authors like Anthony Giddens (1984) and Nicos Mouzelis (1991, 1995) have noted, the dualism of structure and agency (of which the structuralism-instrumentalism battle is merely a reflection) is not only a problem within Marxism but has characterized social and political science since its inception. In the strategic-relational approach it has eventually been transcended in a simple yet sophisticated manner. Though not all will share the analytical, critical and political concerns that animate contemporary Marxist theory, few can help but benefit from the analytical insights it offers.

Jessop's central achievement has been to take Marxist state theory beyond the fatuous question: *is the modern state a capitalist state or a state in capitalist society?* If his work receives the attention it deserves, feminists need not duplicate the errors and deviations of Marxist theory by asking themselves: *is the contemporary state essentially patriarchal or merely a state in a patriarchal society?* Contemporary Marxist theory will probably never get the chance to follow Henry Higgins in transforming the object of its study. But those who might can surely learn a thing or two from its deviations.

Yet this is perhaps to finish on too negative a note. For it is not just from the failings of Marxism analytically that we can learn. We live in an age not just of crisis but of acknowledged crisis – and an age in which few, if any, more mainstream approaches and theories either saw the global financial crisis coming or, even now, have much to say about it. That is not true of Marxism in general; and it is certainly not true of Marxist state theory more specifically. While it hardly predicted the precise form that the crisis was to take, it provides a great variety of concepts which might help us to make sense of the world in which we now acknowledge ourselves to be living and many of the responses to it. Above all, it is the theory par excellence of the endemic tension between the deregulatory disposition of capital and the need for a regulatory oversight that only the state and state-like agencies are capable of providing. Arguably, in this respect at least, it is the theory of our age.

Further Reading

Barrow, C.W. (1993), *Critical Theories of the State: Marxist, Neo-Marxist, Post-Marxist*, Madison: University of Wisconsin Press – Still probably the best accessible guide to contemporary Marxist and neo-Marxist theories of the state.

Gramsci, A. (1971), *Selections from Prison Notebooks*, London: Lawrence & Wishart – Quite possibly the single most important intervention in the development of Marxist state theory in the twentieth century.

Jessop, B. (2016), *The State: Past, Present, Future*, Cambridge: Polity – Jessop's crowning achievement – an extraordinarily rich yet at the same time highly accessible introduction to the strategic-relational approach and the insight it has to offer to analysts of the contemporary capitalist state.

Miliband, R. (1969), *The State in Capitalist Society: An Analysis of the Western System of Power*, London: Weidenfeld & Nicolson – A clear, cogent and remarkably accessible exposition and defence of the 'instrumentalist' conception of the state within Marxist theory.

Poulantzas, N. (1978), *State, Power, Socialism*, London: New Left Books – Probably Poulantzas's greatest work and far more sophisticated than the position he sought to defend in the Miliband–Poulantzas debate. It is, however, characteristically dense and impenetrable at times.

4

Public Choice

Brad R. Taylor and William Bosworth

Introduction

Public choice theory applies the methods and assumptions of economics to the questions of political science. At the heart of economics is a commitment to methodological individualism and the theoretical framework of rational choice theory. Methodological individualism holds that individual human beings should be the basic unit of analysis. Although there are specific technical elements (see Hargreaves-Heap et al. 1992: ch. 1), the essence of rational choice theory can be expressed in two simple assumptions:

(a) Individuals are able to coherently and consistently rank possible states of the world from their most to least preferred.

(b) Individuals make choices in order to secure their most preferred state of the world among the available options.

In this general form, rational choice theory is what Dowding (2016: 72–79) calls an 'organizing perspective' – a set of assumptions and methods which push us as social scientists to focus on particular types of social process but which do not themselves make specific empirical predictions. In this broad sense, rational choice theorists are not committed to making any particular assumptions about the content of what people want – e.g. whether they are selfish or altruistic – but only that individuals have preference rankings which make sense and which form the basis of the choices they make.

The term 'public choice theory' is sometimes used broadly to refer to the general rational choice approach. Many self-identified public choice theorists, and particularly those trained in economics departments, however, take the approach to imply a thicker conception of rationality. Indeed in the opening paragraphs of the revered handbook *Public Choice III*, Dennis Mueller (2003: 1–2) states plainly that '[t]he basic behavioral postulate of public choice, as for economics, is that man is an egoistic, rational, utility maximizer'. In this chapter we use 'public choice theory' to refer to the research programme which applies this thicker conception of rationality as the calculative pursuit of self-interest to the study of politics. As we will see below, this view of humanity as primarily driven by self-interest often leads to a rather bleak conception of politics as plagued by corruption and inefficiency.

So construed, public choice theorists insist that, compared to markets, the institutions of the modern democratic state provide weak or perverse incentives. Following Adam Smith (1776), economists argue that free and competitive markets tend to channel, as if by an invisible hand, individual self-interest in socially beneficial directions. Business owners would like to charge high prices and skimp on quality, but in order to attract customers they need to produce quality products at reasonable prices. Here competitive markets provide incentives that go at least some way towards aligning the self-interest of individual producers and consumers. Public choice theorists argue that state institutions, on the other hand, are rarely up to the task of similarly channelling self-interest into public interest. The efficiency of the private sector will be compromised when market failures like negative externalities, bad information and monopolies exist. But where economists traditionally took state intervention as the key to correcting for such failure, public choice theorists suggest similar inefficiencies will be just as likely (if not more so) for decisions relating to that intervention. In the same way that market failures are described from the assumption consumers are self-interested, public choice theory describes government failure from the assumption that voters, politicians and bureaucrats are similarly self-interested.

If government tends to produce undesirable results relative to the market, according to this argument, we must reduce the size and scope of government and put measures in place to expose public servants to market-like incentives. Public choice theory has thus provided intellectual support for neoliberal reforms for 'hollowing out' (Rhodes 1994) the state and moves towards New Public Management (Pierre 2011; Self 1993). It is arguably also to blame in part for recent declines in political trust and participation (Hay 2007). Indeed, many circles now dismiss public choice theory as biased and ideologically driven.

The inefficient state

James M. Buchanan suggests that the core of public choice theory as a research programme can be summed up in the three-word slogan 'politics without romance':

> Public choice theory has been the avenue through which a romantic and illusory set of notions about the workings of governments and the behavior of persons who govern has been replaced by a set of notions that embody skepticism about what governments can do and what governments will do, notions that are surely more consistent with the political reality that we may observe all about us. (Buchanan 1984: 11)

Buchanan's primary target is what he terms the 'benevolent despot' model of government, prominent in welfare economics and public finance prior to the 1960s (Buchanan 1975). On this view, which was normally implicitly assumed by applied economists rather than explicitly stated and defended, government exists as a welfare-maximizing social planner able to correct market imperfections through well-directed policy interventions. In practice, this involved economists offering policy prescriptions based on deviations from ideal circumstances without considering whether government could in reality do any better. By ignoring the state, economists implicitly assumed it to be a flawless maximizer of the general welfare. By failing to consider the corrupting influence of self-interest we assume benevolence; by failing to consider state capacity and informational constraints we assume omnipotence and omniscience.

Welfare economists have shown theoretically that unregulated markets produce efficient results when certain conditions are met. If we have an adequately competitive market with well-informed consumers and no spill-over effects, markets will roughly produce an outcome which is 'Pareto efficient' – i.e. there is no alternative distribution of resources which would make any person better off without also making someone else worse off. Efficient market outcomes may be problematic in terms of fairness or equality, but they cannot be unambiguously improved upon in narrow welfare terms: any change which helps someone will hurt someone else (Dowding and Taylor 2020: 17–26). When there is an alternative that benefits at least one person without harming another, it seems obvious it would be socially inefficient not to take it. When two individuals want to trade goods and services it would be inefficient to deny them this possibility if the trade would not harm anybody else.

Unfettered markets are not always efficient in this sense, however. Suppose that a paper factory spills contaminated wastewater into a river and thereby harms local residents who swim in the river. This is an 'external cost' – an undesired impact of the production or consumption of a good imposed on a third party (i.e. neither the buyer nor the seller) without their consent. Such bystanders do not have any say on whether the production and sale of a sheet of paper goes ahead, yet they are impacted by it. If the impact on these bystanders is greater than the cost to the buyers and sellers of stopping the pollution, we have a Pareto sub-optimal market failure – a situation which could in theory be improved upon through a series of rule changes and/or side-payments. The unregulated market outcome can thus in principle be improved upon through a well-crafted government intervention (Dowding and Taylor 2020: 26–41).

Buchanan's critique of naive welfare economics is the uncritical move from this identification of a market imperfection to the normative judgement that government should step in to attempt to correct it. There is no guarantee that human beings making decisions on behalf of government will be willing and able to pursue the public interest. The mere existence of market failure, therefore, is not enough to justify government intervention. In addition to market failure, we need to be concerned with the possibility of government failure (Keech and Munger 2015; Le Grand 1991; Tullock, Seldon and Brady 2002). If we assume, as economists typically do, that people are narrowly selfish and calculative when buying and selling goods on the market, this assumption must also be extended to political behaviour – when they enter the voting booth or take a job in a government department – unless we have a compelling argument to the contrary (Brennan and Buchanan 2000: 56–57).

Below, we outline two forms of government failure prominent in the public choice literature: special interest politics and bureaucratic inefficiency.

Special interest politics

The pluralist tradition in political science (see Chapter 1) emphasizes the importance of interest groups in shaping the behaviour of the state. Public choice theorists have been similarly interested in interest groups, but a commitment to methodological individualism prevents public choice theorists from treating groups such as taxpayers or the mining industry as the basic entities of social interaction. According to public choice theorists, these groups are aggregates of individuals, and, strictly speaking, only individuals are capable of taking actions. We thus need to consider the incentives of individual group members to contribute to collective group goals in order to think about which interests are most likely to be represented. This is the basis of Mancur Olson's (1965) *Logic of Collective Action*, which uses public choice theory to consider the relative power of groups (see Hindmoor and Taylor 2015: ch. 6).

All groups face the challenge of 'free riding' in the pursuit of collective goals. Suppose there are twenty members of a group wishing to produce the collective good of a pot-luck dinner. For the dinner to be successful, all or most participants will need to spend time and money producing a quality plate of food. Each member of the group is responsible for paying the full cost of their own contribution (in terms of time and ingredient costs) but they themselves only enjoy one-twentieth of the benefit of their own contribution. If everybody fully and equally contributes this is not a problem, since each member also enjoys one-twentieth of everybody else's contribution. However, if group members are allowed to eat regardless of their own contribution there is an incentive problem. If a guest is considering (in a rational and self-interested way) whether to produce a dish which costs $50 in time and money but adds $100 in total enjoyment to the dinner party as a whole, she will need to pay the full $50 to produce the dish but only enjoy one-twentieth of the $100 benefit, or $5. Since $50 is greater than $5, it would be irrational for the guest to produce the dish. She thus has an incentive to free ride on the contributions of others by turning up empty-handed or with the minimal contribution which will get her through the door (perhaps a packet of malt biscuits). If everyone else makes a strong contribution to the meal, the free-riding guest eats well for free. However, the same incentives apply to all other group members and if they all act selfishly they might arrive at the dinner party to discover an empty table or twenty packets of malt biscuits.

Although a group of friends like this will likely to be able to overcome this collective action problem, many groups will not. Collective goods will often be underprovided when individuals are able to free ride. Olson's key finding for our purposes is that widely dispersed interests (i.e. those held weakly by a large group of individuals) are less likely to be mobilized than concentrated interests (i.e. those held strongly by a small group of individuals). There will be less temptation to free ride in smaller groups, since each member has more impact on the collective outcome and thus captures a greater share of the value of their own efforts. Not all large groups are created equal, however. Some groups may have a large number of members but one or more members with a disproportionately large stake in the outcome. Here, although most members free ride, the most affected are more likely to contribute to group goals.

Interest groups differ in size and concentration of benefits, so Olson's theory predicts that some interest groups will be better able to mobilize members and influence government than others. An example of this is the response of the Australian mining industry to the proposed Resources Super Profits Tax (RSPT). In May 2010, Prime Minister Kevin Rudd announced a planned 40 per cent tax on profits above the normal rate of return on capital. Since Australia at the time was experiencing a long mineral price boom, this would have delivered substantial tax revenue and was argued to more fairly distribute the benefits of high resource prices to the Australian people. There was a swift response from the three largest mining companies and the Mineral Council of Australia in the form of an extensive advertising campaign which claimed that the RSPT would result in job losses, investment moving offshore and higher electricity prices (McKnight and Hobbs 2013). Regardless of the truth of such claims, the mining industry was able to convince many Australians that the RSPT was bad policy, and the government quickly backed down in June 2010 as Rudd lost the Labor Party leadership and position of prime minister to his deputy, Julia Gillard, who immediately negotiated with mining companies and settled on a watered-down version of the proposal (Bell and Hindmoor 2014).

As Gilding et al. (2013) argue, the mining industry's strong response to the RSPT is consistent with Olson's theory. At the time, there were slightly over 1,000 mining companies in Australia. Most of these are small companies focused on exploration and prospecting that earn little revenue. Three companies – BHP Billiton, Rio Tinto and Xstrata – dwarf the others in terms of scale and revenue (Gilding et al. 2013: 504–505). Each of these companies had a very significant interest in avoiding the tax and strong incentives to contribute to the collective response, since each knew that their own contribution would have a major impact on the likelihood of success (Gilding et al. 2013, 505–506). Each member of the public who would benefit from the tax, on the other hand, has only a small stake in the outcome and so mobilization of these interests is much less likely.

The important point here is not that this was in fact good policy overturned by the power of business. Rather, the point is that the mining industry was able to decisively and rapidly influence policy because the large companies were strongly motivated to contribute to their collective goals. This raises obvious concerns about political equality in democratic countries (Gilens and Page 2014; Page and Gilens 2020), but for public choice theorists it also means that many policy decisions are likely to be inefficient. If small and concentrated groups are better able to mobilize resources than large and dispersed groups, the costs of the resulting policies on the general public will often exceed the benefits to the privileged industry.

Gordon Tullock (1967) argues that the inefficiency caused by interest-group influence is even greater than this. Businesses go to great effort in attempting to influence government policy, and this diverts resources away from socially productive uses, such as improving product quality, towards the socially unproductive capturing of excess profits created by government privilege. An industry organization lobbying government for their favoured policy, for example, will devote office space, equipment and labour towards that end. Although this might be a worthwhile investment for the firms involved, any gain is likely to come at the expense of those negatively affected by the policy and from a social point of view this is wasteful. If there are multiple firms competing for government privilege, it may even be possible that the entire value of the prospective privilege is wasted by firms trying to capture it. This has become known as 'rent-seeking' (Krueger 1974), and has spawned a large theoretical and empirical literature (see Hindmoor and Taylor 2015: 167–178; Mueller 2003: ch. 15).

Interest-group influence, then, can result in government failure in a narrow economic sense by resulting in inefficient policies and leading to wasteful lobbying efforts. In both cases there is in principle an alternative situation which would leave some better off and none worse off (e.g. protected industries would give up protection in exchange for a cash bribe from consumers). In a broader sense, interest-group influence shows that rational self-interest can undermine political values such as democratic equality. Many public choice theorists thus worry that many specific regulations are really aimed at enriching special interests and do more harm than good (e.g. Simmons 2011: chs. 9, 10). It is also possible for special interests to pervert the course of well-intentioned and widely supported policies. For example, there is broad and growing consensus that climate change represents an enormous market failure which in principle justifies significant government intervention (see Chapter 7). There are many ways to tackle climate change, however, and we might expect to see policies which favour powerful interests, even if they are less effective at dealing with the problem (Helm 2010). Even when we clearly identify a market failure, then, we cannot guarantee that government action will efficiently solve the problem. Public choice theorists argue that the cure here will often be worse than the disease.

Bureaucratic inefficiency

In public bureaucracies the heads of government departments are the agents of elected politicians and are tasked with efficiently and effectively implementing government policy (Dowding and Taylor 2020: ch. 5). Public choice theorists have argued that, since public bureaucracies lack market discipline or effective mechanisms for oversight, self-interested behaviour in this realm tends to result in inefficiency and excessive government (Niskanen 1971; Tullock 1965; Tullock, Seldon and Brady 2002: ch. 5).

Managers in all organizations have incentives to pursue their own objectives rather than those they are meant to represent. In a corporate setting, CEOs are tasked with representing the interests of shareholders. The shareholders would prefer the CEO do everything possible to increase profit – by, for example, working hard and cutting costs wherever possible. The CEO has a different set of objectives which will at times conflict with those of shareholders. They may prefer to spend time playing golf rather than working and claim that this is an important networking opportunity. They may prefer to hire personal assistants to make their job easier even if the cost of this cannot be justified in terms of increased productivity. In the language on economics, this is known as a 'principal-agent' relationship. The principal (shareholders) hires an agent (the CEO) to work as their representative, but since the interests of the agent are not perfectly aligned with the preferences of the principal they will need to be monitored and incentivized to faithfully execute their duties (Hindmoor and Taylor 2015: 179). Although some degree of slack is likely to remain in corporate principal-agent relationships, shareholders will be able to monitor the performance of CEOs by looking at the objective criterion of profitability and offering incentive contracts. Since most firms face some level of competition, shareholders can also use comparative performance as a yardstick against which to evaluate managers (Laffont and Martimort 2009).

In a market setting, it is clear how many goods or services have been sold to consumers and the price paid for each of these. We can thus objectively measure the productive *output* of a private firm selling goods on a market. For bureaucracies, this is usually not the case. Consider the example of defence. We can conceptually consider the Department or Ministry of Defence as producing the public good of national defence. The inputs in this productive process include soldiers and fighter planes, but it is ultimately the military's ability to protect against foreign attack or project power which is the output of the military. Since this is a collective good which individuals do not purchase or consume, it is difficult to specify the level of output produced. The output of a government department, then, will typically be judged on the inputs to the productive process – the level of *activity* rather than the quantity or value of the outputs produced (Mueller 2003: 362–363).

Bureaucrats, therefore, typically have better information about the minimum cost of their activity than the elected representatives with whom they must negotiate outputs and budgets. Given government departments are created to provide a specific service, be it defence, health or education, they effectively also have a monopoly over their respective area. William Niskanen (1971) argued this gave heads of bureaucracies the ability to make 'take it or leave it' offers to government, which gave them considerably more slack than CEOs to pursue their own self-interest. Shielded from market competition, they will be motivated not by the quality or value-for-money of the department's output, but rather by a variety of factors which benefit them personally, including salary, job perks, power and prestige (Niskanen 1971: 38). Since these are positively related to the department's total budget, Niskanen argued top bureaucrats have an incentive to budget-maximize, creating bloated bureaucracies and considerable government waste.

Tullock (1965) conceptualizes bureaucracy as a hierarchical pyramid through which information and directives must flow. Those near the top of the pyramid – such as the heads of government departments – will rely on their subordinates to gather appropriate information and pass it up the chain. Only with accurate information can senior bureaucrats make the right decisions. Subordinates, however, will be guided by their own interests and may be reluctant to pass on information likely to anger their superiors or cast them in a bad light. Since there are multiple links in the administrative chain, the situation may come to resemble the children's game 'telephone' (or, as it is more problematically known in Commonwealth English, 'Chinese whispers'). Subtle manipulations of information at each level of the administrative hierarchy are amplified and leave those at the top of the chain with a deeply distorted picture of the on-the-ground reality (Tullock 1965: ch. 14). The Soviet response to the nuclear accident at Chernobyl is an extreme example of this dynamic: individual decision-makers within the Soviet hierarchy had incentives to understate risks and damage or otherwise distort information flowing to their superiors. This left senior decision-makers with poor information, contributing to a poor emergency response (Geist 2015; Hoffmann 1986).

The state as a product of political exchange

The most central and perennial question of the state is its justification. A major strand of political theory is based on the broadly contractarian idea that the state is justified by the implicit or hypothetical agreement among those bound by it (Darwell 2002). The question of whether people would or should agree to be bound by the state under various situations can usefully be analysed using the assumptions and tools of economics (e.g. Hardin 1991; Kavka 1983). The most influential public choice justification for the state, however, comes from Buchanan (see especially Brennan and Buchanan 2000; Buchanan 2000; Buchanan and Tullock 1999).

Buchanan starts with the individualist liberal premise that the state must in some way be justified on the basis of the unanimous consent of the governed, and sees politics as essentially a complex form of voluntary exchange. Just as rational individuals trade goods and services for mutual benefit, rational individuals would agree to be bound by rules limiting their freedom in exchange for a similar promise from everyone else.

Like Hobbes (1651), Buchanan (2000: 31–36; Brennan and Buchanan 2000: 5–8) asks whether rational people living without a state would unanimously agree to create one. Hobbes famously assumed that life without the state would be 'nasty, brutish, and short' since without external authority there is nothing to prevent individuals from enriching themselves by stealing from others rather than engaging in productive activities such as growing their own food. If your neighbour puts effort into growing crops, your rational response might be to murder them in their sleep and claim their work as your own rather than tilling your own soil and planting your own seeds. Knowing this, your neighbour will divert effort into protection from you, rather than growing crops, and might even pre-emptively murder you in *your* sleep. Without an external enforcer able to keep the peace, Hobbes argues, nothing much of value will get produced and we could all be murdered at any minute (see also Chapter 10). Hobbesian anarchy is no good for anyone.

Hobbesian anarchy can be modelled using game theory, an economic tool which allows us to examine rational choices in situations of strategic interdependence. We assume that each participant in a social situation (or 'player' in a 'game') can be defined by their preference rankings over possible states of affairs, with each earning a different 'payoff' depending on their own actions as well as the actions of others.

To show how the Hobbesian state of nature can be modelled in this way, we make some simplifying assumptions (Brennan and Buchanan 2000: 5–8). First, we assume that there are only two players, each of whom have the binary choice between working to produce food for themselves and their families ('production') or stealing from the other player ('predation'). We also assume that each player seeks only to maximize their own material welfare and will ruthlessly pursue this goal without concern for justice or the welfare of others. This does not fully capture all the social dynamics which would be at play in the state of nature, of course, but it does offer a lens through which to view the material incentives of each player in a stateless world under the assumptions made by Hobbes and Buchanan.

Figure 4.1 represents this as a normal form game – a type of game in which a decision is made only once and each player chooses simultaneously. Depending on the choices made by each player, both end up in one of the four cells. Each player chooses either production or predation. One of the players (in this case, Will) determines whether the players end up in the top or bottom row. The other (in this case, Brad) determines whether they end up in the left or right column. The four cells, then, represent all possible combinations of choices made by Will and Brad. If Will chooses production (top row) and Brad chooses predation (right column), for example, we end up in the top right cell. Will engages in productive work and Brad murders him in his sleep and steals it all. In strictly material terms, this is a very good result for Brad and a very bad one for Will. This is represented by the payoffs (or preference rankings) inside the cell: the top right cell is Brad's first preference but Will's fourth (i.e. least) preferred outcome.

	Brad chooses Production	Brad chooses Predation
Will chooses Production	Brad's 2nd preference Will's 2nd preference	Brad's 1st preference Will's 4th preference
Will chooses Predation	Brad's 4th preference Will's 1st preference	Brad's 3rd preference Will's 3rd preference

Figure 4.1 'The State of Nature'

The payoffs for other outcomes are shown in each cell, and reflect the assumptions made by Buchanan that each person would be better off materially if they could steal from others who engage in production (Brad most prefers top right and Will most prefers bottom left), but that when everyone tries to steal from one another nothing gets produced and everyone is poor (the bottom right cell is the second worst outcome for both, just ahead of being murdered after working productively). The outcome in which both choose to peacefully produce (top left) is the second best outcome for both players – each would prefer to be the sole predator, but peaceful coexistence is preferable to being at each other's throats or being a passive victim.

Game theory allows us to take this preference ordering and ask what the likely outcome will be if both players pursue their self-interest. The payoffs in Figure 4.1 conform to a much-studied form of game known as 'the prisoner's dilemma' which can be solved by finding a dominant strategy for each player. We can thus predict a specific outcome if we accept the preference rankings of the players as accurate and assume rational maximization of these preferences.

Consider the choice facing Will. He does not know whether Brad will choose production or predation but can ask himself what his best response would be in either case. If Brad chooses production (left column), Will reasons, he can either also choose production and secure his second preference (top left) or he could choose predation and secure his first preference (bottom left). In this case, his best response is to choose predation since it secures his higher ranked outcome. If, on the other hand, Brad chooses predation (right column), Will could either choose production and be murdered in his sleep (the worst outcome for Will, top right) or choose predation and end up in conflict (the next-to-worst outcome, bottom right). On the assumption that Brad chooses predation, then, Will should also choose predation to avoid the worst outcome for himself. No matter what Brad chooses, then, Will's best response is to choose predation. In the language of game theory, this is his 'dominant strategy' and if he is rational he will always take this option. The payoffs here are symmetrical, so predation is also the dominant strategy for Brad. If both players choose their dominant strategies, which game theory says they must, we end up in the bottom right cell – the Hobbesian 'war of all against all'.

The key thing to note about this result is that both Will and Brad will be pretty unhappy with it. It is preferable to the very worst outcome of being exploited by the other, but both consider the equilibrium outcome worse than the top left cell in which both choose production. Moving from the bottom right to top left would be a Pareto improvement since it benefits both Will and Brad and doesn't harm anyone. If they could somehow coordinate their actions to end up in the top left cell (by both agreeing to choose production rather than predation) they would both benefit. Unfortunately, the logic of self-interest in this situation means that this is impossible in the absence of some way of enforcing such an agreement.

For Buchanan, like Hobbes, the state is essentially a way of enforcing the agreement to lay down arms and engage in production rather than predation. The creation of a political association can thus be considered a form of voluntary exchange. Since all rational people in the state of nature would agree to be bound by coercive rules, such rules are justified on the liberal foundation of (hypothetical) unanimous consent.

Hobbes argues that any state capable of enforcing order would be preferable to anarchy and so endorses absolute government power. Buchanan, on the other hand, argues that the power of the state can be limited by constitutional rules. Those in the original position may indeed prefer an unrestrained state rather than anarchy, but an even better option would be a limited form of state forced to pursue the general welfare and respect civil rights. An autocratic ruler obviously has a great deal of power to violate individual rights, but Buchanan also insists that predation persists in democratic governments. Government can facilitate predation in a number of ways. As we saw in the previous section, concentrated and well-organized interest groups can seek favours from policymakers which harm society at large (Olson 1965; Tullock 1989); majorities can extract resources from minorities (Buchanan and Tullock 1999) or force them to behave in accordance with their version of morality (Buchanan 2000: 5–9).

James Madison and the other founders of the American republic were just as concerned with the danger of predation through factions using the machinery of the state as they were of a single tyrant taking control of government. In a letter to Thomas Jefferson, he states quite clearly that 'the invasion of private rights is chiefly to be apprehended, not from acts of Government contrary to the sense of its constituents, but from acts in which the Government is the mere instrument of the major number of the constituents' (Madison 1788).

Rather than one actor dominating others – creating order at the expense of justice – government on this view is characterized by competing factions using political means as a substitute for private violence. As Madison points out in *Federalist 51*, a government in which 'the stronger faction can readily unite and oppress the weaker, anarchy may as truly be said to reign as in a state of nature'. While unrestrained government may remove much of the physical violence of the war of all against all, it does not remove the underlying predation and conflict. Even if each would be better off if they could somehow agree to respect each other's rights, each has an incentive to renege on any such agreement when part of the ruling coalition (Gwartney and Wagner 1988: 18).

Like Hobbesian anarchy, this leads to unproductive expenditure in predation and protection against the predation of others. Tullock's (1967) argument, as outlined in the previous section, that competition for government favours tends to dissipate at least some of the value accruing to eventual beneficiaries reinforces this point. While the potential benefit available to a firm which can convince the state to grant it special favours is large, the socially unproductive lobbying effort removes at least some of this. When all is said and done, the costs of lobbying to the public at large are not fully offset by benefits to well-connected firms. Even those who frequently win government influence might prefer a government which denied them, and everyone else, these opportunities.

In the absence of a stable and homogeneous group which can expect to retain power, Buchanan suggests that rational actors would prefer a binding agreement not to violate the rights of others through the power of the state, just as those in the state of nature would prefer a binding agreement to engage in production rather than predation. The primary difference between Hobbesian anarchy and unrestrained government, on this view, is that lawyers and lobbyists replace swords and spears (Wagner and Gwartney 1988: 36). This provides the impetus for a further political bargain which limits the power of government. By agreeing to constitutional rules, individuals agree to give up the right to violate the rights of others in exchange for a similar promise from everyone else. In game theory terms, the same analysis which Hobbes used to argue for Leviathan over anarchy (see Figure 4.1 above) is used by Buchanan to argue for limited over unlimited government. Again, this justification is based on the supposed unanimous consent of rational actors were they to face such a decision.

When making any collective choice, conflicting interests will lead to disagreement. As every particular political decision benefits some at the expense of others, post-constitutional politics is inherently adversarial. To mitigate this conflict, the rules of politics must be decided separately from everyday politics. Just as unanimity over the rules of a card game is more likely before the cards are dealt, so constitutional choice must take place at a higher level of abstraction than pragmatic politics. Since constitutional rules are long-lasting and apply to a wide variety of particular situations and policy areas, Buchanan argues, individuals will not in general be able to predict which constitutional rules will give them an unfair advantage over others. This will lead people to promote the general good rather than focusing on their own narrow interests at the constitutional level of choice (Buchanan and Tullock 1999: 78–79).

Impartial self-interest will compel individuals to favour restrictions on the power of majoritarian democracy. Everyone is in the majority at some times on some issues and in the minority on others. All things considered, people will agree to limit state power in a way which is mutually beneficial, and the state which is justified for Buchanan is a fairly minimal one which enforces property rights and produces public goods but otherwise does very little (Buchanan 2000).

This case for the legitimacy of limited government is based on the individualistic assumption of unanimous consent as the justification for coercion. Using the concept of Pareto efficiency which grounds Buchanan's analysis, we can say that a move from one situation to another is an improvement if it benefits at least one person without harming anyone else. It does not tell us any more than this; in particular, it does not allow us to say that one Pareto-efficient situation is preferable to another. Buchanan's argument is that the minimal state is preferable to anarchy in this sense, but that the move from the minimal to a more expansive state cannot be justified in the same way. Since this would presumably involve some people being predictably benefited and others predictably harmed, it would not be a Pareto improvement. We need to be careful in interpreting precisely what this means, however. To say that a move from the minimal to an expansive state is unjustified on Pareto grounds in no way implies that the former is preferable to the latter; it simply implies that the two states cannot be compared to one another in terms of Pareto dominance (Dowding and Taylor 2020: ch. 2). To claim that the minimal state is justified over a more expansive one would require further normative justification.

Buchanan and other public choice theorists do tend to favour a state which is smaller and more tightly constrained than those we see in, for example, the United States and the UK today. This argument goes beyond the constitutional logic described in this section, however, combining government failure arguments like those in section 2 with a philosophical commitment to classical liberalism and economic arguments emphasizing the advantages of markets (Buchanan 2005).

Conclusion

The picture of the state presented above reflects the more general view of economics as the study of spontaneous order. The state, like the market, is not a unitary actor with preferences of its own but rather a field of social interaction. To think about aggregate behaviour of the state we need to begin with the motives and opportunities of political actors (Schelling 1978). In economics this approach is associated with Friedrich Hayek, but can be traced back to the Scottish Enlightenment thinking of Adam Smith, David Hume, and Adam Ferguson (see C. Smith 2006). On this view, states, like markets and other social institutions are 'the result of human action, but not the execution of any human design' (Ferguson 1782: pt 3, sect. 2, para. 7). The decisions the state ultimately reaches are not consciously chosen by any individual.

Although public choice theorists are by no means uniformly in favour of free markets and opposed to expansive government (see Dowding and Hindmoor 1997), the most common view is that market institutions channel self-interest in socially beneficial directions by decentralizing decision-making power. Public choice theory tends to emphasize the shortcomings of centralized government and favours a tightly constrained state (e.g. Tullock, Seldon and Brady 2002; Simmons 2011).

Public choice theory has been highly influential in libertarian and conservative thought (Ashford and Davies 2012: 214–216; Boettke and Piano 2019) and served as one of the intellectual pillars of the widespread neoliberal reforms and the emergence of New Public Management across many countries in the 1980s and 1990s (Pierre 2011; Self 1993; Hay 2007: ch. 3). As we saw in section 2, public choice theorists conclude that centralized states and bureaucracies tend to be inefficient and regulatory decisions will often serve the interests of well-connected firms rather than the general welfare. This provided intellectual ammunition for those seeking to reduce the size and scope of government through privatization and deregulation, transfer policymaking power to independent agencies, devolve responsibilities to subnational governments, and introduce market-like incentives into the public service. Thatcher's call to roll back the frontiers of the state and Reagan's view of government as a problem rather than a solution found a convenient ally in public choice theory, which provided both intellectual justification as well as policy specificity. William

Niskanen, an influential public choice theorist whose work on bureaucracy we encountered in section 2.2, was a member of Reagan's Council of Economic Advisors and played an important and active role in designing the public sector and economic reforms which constituted Reaganomics (Niskanen 1988).

Some have argued that these neoliberal reforms have 'hollowed out' the state (Rhodes 1994). On this view, the state lost some of its capacity to govern; its ability to steer the social and economic direction of the country has been reduced with privatization and the transfer of power to lower levels of government and independent agencies. Although there remains a great deal of public-sector governance, this has become decentred as the role of the centralized state has declined (Bevir 2002).

Neoliberal ideas, partly grounded in public choice theory, have certainly succeeded in influencing policy and restricting the ambitions of the state in a number of countries, but we must be careful to specify exactly what we mean when we say that public choice theory has contributed to a hollowing out of the state. Here, we need to distinguish between the size and scope of government on the one hand and *state capacity* on the other. By 'state capacity' we mean the ability of the state to make and effectively enforce rules. This depends on, among other factors, the policy instruments available to the state and the strength of its administrative apparatus (Bell and Hindmoor 2009: 59–66; Johnson and Koyama 2017; Skocpol 1985). Although alternative governance mechanisms such as markets and networks have become more predominant, this does not necessarily reduce state capacity. The state retains a predominant position in society, although it has a wider variety of governance tools at its disposal and must often make policy in partnership with other actors and organizations (Bell and Hindmoor 2009: ch. 8). Indeed, it can even be argued that many of these neoliberal reforms have in fact *increased* state capacity by providing additional governance tools, such as independent central banks able to more effectively control inflation and enabling great public-sector efficiency (Bell and Hindmoor 2009: 23–27). Public choice theory has contributed to a decentring of the state, but not to a general decline in state capacity.

More generally, public choice theory has reinforced and added legitimacy to the view common in the public that politicians and bureaucrats are only out for themselves rather than serving the public interest. In one sense, this increased scepticism of the motivations of political actors can be interpreted as a sensible form of critical engagement with politics. Democracy requires critical citizens, and assuming the worst is valuable in so far as it draws our attention to worst-case scenarios (Brennan and Buchanan 1983; Gershtenson and Plane 2015). On the other hand, Hay (2007) argues that the self-interest assumption is overly cynical and contributes to the disenchantment with politics and a dangerous disengagement on the part of democratic citizens. If citizens withdraw from politics, increased scepticism is unlikely to result in greater accountability.

Although it is worth pointing out that the methods of public choice theory do not necessarily lead to neoliberal conclusions and can in fact be used to ground left-of-centre and even Marxist analyses (Dowding and Hindmoor 1997; Elster 1985), it is fair to say that mainstream public choice theory is based on sceptical assumptions about the state and thus tends to produce anti-state and pro-market conclusions. This has contributed to a rightward shift in public policy and growing cynicism about the motivations of politicians.

Is public choice theory simply an analytic smokescreen used to justify an ideologically driven commitment to neoliberalism or an interest-driven commitment to policies which benefit business? We think not. Public choice theory has identified genuine shortcomings of centralized government which ought to be factored into institutional and policy decisions. Bureaucracies do often suffer from information and incentive problems, and public choice theory helps us understand these and consider mechanisms, such as quasi-markets, which might help solve these problems. In this way, public choice theory provides a useful sceptical lens through which to view the state.

This is not the only useful lens through which to view the state, of course, and a reform agenda grounded entirely on public choice theory to the exclusion of institutionalism (see Chapter 5) or poststructuralism (see Chapter 8) will be necessarily incomplete. The assumptions and methods of public choice theory focus our attention on particular sorts of social processes – those driven by calculative self-interest – but tend to neglect other factors such as the causal role played by ideas and the normative importance of power relations. Self-interest is a real force in the political world, but not the only one. Political phenomena are overdetermined: many factors are at play simultaneously, and no single approach, much less any particular model, is able to fully predict outcomes or explain the world in all its complexity.

Further Reading

Brennan, G. and J.M. Buchanan (1985), *The Reason of Rules: Constitutional Political Economy*, Cambridge: Cambridge University Press. Available at https://www.econlib.org/library/Buchanan/buchCv10.html

Green, D.P. and I. Shapiro (1994), *Pathologies of Rational Choice Theory: A Critique of Applications in Political Science*, Cambridge: Cambridge University Press.

Hindmoor, A. and B. Taylor (2015), *Rational Choice,* 2nd edn, London: Palgrave Macmillan.

Mueller, D.C. (2003), *Public Choice III*, Cambridge: Cambridge University Press.

Olson, M. (1993), 'Dictatorship, democracy and development', *American Political Science Review*, 87, 567–576.

Ostrom, E. and V. Ostrom (2004), 'The quest for meaning in public choice', *American Journal of Economics and Sociology*, 63(1), 105–147.

Shepsle, K.A. (2010), *Analyzing Politics: Rationality, Behavior and Institutions,* 2nd edn, New York: W.W. Norton.

5

Institutionalism

Vivien A. Schmidt

Introduction

The so-called 'new institutionalism' is no longer such a new addition to the pantheon of theories of the state and, like some of the other perspectives considered in this volume, it is by no means *only* a theory of the state. The origins of the new institutionalism, as explained in the introductory chapter, lie in the attempt to 'bring the state back into' mainstream political science by a range of theorists critical of the dominant agent-centred and behaviouralist approaches of the time (see, for instance, Evans et al. 1985). Such scholars argued for the need to contextualize politics institutionally – in other words, to see the conditions of political opportunity as being, to a significant extent, set institutionally. As such, new institutionalism is actually more of a methodological theory about how to study the state than a substantive theory about it, even if the various new institutionalist approaches to explaining the state contain presuppositions about its nature and scope. That said, the state still lies at the heart of new institutionalist scholarship – even if not always labelled as such.

Institutionalism is characterized, unremarkably perhaps, by its emphasis upon the institutional context in which political events occur and for the outcomes and effects they generate. In contrast to earlier behaviouralist and rational choice orthodoxies, it emphasizes the extent to which political conduct is shaped by the institutional landscape in which it occurs, the importance of the historical legacies bequeathed from the past to the present and the range of diversity of actors' strategic orientation to the institutional contexts in which they find themselves (Hay 2002: 14–15). As such, each contributes its own distinctive view of the state.

Since the mid-1990s, 'new institutionalism', which involves 'bringing institutions back in' to the explanation of politics and society, has gained increasing currency in political science. What political scientists mean by new institutionalism, however, depends upon their preferred methodological approach to political science, and its particular epistemological and ontological presuppositions. This in turn has significant implications for the study of the state. There are three main new institutionalisms – rational choice, historical and sociological institutionalism – plus a fourth newer 'new institutionalism' – discursive institutionalism. Each has different objects and logics of explanation, along with very different philosophical presuppositions about the nature of human agency and institutions. This makes for very different approaches to the state, and each has advantages and disadvantages with regard to its analyses of the state.

Rational choice institutionalism (RCI) portrays the state either as itself a rational actor pursuing its interests following a 'logic of calculation' or as a structure of incentives within which rational actors follow their preferences. Historical institutionalism (HI) concentrates instead on the origins and development of the state and its constituent parts, which it explains by the (often unintended) outcomes of purposeful choices and historically unique initial conditions in a 'logic of path-dependence'. Sociological institutionalism sees the state as socially constituted and culturally framed, with political agents acting according to the 'logic of appropriateness' that follows from culturally specific rules and norms. Finally, the newest of the 'new' institutionalisms, 'discursive' institutionalism, considers the state in terms of the ideas and discourse that actors use to explain, deliberate, and/or legitimize political action in an institutional context according to the 'logic of communication'.

From the 'old institutionalism' to the 'new institutionalism'

'New institutionalism' began in the late 1970s and early 1980s with the desire by a wide range of scholars to bring the institutions of the state back into the explanation of political action. It was less focused on rejecting the 'old institutionalism' – which studied the formal institutions of government and defined the state in terms of its political, administrative and legal arrangements, and which it treated as background knowledge – than on providing a counter to behaviourism. Behaviourism itself was by now under attack from the inside as well as from the outside because it was perceived as plagued by over-quantification and undertheorizing, without much cumulation of knowledge into a coherent body of theory (see, e.g. Wahlke 1979; Ostrom 1982).

'New institutionalism' was a response to the absence of institutional analysis, of considering collective action *qua* collective – through composite or institutional actors – rather than reducing political action to its methodological individualist parts. The theoretical core uniting the very disparate kinds of institutionalisms that emerged rejected the proposition that observable behaviour was the basic datum of political analysis and argued instead that behaviour cannot be understood without reference to the 'institutions' within which such behaviour occurs (Immergut 1998: 6–8).

But while the new institutionalists have been united on the importance of institutions and in the rejection of behaviourism, they have been divided along a number of other dimensions. These include first and foremost the way in which they define the state – understood now as the whole range of governing structures in and/or through which political actors, governmental as well as non-governmental, interact – and the logic of political action. But new institutionalists have also been divided along continua ranging from universalistic to particularistic generalizations, from positivism to constructivism, and from static to more dynamic explanations of political action. We begin here with the ways in which these four institutionalisms were initially defined, and the ways in which they sought to remedy perceived problems.

Rational choice institutionalism (RCI)

Rational choice institutionalism in political science has its roots in the problems encountered by rational choice analysts (see Chapter 4), in particular those interested in American congressional behaviour. Because conventional rational choice analyses predicted instability in congressional decision-making due to uncertainties resulting from the multiplicity of individual preferences and issues (e.g. Riker 1980), how could it explain the unexpected stability of outcomes? The answer was found in the institutions of the state, in particular in the rules of procedure in Congress that lowered the transaction costs of making deals, thereby solving seemingly unsolvable collective action problems (Shepsle 1986).

In short, rational choice institutionalists brought the state back in as a way of explaining outcomes that could not be explained by universal theories of rational action without reference to institutional context. But rather than asking about the context itself, meaning the state, they generally took the institutions as given and asked about the nature of rational action within such institutions. As such, institutions represented either the formal structures that set the 'rules of the game' played by rational actors or the less structured patterns and practices of the actors playing the game (Shepsle 2008). In either case, those rational actors were seen as having fixed preferences which they seek to maximize via strategic calculations within such institutions. And where any such institutions failed to promote complementary behaviour through coordination, rational actors would confront collective action problems such as the 'prisoner's dilemma' and the 'tragedy of the commons', where individual actors' choice can only lead to sub-optimal solutions (Elster and Hylland 1986; Ostrom 1990).

In American politics, rational choice institutionalist analyses are found in principal-agent theories of how 'principals' – e.g. Congress, the executive or political parties – maintain control or gain compliance from the 'agents' to which they delegate power – e.g. bureaucracies, regulatory agencies, or courts (e.g. McCubbins and Sullivan 1987; see also Chapter 4). In comparative politics, rational choice institutionalists consider delegation between European Union institutional actors (Pollack 1997; Moravcsik 1998), the European Parliament as agenda setter (Tsebelis 2002), and the collective decision-making traps in Europe (Scharpf 1999), while in international relations they examine delegation in international organizations (Martin 2000) or use a game-theory approach to democratic transitions (Przeworski 1991).

Rational choice institutionalism works best at identifying the interests and motivations behind rational actors' behaviour within given institutional settings. The deductive nature of its approach to explanation means that it is tremendously helpful at capturing the range of reasons actors would normally have for any action within a given institutional incentive structure as well as at predicting likely outcomes, even if future-oriented predictions are rarely offered. It is also good at bringing out anomalies or actions that are unexpected given the general theory. However, for the most part it cannot explain these anomalies if they depart radically from interest-motivated action, and therefore might better be explained in sociological, historical or discursive institutional terms (Scharpf 1997). Moreover, where the push is toward universalistic generalizations, problems with overgeneralization abound.

The deductive nature of rational choice institutionalism, along with a theoretical generality that starts from universal claims about rationality, also makes it difficult if not impossible to explain any one individual's reasons for action within a given context or any particular set of real political events (Green and Shapiro 1994). Because rational choice explanation works at such a high level of abstraction, it offers a very 'thin' definition of rationality in which individuals *qua* individuals are not considered. Moreover, because it has a rather simplistic understanding of human motivation, it misses out on the subtleties of human reasons for action (see Mansbridge 1990).

The rational choice institutionalist approach is also often highly functionalist because it tends to explain the origins of an institution largely in terms of its effects; highly voluntarist because it assumes that rational actors not only perceive the effects of the institutions that affect them but can also create and control them. Such voluntarism comes not only from the fact that rational actors are assumed to be able to act outside the institutions by which they are supposed to be bound but also because they see institutional creation as a quasi-contractual process rather than as affected by asymmetries of power (see Hall and Taylor 1996: 952; Bates 1987).

In addition, rational choice institutionalist explanation is static (see Green and Shapiro 1994; Blyth 1997). Because it assumes fixed preferences and is focused on equilibrium conditions, it has difficulty accounting for why institutions change over time other than in purely functionalist terms. Recent attempts to 'endogenize' change have involved paying more attention to political coalitions and the formal electoral institutions that act as incentive structures to their creation and policy focus (e.g. Iversen and Soskice 2006). The problem with this approach is that it remains highly deterministic, as institutions are portrayed as determining politics which in turn determine political outcomes; and it still cannot explain the origins of the institutions or of the political coalitions that created them, let alone why institutions or policies might change over time.

Moreover, rational choice institutionalists' emphasis on the self-interested nature of human motivation, especially where it is assumed to be economic self-interest, is value-laden and can appear economically deterministic. The normative assumptions lie in positing political action as motivated by instrumental rationality alone, and thereby risk making the utilitarian calculus within established institutions the universal arbiter of justice (e.g. Elster and Hylland 1986: 22 – see the critique by Immergut 1998: 14). What is more, despite the fact that rational choice institutionalists could question the institutional rules within which rational actors seek to maximize their utility, either in terms of the justness of the institutional rules or of the exercise of institutional power, they generally do not (see Immergut 1998: 13). They do not even question them in terms of efficiency (e.g. North 1990)! Instead, as Terry Moe complains, they tend to see institutions 'as good things, and it is their goodness that ultimately explains them: they exist and take the forms they do because they make people better off' (2003: 3 – cited in Thelen 2004). A notable exception is Margaret Levi's Marxian rationalist analysis of the 'predatory' state with regard to tax collection (1989). But mostly, institutions – and with them the state – are assumed to be good things that create greater stability for rational actors' utility maximization.

Rational choice institutionalism, thus, suffers from a wide range of problems, including too much determinism and its inverse, too much voluntarism, along with excessive universalism as well as a tendency to reify the status quo. Rational choice institutionalists have long shrugged off many of these problems, whether raised from the inside, by fellow travellers seeking to perfect the approach, or from the outside, by critics supporting alternative approaches. As Kenneth Shepsle (2008: 33–35) concluded in a discussion of the 'limitations' of rational choice institutionalism, the so-called limits are themselves 'liberating', since they paved the way for new developments, including bounded rationality, which loosened the strictures of the approach; behavioural economics, which focuses on its cognitive psychological limitations; transaction cost economics, centred on the political costs of economic exchange; and analytic narratives, which use analytical models set in historical context. It is useful to note that all these are still very much steeped in the premises of rational choice, with little move toward engagement with the other institutionalisms.

Nonetheless, some rational choice institutionalists have sought accommodation with other neo-institutionalisms to solve some of their most intractable problems, most notably with historical institutionalism (e.g. Katznelson and Weingast 2005). For example, to endogenize change, Avner Greif and David Laitin (2004) sought to build historical institutionalist insights into game-theory analysis by redefining the goal of institutions – from 'self-enforcing' to self-reinforcing or self-undermining institutions – and their effects – as 'parametric' in the short term, meaning exogenous and fixed for agents who act on self-enforcing beliefs, but only 'quasi-parametric' in the long run, meaning endogenous and variable as individuals are led to act in a manner that does not reproduce the associated beliefs. The problem here is that we are still left with the irrationality of the choice of institutions to begin with; the deterministic trajectory of change over time, now for better or worse; and the limited rationality of these supposedly 'rational' actors at any given point in time. The basic assumptions of rational choice institutionalism, in short, are not compatible with historical institutionalism, as we will see in what follows.

Historical institutionalism (HI)

Historical institutionalism is arguably the institutionalism most influenced by the old institutionalism as well as by political systems approaches, both structural-functional and Marxian approaches. From the old institutionalists came the continuing interest in the state and the formal institutions of government; from the structural functionalists, the emphasis on structures (but not functions); and from the Marxists, the focus on power, with the state seen 'no longer as a neutral broker among competing interests but as a complex of institutions capable of structuring the character and outcomes of group conflict' (Hall and Taylor 1996: 938; see also Chapter 3). Thus, historical institutionalism, unlike rational choice institutionalism, focuses most explicitly on the state and its institutional development – with the state just as problematic as the action within it.

Historical institutionalism began in the late 1970s with the works of comparativists like Theda Skocpol (1979) and Peter Katzenstein (1978), international relations scholars like Stephen Krasner (1980), and Americanists like Stephen Skowronek (1982), all of whom were intent on 'bringing the state back in' (Evans et al. 1985). These scholars argued that political action could not be reduced to individual behaviour alone or even to group activity because of the importance of how the state structured action and of how state capacity and policy legacies structured outcomes. Their work formed the basis for the subsequent, more self-consciously historical institutionalist body of literature, in which they tended to disaggregate the state into its component institutional parts (see Blyth and Vargwese 1999). Among these, Peter Hall (1986) explained the different trajectories of British and French political-economic development as the result of the structural constraints implicit in their socioeconomic organization; Peter Katzenstein (1985) demonstrated that the economic openness of small states combined with strong welfare states could be explained by historically developed, corporatist institutional structures; while Paul Pierson (1994) showed how past welfare state policies set the conditions for future policies in a comparison of the United States and Britain.

Institutions, for the historical institutionalist, are understood not as rationalist structures of incentives but rather as sets of regularized practices with rule-like qualities that structure action and outcomes (see Hall and Thelen 2009). Moreover, institutions are historical institutionalists' primary concern, with their focus the origins and development of institutional structures and processes over time. Historical institutionalists emphasize not just the asymmetries of power related to the operation and development of institutions but also the path-dependencies and unintended consequences that result from such historical development (Hall and Taylor 1996: 938; Steinmo et al. 1992; Thelen 1999). Path-dependency ensures that rationality in the strict rational choice sense is present only in so far as institutions are the intended consequences of actors' choices. But this is often not the case, given the unintended consequences of intentional action and the unpredictability of intervening events. As a result, the institutional structures of the historical institutionalists are not as efficient as they appear to rational choice institutionalists.

Interests, moreover, rather than being universally defined, are contextual (Zysman 1994; Thelen 1999). Compared to rational choice institutionalism, historical institutionalism tends to be less universalistic in its generalizations and more 'mid-range' in its theory-building, by focusing on changes in a limited number of countries unified in space and/or time or on a specific kind of phenomenon that occurs in or affects a range of countries at one time or across time (Thelen 1999). But although more particular in its generalizations, the 'new' historical institutionalism rarely stays at the level of the 'mere storytelling' of which it is sometimes accused by rational choice institutionalists. Noticeably absent is the focus on 'great men' or 'great moments', characteristic of more traditional historical approaches in the old institutionalism. In fact, the macro-historical approach prevalent in most accounts tends to emphasize structures and processes much more than the events out of which they are constructed, let alone the individuals whose actions and interests spurred those events. Here too, then, there are no individual actors as such. What is more, any 'micro-foundational logic', as rationalists put it, is generally missing from this macro-historical work.

Instead, it follows the logic of path-dependency. Rather than appearing economically deterministic, therefore, historical institutionalism can appear historically deterministic or even mechanistic where it focuses exclusively on continuities and path-dependencies. The 'critical junctures' literature that looks at 'configurative' moments (e.g. Gourevitch 1986; Collier and Collier 1991) or 'punctuated equilibrium' (Krasner 1988) is something of a corrective to this problem; but it still has difficulty explaining what brings about the crisis that spurs change. Moreover, it assumes that change comes only in bursts, with stasis in between, and cannot account for incremental change or human agency (Thelen and Conran 2016).

Historical institutionalists who sought a way out of the impasse brought about by the early reliance on path-dependency subsequently turned to the study of gradual institutional transformation. As Kathleen Thelen and Wolfgang Streeck (Thelen 2004; Streeck and Thelen 2005) argue in an important revision of historical institutionalism, institutional evolution can be explained by way of certain mechanisms of change such as the 'layering' of new elements onto otherwise stable institutional frameworks, the 'conversion' of institutions through the adoption of new goals or the incorporation of new groups, or even the 'drift' resulting from deliberate neglect in updating institutional rules. But even here, how change is instigated – through layering, conversion or drift – remains unclear without adding elements from other analytic approaches. Moreover, although Thelen and Mahoney (2010) subsequently bring agency into the very definition of actors when they categorize them by their active roles in political-economic transformation (e.g. as insurrectionaries or parasites), they do little to explain how they become change-agents, including how they mobilized and persuaded others to join them.

The main problem for the historical institutionalists, given their emphasis on structures, is how to explain human agency. For this, historical institutionalists mostly turn to analyses that add what Peter Hall and Rosemary Taylor (1996: 940–941) have termed either a 'calculus' or a 'culture' approach. The calculus approach puts the historical institutionalists closer to the rational choice institutionalists, with a materialist reading of human behaviour, albeit still with a primacy to historical structures that shape actors' interests. The 'culture' approach puts historical institutionalists closer to the sociological institutionalists, although here historical structures add to norms to give meaning to actors' interests and worldview.

Examples abound on the combination of historical institutionalism with rational calculus, with contemporary historical institutionalism largely materialist in its approach to human agency. Most notable in the study of comparative political economy is the Varieties of Capitalism approach (Hall and Soskice 2001) that embedded a rationalist analysis of firm-centred coordination in a historical institutionalist analysis of the binary division of capitalism into liberal market economies (e.g. Britain) and coordinated market economies (e.g. Germany). Paul Pierson (2004), in his study of the dimension of time in political analysis, has also combined the two, using historical institutionalism to provide a temporal dimension to rational choice institutionalism (2004).

In contrast, there have been many fewer historical institutionalist combinations with the 'culture' approach, or what has come to be known as sociological institutionalism. And most of these have been by sociologists (e.g. Campbell 2004). Over time, however, historical institutionalists have increasingly engaged with sociological institutionalism, adding norms and culture along with social agents to their historical institutionalist approach (e.g. Hall and Lamont 2013). As we shall see below, there are also a number of historical institutionalists whose work, because of their focus on ideas, no longer fit under the mainstream definitions of historical institutionalism, and whom we therefore discuss under the rubric of discursive institutionalism.

Sociological institutionalism

Sociological institutionalism, much like historical institutionalism, had its beginnings in the late 1970s, mainly in the sociological sub-field of organizational theory. Sociological institutionalists also rejected the older methodological approaches, including behaviourism and systems approaches, as well as rational choice analyses. Against Weberian assumptions about the rationality and efficiency of organizations in particular, sociological institutionalists turned to the forms and procedures of organizational life stemming from culturally specific practices. Sociological institutionalists' institutions are cast as the norms, cognitive frames and meaning systems that guide human action as well as the cultural scripts and schema diffused through organizational environments, serving symbolic and ceremonial purposes rather than just utilitarian ones. Here too, then, much like rational choice institutionalism, the state is the taken-for-granted environment in which action occurs – but the sociological institutionalist's state looks very different from the rationalist's state, as cultural practices rather than rational action infuse it with meaning.

Rationality for sociological institutionalists is socially constructed and culturally and historically contingent (see also Chapter 8). It is defined by cultural institutions which set the limits of the imagination, establishing basic preferences and identity and setting the context within which purposive, goal-oriented action is deemed acceptable according to a 'logic of appropriateness' (see Meyer and Rowan 1977; DiMaggio and Powell 1991; March and Olsen 1989; see also the discussions in Hall and Taylor 1996: 947–948; Campbell and Pederson 2001: 7–8; Campbell 2004). Sociological institutionalism is thus in direct contradiction to rationalists' views of human behaviour as following a 'logic of interest' which is prior to institutions, by which individuals may be affected but not defined.

Sociological institutionalist analyses that are particularly significant for political scientists include Frank Dobbin's (1994) study of nineteenth-century railways policy, where reasonably similar policies were 'concealed' as state actions in the United States but 'revealed' as state actions in France; Neil Fligstein's (1990) account of the transformation of corporate control as resulting from change not just in economic environments but also in corporate leaders' perceptual lenses; and Yasemin Soysal's (1994) contrast of immigration policy in Europe and America, which showed the importance of distinctive 'incorporation regimes' for absorbing immigrants based on differing models of citizenship. In political science itself, the seminal work is by James March and Johan Olsen (1989), who argued that cultural as well as historical structures matter, and who were therefore claimed as one of their own by historical institutionalists as much as by sociological institutionalists. Subsequently, a number of political scientists moved to sociological institutionalism (see Finnemore 1996a), in particular in international relations, where they called themselves 'constructivists'. Most notable was Peter Katzenstein's edited volume (1996) that focuses on how interests develop from state identities, with norms acting as collective expectations about the proper behaviour for a given identity, and with state identities structuring national perceptions of defence and security issues. But while most sociological institutionalists have centred their attention on meaning structures and social norms as the primary drivers of behaviour, some have more recently taken the 'practice turn', centred on everyday politics (Adler-Nissen 2016; Saurugger 2010). Kathleen McNamara (2015), for example, has focused on identity-building in the EU by exploring the cultural and social processes that create the EU as a political authority while changing the lived experience of Europeans via symbols, practices and techniques focused on 'constructing Europeans'.

Sociological institutionalism works best at delineating the shared understandings and norms that frame action, shape identities, influence interests and affect what are perceived as problems and what are conceived as solutions. It stands in direct opposition to rational choice institutionalism in its assumption that norms, identities and culture constitute interests, and are therefore *endogenous* because embedded in culture, as opposed to seeing interests as *exogenous* and culture, norms and identity as epiphenomena that follow from interests rather than preceding them (see Ruggie 1998; Wendt 1987).

But as a result, rather than being too general, it is sometimes accused of being too specific, and the 'cultural knowledge' it provides useful mainly as preliminary to rational choice universalization. However, when the objects of sociological institutionalism are subsumed under rational choice explanation, often the very essence of sociological institutionalism – the norms, rules and reasons which are culturally unique or anomalous because they do not fit generally expected interest-motivations – gets lost. Because such explanations are arrived at inductively rather than deductively, they can lend insight into individuals' reasons for action in ways that rational choice institutionalism cannot, whether they fit the norm or depart from it. Moreover, because such explanations account contextually for individuals' reasons for action, sociological institutionalism is better able to explain the events out of which historical institutional explanations are constructed. And because sociological institutional explanations emphasize the role that collective processes of interpretation and legitimacy play in the creation and development of institutions, they can account for the inefficiencies in institutions that rational choice institutionalism cannot (Meyer and Rowan 1977; see discussion in Hall and Taylor 1996: 953).

However, because sociological institutionalism makes no universalistic claims about rationality and is generally focused on explanation within rather than across cultures, it risks an implicit relativism which leads one to question whether sociological institutionalism allows for any cross-national generalizations at all. In fact, generalizations are possible here too, by invoking similarities as well as differences in cultural norms and identities, much in the way of historical institutionalism with country-specific institutional structures and processes. The resulting explanation, however, involves a lower level of generality and less parsimonious, 'thicker description' than in historical institutionalism, let alone rational choice institutionalism.

Finally, rather than appearing either economically or historically deterministic, sociological institutionalism can appear culturally deterministic where it emphasizes the cultural routines and rituals to the exclusion of individual action which breaks out of the cultural norm, i.e. rule-creating, as opposed to rule-following, action. Moreover, its emphasis on macro-patterns may make it appear like 'action without agents' (Hall and Taylor 1996: 954) or, worse, structures without agents (see the critique by Checkel 1998: 335). And like the rational choice approach, it too can be too static or equilibrium-focused, and unable to account for change over time – although where it adds a historical perspective, it can also show how norms are institutionalized, as in the case of the police and military in post-war Japan and Germany (Katzenstein l996b), how state identities can change and pull interests along with them, as in the case of anti-militarism in Germany and Japan (Berger 1998), or how a thin European identity can develop (McNamara 2015).

Discursive institutionalism

Discursive institutionalism is the term I use for the fourth and newest of the 'new institutionalisms' (Schmidt 2002, 2008, 2010; see also Campbell and Pederson 2001). It can be seen as an umbrella concept (Schmidt 2010) for a wide range of approaches. These go from a focus on ideas – as in the 'ideational turn' (Blyth 1997) or 'ideational constructivism' (Hay 2006) – to discourse. Discourse encompasses not just the representation or embodiment of ideas – as in discourse analysis (following, say, Foucault 2000, Bourdieu 1990 or Laclau and Mouffe 1985; see also Chapter 8) – but also the interactive processes by and through which ideas are generated in the policy sphere by discursive policy communities and entrepreneurs (e.g. Haas 1992; Sabatier and Jenkins 1993) and communicated, deliberated and/ or contested in the political sphere by political leaders, social movements, and the public (e.g. Habermas 1989; Mutz, Sniderman and Brody 1996). More recently, feminist institutionalism has also made its appearance as a distinctly ideational and discursive project, although sometimes also conjoined with historical institutionalism (Mackay, Kenny and Chappell 2010; Kulawik 2009).

This approach has grown out of scholars' concern with the seeming unwillingness of the three older new institutionalisms to deal with real agents' ideas and discourse as well as with their inability to explain change, given their often very static view of institutions. The problem with the other approaches was first brought home as a result of real events, in particular as communist states collapsed following the fall of the Berlin Wall, giving the lie to the static presuppositions of all three approaches (see Blyth 2003), and as the rationalist presuppositions of neoliberalism encountered problems with democratic transitions (Campbell and Pederson 2001: 7–8; Campbell 2004). The recurrent crises that states have had to confront since then, especially beginning with the financial crisis in 2008, followed by the Eurozone crisis in 2010, recurring migration crises, the climate crisis and the Covid-19 health pandemic, capped by the populist challenges to liberal democracy and the state, all contribute to the recognition that institutions are much less stable than theorized, and that ideas and discourse matter a lot more than traditional neo-institutionalists have recognized.

The turn to the role of ideas and discourse was also a natural next step for scholars immersed in all three of the new institutionalisms but concerned to explain changes within the state and to the state. In so doing, most added the institutional context of their own preferred approaches. But while, for some, turning to ideas meant staying within the initial constructs of their own institutionalist approach, others moved beyond, into discursive institutionalism, and a primary concern with the substantive content of ideas and/or how they are communicated through discourse in discursive interactions in the policy and political spheres.

For all such scholars, institutional context refers first and foremost to the structure, construction, and communication of meaning by sentient agents who convey substantive ideas through the interactive processes of discourse following (contextualized) 'logics of communication'. In consequence, discursive institutionalists all question the older neo-institutionalists' primary view of institutions as constraints – whether as rationalist incentive structures, historical path-dependencies or cultural frames – and of agents as largely determined by those institutions – whether as rational actors driven by interests, corporate actors shaped by path-dependent rules, or social actors framed by cultural norms. Discursive institutionalists focus their attention instead on the dynamics of change (and continuity) through sentient agents' ideas and discourse-driven (re)construction of interests, (re)shaping of historical paths, or (re)framing of culture (see also Chapter 8).

Ideas in neo-institutionalist perspective

The ideas and discourse considered by discursive institutionalists may come in different forms and types at different levels of generality. The different forms of ideas and discourse include narratives, frames, storytelling, argumentative practices and discursive struggles (e.g. Roe 1994; Hajer 2003; Fischer and Forester 1993; Stone 1988). The types encompass cognitive ideas justified in terms of interest-based logics (e.g. Jobert 1989, Hall 1993; Schmidt 2002: ch. 5) and normative ideas legitimated through values-based logics of appropriateness (e.g. March and Olsen 1989; Schmidt 2000). The different levels of generality go from the most immediate level of policy ideas (e.g. Kingdon 1984) to the intermediate level of programmatic ideas or 'paradigms' (e.g. Berman 1988; Jobert 1989; Hall 1993) to the deeper level of philosophical ideas, including ideology (Freeden 2003), hegemonic discourse (Gramsci 1971) and public philosophy (Campbell 2004).

Only a few RCI scholars have turned to ideas to account for institutional change (e.g. Goldstein and Keohane 1993). But they never took ideas very seriously, since ideational explanation was deemed useful only when and if explanation in terms of 'objective' or 'material' interests was insufficient, at which point ideas could be seen as 'road maps', 'focal points', or even, following the work of Douglas North (1990), 'shared mental modes'. The problem for RCI scholars is that they could not continue to maintain the artificial separation of 'objective' interests from the 'subjective' ideas about interests, i.e. beliefs and desires. These threatened to undermine the 'fixed' nature of preferences and the notion of outcomes as a function of pre-existing preferences that are at the basis of the rationalists' thin model of rationality (see Blyth 2003). But without taking ideas seriously, it becomes very difficult to explain change, since RCI cannot explain how interests are reconceptualized or new coalitions formed. This helps explain why most rational choice institutionalists quickly abandoned the pursuit of ideas, other than sometimes seeing them as pre-existing beliefs or preferences to be recognized as such, but not investigated.

It is important to note, however, that more recently the very sources of rational choice institutionalist inspiration, economists, have come to emphasize the importance of ideas. North (2010), for example, suggested that economics needed to be revised to take into account how humans cannot know the 'reality' of their political-economic system but nonetheless 'construct elaborate beliefs about the nature of that "reality"' which result in the 'elaborate structure of institutions that determine economic and political performance'. Jens Beckert (2011) went even further, using the concept of 'fictionality' to suggest that market actors, instead of being economically rational, elaborate 'imagined futures' about what might happen and organize their activities based on such 'mental representations'. Donald MacKenzie (2006) similarly shows that financial actors embed their presuppositions in the very instruments and analytic tools that serve to reshape rather than simply reflect the markets, like 'an engine, not a camera'. But even economists who may continue to use rational actor theory in their models have discovered behavioural economics, including 'irrational exuberance' and 'animal spirits' (Akerlof and Shiller 2009), which enables them at the very least to explain why their models stopped working. Even in political science, an increasing number of scholars in the rationalist tradition have turned to investigating its limits, such as James Druckman (2004), who argues that 'framing effects', that is, meaning contexts, matter.

For those relatively few political scientists in the rational choice tradition who took ideas seriously, subjective interests replaced the objective ones, as ideas about interests. In international political economy, for example, Woll (2008) demonstrates that firms' ideas about which utility to maximize (interests) in international trade in services, how to maximize it (strategies), and to what end (goals) explain changes in their identity, as they moved from seeing themselves as national champions to global players. In comparative political economy, moreover, Rothstein (2005) shows that institutions such as those of Sweden's collective bargaining system should not be treated as neutral structures of incentives but, rather, as the carriers of ideas or 'collective memories' which make them objects of trust or mistrust and changeable over time as actors' ideas and discourse about them change in tandem with changes in their performance.

In the historical institutionalist tradition, the move into ideas has been more widespread. Here, the question is really where the tipping point is between historical institutionalists who continue to see institutions as constitutive of ideas, determining which ideas are acceptable, and those who might better be called discursive institutionalists within a historical institutionalist tradition because they see ideas as constitutive of institutions even if shaped by them. Interestingly enough, even in the book that gave historical institutionalism its name (Steinmo et al. 1992), the few chapters that were focused on ideas – those of Peter Hall, Desmond King and Margaret Weir – went beyond historical institutionalism. These authors also went beyond HI in their subsequent work (e.g. Hall 1993; King 1999; Weir 2006).

Within the historical institutionalist tradition, in fact, much work focused on ideas tips into what I call discursive institutionalism – although the dividing line is admittedly fuzzy. What defines these is the focus on ideas as explanatory of change, often with a demonstration that such ideas do not fit predictable 'rationalist' interests, are underdetermined by structural factors, and/or represent a break with historical paths (see discussion in Blyth 2003). Early examples include Sheri Berman's (1998) historical contrast between the German Social Democrats' capitulation before Nazism, in large measure because they could not think beyond their long-held Marxist ideas, and the Swedish Social Democrats' success because they were free of any such ideational legacy and able to reinvent socialism; Mark Blyth's (2002) analysis of the role of foundational economic ideas at moments of economic crisis first in 'embedding' liberalism in the 1930s and then 'disembedding' it beginning in the 1970s in Sweden and the United States; and my own analysis (Schmidt 2002) of the political economies of Britain, France and Germany, in which I begin with a historical institutionalist examination of the evolution in the three countries' economic practices followed by a discursive institutionalist discussion of the changing ideas and discourse in the politics of economic adjustment.

More recently, traditional historical institutionalists concerned with 'endogenizing' incremental institutional change and bringing agency back in have turned to ideas in increasing numbers. For example, at the end of a discussion of what rationalist approaches could gain from historical institutionalism, Hall (2010) included a lot of the stuff of sociological institutionalism and discursive institutionalism when he emphasized instrumental and normative beliefs, identity, framing effects, 'debates' that engage identities, and the 'politics of ideas' that is 'intrinsic, rather than epiphenomenal, to the processes of coalition formation that underpin change' (Hall 2010: 212). In a similar vein, and even more recently, Giovanni Capoccia (2016) has emphasized the ideational factors in political battles over the meaning of institutions to explain their transformation.

Most ideational approaches that are within the sociological institutionalist tradition, by contrast, sit closer to the constructivist end, and are mostly found in international relations. In these approaches, ideas constitute the norms, narratives, discourses, and frames of reference which serve to (re)construct actors' understandings of interests and redirect their actions within the institutions of the state. The focus here is on the normative aspects of discourse, that is, how and why new ideas 'resonate' with national values, and how they may 'revaluate' values, all within a logic of appropriateness (March and Olsen 1989; Rein and Schön 1991; Schmidt 2000).

In the sociological institutionalist tradition, one cannot talk about a move into ideas as such, since ideas have always been at the basis of the approach – as norms, cognitive frames and meaning systems. However, there is also a tipping point here. On the one side are those scholars who see ideas more as static ideational structures, as norms and identities constituted by culture, and thus remain largely sociological institutionalists as per the earlier definition. These include 'constructivists' like Katzenstein and colleagues (1996) who stay largely within sociological institutionalism because they 'cut into the problem of ideational causation at the level of "collective representations" of ideational social facts and then trace the impact of these representations on behavior' (Ruggie 1998: 884–845). On the other side are constructivists who more clearly fit under the rubric of discursive institutionalism because they present ideas as more dynamic, that is, as norms, frames, and narratives that not only establish how actors conceptualize the world but also enable them to reconceptualize the world, serving as a resource to promote change (e.g. Wend 1987:359–360). Scholars who first explored this more dynamic dimension empirically include Martha Finnemore (1996b), who examines the diffusion of international norms to developing countries, and Thomas Risse (2001) who considers the ways in which different European countries successively constructed and reconstructed their state identities and ideas about European integration. My own work on the differential impact of European integration on national democracy (Schmidt 2006) similarly focuses on state reconstructions of identity over time, showing that, while historical institutionalist attention to state design helps account for why simple polities such as France and the UK had greater difficulty adapting to the highly compound EU than similarly compound polities like Germany and Italy, it cannot explain these countries' differing responses to the EU without discursive institutionalist analysis of the role of legitimizing ideas as well as persuasive discourse in promoting (or not) public acceptance of European integration.

Discursive processes of interaction

Most of the discursive institutionalists just discussed – whether in the historical or sociological institutionalist tradition or straddling the two – tend to deal mainly with ideas, leaving the interactive processes of discourse implicit as they discuss the ideas generated, accepted and legitimized by the various actors. Some scholars, however, have gone farther to formalize the interactive processes of idea generation, acceptance and legitimization, and to clarify how they are structured. They tend to see discourse not only as a set of ideas bringing new rules, values and practices but also as a resource used by entrepreneurial actors to produce and legitimate those ideas. Their approaches can be divided into those focused on the 'coordinative' discourse among policy actors and those more interested in the 'communicative' discourse between political actors and the public (see Schmidt 2002: ch. 5, 2006, 2008, 2010).

In the coordinative sphere, discursive institutionalists tend to emphasize primarily the individuals and groups at the centre of policy construction who generate the ideas that form the bases for collective action and identity. Some of these scholars focus on the loosely connected individuals united by a common set of ideas in 'epistemic communities' in the international arena (Haas 1992). Others target more closely connected individuals united by the attempt to put those ideas into action through 'advocacy coalitions' in localized policy contexts (Sabatier and Jenkins-Smith 1993) or through 'advocacy networks' of activists in international politics (Keck and Sikkink 1998). Yet others single out the individuals who, as 'entrepreneurs' (Fligstein and Mara-Drita 1996; Finnemore and Sikkink 1998) or 'mediators' (Jobert 1992; Muller 1995), draw on and articulate the ideas of discursive communities and coalitions in particular policy domains in domestic or international arenas.

In the communicative sphere, discursive institutionalists emphasize the use of ideas in the mass process of public persuasion in the political sphere. Some of these scholars focus on electoral politics and mass opinion (Mutz, Sniderman, and Brody 1996), when politicians translate the ideas developed by policy elites into the political platforms that are put to the test through voting and elections; others are more concerned with the 'communicative action' (Habermas 1996) that frames national political understandings; yet others, on the more specific deliberations in the 'policy forums' of informed publics (Rein and Schön 1991) about the ongoing policy initiatives of governments. This communicative discourse may be seen as top-down, as elites seek to form mass public opinion or legitimize public policy; at the top among policy and political actors, as elites debate ideas in national or global expert forums (Seabrooke and Wigan 2016); at the bottom among everyday actors engaged in deliberative democracy or in expressing ideas through their everyday practices; or bottom-up, as social activists attempt to influence national and international debates (Finnemore and Sikkink 1998).

One example of this is Charlotte Epstein's (2008) account of the success of the discourse of the 'Save the Whale' movement, which was extremely effective in a relatively short span of time in moving ideas about whales from nasty, dangerous creatures (as Moby Dick) to endangered species worthy of protection and even affection (as Moby Doll).

Finally, more recently scholars have tended to bring the coordinative and communicative discourses together, while considering historical development over time. A particularly good example is that of King and Smith (2014) in their analysis of a critical ideational development in American race policy, where they show that change results not only from a coordinative discourse that succeeds in coalescing a new coalition of policy actors around a set of ideas but also from the translation by political leaders of those ideas into a persuasive communicative discourse to the public that wins elections. Another is that of Wesley Widmaier (2016), who traces change in economic ideas about how to govern the economy from the 'rhetorical construction' of an economic policy order by a 'rhetorical' political leader who commands authority and public trust, through intellectual conversion of that order by technocratic elites (mainly economists) engaged in technical fine-tuning, to crisis of the economic policy order that may lead to its replacement by another such order, promoted by another rhetorical leader.

Conclusion

The study of the state, as we have seen, is very different depending upon the kind of new institutionalism. Each has a different object of explanation – whether rational behaviour, historical structures, norms and culture, or ideas and discourse; a different logic of explanation – whether interests, path-dependency, appropriateness or communication; a different emphasis on continuity or change – whether on continuity through fixed preferences, through path-dependency, through cultural norms, or on change through ideas and discursive interactions (see Table 5.1). The result is that there are very different kinds of institutionalist studies of the state, many of which focus little on the state itself but, rather, on different kinds of action within the state.

Among the questions that remain to be answered is one crucial one: can these four new institutionalisms fit together? Can empirical studies of any one issue mix approaches? Many of the most theory-driven of new institutionalists would answer in the negative, because their purpose is to

Table 5.1 The Four New Institutionalisms

	Rational Choice Institutionalism	Historical Institutionalism	Sociological Institutionalism	Discursive Institutionalism
Object of explanation	Rational behaviour	Historical structures	Norms and culture	Ideas and discourse
Logic of explanation	Interest	Path-dependency	Appropriateness	Communication
Ability to explain change	Static – emphasis on continuity through fixed preferences	Static – emphasis on continuity through path-dependency	Static – emphasis on continuity through cultural norms	Dynamic – emphasis on change and continuity through ideas and discursive interaction
Examples	Principal-agent theory; game theory	Historical institutionalism process tracing varieties of capitalism	Constructivism; norms; cultural analysis	Ideas; discourse; constructivism; narratives; frames; advocacy coalitions; epistemic communities

demonstrate how their particular approach is the best way of explaining politics. More problem-oriented scholars mix approaches all the time, using whichever approaches seem the most appropriate to explaining their object of study. For a theoretical answer to the question of how the various approaches fit together, new institutionalists need first to stop seeing their relations with rival approaches as methodological wars where the battles are fought over conceptual territory. They would do better to declare peace, and begin exploring areas of mutual compatibility along their borders. This would surely move all four new institutionalisms forward theoretically, while providing the greatest benefits for empirical research.

Further Reading

Blyth, M., O. Helgadottir and W. Kring (2016), 'Ideas and Historical Institutionalism'. in O. Fioretos, T.G. Falleti and A. Sheingate (eds), *The Oxford Handbook of Historical Institutionalism*, 142–164, Oxford: Oxford University Press.

Carstensen, M. and V.A. Schmidt (2016), 'Power through, over and in ideas: Conceptualizing ideational power in discursive institutionalism', *Journal of European Public Policy*, 23(3), 318–337.

Hall, P. and R. Taylor (1996), 'Political science and the three new institutionalisms', *Political Studies*, 44(5), 952–973. The most readable account of the three 'new institutionalisms', and the first to identify them clearly.

March, J.G. and J.P. Olsen (1989), *Rediscovering Institutions: The Organizational Basis of Politics*, New York: Free Press. The groundbreaking work that introduced sociological institutionalism to political science.

Pierson, P. (2004), *Politics in Time: History, Institutions, and Social Analysis*, Princeton, NJ: Princeton University Press. A book that brings together rational choice and historical institutionalism.

Schmidt, V.A. (2008), 'Discursive institutionalism: The explanatory power of ideas *and* discourse', *Annual Review of Political Science*, 11, 303–326.

Somit, A. and J. Tanenhaus (1982), *The Development of American Political Science from Burgess to Behavioralism*, New York: Irvington. An insightful history of the old institutionalism and its replacement with systems analysis and behavioural approaches.

Thelen, K. (1999), 'Historical Institutionalism in Comparative Politics', in *The Annual Review of Political Science*, Palo Alto, CA: Annual Reviews. The last word on historical institutionalism.

6

Feminism

Johanna Kantola

Introduction

The state fundamentally shapes gender and gender relations in different societies. States are neither gender neutral – treating different people as if they had no gender, race, ethnicity or class background – nor gender equal – having adequate policies, institutions and processes in place to ensure equal opportunities and outcomes for all. With laws and policies, states can indeed advance or hinder gender equality in the society. From a feminist perspective, states are contradictory. For example, welfare states have provided (some) women with jobs and services, which has increased equality and, at the same time, cemented gendered labour markets where women have been trapped in public-sector jobs and low levels of pay. Different models and levels of democracy either give a voice to women and minorities as political decision-makers, citizens and civil society actors or exclude them from decision-making.

Such contradictions explain why feminist theories on the state were long dominated by a deep uneasiness about the state which was seen as patriarchal and therefore beyond feminist politics. This discomfort culminated in arguments that feminists did not have a theory of the state (MacKinnon 1989) and that it was not a feminist concern to theorize the state (Allen 1990). Judith Butler (1997) too, whose gender theory has been so influential among poststructural feminists and beyond, has conceptualized the state in a strongly anti-statist way – in contradiction with her other anti-essentialist thinking (Lloyd 2007). Despite these tendencies, a variety of feminist perspectives on the state exists. The 'canon' includes liberal, radical, Marxist/socialist, Nordic, poststructural feminist perspectives, and, most recently, new materialist and postcolonial feminist perspectives on the state (see e.g. Chappell 2013; Kantola 2006, 2016). Alternatively, in our recent book, we discern how the analytical perspective on the state changes depending on one's conceptualization of gender. We distinguish between five perspectives: women; gender; deconstruction of gender; intersectionality; and postdeconstruction (Kantola and Lombardo 2017).

The different feminist perspectives on the state have continuously tackled some key issues. Traditionally, key feminist questions in relation to the state have included analyses about paradoxes and dichotomies such as the public-private, in and out of the state, and relationships of the state to feminist politics and struggles (Banaszak, Beckwith and Rucht 2003; Banaszak 2010). Although the different perspectives on the state continue to coexist, it is possible to discern some general trends in feminist debates (see Kantola 2016). Feminist debates have, first, moved away from *essentialist* notions about women and men, and the state and nation. Black feminist theorizing about gender, race, ethnicity, sexism and racism (hooks 1984; Hill Collins 1991) has become more mainstream with the popularity of the notion of intersectionality (Crenshaw 1991) that highlights how gender intersects with race and ethnicity, sexuality, disability, class and other inequality categories.

Second, instead of the state being a real essentialized object, feminist theories tend to explore the ways in which states need to be constantly *reproduced* through discourses, practices or material circuits (see also Chapter 8). Feminist scholars explore the power relations behind these constructions, the femininities and masculinities that they rely upon and reproduce, and their differentiated gender impacts. State processes, policies, institutions, discourses, practices and norms are shown to be gendered and gendering and constitutive of gender orders. States are also racialized and sexualized in that they use norms around heterosexuality to reproduce the state and nation. Feminist scholars have coined the terms homonationalism and homoprotectionism to illustrate how the states and nations draw new boundaries between 'us' and 'them', the Others (Puar 2007). In these approaches, state interests are constructed in the very processes where they are represented or articulated (Kantola 2007).

Third, the state and related concepts are now theorized as highly *context specific* rather than universal. Context-specific states are termed abusive, women-friendly, developmental, fragile, coercive, postmodern, central or postcolonial in feminist debates to reflect both the differences between and within states and state institutions (Bumiller 2008; Prügl 2010; Kantola and Dahl 2005). The 'affective turn' in feminist theory, in turn, points to the role of emotions in holding nations and states together (Ahmed 2004). Finally, the *changing political and societal context* is reflected in the feminist debates about the state. What was first discussed as 'globalization' has now been specified as neoliberalization that takes different forms in different parts of the world. Neoliberal governmentality reflects the infiltration of market-driven truths and calculations into the domain of politics (Ong 2007: 4). A cross-cutting theme in current feminist research is the manifold impact of neoliberalism and its manifestations in states and feminist engagements with them to the extent that we can talk about a move towards 'market feminism' (Kantola and Squires 2012). Feminist scholars explore, in particular, the ways in which neoliberalism is often combined with other ideologies such as conservatism, radical-right populism or homonationalism, and the gendered outcomes of this (Brown 2018; Elomäki and Kantola 2018).

This chapter discusses feminist theories of the state by focusing on some key questions such as: What is the state? How is it gendered, racialized, classed and sexualized? What do states do and with what effects? What roles do states play in advancing equalities/perpetuating inequalities? The chapter begins by focusing on feminist conceptualizations of the state as neutral and benign, then moves on to discuss the state as capitalist and patriarchal, postcolonial, poststructural and, finally, from new materialist perspectives. The chapter finishes with some reflections on feminist empirical research on the state, including the challenges created by the impact of radical-right populism.

Neutral and benign state

For some feminist scholars, the state represents a neutral institution that can be targeted and lobbied to achieve progressive gender equality legislation. The state is an institution that is a source of potentially women-friendly legislation and policies. For example, in the liberal feminist classic Betty Friedan's *The Feminine Mystique* (1962), equality of opportunity for women is to be achieved through changing legislation on equal pay and working hours, and outlawing discrimination in workplaces. Women's access to the state in terms of political institutions (parliaments, governments, bureaucracy) becomes an important political question and goal.

While liberal feminists recognize that state institutions are dominated by men and that policies reflect masculine interests, they argue that the state is to be 'captured back' from the interest group of men (see Kantola 2006). In other words, the state is a reflection of the interest groups that control its institutions, a notion that resembles pluralist state theories in political science. The notion of the state put forward by liberal feminists is symptomatic of liberal feminist appropriation of key concepts in general: they take the existing ideas and apply them to the case of women (cf. about power Lloyd 2013: 113). More women in the state would entail more women's policy, a presumption that has since been challenged in the debate about women's substantive representation where it has been shown that the link between increases in women's descriptive representation do not automatically translate to feminist policy (Celis et al. 2008). The benign notion of the liberal state informs the work of Susan Moller Okin (1989) too who argues that the liberal models of justice are to be extended from the sphere of the benign state to the sphere of the family and she criticizes the state's indirect role in the reproduction of inequalities in families. For Okin, the solution to these problems lies within the liberal state: in its public policies and reforms of family law. The arguments about the benign liberal state have surfaced in recent debates about feminism and multiculturalism. Okin (1999) argues that the liberal state should set boundaries to multicultural group rights when these rights harm women.

A similar benign notion of the state can be discerned from a different feminist tradition, namely Nordic theorizing of women-friendly welfare states. Helga Maria Hernes (1987) defined Nordic states as potentially women-friendly societies, which signified that women's political and social empowerment happened through the state and with the support of state social policy. The social democratic citizenship tradition results in an optimistic acceptance of the state as an instrument for social change. For Hernes, Nordic women acted in accordance with their own culture in turning to the state, even in those instances where they wish to build alternative institutions. Studies of the Nordic women-friendly welfare states argue that women become empowered as political subjects through the institutionalization of gender equality. This drew attention to women's contributions and roles in both maintaining and changing gender relations (Siim 1988). Early debates on women-friendly welfare states highlighted the contradictions, where the private dependency of women on individual men was argued to be transformed into public dependency on the state in the women-friendly welfare states (Dahlerup 1987). The expansion of the public sector, even if it benefits women, is planned and executed by a male-dominated establishment. Thus, women were the objects of policies. The tendency was exacerbated by the observation that women's lives were more dependent and determined by state policies than men's and the Nordic welfare states are based on a gendered system of power and hierarchies.

The women-friendly welfare state has since come under even more intense criticism from feminist scholars in the Nordic countries. First, the women-friendly welfare state has been shown to benefit only some women and men (e.g. white and middle-class) and to be constructed on inequalities based on race and ethnicity, sexuality and class. As a powerful discourse, the 'women-friendly welfare state' may even mask these inequalities by creating an impression that equality has been achieved for all (Kantola 2006; Martinsson et al. 2017). Second, Nordic welfare states have been strongly influenced by the processes of neoliberalization and economization, which intensified during and in the aftermath of the 2008 financial and economic crisis. These states have become more neoliberalized in terms of policymaking norms and processes and the effects have been gendered and racialized – an issue pertinent to so many states that it is discussed in more detail in the final section of this chapter (Elomäki and Koskinen Sandberg 2020). Third, the Nordic welfare states are highly corporatist, meaning that a number of gender equality issues, especially those related to the labour market, continue to be decided in complex negotiations between the labour market organizations – out of the reach of parliamentary politics (Elomäki et al. 2021; Elomäki et al. 2022; Saari et al. 2021). While Nordic countries continue to perform comparatively well in terms of achievements on gender equality, highly understudied corporatism has in many cases been detrimental to gender equality too.

Patriarchal and capitalist state

Theorizing the state as patriarchal and capitalist has occupied an important place in feminist debates. These critiques of the state come from very different theoretical traditions, ranging from Catharine MacKinnon's radical feminism to Marxist and socialist feminism and to Judith Butler. The state is theorized to work together with ideologies or modes of governance such as neoliberalism or capitalism to appropriate feminist movement goals – for example, in relation to sexual violence (Bumiller 2008).

Radical feminists stress the patriarchal nature of the state which requires analysing the roles of the state in perpetuating gender inequalities. The state is not an isolated, neutral and narrow institution but rather is embedded in broader gendered societal structures that in turn shape women's engagements with the state and the policies that emanate from it (Eisenstein 1986: 181). With Kate Millett, the concept of patriarchy acquired a new meaning (1970). Until her *Sexual Politics*, patriarchy had signified the rule of the father or the rule of the head of the household. Millett argued that what patriarchy is actually about is the rule of men – male supremacy – the most fundamental form of oppression. The concept of patriarchy captured the insight that the oppression of women is not haphazard or piecemeal but, rather, that the diverse forms of oppressions were interconnected and mutually sustained. The radical nature of this feminist analysis stemmed from the claim that the state is not only contingently patriarchal, but essentially so. Furthermore, patriarchy was global and universal. The particular forms that states took were not particularly significant as all were patriarchal states.

Catharine MacKinnon (1987, 1989) articulated a radical feminist stance on the state. She argued:

> The state is male in the feminist sense: the law sees and treats women the way men see and treat women. The liberal state coercively and authoritatively constitutes the social order in the interest of men as a gender – through its legitimating norms, forms, relations to society, and substantive policies. (1989: 161–162)

Feminists could not expect the state to liberate women because it is impossible to separate state power from male power. MacKinnon directed her critique at the liberal state in particular and criticizes its laws and policies. According to her, even if the laws on rape, abortion and pornography were formally there, they were never fully enforced. At the same time, states enforced the equation of women with sexuality, which adds to their oppression. For Carole Pateman (1988), the origins of patriarchy lay in the social-sexual contract that gave men the political right over women and access to their bodies. An exclusive focus on integrating women into state institutions produced a situation that perpetuated dominant patriarchal discourses and norms rather than challenged them.

While liberal feminists understand the state in terms of its political institutions, radical feminists extend their focus to the wider structures of the state and society. Radical feminist work shows the patriarchal nature of the formal and informal practices of politics and connects this to the 'personal' – families, sexuality, intimate relations, violence – which significantly expands the scope of what is studied as politics and the political. The concept of patriarchy informs feminist strategies and political goals: the whole structure of male domination must be dismantled if women's liberation is to be achieved (Acker 1989: 235). Civil society, rather than the state, is the sphere in which women should concentrate their energies in order to challenge patriarchy. Via consciousness-raising, it becomes possible to rediscover what is truly female and to struggle to speak with women's own voice.

Whereas for radical feminists, the state was patriarchal, for Marxist feminists, the state was essentially capitalist (McIntosh 1978: 259). The state was not just an institution but also a form of social relations. Women's subordination played a role in sustaining capitalism through the reproduction of the labour force within the family. Women were oppressed in work and in exclusion from it and Marxist feminists argued that the familial ideology was to blame. When criticizing welfare states, Marxist feminists argued that the state helps to reproduce and maintain the familial ideology primarily through welfare state policies. In contrast to radical feminism, Marxist feminists argued that women were important in the struggle against capitalism as workers, not as women (McIntosh 1978) and the category of women was employed in reproductive terms (Sargent 1981: xxi).

Socialist feminists attempted to combine the insights of both Marxist and radical feminism. From radical feminists, socialist feminists derived the understanding of the system of oppression called patriarchy, and from Marxist feminists the importance of the class oppression defining the situation of all workers. The two approaches were combined in analyses of this 'dual system' of capitalism and patriarchy. For Zillah Eisenstein, the notion of capitalist patriarchy captured the 'mutually reinforcing dialectical relationship between capitalist class structure and hierarchal sexual structuring' (1979: 17). Michèle Barrett, in turn, identified a number of ways in which the state promoted women's oppression: women were excluded from certain sorts of work by protective legislation, the state exercised control over the ways sexuality was represented through pornography laws, and the state's housing policy was resistant to the needs of non-nuclear families (1980: 231–237). The socialist feminist debates revolved around the relative autonomy of the two systems. Some theorists argued that patriarchy had causal priority over capitalism and others that capitalism was more autonomous. For Eisenstein (1979:196), the capitalist class did not rule the state or government directly but instead exercised hegemony. A large part of the mystificatory role of the state was in this seeming identification of male interests and bourgeois interests.

Many of the ideas that radical, Marxist and socialist feminists held especially about women, men and gender have been challenged and critiqued as gender theory has progressed. One of the most influential parts of this critique has come from the political theorist and philosopher Judith Butler who in her *Gender Trouble* (1990) showed how both 'sex' and 'gender' are effects of heterosexual power relations. Interestingly, in relation to the state, Butler's work (1997) evidences an anti-state account that is critical of the legalization of politics and is based on the belief that democratization works best through civil society. In *Excitable Speech*, Butler is critical of feminists who want to criminalize hate speech and argues instead that other forms of politics are more effective: 'nonjuridical forms of opposition, ways of restaging and resignifying speech in contexts that exceed those determined by the courts' (Butler 1997: 23). Butler is suspicious about the arbitrary nature of state power and, for her, the regulation of hate speech is an example of a means by which the state can extend its power (Lloyd 2007: 127). As Moya Lloyd explains in her interpretation of Butler: constructs such as hate speech become legal mechanisms for the state through which it can 'extend its own racial and sexualized discourses', which in turn result in inclusions and exclusions (Lloyd 2007: 129). These forms of state regulation curtail the opportunities of resignification in civil society. In sum, Butler's position stresses the productivity of state discourse and calls for understating the ways in which laws can be misappropriated and used in anti-progressive ways (Lloyd 2007: 129).

Critical commentators have suggested that Butler assumes that legal protection is necessarily reactionary and hence dismisses the ways in which states may promote progressive equality politics (Lloyd 2007; Passavant and Dean 2001). Butler's notion of the state is also contradictory, signifying at times a very narrow judicial institution and, at other times, a broader set of conflicting institutions, practices and discourses. In her later work, Butler offers a qualified definition of the state and suggests that the state 'is not reducible to law' and that it comprises plural institutions whose interests do not always coincide, and where there are, consequently, multiple sites for political resistance (Butler 2002: 27; see Lloyd 2007: 131). However, Moya Lloyd suggests that Butler's scepticism towards the state remains. Lloyd argues that there is indeed a fundamental paradox in Butler's account of the state: she implies that 'hate-speech and pornography can be radically recited but denies this possibility to state speech, or rather she allows that it can be recited but only in anti-progressive directions' (Lloyd 2007: 132). The debate around Butler's conceptualization of the state illustrates the long shadows of the contradictions faced by feminist scholars writing about it.

Postcolonial state

Feminist theorizing on the state, such as the conceptualizations discussed above, often comes from specific (Western) contexts that are not always made explicit. There is a strong body of feminist work on the state that stresses the importance of different contexts where the states are theorized as well as the linkages between theory and practice. Development scholars too point to the fundamentally different meaning of the state in non-Western countries (Afshar 1996; Alvarez 1990; Dore and Molyneux 2000; Rai and Lievesley 1996; Visvanathan et al. 1997). Like Western debates, these literatures are concerned to examine the processes of state institutions in exercises of power in various areas of the public and private lives of women and women's resistance to these intrusions (Rai and Lievesley 1996: 1). However, there are important differences.

In terms of key issues, postcolonialism, nationalism, economic modernization and state capacity emerge as important, whereas Western feminists often take these issues for granted, focusing instead on how best to engage with the state (Chappell 2000: 246). For example, in Indonesia, the colonial state introduced the emphasis on motherhood and the domesticity of women that was characteristic of Victorian European societies (Wieringa 2002: 47). During the process of decolonization, women were first urged to join the battle against the colonizers but later their rights were forgotten or put aside, leading even to more conservative construction of women's roles in the state (Wieringa 2002: 47). When exploring women's activism, for example, in Africa, the ways in which patriarchy is combined with the (neo)patrimonialism in the state become central (Tripp 2001; Njagi 2013). In neo-patrimonial states, 'claims to authority are based on personal relations of loyalty and dependence that stand above the law' (Tripp 2001: 106) and when combined with patriarchy can exacerbate women's positions and chances in the states (Njagi 2013). Hence, questions of women's autonomy acquire a different significance from those of Western states. For example, the Ugandan women's movement has been able to claim a greater degree of autonomy from the state, which has been critical to its success

(Tripp 2001: 105). Again, these practices vary greatly between states and need to be studied contextually.

In postcolonial states, the colonial past and anti-colonial struggles are present in different ways and shape the ideologies, governance and institutional structures of such states (Parashar 2018: 162). For many, the nation-state presented an idealized form of self-rule, a structure where anti-colonial nationalism could be manifested (Parashar et al. 2018: 8). For critics, such as Ashis Nandy (2003), 'the state' shares 'the white man's burden' as it controls and civilizes societies towards modernization through, for instance, development policies. For postcolonial states, in particular, it is an acute paradox that, while anti-colonialist struggles aimed for the idea of the sovereign state as a solution to colonialist abuse, 'many of these postcolonial states became perpetrators of gross human rights violations, particularly against women and minorities, violences that have been largely unseen or silenced, neither reported, recorded nor recognized' (Parashar et al. 2018: 1). Political and armed conflicts in Africa, Asia and the Middle East fuel and are fuelled by weak, non-existent state structures, making the achievement of human rights, women's rights and equality through sovereign states seem like a distant goal.

Poststructural state

Poststructural feminists have sought to deconstruct the internal unity of the state and to theorize the differentiated state as a diverse set of institutions. Rosemary Pringle and Sophie Watson challenged the unity of the state and argued that the state consists of a set of arenas that lacked coherence (1990, 1992) and Elisabeth Prügl defined the postmodern state as 'a decentered state in which authority is shared by multiple levels of government' (2010: 448). In poststructural analyses, then, the state is a differentiated set of institutions, practices, agencies and discourses, and politics and the state are conceptualized in broad terms (see also Chapter 8). The state is depicted as a discursive process, meaning, for example, that the state's unity and identity are reproduced discursively (see e.g. Kantola 2007; Kantola, Norocel and Repo 2011).

The state is not inherently patriarchal but was historically constructed as patriarchal in a political process whose outcome is open. The patriarchal state can be seen, then, not as the manifestation of patriarchal essence, but as the centre of a reverberating set of power relations and political processes in which patriarchy is both constructed and contested (Connell 1987). Particular discourses and histories construct state boundaries, identities and agency (Kantola 2006, 2007). Masculinity is central for understanding 'the multiple modes of power circulating through the domain called the state' (Brown 1995: 177).

Wendy Brown's poststructuralist approach draws attention to the constitutive character of the state's gender orders, to contradictions inherent in them and to the ways in which state processes occur across very different sites (Brown 1995: 167). Elisabeth Prügl (2010), although inspired by her work, critiques Brown for giving insufficient attention to feminist struggles and to the ways in which these have been institutionalized in state-based laws and policies. A number of other poststructural feminists have asked what the most effective strategies are for empowering women in their engagements with the state. In other words, the feminist aim becomes to make sense not only of the state's impact on gender but also of the ways in which the state can be made use of and changed through feminist struggles (Kantola 2006). The analyses allow the complex, multidimensional and differentiated relations between the state and gender to be taken into account. They recognize that the state can be a positive as well as a negative resource for feminists, thus deconstructing the dichotomy between 'in' and 'out' of the state. Within a framework of diverse discourses and power relations, gender diversity and differences in women's experiences come to the fore (Kantola and Dahl 2005).

New materialism and the state

'Renewed materialist feminism' suggests that the state and its effects cannot be understood merely in terms of discourses. Instead, these approaches stress that states are embedded in material phenomena and processes (Coole and Frost 2010: 2–3). The renewed material feminism accepts social constructionism but conceptualizes the material realm as irreducible to culture and discourse (Coole and Frost 2010: 27; for debates about feminist new materialism see Ahmed 2008). In terms of the state, this signifies combining the 'Weberian insights of critical theory regarding the bureaucratic state, whose tentacles reach increasingly deeply to control ordinary lives through governance and governmentality, and aspects of

Foucauldian genealogy that describe how the minutiae of power develop and practically manage embodied subjectivities' (Coole and Frost 2010: 27). When explaining the renewed scholarly interest in materialism, Diana Coole and Samantha Frost single out not only the advances in natural sciences and biopolitical and bioethical issues but also the global political economy and understanding its structural conditions such as neoliberalism (Coole and Frost 2010: 6–7).

From the point of view of theorizing the state, what becomes important is the biopolitical interest of the modern state: the state's role in managing the life, health and death of its populations –the management of 'fertility rates, marriage and funeral rites, epidemics, food hygiene, and the nation's health' (Coole and Frost 2010: 23). Seemingly technical questions about biological life processes enter the political order because the state must make decisions about the worth of different lives (Coole and Frost 2010: 23). In this way, states exert powers in shaping, constraining and constituting life chances and existential opportunities. The exercise of these powers takes place in complex circuits 'whereby discursive and material forms are inextricable yet irreducible and material structures are simultaneously over- and undermined' (Coole and Frost 2010: 27). While economic factors and capitalism become central, the capitalist system is not understood in a narrowly economic way but rather 'as a detotalized totality that includes a multitude of interconnected phenomena and processes' (Coole and Frost 2010: 29) This view encourages us to take seriously Foucauldian analysis of governmentality, biopolitics, and the role of discourse in maintaining social order, and incorporating the state's role in maintaining the conditions of capital accumulation into the analyses (Coole and Frost 2010: 30).

Feminist political analyses of the state

Feminist political analyses of the state powerfully demonstrate the multiple ways in which states continue to be gendered. Comparative state feminist literature has studied the ways in which women's movements engage with one branch of the state – women's policy agencies – and evaluated the factors that impact on the successes and failures of these engagements for overall gender policy in the state (see McBride Stetson and Mazur 1995; McBride and Mazur 2010). Lee Ann Banaszak (2010) conceptualizes the state in terms of its organization and bureaucracy and explores the favourable locations for gender activists and the impact of changes in these for feminist struggles. Intersectional analyses of the state have explored how LGBT activists have changed state relations and how the state has structured opportunities for lesbian and gay communities all over the world (Ayoub and Paternotte 2014). An important shift in Europe has been states' engagements with political intersectionality that has expanded state policies on different inequality categories from gender and race to, for example, sexual orientation, age, disability, and religion and belief in a contested political process that has been termed by feminist scholars 'institutionalizing intersectionality' (Kantola 2010; Krizsán, Skjeie and Squires 2012). Feminist new institutionalists, in turn, study the state as a variety of separate institutions that include both formal and informal institutions such as norms and rules (Chappell 2013: 607; Chappell 2002). The body of work draws attention to the importance of institutional legacies, path-dependencies, and possibilities for change (Chappell 2013: 608).

Two global developments vis-à-vis states have been particularly intensely analysed from feminist perspectives: neoliberalism and the rise of radical-right populism. First, neoliberalism has become an important theme for feminist analysing of gendered states as it has so fundamentally shaped the opportunities for gender and equality policies and feminist engagements with the state. Neoliberalism has signified the marketization of public services, transferring of costs and risk from the state to individuals and families, employment and social policies that make individuals responsible, and governance reforms that extend private-sector management practices to the public sector (Elomäki and Kantola 2018). The effects have been gendered. While neoliberal discourses and policies portray both women and men as rational economic actors and push women to the labour market, policies that dismantle the welfare state and reprivatize and informalize care rely on and intensify women's unpaid or poorly compensated work, increasing class-based and racialized inequalities among women (Bakker 2003; Brown 2015).

Feminists are faced with new challenges when the state becomes a 'competition state' or a 'strategic state' as a result of the impact of neoliberal ideologies and modes of governance. At a practical level, lower levels of funding of state-based bodies have resulted in the dismantling of state gender equality architecture too and also in defunding women's organizations (Kantola and Lombardo 2017). Neoliberalism has also been conceptualized as a new relationship between government and knowledge through which governing activities are recast as nonpolitical and non-ideological problems that need technical solutions (Ong 2007: 3). Dedemocratizing shifts in economic governance have narrowed down democratic debate and civil society participation. These changes in the states are also transforming state-based feminist strategies and practices from previous 'state feminism' to 'market feminism' (Kantola and Squires 2012) or governance feminism (Prügl 2011), where feminist knowledge is appropriated and transformed to the service of neoliberal states.

Radical-right populism (see also Chapter 14) is changing feminist politics in relation to states too. Radical-right populists have had important electoral victories coming to power in a number of European states, most visibly for gender equality in Hungary and Poland. Even in countries where they are in opposition, the ways in which they oppose gender equality and LGBTQI rights is having an impact on debates on gender equality, making them less legitimate (Verloo 2018; Kantola and Lombardo 2019 and 2021; Kuhar and Paternotte 2017). New forms of opposition to gender equality include the construction of the concept of 'gender ideology' where radical-right populists construct advancing gender equality as a harmful elitist ideology, argued to be imposed on member states by the European Union (Kantola and Lombardo 2019). In addition to the rhetorical impact, Viktor Orbán's Fidesz in Hungary has transformed the democratic principles of the state, curtailing the independence of media, civil society and the courts. Feminist activists, like others, are faced with engaging the new illiberal politics of the state (Krizsán and Roggeband 2018). In other contexts too, the combined effects of neoliberal austerity politics, shift to conservative values, and nationalism are challenging traditional ways of feminist engagement with the state (Elomäki and Kantola 2018).

Conclusion

The state continues to play a key role in upholding and challenging gendered, racialized and sexualized hierarchies in contemporary societies. Feminist scholarship theorizes the state as a powerful construct where gender, race, class and sexuality occupy a central position. Feminist answers to the 'where are the women?' question (Enloe 1989) exposed the power of the public-private distinction that had traditionally kept women outside the state in the private sphere. At the same time, this research showed women's active roles in states. A fundamental shift in feminist theory to study gender instead of women transformed the feminist study of states too. Theoretically, it required focusing on both femininities and masculinities, on the broader power relationships in societies, and on structural and institutionalized hierarchies in states. The power relations between gender and the state were no longer theorized as either top-down or bottom-up, but co-constitutive and complex. The relations that shape gendered states also go beyond traditional state boundaries, to the supra-national, international and local levels and spheres. Later Judith Butler's (1990) influential work on the performativity of gender impacted on feminist theories about the state too. Gender and the state were now theorized in terms of doing rather than being: they need constant repetitive acts by subjects to uphold them. The states are discursively produced in processes where gender, race and ethnicity, sexuality and class play a central role. The new materialist turn in feminist theorizing suggests that these processes are not just discursive but material and bodily, and affects and emotions strengthen the ties between them and make change harder. The contemporary challenges from neoliberalization and radical-right populism call for applications of the theories and perspectives to make sense of the changes for social justice.

Further Reading

Allen, J. (1990), 'Does Feminism Need a Theory of "The State"?', in S. Watson (ed.), 21–37, *Playing the State*, London: Verso.

Chappell, L. (2013), 'State and Governance', in G. Waylen, K. Celis, J. Kantola and L. Weldon (eds), *The Oxford Handbook on Gender and Politics*, 603–626, New York: Oxford University Press.

Hernes, H.M. (1987), *Welfare State and Woman Power*, Oslo: Norwegian University Press.

Kantola, J. (2006), *Feminists Theorize the State*, New York and London: Palgrave Macmillan.

MacKinnon, C. (1989), *Towards a Feminist Theory of the State*, London: Harvard University Press.

Prügl, E. (2010), 'Feminism and the postmodern state: Gender mainstreaming in European rural development', *Signs*, 35(2), 447–475.

7

Green Theory

Annica Kronsell and Roger Hildingsson

Introduction

In the scholarly literature on the state's role in governing human societies towards ecologically sustainable ends, there are various approaches ranging from liberal environmentalist accounts of ecological modernization to more radical and post-liberal accounts of ecologism and ecological democracy. While asking what the role of the state is in responding to multiple problems relating to environmental change and to the current ecological, climate and sustainability crises and how to address ways for greening the state, scholars of green political thinking and green social movements have an ambivalent relationship to the state. On the one hand, the state is problematic in terms of reproducing structures of dominance that generate environmental change and promote activities that lead to environmental degradation. On the other hand, greens have called for better and stronger state involvement in governing responses to environmental change.

Some green political thinkers view the state as lacking the capacity to handle problems of the complexity and magnitude that humankind is witnessing, problems ranging from rising temperatures and increased frequency of extreme weather, floods and droughts (IPCC 2014, 2018) to the continuous overuse of natural resources like water, land and forests, the unprecedented depletion of biodiversity (IPBES 2019; UNEP 2012) and the spread of zoonotic diseases (Gibb et al. 2020). Many scholars are highly sceptical of the state's ability to mobilize societal action or the resources required to take on the challenge of such a daunting task, particularly since the state is deeply entrenched in a capitalist economic system (see also Chapter 3) and dependent on production processes that caused the problem in the first place. Barry (2012) speaks of the centrality of the economic imperative of growth to industrialized states in the Global North which has led to an unsustainable economic system that has created affluence through globalization, exploitation of resources and wage differences (see also Harvey 2010). This economic imperative is highly problematic from an ecological perspective (Eckersley 2004) and remains tenacious for the state's involvement in environmental and sustainability issues. Hence, in some of the relevant literature on environmental governance, there is a lack of faith in the state's capacity to deal with these problems.

For issues of climate change in particular, rather than putting their faith in the state, scholars look to the possible transformations of the economy (Paterson 2007; Newell and Paterson 2010; Klein 2014), while others find more hope in non-state actors and transnational governance arrangements (Bulkeley et al. 2014; Hoffman 2011; Stripple and Bulkeley 2013) that take on important governance functions, and compensate for implementation and legitimacy deficits when states fail (Biermann and Pattberg 2012; Bäckstrand et al. 2010). Yet others call for a reformed United Nations (Biermann 2014), or a strong EU polity and leadership (Biedenkopf and Dupont 2013; Wurzel and Connelly 2011), while even others highlight the importance of cities and municipalities in advancing climate transitions in urban areas (Bulkeley et al. 2010). While these literatures sidestep the state, or even ignore it, they still implicitly assume a functioning state (cf. Lövbrand and Linnér 2015) or, alternatively, a state entrenched in late-modern capitalism, void of agency (cf. Blühdorn and Deflorian 2019).

Clearly, it is relevant to recognize how the state is problematic in terms of promoting activities that lead to environmental degradation and reproducing structures of dominance that generate environmental change. However, when the state responds to environmental change, it does so as one of the most important and powerful political organizations, with substantial capacities and endowed with the kind of legitimacy that other organizations rarely possess (Bäckstrand and Kronsell 2015). This insight is supported by the empirical observation that environmental management and protection is increasingly becoming a core area of state responsibility, not only in liberal welfare states but in many countries around the globe (Death 2016; Lim and Duit 2018; Sommerer and Lim 2016). It appears that the state is the only entity with the kind of power and authority needed to orchestrate collective responses to current environmental problems (cf. Johnstone and Newell 2018; Hale and Roger 2014).

A focus on the state implies a focus on the polity, the collective of state institutions, administrations and principles for decision-making. In this chapter we take stock of the green state literature and discuss different views on the role of the state in greening human societies, economies and politics. We begin by discussing the meaning of a green state in relation to the scholarship that has so far emerged. We then probe the ways in which a green(er) state rationality is evolving within the realms of the modern state through advances in environmental governance, making states more responsive to ecological concerns over time. In particular, comparative research on the green state suggests that advanced welfare states have stronger institutional capacities and legitimacy to intervene in economic relationships and to negotiate compromises between societal interests. Then we explore three particular challenges for the green state: its relation to the economy, how transformative change can occur and how democracy is conceptualized in the green state. These three areas are all in need of further exploration and research so as to advance more progressive forms of environmental politics and governance in efforts to green the state and human societies.

What is a green state?

Scholars in the field have used a variety of expressions to describe the phenomena of state responses to environmental change. This includes the 'green state' (Dryzek et al. 2003; Eckersley 2004; Christoff 2005; Huh et al. 2018), the 'ecological state' (Lundqvist 2001), the 'environmental state' (Mol and Spaargaren 2002; Meadowcroft 2012; Duit et al. 2016), the 'ecostate' (Duit 2014), and the 'eco-social state' (Koch and Fritz 2014). While being frequently used as interchangeable terms, these concepts originate in different traditions. One tradition emerges from green political theory which stipulates the normative features of a green state, including typologies, ranging from a green state committed to biocentric and eco-citizenship values to a neoliberal environmental state that is market-oriented and relies on weak ecological modernization (Christoff 2005: 42–43; Hysing 2015). In this vein the green state is a normative ideal, with ecological sustainability and biocentric values as state objectives and the foundation for social, economic and political transformations.

Another tradition is empirically oriented and found in comparative environmental politics that analyse the response of states to ecological pressures in terms of regulation and institutional output (Duit 2014). Emerging since the 1960s, environmental policy has become a core domain of state activity as the state has gradually taken on responsibilities such as limiting the pollution of water and air, adopting goals of sustainable development and, more recently, steering society through transformations of the fossil energy system and economy. This development has established environmental management as an 'essential component of state activity' to the extent that it is 'publicly recognized as a fundamental part of what a civilized state should do' (Meadowcroft 2012: 67). Nowadays, most states devote public spending to environmental protection, monitoring and education and have developed considerable administrative, institutional, regulatory, legislative and redistributive capacities for environmental protection, although unevenly institutionalized (Mol 2016), all while continuing their unsustainable practices in many areas of consumption and production. Political greens and green parties monitor this and call for better and stronger state involvement in governing responses to environmental change. Approached as an empirical phenomenon evolving and emerging over time, the green state is often studied in relation to how other states have performed, typically in large-n studies on environmental statehood measured, for example, in terms of certain institutions of the state (e.g. environmental ministries), policies (e.g. environmental taxation and spending) or environmental performance (e.g. ecological footprints) (see e.g. Duit 2016; Koch and Fritz 2015; Povitkina 2018).

Although states are still far from the normative ideals of the green state, many states are responding to environmental change in an increasingly progressive manner. A combination of the normative and the empirical approaches to the green state is most useful, as it allows for counterfactual ideals to be critically assessed against actual achievements and performance, while at the same time mapping and comparing those achievements. Thus, contemporary states are emerging as green states, or environmental states, albeit in an often cumbersome and far from perfect way.

To be concrete, the emerging green state has a significant set of institutions and practices dedicated to the management of the environment and societal-environmental interactions in place. Typically, this includes: environmental ministries and agencies; framework environmental laws; air, water, land and waste management rules and regulations, associated regulatory bodies, mechanisms and policy instruments; dedicated budgets and environmental funding and tax provisions; scientific advisory bodies, councils and research organizations. Thus, the green state is associated with a distinctive sphere of environmental governmental activity while environmental problems and what governments should do about them constitute an issue of ongoing debate and protracted political struggles. Adhering to such a definition allows for empirical analysis of existing states but can also support too minimal a definition, whereby most states in the industrialized world (and many developing states) with environmental legislation and administrations would qualify as green states, even when environmental regulations and institutions are not matched by strong environmental performance for reaching sustainability objectives.

Thus, the normative contributions of green scholarship are important correctives, useful as a heuristic to critically examine green states – as Peter Christoff (2005) did, for instance, by assessing green states on a continuum from strong to weak types of green state, each with specific characteristics. Green states, he argued, demonstrate high levels of state capacity and intervention, eco-citizenship, strong commitment to biocentric values, human welfare and ecological protection. With his definition, no existing state merits the label green state. Environmentally pioneering welfare states (e.g. Sweden and the Netherlands) have weaker institutionalization of ecological values, moderate values of eco-citizenship and environmental capacity for state intervention but are not proper green states (cf. Tobin 2015). Environmental neoliberal states (e.g. the United States and Australia) are defined by strong market orientation, weak ecological modernization and low budgetary commitment to social and environmental welfare protection. Such typologies become valuable when employed in comparative political studies to empirically assess degrees of 'greenness' of states. While seldom translating into real-world cases, they entice us to think more deeply about what the elements are that are needed for states to live up to ideals of green statehood. As such, they might work as counterfactual ideals against which to assess how states are emerging as green states or are institutionalizing key features of ecological democracy.

Empirically, there has even been a propensity to study Scandinavian states, likely because they most closely resemble the ideal of a green state (see e.g. Hildingsson and Khan 2015; Hysing 2015; Teräväinen-Litardo 2015; Tobin 2015). Andersen and Liefferink (1997) championed Nordic countries as environmental pioneers and leaders on empirical grounds. Bäckstrand and Kronsell (2015: 4) argue that, while the Nordic welfare countries are atypical, their experiences with environmental governance are relevant and provide a test bed for examining processes of green statehood. Scholars who have explored environmental leadership in international climate negotiations argue that the EU, United States and also China are perceived by others as leader states (Karlsson et al. 2011), but to be a leader does not assure green statehood. Although its member states' climate ambitions vary greatly, the EU has been able to address leadership in climate politics (Wurzel and Connelly 2011). In recent years, the EU has taken an active leadership around the Paris Agreement as well as with the European Green Deal championed by the von der Leyen Commission. Eckersley's work (2016) on Norway and Germany as climate leaders develops the concept of leadership from the perspective of the green state and centres on how a green leader state serves both the national and international community in furthering climate protection. They do so by legitimizing climate concerns internally using green growth and ecological modernization strategies tied to national identity conceptions, with international engagement flowing naturally from these conceptions and norms, thus simultaneously providing a rationale for fulfilling global obligations.

Finally, regarding the empirical scope of green state research, it is predominantly advanced industrialized democracies (Huh et al. 2018) and welfare states that have been investigated empirically. But in recent years we have seen an emerging literature looking beyond OECD countries to study the development of green state arrangements also in authoritarian, postcolonial and developmental contexts. Sommerer and Lim (2016) demonstrate a diminishing gap between Western and a selected sample of non-Western states when it comes to environmental policy developments. Death (2016) is critical to previous research and shows how green state practices in Africa have been largely neglected and that African states' environmental ambitions have reflected colonial practices of nature conservation. Chandrashekeran et al. (2017) demonstrate the usefulness of a green state perspective in assessing South Africa's progress on environmental action, which showed some green state capacity but with weaknesses in implementation and in the lack of budgetary commitments. China is an exemplar of an authoritarian environmental state potentially featuring as an eco-fascist green state along the lines of Ophuls (1973). But, as Lo (2015) shows, while China conforms to an authoritarian green state at the national state level, it resembles a liberal state at local levels in implementing environmental policy while being responsive to citizens' demands under certain circumstances (Kostka and Zhang 2018). The complicit role of the state in resource extraction practices is a key feature of developmental states that also undermines sustainability and environmental efforts as exemplified in Sumatra (Pramydia et al. 2018) and in Colombia (Sankey 2018).

Greening the welfare state?

States have dealt with great societal transformations before, and the transformations called for in response to environmental change are likely of a similar magnitude to the rapid industrialization at the beginning of the last century, the emergence of the nation-state system, liberal democracy or the market economy. When the welfare state once developed as a political and societal response to the challenges and externalization of social costs (Polanyi 1944), the state was the only actor with sufficient clout to counter the market's inherent anarchical and chaos-creating tendencies. The emerging green states can be viewed as similar responses to the problem of the market's externalization of environmental costs. Even more so in current times, when several related problems come together: climate change, biodiversity depletion, species extinction and the spread of zoonotic viruses affecting human health. For instance, the comprehensive responses taken by many states to the Covid-19 pandemic suggest advanced welfare states hold strong capacity for rapid transitions in response to such problems.

In green state theory, James Meadowcroft (2005) was the first to draw parallels between the genesis of the welfare state and the emergence of the environmental state, the two having in common the extension of state authority in new social and political domains as a response to market failures and lack of voluntary action. The welfare state has historically dealt with the negative externalities of the market and the social and human costs arising from it and have in response to this developed capacities to act with the institutions, processes and policies in place. In a similar vein, the authority and capacity established in welfare states have made it possible for state institutions to intervene in economic relations to correct for environmental externalities and to secure the provision of environmental public goods. Over time, evolutions in environmental policy and governance have led to a gradual institutionalization of environmental management and regulation, which have contributed to the development of a *de facto* emerging green state (Meadowcroft 2012). The emerging field of comparative green state studies confirms this greening of state capacities and institutions (see e.g. Duit 2014;

Lim and Duit 2018; Huh et al. 2018), including for a selection of developing states in Asia and Latin America (Sommerer and Lim 2016). Interestingly, they also provide support for Meadowcroft's proposition about synergies between welfare state arrangements and environmental policy developments. For instance, Lim and Duit (2018: 233) show that 'the environmental state has emerged as an additional layer on top of the welfare state' and that 'the welfare state plays a pivotal role in translating demands for state action on environmental problems into regulatory responses'.

Lennart Lundqvist (2001) also sees this potential in the welfare state. In his article 'A Green Fist in a Velvet Glove' he writes that the normative criterion for a green state is a state with a fairly strong degree of authority in decision-making at multiple levels – the green fist – employing resource management and comprehensive ecological planning, but that this necessarily has to be coupled with a strong democratic state – the velvet glove – with broad deliberation on scientific expertise and knowledge on ecological issues in various democratic settings from the local to the global. For Lundqvist, economic growth and ecological concerns are neither conflictual nor mutually exclusive. Quite the contrary, he views greening as successful when ecological evaluations have become as important as economic ones (Lundqvist 2001: 469), while also addressing the need for the welfare state to become more inclusive of various interests.

Returning to Polanyi (1944), his interest was directed towards the (first) decommodification which created welfare states with social benefits provided by public authorities and paid for by taxes. The green transformation of the state (Scoones et al. 2015) would entail a second stage with 'a move towards de-commodified production – reducing working hours and commodity purchases, developing co-production (comprising civic and household economies), and fostering preventive social behavior' (Gough and Meadowcroft 2011: 501). Gough (2017) developed this further, focusing on the social dimension of climate change, drawing on human needs theory and the 'doughnut model' for social and ecological sustainability (Raworth 2012).

Kronsell and Stensöta (2015), too, argue that welfare states may be better suited to deal with sustainability challenges because of their potential capacity as representing a state that cares. In the welfare state, care for human needs has been emphasized – for example, by ensuring that the weak, the vulnerable and the young are taken care of; this has the potential to be extended to general caring, for the environment, the planet and future generations. The Covid-19 pandemic accentuated the crucial role of the caring sector in the maintenance of welfare functions and the economy. While the final extent of this remains to be seen, the notion of care could be cultivated as a useful normative foundation for the green state in order to develop co-production and foster preventive behaviour (Kronsell and Stensöta 2015) as a part of the decommodification process that Gough and Meadowcroft (2011) are after. The notion of care is a core human principle experienced by everyone that can be extended to non-humans and future generations. Also Bailey (2015: 805), who is critical to the capacity of the welfare state on other grounds as we will see below, reckons that the mark of a robust welfare state is that it modifies 'how citizens relate to each other and the planet', engendering a 'sense of community and the public good'. Further, he suggests that values that 'underpin an effective response to climate change' also 'promote the core values underpinning public welfarism' (Bailey 2015: 806).

There are several critics of the prospects for greening the welfare state, as several features speak against welfare states emerging as green states. First, the welfare state's dependence on economic growth (Bailey 2015) and the centrality of the economic imperative to the state (Eckersley 2004; Hildingsson et al. 2019) make the task of responding to environmental change particularly challenging. Historically the welfare state has been viewed as a complement to a growing economy, while in the green state unconstrained economic growth and material throughput are not possible as consumption and production patterns must be kept within ecological limits or 'planetary boundaries' (Steffen et al. 2015). This tension can be exemplified with the case of Sweden, a developed welfare state, even dubbed a leader and forerunner due to its pioneering environmental output. While heavily engaged in progressive environmental and climate policy developments at local, national and international levels and, for instance, being successful in decarbonizing power generation and heating, Sweden is simultaneously continuing on a path of resource depletion, escalating consumption-based emissions and increasing ecological footprint (Hildingsson and Khan 2015; Tobin 2015).

Second, the constituencies that can be mobilized for the welfare state and the green state differ: the working class and trade unions for the welfare state, and environmental movements and green parties for the green state. Decision-making typically takes place through strategic bargaining, which tends to be reactive or preventive at best (Eckersley 2004: 85–104), and environmental interests and long-term concerns are only weakly represented, if at all (Kronsell et al. 2019). Further, the policy process tends to be guided by administrative rationality, which considers ecological risks only to a limited extent (Kronsell and Bäckstrand 2010). The welfare state's scope is primarily nationally oriented, while the green state acts collectively with other states in a global and multilateral setting as environmental problems are often transboundary in character, which motivates international engagement (Meadowcroft 2005:12). Furthermore, Lövbrand and Linnér (2015) raise a critical point related to the particular historical experience of liberal or social welfare states, which they emphasize have become normative for the scholarship. What we learn from most studies is less applicable beyond advanced welfare states and the features found important may have limited relevance for other types of state. While this questions the generalizability of the findings it also points to a need to develop green state theory, to include, reflect and speak to the heterogeneous category of states – for instance, those struggling with legacies of colonialism, authoritarian rule and societal-state struggles.

Key challenges for the green state

The green state and the economic imperative

The function and prospects of economic development remain central in the debates on green statehood and many have argued that the core imperative of the modern state is to promote economic growth and capital accumulation, which presents a major obstacle to the progress of green states. The centrality of the economic imperative for the modern state has entangled it in an unsustainable economic system reproducing structures of domination and overexploitation of material and human resources (Barry 2012; Barry and Eckersley 2005: 260–263). When it comes to environmental change, the critical issue is whether the current economic system can be tweaked to meet sustainability ends – for instance, by means of ecological modernization – or whether it needs to be reconstructed and transformed – for instance, towards a steady-state economy by means of degrowth measures.

Proponents of ecological modernization are optimistic about the ability of the market to solve environmental problems and view the green state as a significant actor that can intervene productively in the market to achieve environmental objectives. Ecological modernization is grounded in a view that the economy evolves over time, to become increasingly efficient and less resource intense, eventually leading to decoupling, i.e. that the economy can continue to grow while diminishing environmental damage (for an overview see Mol et al. 2009). In this perspective, economic growth goes hand in hand with lowering emissions and protecting the environment. Technological change is fundamental and environmental policies and regulations are seen as drivers for innovation, through which ecologically benign performance becomes integrated in production, resulting in energy and resource efficiency and simultaneously lower costs (Porter and van der Linde 1995; Jänicke 2012). Ecological modernization fits with a win-win discourse, reconciling economic and ecological concerns and, according to which, pollution prevention pays off in terms of both ecological performance and economic efficiency (Hajer 1995). In such a weak conception of ecological modernization (Christoff 1996), environmental protection through state intervention can align with the market economy and contribute to restructuring and reforming the state to reflect ecological values. Concepts like *green economy* and *green growth* represent efforts to reconcile economic growth and environmental protection (see further e.g. Bina 2013; Fiorino 2017). Ecological modernization remains the prevailing norm in public policy circles and public discourse, it thus being assumed that states will act on and regulate environmental change by incentivizing market actors and correcting for market externalities, but without intervening too much in current business practices.

Green state scholarship (e.g. Barry and Eckersley 2005; Eckersley 2004; Meadowcroft 2012) has less faith in the narrative of ecological modernization because of the way ecological and economic values are presumed to work in tandem, when ecological values ought to take priority. They have little enthusiasm for the values of efficiency, profit and growth that steer liberal markets and are more agnostic about the role of technical innovation for the green state while recognizing the need for market mechanisms (Christoff 2005; see also Spaargaren and Mol 2010). Yet other scholars, often Marxist-inspired (see Chapter 3), are highly sceptical toward any prospect of the state being able to reconcile the production and consumption patterns essential to the capitalist economy with the protection of the climate and the environment (see e.g. Koch 2011; Koch 2020). Examples of this can be found in comparative studies (e.g. Koch and Fritz 2015; Fritz and Koch 2016) that conclude that the coexistence of environmental problem pressures and advanced levels of green regulation – evident in advanced social democratic welfare states – has not improved environmental performance in terms of, for instance, ecological footprints. They predict conflict between winners and losers when states increasingly regulate and intervene in the area of climate change and environmental management. They also challenge the ecological modernization thesis, arguing against a win-win between growth and ecological integrity since *absolute* decoupling between economic growth and environmental performance is seen as impossible to achieve (Jackson 2009; Victor 2008), while accusing green state theorists of taking the problem of capitalism too lightly. Instead, they side with calls for a transformation towards a steady-state economy (Daly 1977) found in degrowth segments of the environmental movement (Latouche 2010; D'Alisa et al. 2015; D'Alisa and Kallis 2020; see also Büchs and Koch 2017).

Democratic welfare states, argued to be the most likely candidates to conform to ideals of green states, also rely on the idea that continuous economic growth is possible and desirable. On the implications of the post-growth scenario on welfare states, Daniel Bailey (2015: 802) points to a significant conundrum: 'The end of growth provokes a point of enormous tension between the left's environmental sympathies ... and the left's deep-seated tendency to view the state as an instrument of progressive politics and welfare provision.' When (taxable) economic activities – reliant on growth – decrease, it implies a shrinking tax base and the state risks losing what has been its most potent tool, the potential to mitigate the effects of the market. To be able to mitigate the effects of environmental change, the state is likely dependent on resources that can be distributed and redistributed. Bailey (2015) suggests that there is a general reluctance to seriously address the conflictual and problematic inherent relation between environmental protection and economic growth. Similar concerns have recently been addressed in a special issue on the 'glass ceiling' of the green state, edited by David Hausknost and Marit Hammond (2020). Envisaging structural barriers to sustainability transformations as an invisible glass ceiling (as applied in feminist studies), Hausknost (2020) argues along with other authors (see e.g. Blühdorn 2020; Machin 2020; Hammond 2020) that institutional structures, the inherent nature of state imperatives and, in particular, the legitimation imperative of liberal democratic states prevent modern states from handling the ecological crisis to a sufficient extent and addressing systemic transformations towards sustainability.

However, in a retort to Bailey (2015, 2020), Eckersley (2018: 4) considers this view overdetermined, and proposes that green states, when and if they emerge, 'will always be works in progress or works in regress', and further argues that:

> There is no reason why the positive connotations of growth cannot be harnessed, but with different adjectives and therefore different meanings.

> These might then provide a warrant for governments, as economic managers, to orchestrate good/healthy/desirable growth and de-orchestrate bad/ unhealthy/harmful growth – in short, grow the good *and* degrow the bad. (Eckersley 2018: 5)

This implies an economic strategy in the green state that would encourage growth in economic activities and industrial practices that contribute to the production and provision of environmental public goods, while overseeing the gradual elimination of polluting, harmful and risky industries and business practices. The latter would imply going beyond green growth by encouraging entirely new patterns of supply and demand (Craig 2019). These would be challenging practices but they could build on capacities and practices of emergent green states – for example, by relying on and encouraging the reflexive capacity of governance systems (Eckersley 2018).

In sum, the economic imperative remains a highly contested issue in the context of green states, and many contrasting perspectives on the possibility of growth in the green state have been vented, including in relation to the growth-dependent legitimation imperative of democratic welfare states. Responses to this challenge lean towards a need for systemic changes but it is unsettled whether it is possible to achieve the required transformations in a capitalist social order by means of ecological modernization, or whether it calls for systemic change based on de-growth or post-growth, or whether economic growth, technological change and environmental protection, climate and sustainability objectives can be made compatible with advancing the green state through a reflexive approach to systemic change. What is clear is that transformative change is necessary, but how is the green state able to handle or instigate such change?

Green states, change and transition

That contemporary challenges of environmental change require transformative responses is getting widespread attention (Scoones et al. 2015; Linnér and Wibeck 2019). However, green state theory with its emphasis on ideal types is a static conception and there has been limited attention given to the potential for changes from one state type to another. Therefore, environmental politics scholars have looked for inspiration in other fields, such as policy theory (e.g. Levin et al. 2011), IR theory (e.g. Bernstein and Hoffmann 2019) and political economy (e.g. Paterson 2016; Johnstone and Newell 2018) and sustainability transition research (see e.g.

Bäckstrand and Kronsell 2015), of which the latter received wide traction across various fields.

In the transdisciplinary field of sustainability transition research, the topic of system change is addressed and offers an understanding of how societal systems and state institutions can be transformed to accommodate climate and sustainability objectives (see e.g. Bäckstrand and Kronsell 2015). Sustainability transition studies (Geels 2010; Grin et al. 2011; Markard et al. 2012) deal with the dynamics of change between, on the one hand, powerful state and sub-state actors (regime actors) supporting the status quo and, on the other hand, change-agents (niche actors) representing new ideas and practices (Schot and Geels 2008). Transition studies originated in technological innovation studies with its emphasis on sociotechnical change, while not questioning the economic system as such. Yet, as emphasized already by Rotmans et al. (2001), transition scholars view transformations as evolutionary processes of change, i.e. processes of sociotechnical transition from redundant to new systems by means of innovative practices, institutional change and new constellations of actors. Thus, it entertains the possibility of systemic change. At a minimum, transition theory provides an important additive to green state theory in conceptualizing how technological innovation and sociotechnical system change can further sustainability in the provision of environmental public goods, though it sidesteps the question on the role of economic growth (see e.g. van den Bergh 2011).

Sustainability transition scholars study the conditions for change and systemic transformations over time and are concerned with governance for transformations towards sustainability. Their view on transformation is particularly interesting; it is said to happen in the interaction between structural levels (regimes, niches and the landscape) according to the multi-level perspective (Grin et al. 2011; Geels 2010). Regimes and niches are embedded in the landscape which provides the context for transformation. This means that transitions always occur in an environment structured by an institutionalized configuration of norms, beliefs and dominant discourses that order society and culture. Significance and legitimation are given to, as well as framing, issues and discourses of regime actors (Geels 2010; Smith et al. 2010). For instance, Smith and Kern (2009) related the landscape concept to state theory, suggesting landscape be understood as the structural factors affecting the polity, such as path-dependencies and institutional conditions for the transition. Important lessons for green state theory are that transformation takes place in the dynamic relation between activities, institutions and norms at the niche, regime and landscape levels, and that change can emerge from niche practices.

A regime consists of 'the (network of) actors that exercise constitutive power' (Avelino and Rotmans 2009: 560), i.e. a regime has the power to establish or enact a social order tied to a certain distribution of resources, and institutions and power structures. Its power is exercised through practices that distribute privileges and resources, but also in more subtle ways by adhering to and applying the normative power of the social order (landscape). Relevant regimes can be found by studying which actors benefit from production, innovation and market solutions (Meadowcroft 2009; Smith and Kern 2009; Smith and Stirling 2010; Voss and Bornemann 2011). In particular 'old' sociotechnical systems with related investments and institutions are viewed as obstacles for transformation, and such incumbent regimes consist of alliances of policymakers and business actors that mobilize various power strategies to resist change (Geels 2014). Transition studies focus on how such regimes, for example in transport and energy systems, can be circumvented and changed through innovation generated from niches. Accordingly, change takes place as incumbent regimes are weakened by the influence of these niches, i.e. places where new ideas that encourage change flourish. Many argue that niches exist outside and are independent of the regimes (Schot and Geels 2008), while others have demonstrated that niches can also develop within incumbent regimes (Hildingsson et al. 2019).

Niche actors are those who have the desire to challenge and transform the current system and the expertise, knowledge, and motivation to act (Loorbach and Rotmans 2010). Niches can be encouraged by creating participatory arenas where relevant actors can meet, deliberate and generate innovation potentially leading to transitions (Kemp et al. 2007; Loorbach 2010). Related ideas are found in environmental political scholarship that stress the need for inclusive policy processes, allowing for a broad range of societal actors to be engaged in processes of communication, democratization and deliberation (Baber and Bartlett 2005; Dryzek 2005) or as a way to safeguard legitimacy for the kinds of transition required to reach sustainable objectives and to secure compliance and implementation (Bäckstrand et al. 2010; Dobson and Bell 2006). However, in transition studies, niches can be organized and are often viewed as parts in a process of change which can and should be designed. As transition theory has developed in a multidisciplinary direction, the niche concept has been used generously, to include forms of experimentation, e.g. in local social movements and in cities.

The contribution of transition studies to green state theory is twofold. First, its attention to the relationship between the polity (i.e. incumbent regimes) and innovative practices and actors (i.e. niches) can help us understand how that interaction can contribute to transitions towards a greener state. Second, it breaks down the state along sociotechnical systems, and views the state polity as a diversified entity composed of overlapping regimes. These are often constituted by alliances between policymakers and economic actors in sectors like energy, transport, housing or conservation, of which some act as incumbents resisting change while others are more open to transforming the existing regime. Following from this, transitions towards greening the state may be expected to happen in a sector-by-sector fashion rather than as a wholesale reform of the welfare state.

Transition studies also has its limitations, one being its approach to governance. Studies often depart from a simplistic managerial perspective, leaving political dynamics and the role of governments and state institutions largely unexplored, although studies are becoming increasingly sophisticated (cf. Frantzeskaki et al. 2012; Fuenfschilling and Truffer 2014; Johnstone and Newell 2018; Meadowcroft 2011). The empirical focus has been overwhelmingly on the energy sector, and transition studies often work with an assumption of prevailing market and regulatory mechanisms for innovation and sociotechnical change. Processes of de-/realignment of new sociotechnical pathways (Geels and Schot 2007) are viewed as contributing to economic renewal, increased efficiency and strengthened competitiveness as well as to better environmental performance without increasing ecological footprints or exhausting resources. However, as shown in the previous section, critical green scholars strongly disagree with assumptions in line with ecological modernization and have severe doubts that environmental challenges can be solved within a system characterized by capitalist economic structures.

Green states and democracy

The green state develops ways that sustainability and environmental governance can be conducted in democratic politics as 'democracy has been part of the modern environmental movement from the outset' (Fischer 2018: 257). There is an extensive literature on ecological democracy, a literature that we discuss here in so far as it relates to the state. The green state encourages democratic politics within state institutions while also guarding the green public sphere. Through this, the state can gain legitimacy and has a unique capacity to foster and lead the transition towards a more sustainable society (Melo-Escrihuela 2015).

A crucial element of democracy is the potential to be inclusive of the needs and wants of various constituencies, in terms of equal representation, voice and justice. In liberal democracies, representation gives priority to individual short-term interests over common interests; therefore, green values and the common environmental good are less likely to be on the agenda. In contrast, ecological democracy endorses a wider notion of political community and a long-term perspective. It requires 'that the opportunity to participate or otherwise be represented in the making of risk generating decisions should literally be extended to all those potentially affected, regardless of social class, geographic location, nationality, generation, or species' (Eckersley 2004:112). Thus, a green democracy needs to find ways to attend to and enact representation in more ways than in terms of humans, including other species and ecosystem integrity, and for the rights of future generations, as well as seeking acceptance for long-term objectives over short-term goals and immediate interests.

There are few ways of representing non-humans in contemporary democratic politics.[1] However, green parties and other parliamentarians with environmental issues on their agenda have been assumed to be representative of such concerns. Long-term objectives may be assured through, for instance, climate laws as seen, for example, in Britain, New Zealand and Sweden, or by giving legal standing to environmental movements and scientific advice from expert authorities. Although, in democracies, green political constituencies with green votes and values can provide the political capital necessary for transforming production and consumption patterns in ecologically sustainable directions (cf. Tobin 2017), there are particular difficulties regarding the need to be inclusive of the concerns for non-human species, earth others or natural systems, and how their inclusion can be secured in governance terms to advance democratic processes, institutions or policy (Eckersley 2019: 17; Bäckstrand et al. 2010). As representative politics is not sufficient for including ecological values, a certain scepticism toward the potential for the state to ensure democratic practices has been voiced already by Goodin (1992: 168): 'To advocate democracy is to advocate procedures, to advocate environmentalism is to

---

[1] The granting of legal personhood to rivers and nature across the world may be such a feature, as it sets up unique institutional arrangements of guardianship within the state.

advocate substantive outcomes. What guarantee can we have that the former procedures will yield the latter sort of outcome?'

Indeed, the environmental movement has been ambivalent regarding the prospect for the state to foster ecological democracy. For one, there has been the well-grounded fear that a state that encourages engagement of civil society may actually absorb and co-opt green civil society and compromise its ability to independently challenge unsustainable state practices. However, the relations between the state, the public and citizens vary empirically, often depending on the type of state. In some welfare states, civil society relations are formalized and the environmental public is institutionalized through formal or informal processes (as demonstrated by Dryzek et al. 2003; Kronsell et al. 2019). Meanwhile, in liberal democratic states, like the United States, with a public discourse that entertains a view of the state as devoid of trust and legitimacy, the environmental public is often positioned in opposition to the state (Bomberg 2015). Further polarization in the United States during Trump's presidency and the rise of anti-environmental populism have turned democracy into a tool for 'the politics of unsustainability' (echoing Blühdorn 2020) and to antagonistic forms of democracy (Machin 2020).

In green theory, deliberation has been suggested as a productive way to include consideration of a broader set of interests in ecological governance (see Hammond 2020; Lövbrand and Khan 2010). To represent those currently marginalized from the polity, non-human species and entire ecosystems, also in the future, requires a high degree of reflection, imagination and openness in thinking and listening (Eckersley 2004: 111–138; Dobson 2010). In response to Goodin's query above, such deliberative designs of ecological democracy can foster a culture of reflexivity on both the means and ends of environmental politics and governance, thus holding the potential to strengthen environmental performance and generate ecologically benign outcomes. In such a perspective, a green theory of the good becomes reconciled with a green theory of values in a deliberative process of ecological emancipation and reflexivity.

The appeal of deliberative democracy to environmentalist scholars and practitioners is that it moves away from the short-term strategic bargaining between what are assumed to be self-interested actors in liberal democracy to reflective deliberations that centre on questions of value and common problems in a long-term and future-oriented perspective. Through open and unconstrained, respectful and informed dialogue, deliberation puts communication and reflection at the centre of democracy (Dryzek 2010: 3), thus turning decision-making into a process of preference transformation rather than simply a process of preference aggregation. As Hammond (2020) argues, sustainability is about meaning-making and deliberation can reorient people's fundamental norms and outlooks. Deliberation also fosters ecological citizenship by encouraging reflection and learning. There is an educative potential, in that citizens can learn about what it means to act as an ecologically responsible citizen (Melo-Escrihuela 2015).

Deliberative democratic theory emphasizes the need for inclusive policy processes that allow a broader range of societal actors to be engaged in processes of communication and deliberation (Baber and Bartlett 2005; Dryzek 2005). The broad inclusion of various stakeholders and citizens, together with experts and government representatives, can be a way to safeguard legitimacy for the kinds of transition required to reach sustainability objectives and to secure compliance and implementation (Dobson and Bell 2006). Environmental decisions and policies are often dependent on scientific knowledge – a prominent example is the relation between the understanding of climate change and the scientific community in the IPCC – as well as struggles around the relationship of citizen involvement and scientific experts in participatory processes (Fisher 2018: 261–262; Schlosberg et al. 2019) as experts may have closer access to the state than do citizens. Hammond (2020: 185) speaks of the need for deep reflection, but also attends to the difficulty in creating this in technocratic and scientific settings, and suggests that inclusive public debates can provide the space where 'fuller' information and alternatives are vented.

There is also a critique against the prevalence of deliberation as the preferred model for ecological democracy, which aligns with Chantal Mouffe's (2005) view on democracy as one of agonisms, i.e. a democratic politics of struggles between different interests, alternatives and groups, recognizing how perpetual conflicts or agonisms tend to be smoothed over through deliberative democratic attempts by marginalizing and making invisible important differences that are inherently part of politics. This risks resulting in antagonistic relations, when there are no legitimate channels for dissenting voices (Machin 2020: 163). Such channels for democratic participation within the state would take account of the fact that differences in opinions and views will always exist, thus recognizing up-front the intersectional categories involved in ecological democracy, noting possible winners and losers over specific policy initiatives or solutions as well as opening up for alliances across groups (Kaijser and Kronsell 2013). As Machin (2020: 165) stresses, it can revitalize environmental politics to nurture agonistic disagreement. Such efforts avoid antagonistic fighting and acknowledge the existence of political adversaries, turning the green public sphere into a generative force for democracy which can be organized through the state.

Deliberative models have not necessarily been designed within state institutions but often outside them. When designed within the state, the deliberative character is often weakened (see Bäckstrand et al. 2010). Yet engaging citizens and civil society is a crucial dimension in transformations towards a green state. As climate and environmental governance initiatives are not concentrated at state level but shaped in relation to subnational levels, local initiatives and civil society, fostering ecological citizenship is one of the green state's essential components.

In cases where ecological democracy is undermined or non-existent, Eckersley suggests it is necessary to build 'resonance between environmental issues and publics via the material practices of everyday life' (Eckersley 2019: 17). This is similar to what White (2019) presents as 'radical design' from a bottom-up perspective. This version of ecological democracy takes issue with how the environmental movement has envisioned a greener future in terms of limits, expressed as a kind of antagonism towards the state and its practices, often set in opposition to civil society and ecological citizens with little faith in any productive engagement from the state institutions and practices. White's (2019) radical design of democracy steps completely outside of these framings. It is set in a critical pragmatism whereby 'building survivable futures on a restless warming planet cannot involve some settler-colonial myth of return to the stable nature we have lost. Rather, it is going to entail recognizing that we constantly and persistently make and remake climate-adaptive socio-ecological worlds we find ourselves occupying' (White 2019: 13). Eckersley (2019: 8) follows up on this by arguing that sustainability is not an end state but a continuous process of adaptation to environmental change. While productive forms of democracy require 'strategies of iteration, experimentation, prototyping, failing and then starting again' (White 2019: 14), this approach also connects democracy to everyday life in the creation of more ecologically responsive 'material practices in collective, embodied, and prefigurative ways' (Eckersley 2019: 10). These processes can be highly complex but also have to be democratic, and include representation of informed publics and experts at the local level, simultaneously imagining and enacting alternative sustainable politics around material flows (Schlosberg and Craven 2019). Such processes can do with the support of strong but flexible state institutions that can facilitate the transition process – for example, by joining up local efforts. These alternative views of a future ecological democracy are likely needed, in order to both broaden the inclusion of various interests and foster a culture of ecological responsiveness and should, thus, be able to work together to make a greener state flourish.

Conclusions

The relationship to the state has been ambivalent among green political scholars and thinkers, while the struggles over and responses to environmental change over time have contributed to the *de facto* development of green state institutions. This indicates that the state matters in environmental and climate politics as a site for progressive action because it possesses authority, capacity and steering mechanisms to enable policies and governance paths towards ecologically sustainable ends. Potentially, this provides some hope that strategies for greening the state can build a more sustainable future by relying on the institutional capacities of state institutions. In our review of the literature on the green state, we find that welfare states are seen to be well-suited to engage with this gargantuan task, although most studies of the green state have hitherto focused on liberal democratic states and only recently have there been emerging studies of authoritarian, postcolonial and developmental green states. The normative ideal of the green state provides an important critique and corrective against which emerging state practices of environmental management and governance can be assessed for their sustainability qualities, and minimalist and maximalist states can be sorted on a scale of greenness.

A key challenge for greening the state is the centrality of the economic imperative of the late-modern state as well as its dependence on growth to generate revenues to maintain the welfare and well-being of its population. It appears that the state will not be able to achieve a green transformation of society unless it takes on this challenge and finds ways to resolve the tensions between economic and ecological concerns. This requires a state that is open to change and transformation, notably by being responsive to different interests and by including a diverse set of actors, particularly those capable of generating the technological, economic and social change needed. It is beyond doubt that a green transformation is necessary and the state can offer new imaginaries, possibilities and visions in the transition to global sustainability and planetary protection. However, the state can hardly achieve this task on its own, or in a top-down manner of politics. If efforts at greening the state are to become successful there is a need to reframe and reconstruct the rationalities of the state and its relationship to its citizens. Efforts to encourage an ecologically democratic state can emerge in line with classic environmentalism, if this provides meaningful representation of various interests and of those potentially affected as well as the means for taking the interests of non-human nature and future generations into consideration. However, this will likely require the exploration of new procedures, such as deliberative or radical democratic designs and other experimental forms of governance, where change, imagination and engagement take place around localized material practices for the benefit of the many, here and now as well as for the future.

Further Reading

Bäckstrand, K. and A. Kronsell (2015), *Rethinking the Green State: Environmental Governance towards Climate and Sustainability Transitions*, London: Routledge.

Barry, J. and R. Eckersley (2005), *The State and the Global Ecological Crisis*, Cambridge, MA: MIT Press.

Death, C. (2016), *The Green State in Africa*, New Haven, CT: Yale University Press.

Dryzek, J., D. Downies, C. Hunold, D. Schlosberg and H. Hernes (2003), *Green States and Social Movements: Environmentalism in the United States, United Kingdom, Germany and Norway*, Oxford: Oxford University Press.

Duit, A., P.H. Feindt and J. Meadowcroft (2016), Greening Leviathan: The rise of the environmental state? *Environmental Politics*, 25(1): 1–23.

Eckersley, R. (2004), *The Green State: Rethinking Democracy and Sovereignty*, Cambridge, MA: MIT Press.

Lundqvist, L.J. (2001), 'A green fist in a velvet glove: The ecological state and sustainable development', *Environmental Values*, 10(4), 455–472.

Mol, A.P.J. and G. Spaargaren (2002), 'Ecological Modernization and the Environmental State', in A. Mol and F. Buttel (eds), *The Environmental State under Pressure: Research in Social Problems and Public Policy*, 33–52, Bingley: Emerald Publishing.

8

Poststructuralism

Alan Finlayson and James Martin

Introduction

This chapter explores and evaluates 'poststructuralist' approaches to the theory and analysis of the state. Central to these is the claim that politics (or 'the political') is a *cause* of events and phenomena rather than merely an *effect* of forces perceived as 'non-political'. Accordingly, poststructuralists conceive of the state not as a precise 'thing' but as an activity – a practice – indeed, an 'ensemble' of practices which produce and are the product of politics. The study of these focuses especially on the concepts, identities and ideologies that define and name states and state practices, how these have been reshaped (or 'rearticulated'), and their specific tendencies (or 'logics') (see Glynos and Howarth 2007).

To explain this fully we will first put poststructuralism into context, taking some time to explain its distinct way of approaching the state while also linking it with philosophical and sociological debates about the theory and history of political rationality and showing how it overlaps with, but also departs from, other 'interpretive' approaches. We then introduce some varieties of poststructuralist political theory and analysis of politics and of the state: the discourse theory developed by Laclau and Mouffe and their concept of 'articulation'; critical theories of international relations and poststructuralist concepts of 'sovereignty'; and Foucault's concept of 'governmentality'. Along the way, we show how these concepts and methods have stimulated critical research on the politics of the state.

Poststructuralism and reason

Some of the most important propositions of poststructuralist approaches to politics are simply stated: rationality has a history and at any historical moment a particular form of rationality is dominant, but contested, and this is fundamental to politics; our theories and methods for studying this history are also part of it (and that must affect our methodologies). Let us explain these claims further.

In his *Critique of Pure Reason*, Immanuel Kant describes his time – the period of the European Enlightenment – as one with a 'ripened power of judgement'. 'Ours' he says, is 'the genuine age of criticism, to which everything must submit', including religion, the law and monarchy. If such institutions will not submit to critique then they 'cannot lay claim to that unfeigned respect that reason grants only to that which has been able to withstand its free and public examination' (A, xi). In other words, public institutions must justify themselves. What is distinct about the present – about 'modernity' – is that in justifying themselves institutions cannot rely on assertions about tradition or dogmatic appeals to superstition; they must show how they conform to the criteria of human rationality. Kant's vision was part of a radical and transformative moment in political history. It shared in the view that political authority, instead of subsuming all individuals into an organic and rigidly structured whole, should ensure that each can exercise their power of reason, subjecting institutions and the principles behind them to critical scrutiny, so that together they might establish a rational state in harmony with 'eternal and unchangeable laws' (A, xii).

Contrary to a common mis-reading, poststructuralist theorists do not reject this critical impulse of the Enlightenment. They simply note that history (including the history of the state) did not come to an end with the birth of the Enlightenment. Reason has a history – the development of one set of ideas enables the development of others, which in turn supersede what made them possible. It also has a social history – the forms, applications and reception of reason change over time along with wider changes in technology, social organization and political arrangements. With this in mind, poststructuralists take reason very seriously – so seriously that they propose something which at first seems paradoxical: that criticism must itself be criticized and reason submit to the test of rationality (and that this is part of what politics is all about).

What that means, for poststructuralists, is that we can and should enquire into the conditions and contexts of reason and its 'laws'. Reason and reasoning have a past, which helps explain our present. They also have a future, which has not yet been determined, is not guaranteed and is a matter of political contestation. History is not the inevitable forward march of only one way of thinking. Alternative rationalities coexist, sometimes ignoring each other, sometimes in conflict, often unable to recognize or understand each other. In the history of reason, things are not smooth but discontinuous: some reasonings are forgotten, lie dormant and can be reactivated; there are unexpected developments and some rationalities spread laterally rather than forward. The principles and reasons that may dominate do so because of battles that were not necessarily conducted in a rational way or organized according to the rationale to which they give rise. All of this is simply to say that, from the perspective of the study of politics, reason, truth and the states for which they provide justifications have a political history that it would be irrational and untruthful to ignore.

For Kant, reasoning involved identifying a universal principle to follow: something that applies across specific cases, independently of them. When enlightened states first granted rights to citizens, they did so by proclaiming that such rights belonged to all, because all were capable of sharing in rationality. But, of course, 'all' did not mean all. The propertyless, the working class, women, slaves, ethnic and religious minorities, and colonized peoples were not part of 'all'. The capacity to reason was not thought to be found equally developed everywhere. The political history of modern Europe and of the world is a history of attempts to increase the numbers and expand the kinds of people deemed capable of reasoning, deserving of civil and other such rights, and to whom states must justify themselves. It is also the (ongoing) history of attempts to oppose this.

Contemporary political ideologies tell different stories about this history. Liberalism thinks of it as the progressive realization of what was always implicit in the Enlightenment and is now embodied in the *Universal Declaration of Human Rights*. Conservatives, by contrast, present it as a history of decline – the corruption of reason by 'fashionable' demands about equality or identity. Socialists criticize liberals for imagining that its ways of living, being and thinking were the only – the *universal* – ways, noting that in order to sustain that belief, liberalism could not acknowledge its own roots in class exploitation. Feminists argue that the exclusion of women by early Enlightenment thinkers was not a mistake but one of its defining features. And ecologically minded critics have proposed that our ways of reasoning have been based on a particular (and ultimately irrational) attitude towards the natural world, and that this must be overcome. For all these critics, reason has too often been conceived as 'instrumental', as a tool, a means for achieving ends in a narrow manner, rather than a manner of thinking about what our ends should be (see Adorno and Horkheimer [1944] 1973; Held 1980).

For poststructuralism, that history of political struggle over rationality, of critique and counter critique, is something we must study – not least because it is still happening. The difficulty of maintaining a dominant conception of rationality, and of proving that a state embodies it, is a defining feature of contemporary politics. The immense complexity of the global division of labour gives rise to very specialized activities that tend to produce their own forms of rationalization (in finance, logistics, management, teaching, farming or medicine). Commodification – the conversion of objects and activities into things for sale – has replaced traditional relationships with market relations in which price displaces other kinds of valuation, upending received moralities and routines of justification. Once relatively closed communities (from rural America to urban Afghanistan) are now connected with each other and exposed to international political, cultural and economic forces that disturb settled ways of life. The ever-increasing speed, volume and fragmentation of the means of producing and communicating information and ideas have affected our conceptions of time and space (Giddens 1991; Beck, Giddens and Lash 1994), how we relate to or identify with the places in which we live, and our mental environment which, filled with images, sounds and meme fragments, is radically different from that of the literate cultures of just a century ago (see McLuhan 1964) and becoming different from that of barely a generation ago. In this context, the very different rationalities that political classes or cultures employ when making or justifying decisions have been foregrounded and made the focus of political dispute.

Poststructuralism, then, proposes that reason has a history, the study of which is important for political analysis and, consequently, for any critical grasp of the state and its operations. In identifying how intellectual or ideological critiques of reason are staged, and the ways that dominant rationalities are organized, contested and defended, we are studying a fundamental dimension of politics. We are also participating in an important form of social criticism. Dominant forms of reasoning are often sustained and justified by treating opposed forms as irrational and thus unsuitable to serve on the 'tribunal' of reason. Such exclusions lead to contradictions and social conflicts, which follow a logic of their own and drive events in distinct directions. Any political theory or political science that ignores or downplays this is either ignoring reality or taking up a position in real political conflicts.

Poststructuralism and interpretivism

Poststructuralism is not the only approach to the study of the state which emphasizes the history of ideas or mentalities that shape political action and the cultural context of events. Various 'hermeneutic' or 'interpretive' approaches in political science also disagree with those who take individual 'preferences' as given – as 'inputs' into a political system that then determines what comes out. For us, such preferences are outcomes of intellectual, deliberative, cultural and ideological processes that we want to understand.

Interpretive methods start with the fact that human beings are conscious, reflective and reflexive creatures. We experience the world through our bodies and in our minds as meaningful and not only as various stimuli to which we instinctually respond. Things and experiences have names and belong to categories that assign them value. There are rules about which things and which categories go together and which must stay apart. Names, categories and rules are not immaterial, existing only 'in' our minds. They take a very material form as speech, writing, performance and visual representations. They exist in the world as actions (ordering, demanding, insulting) and as objects (books, banners and artistic works which store, circulate and communicate meaning). Such communication is possible, however, only because it draws on 'language', in the broadest sense of that term – a 'system' of rules for the meaningful arrangement of signs and sounds, words and other expressions. To participate in a culture (a society, a political party, perhaps a profession) is to know the rules of its language and to share in using it with others – but also to submit to it if we are to communicate successfully. By studying such systems, interpretivists hope, we may gain insight into the modes of reason particular groups employ and explain why they acted as they did (or at least what they thought they were doing) (see Bevir and Blakely 2018).

Interest in meanings has become increasingly common in political science and studies of governance because to understand social interactions in government bureaucracies, or politicians negotiating over policies, we must also understand the languages in use, the relations between them and the ways they influence rationality (Bevir et al. 2004; Bevir and Rhodes 2015). Some forms of 'new' institutionalism, for instance, examine the informal norms, values and symbolic forms that shape institutions (see Chapter 5; Lowndes 1996: 182; 2002), including ideas that supply institutionalized 'templates' for action. Bevir and Rhodes (2003, 2010) emphasize the 'narratives' that political actors (and political scientists) employ when making sense of governance, insisting that actions can only be understood by grasping the beliefs and values that motivate them, which means examining the 'inherited beliefs and practices' that establish traditions. Poststructuralism also examines the inherited frameworks of meaning within which actors act. But it does so in a distinct way.

A key claim of poststructuralists is that the rules of thought or language that underpin political institutions, cultures and groups are neither fixed nor unitary (see Derrida 1978). The reason poststructuralists are so called is that they argue that no system, no structure of meaning, is ever perfect or closed. It cannot account in advance for everything that might be said. Words can always be put together in new ways and things outside the system will always impinge on it (such as other languages, new technologies of expression, unforeseeable events). Human action is not like a chess game. The rules and pieces in chess constitute a system that assigns meanings or values to the pieces and specifies what they are and are not allowed to do. That constrains players (who can't do just anything) but it also produces possibilities from among which they choose. Estimates suggest that the lower limit of possible chess games may be as high as 10 to the power of 120. It is tempting to think of a culture, a language, a system of meaning in this way. What poststructuralism points out is simply that people often play chess 'wrongly'. They break or misunderstand the rules; they play 'suicide chess' and try to lose; they use the pieces for draughts or to make up for a missing piece in some other board game. Such activity is not entirely random or lawless. It comes out of extant rules and sometimes what starts as a breach of rules becomes permissible, changing a system in a small way, perhaps in time becoming a new rule – like using a split infinitive, or the 'tradition' of Prime Minister's Questions (PMQs) in the House of Commons.

For poststructuralism, we inhabit systems of meaning that are unstable, open to revision from within, and sometimes forced to change from without. Such change is often resisted. Some will try to maintain the rule about infinitives or to assimilate PMQs to executive power. Such contestation is a driving force of cultural history and it is thoroughly political. Social orders – often backed by the state – assign people to particular places (perhaps to do with the kind of work they do, their gender, their country of origin) and give different values to such places and different kinds of room for manoeuvre. But sometimes people fall out of their allotted place or actively push against it. Those with power will try to defend the system with violence. Sometimes the system will win, or maybe it will adapt or change, perhaps dramatically. The key thing is this: where interpretivism wants to know how meaning works, poststructuralism also wants to know how meaning *does not* work.

Moreover, poststructuralism is distinct in the way it conceives of the identity of the individuals or agents involved in political action. In political analysis we often proceed on the basis that within a polity there are individuals or groups with a clear identity – the working class, investors, Christians – which is linked to some set of ideal or material interests that, in turn, gives rise to certain demands: better pay, higher returns, the right to proselytize. What poststructuralists point out is that there are lots of people who could be all of these simultaneously – working-class Christian investors, for example. Political analysis that starts from the assumption that it is just 'obvious' what categories apply misses how it is that people come to see their identity and their interests as being one thing over others. Poststructuralists argue that how we see our identity and our interests is the outcome of an unpredictable process, a power struggle to organize the systems of meaning through which we act. Individuals achieve an identity through their position within a broader politicized system of meaning. Many actors and institutions play a role in organizing social systems that naturalize and legitimate political claims, making the 'rules of the game' and how we 'naturally' and 'normally' act seem inevitable and immovable. These are 'discourses' or 'discursive structures' that draw lines of exclusion and inclusion, determining what is and is not a legitimate 'move in the game' or an identity that matters, 'drawing ... political frontiers between "insiders" and "outsiders" ... excluding certain options and structuring relations' (Howarth, Norval and Stavrakakis 2000: 4; see also Howarth 2013).

From this point of view, when we look at 'the state' what we see is a complex variety of discourses that lay claim to an unassailable rational and legal authority, assigning identities and interests, organizing things into categories, establishing boundaries between things and managing their frontiers. In order to act within the state, one has to think and act within such discourses. State bureaucracies, for example, are domains built around numerous professional codes and presuppositions – concerning what is foreign and domestic policy, what is health and what welfare, what is a legitimate proposition and what is not, who can speak about what, when and where (see Cooper 2019). In a sense, state actors act on the basis of an implicit yet unexamined social theory. Poststructuralists investigate such discourses in order to perceive the structure, rules of performance and institutionalization of the 'theory' that underpins it. But we do this not to uncover a fixed structure of propositions which can then be verified or falsified but to establish what has been excluded and how, and to try and make something new thinkable: that is 'critique'. 'Discourses' are open-ended systems, always productive of new possibilities. 'Authorities' of various kinds may seek to control language, meaning and identity within narrow, stable parameters but meaning always exceeds such control. There is not one discursive structure in society as a whole, or even just within the governmental domain, but multiple, overlapping 'language games' (Wittgenstein 1958) and multiple rationalities that may contradict or clash. This tension between openness and closure is at the heart of political struggle and it is from that perspective that poststructuralists study the phenomenon of the state.

Articulation

The 'discourse theory' associated with Ernesto Laclau and Chantal Mouffe (1985) represents a significant attempt to apply poststructuralist insights to political theory and to the analysis of states and governments. Laclau and Mouffe conceive of society as a complex ensemble of overlapping, mutually limiting and modifying discursive practices. These, they argue, are never organized from a fixed centre. In fact, Laclau and Mouffe argue that society is premised on the *absence* of such a centre. Society, they declare, paradoxically, is 'impossible'. What they mean is that it is never a completed, finished entity and it cannot be explained by referring to a single, controlling principle (1985: 111), be it the economy, human nature or biology. There is only 'the social': a process of ongoing creation consisting of attempts to provide an anchor for society, an incontestable point of reference, that will join together and tie down its various elements, specifying what they are and how they relate. Political analysis can thus examine 'the social' by exploring how its elements are articulated (combined and recombined) and social identities and interests formed, and how states are involved in managing or policing it all. Moreover, it can do this with a view to clarifying the opportunities to challenge and radically transform how politics is done.

For instance, in developed states and economies such as the United States or the UK, we find the 'articulation' of capitalist production and exchange with liberal individualism and representative forms of democracy. This is not merely a coincidental alignment of distinct phenomena (a mode of production, an ideology of personhood and a political system). The theory of 'articulation' says that, when combined, such phenomena are themselves modified. There is no unchanging 'essence' to capitalism, individualism or representative democracy. Their articulation creates a new form, or 'regime', that combines opposing logics: the state of capitalist liberal democracy (see Mouffe 2000). It is important, then, not only to study what we imagine to be political 'things in themselves' but also the relations between them. For instance, capitalist production may also be articulated with ethnic nationalism and a political structure centred on an authoritarian personality cult – Fascism. Laclau and Mouffe's discourse analysis is interested precisely in the way such articulations produce distinct formations from conditions of antagonism and conflict. It does not see these as naturally or necessarily given forms but as the 'condensation' of political practices and struggles to define society by combining its elements (including economics, individuals and the political system) in particular ways.

Laclau and Mouffe employ Gramsci's term 'hegemony' to define this process of fixing and associating elements and identities, imposing a dominant meaning on social practices to sustain but also limit the range of possibilities within a given structure (see Gramsci 1971; Martin 2019). Importantly, though, discourse analysis highlights what is excluded in the attempt to create unity. Again, the emphasis is on the relations between things. If we want to understand something such as 'the state' we need to know not only what is going on inside it but also what it is outside. Some movements try to articulate with each other to form a larger political coalition. Feminism, for example, might be articulated with socialism, liberalism or conservatism but in each case the nature of each ideology is changed. Laclau argued that hegemony is always a process whereby a range of subjective identities are related to each other such that they seem to be joined by some kind of universal category (see Laclau 1996). For instance, when President George W. Bush declared a 'war on terror', he shaped policy on the basis of an 'axis of evil' and sought to constitute a 'coalition of the willing' where 'you are either for us or against us'. State alliances were thereby constituted in terms of a specific, exclusionary, set of identities and relationships. On the one side were 'friends' who are for freedom and democracy, and who, despite their differences, are united under these 'universal' categories; on the other, the 'enemies' associated with the categories of dictatorship and evil. On each side, discursive 'relations of equivalence' effect a unity by virtue of a universal element in which all share equally. This discourse constitutes a political logic that orders the inter-state field in a particular if limited way and from that stark arrangement certain political behaviours must seem necessary.

The state, then, is not a discrete object or unified phenomenon. For Torfing (1991) it should be conceived as a complex ensemble of discursively formed rationalities: law, sovereignty, claims to expertise, information and knowledge, types of communication as well as institutions, departments, bureaucracies, ritualized habits of legitimation, organizations of coercion and control. Political analysis can look at how these are combined and recombined, asking what effects they have upon each other. That might enable us to describe, for different states, the ways the 'centre' is organized, imagined or even 'fantasized'.

For instance, in some states the systems of law, government and military may be articulated directly with 'the people' whose interests they are held to express. This is a formation we often call 'totalitarian' and contrast to the liberal democratic regime in which there is no unified people, only independent individuals who are not directly articulated to the government. Fascist parties (and, increasingly, populist movements) aim to articulate the idea of the people with government by defining the people in opposition to other, 'unacceptable' peoples such as refugees or immigrants. Other states imagine their unity by an articulation with God, and the 'people' may be conceived in religious terms, leading to a different series of relations with the law or the military. In the Islamic Republic of Iran, for example, the state is organized according to a principle of divine sovereignty. Society, law, politics and military are articulated under the sign of this one overarching principle. But in all cases, the state has an evolving and potentially unpredictable character. Its policies, ministries, bureaucracies and personnel are always facing the possibility of conflict and the threat of disaggregation.

The state, then, is never a single 'institution' or even a number of 'institutions' joined without remainder but, rather, a relatively open field of practices, actions and reactions that draw from 'traditions' and 'habits' but also redraw them – rearticulate them – in every new action. For the theory of hegemony, the state is both a primary site and an outcome of such articulatory practices; it is the location of ongoing strategies to unify by 'hegemonizing' the unavoidable plurality of its apparatuses and the society it seeks to govern.

Thus the focus of discourse-theoretical approaches, following Laclau and Mouffe's innovations, has been on the antagonisms and discursive vocabularies that shape struggles and strategies for hegemony across diverse contexts, rather than 'the state' conceived as a unity (see Howarth, Norval and Stavrakakis 2000; Bastow and Martin 2003; Howarth and Torfing 2005); on how these shape the challenges to a particular state (or to the state as such) and how states and governments try to contain or resist such criticism and contestation. Such theorists also often advocate 'radical democracy' (and, more recently 'left populism') – a critical, egalitarian project of coalition-building that promotes the expansion of 'the political'. They argue for an increase in the diversity of participants in politics and embrace the potential for 'agonistic' conflict, rather than limiting democracy to elite-led practices of state-centric technocratic reform (see Mouffe 2013, 2018; Tonder and Thomassen 2014).

Sovereignty

Laclau and Mouffe's approach tends to focus on types of hegemonic activity found within specific fields and to assume the nation-state as the terrain of hegemonic struggle (see Nash 2002). But states also exist in relation to other states. Can a poststructuralist approach to the multiple rationalities of statehood tell us anything about politics at the international level?

The concept of hegemony (see also Chapter 3) has long had significance for the study of international relations where it has been used to describe how states dominate others in a 'state system'. In such theories the state is taken more or less as a given. It is a corporate actor with its own interests and capacities for strategic calculation. That idea of a singular, unified 'actor' and its complement – a number of such actors contending for power in an essentially anarchic 'international arena' – have been questioned by numerous 'critical' theories of international relations (see Edkins 1999). These challenge the very idea of sovereign statehood (see Chapter 9), exposing its limits and investigating the reasonings they presuppose.

For instance, in his critique of realist and neo-realist literature, Richard Ashley (1988) argues that the discourse of national sovereignty *requires* the concept of international anarchy. Sovereign states with authority over their domestic interiors are taken as the foundational elements of theories of international politics. The world 'outside' states is imagined as an unregulated, anarchic space within which a multiplicity of forces either compete or cooperate. Anarchy, then, is the 'other' of sovereignty, against which it is defined. This lays the basis for a rationality that constantly asks of the international arena 'how is order possible?'; 'how can order be maintained?'; 'how can policy be coordinated'? Rational and self-interested 'state-agents' face an ambiguous, uncoordinated environment against which they must range. Corresponding theories of the 'balance of power' and its maintenance become the basis for state policies. But the state itself is unquestioned since it is a 'rational presence already there, a sovereign identity that is the self-sufficient source of international history's meaning' (1988: 231). But, Ashley continues, this rigid dichotomy between sovereignty and anarchy creates the very environment it claims to describe (1988: 243). Ambiguous practices that undermine the assumption of the sovereign state in an unstable environment are downgraded and ignored. Non-state actors, agencies that compete with states, even the distinct branches of the state bureaucracy itself, all complicate the idea of unitary actors and may even work against it. The state coexists alongside transnational corporations, political movements and NGOs, all of which transcend and disrupt state boundaries while the migration of populations or refugees problematizes state responsibility for citizens (Innes 2015). All these things lie beyond the boundaries of unitary sovereignty and bring into question that very concept of bounded statehood demarcated through the distinction between a domestic 'inside' and an international 'outside' (see Walker 1993). As a result, international relations are dominated by assumptions about conflict and order that derive from a presumption of rationality rather than from an examination of the possibilities contained within the complex multiplicities of world politics.

Poststructuralist critics, then, take a 'constructivist' approach to international relations. That is to say, they are interested in how concepts and practices of sovereignty or inside/outside distinctions are created through, for example, mutual recognition by other states of national identity, territorial integrity and border management (Vaughan-Williams 2012) or assumptions concerning trade in capitalist markets (see Biersteker and Weber 1996). In articulating its authority through claims to national purity or economic success, the state continually confronts resistance to its efforts (often as a consequence of its own interventions) that expose the partiality and contingency of its claims. Poststructuralists draw attention to the role of power and exclusion in this process, underlining its *political* nature (Edkins 1999; Aradau 2010). The concept of the state as a sovereign entity in an open international environment is a myth dependent on ongoing processes that distinguish its 'inside' and 'outside' by practices of exclusion that create the very environment within and through which the state is then deemed to act.

But that does not mean that defining the state and 'its' interests is a matter of inventing 'mere' fictions. Typically, it involves very material forms of violence against bodies and identities. Poststructuralist thinkers (among others) draw attention to the 'securitization' of the international environment through which subjects and identities are constituted in relation to other identities, boundaries and 'threats'. For example, David Campbell (1992) argues that foreign policy should be understood not as the more or less successful expression of a state's given interests and identity but as part of the ongoing attempt to establish that identity and those interests through, for example, the constitution of enemies and dangers against which state action can be ranged and defined. As Campbell puts it: 'the inability of the state project of security to succeed is the guarantor of the state's continued success and impelling identity' (1992: 11–12). Increased securitization and expansion of techniques of surveillance in relation to terrorism, migrants and fleeing refugees can be conceived not as merely rational reactions to isolated situations but as comprehensive strategies to reassert state power by redefining the disorder that threatens it (see also Hansen 2017). Sovereignty is, at a fundamental level, a claim to autonomy that can only be demonstrated by controlling others, and particularly by enacting (or threatening) violence on the bodies – or what Giorgio Agamben calls the 'bare life' – of other subjects (see Agamben 1998).

One may well ask, for instance, precisely where is the border of the sovereign state? State power never entirely coincides with a delineated territory since states undertake actions overseas (in embassies and through forms of cooperation with other agencies or by interventions in other territories). The various borders surrounding and separating off the state from what is non-state are never simply empirical but bound up with legal and political reasonings that project sovereignty well beyond territorial space (see Vaughan-Williams 2009 and Chapter 11). In the study of 'geopolitics', writers such as Gearóid Ó Tuathail (1996) and John Agnew (Agnew and Corbridge 1995; Agnew and Ó Tuathail 1992) examine the ways in which international space is rendered both meaningful and practically governable through discursive representations. These are embodied in various forms such as maps, public 'common sense', types of intellectual reasoning, which contribute to a vision of the international order favourable to certain kinds of action rather than others. The Cold War, for example, involved efforts to envision a dichotomous division of space into broadly homogeneous, antagonistic camps, thus obscuring the very real differences between states presumed to be on the same 'side'. The spatial discourse of 'East vs. West' validated some identities and a selective understanding of the purpose and function of other states. It made it possible to imagine the United States as the 'defender' of Western civilization and to interpret events anywhere in the world in terms of that overriding dichotomy (as if the Middle East or South East Asia were merely a theatre for the Cold War).

In more recent years, however, the representations and rationales of states in the 'geopolitical imaginary' have altered in light of the end of the Cold War and the intensification of 'neoliberal' forms of globalization (see also Chapter 11). Not only have structures of international cooperation and divisions changed but the organizing principles of statehood have begun to alter with them, often in quite contradictory ways as increased marketization diminishes the capacity for maintaining social solidarity and security. State boundaries are no longer static territorial contours but moveable borders *inside* states as well, as perceived threats are seen to operate within and across traditional boundaries. New anxieties about immigration and terrorism, especially, have dramatically heightened attention to domestic techniques of monitoring and control of individuals within territories – for example, by building walls or utilizing technologies for surveillance (see Brown 2010). States have also increased their use of 'offshore' border systems (such as the use of Guantánamo Bay Naval Base by the United States) to filter, detain or repel suspect individuals, typically by placing them in legally ambiguous zones classified as 'exceptions' to the regular restraints of domestic and international jurisdiction (see Agamben 2005). Obsessed with potential risks, new agencies and technologies have been deployed to pre-empt security threats and distance them from national populations, though often with severe implications for individual civil liberties (Vaughan-Williams 2009). In these new border regimes, sovereign power and authority have significantly reorganized what counts as inside/outside, legal/illegal and public/private, often without effective critical oversight by democratic representatives.

Poststructuralist analyses of international state sovereignty expose the arbitrary, shifting boundaries beneath the supposed stability of the state as a principle and guarantor of order. The rationality of neoliberal sovereignty places complex decisions and judgements within a frame whose intrinsic unity is typically presupposed and therefore not open to debate and contestation by a 'demos' (see Brown 2015). In the very moment in which 'it' takes a political decision, the state itself is depoliticized.

Governmentality

We have seen how poststructuralists want to 'open up' the state by unpacking the competing rationalities that constitute it. By looking at the discourses that invoke the state as a centre to social life, they have *decentred* the idea of a singular political power acting as if it were a unitary agent. The notion that the state, or indeed sovereignty, should be at the centre of political analysis is made problematic and the very object and method of enquiry destabilized. This is the moment to turn to the work of Michel Foucault.

Foucault polemically challenged political theory and analysis by inveighing against the notion of sovereignty. 'Political theory', he suggested, 'has never ceased to be obsessed with the person of the sovereign' (1980: 121). It is concerned with the single location and origin of power and with secondary questions as to how it may be legitimately exercised, contained and directed. Further, sovereign power is taken to express itself through the setting of limits, typically expressed as laws prohibiting what can be done. It was just this claim – shared by classical liberals and Marxists alike – that Foucault disputed, problematizing the idea of sovereignty in order to examine the peculiar strategies and practices that comprise contemporary power (see Foucault 1980, 1991). The reduction of power to a state construed as a rational subject writ-large obscures the organizational continuity between state and non-state agencies that work throughout society to administer 'disciplinary' and 'normalizing' techniques of governance. Foucault sought a 'political philosophy that isn't erected around the problem of sovereignty, nor therefore around the problem of law and prohibition' and declared that 'We need to cut off the king's head: in political theory that has still to be done' (Foucault 1980: 121).

From this perspective, our object of analysis ceases to be simply 'the state' and becomes the diverse range of agencies, apparatuses and practices producing mechanisms of control and forms of knowledge that make aspects of social life available for governing – and not only by government. Importantly, Foucault conceived of power as 'productive' and not only 'repressive'. It does not just prohibit, it also gets us to do things, often willingly, and in particular ways. Such power is dispersed across society and affects people within the state as much as those subject to state intervention. That is because power works through and out of an ensemble of authorities, knowledges and fields of expertise (medical, academic-intellectual, economic and so on) on which government then draws.

In historical studies, Foucault traced the emergence of modern techniques of control, surveillance and discipline, showing how these were adopted within numerous institutional settings in the eighteenth century: prisons, schools, factories, hospitals. These practices made possible new types of knowledge about human behaviour, leading to the codification of procedures to monitor and observe subjects: to interview them, to gather information, document and tabulate the results. That knowledge enabled techniques to mould behaviour and produce new kinds of person: useful, obedient and self-monitoring. This type of social control, more subtle than brute force, became increasingly generalized, forming a 'microphysics of power' in which the human body is the object of knowledges that categorize, problematize, discipline and normalize (Foucault 1977: 24–31).

Foucault later drew attention to the exercise of what he called 'bio-power'. In the classical theory of sovereignty, a basic power of the sovereign is that over life and death. The sovereign wields the power to decide who shall live and who shall die. Liberal political theory and analysis were concerned precisely with supervising the exercise of that power, regulating the right to restrict, restrain and ultimately to kill. But in the modern era, argues Foucault, governmental power concerns not only individuals but 'the nation' or 'the mass' and 'the people' as a whole, and it makes the conditions of the population (its size, its health, its environment) into objects of policy. No longer is power concerned only with death; it administers the conditions and processes of life itself. For instance, the study of the ratio of births to deaths helps policies of population management; demography, epidemiology and actuarial inquiry produce knowledge and information making intervention into living populations possible. Public hygiene becomes a matter of governmental concern and its management involves the centralization of power and the development of associated knowledge and applied rationalities. Illness becomes a social and not merely a personal problem, in need of a societal solution, particularly in the case of old age and infirmity. Such sickness requires rationally organized systems of insurance or pensions that the state underwrites. There is also systematic intervention with rational intent into the environment: irrigating, draining and redirecting water flows so as to manage the urban environment with sewage systems or making air quality a policy goal. This creates a relation of state to society or to social action that is not simply repressive or disciplinary. Nor is it easily described in terms of rights. It involves the management of a population and its doings, legitimating and making possible widespread intervention. When population size is an object of policy, intervention into sexual reproduction itself becomes a necessity (as, for example, in the case of China's 'one-child' policy) (see Thompson 2012).

Such activity is not made possible or directed from a single locus of sovereign power. For Foucault it is more like the declaration of a general and permanent state of emergency in society with many agencies, institutions and actors continually developing new techniques and identifying new areas that require examination and intervention. As Foucault put it:

> security mechanisms have to be installed around the random element inherent in a population of living beings so as to optimise a state of life ... using overall mechanisms and acting in such a way as to achieve overall states of equilibrium; taking control of life and the biological processes of man-as-species and ensuring that they are not disciplined, but regularized. (2003: 246–247)

Such power cannot be referred back to some prior agency that 'wields' it, for its agents are also effects of the practices and knowledges in question (1977: 27–28). Understanding and analysis require examination of the rationalities enabling specific interventions, their historical emergence, the reactions they engender and their reformulation.

Foucault's writings on 'governmentality' are thus concerned not with the disciplinary practices of specific institutions but with techniques for administering whole populations, shaping and guiding the behaviour of subjects who, in modern liberal society, are formally free yet still objects of social policy (see Foucault 1991; Dean 2009, 2013). Individual conduct is not itself the object of policy but, rather, 'the conduct of conduct'; that is, ways of shaping the exercise of freedom (see Joyce 2003). Liberalism is more than just an ideology or political philosophy; it is also a 'rationality of government': 'a system of thinking about the nature and practice of government ... capable of making some form of that activity thinkable and practicable both to its practitioners and to those upon whom it is practised' (Gordon 1991: 3). Governmental rationalities constitute the objects of government as questions to be solved or failures to be rectified, inviting the formulation of 'programmes' and 'initiatives' that justify the utilization of 'technologies', be they financial measures, legal controls, bargaining procedures, policies of criminalization, efforts to influence diet, exercise and so forth).

Such studies of governmentality demonstrate how the state is one of a number of settings within which the operations of government are exercised. The state does not have a single grand function (such as to maintain capitalism or represent the public). Rather, it grants rationalities 'a temporary institutional durability'. The state, or more particularly the discourses that shape it, are, as Rose and Miller put it, 'an historically variable linguistic device for conceptualising and articulating ways of ruling' (1992: 177). Poststructuralism thus highlights the complex and irreducibly plural nature of state practices, showing how the state can be a variety of porous mini-authorities utilizing knowledge to categorize and shape the subjects. Attention to this complexity has been important in qualifying accounts of the state. Both Marxists and feminists have made use of Foucauldian ideas to steer away from purely repressive conceptions of political power (see Poulantzas 1978; Jessop 1990; Pringle and Watson 1992).

The substitution of the state by the study of the rationalities operative within it, which may also exceed it, is a bold move for political analysis and research, extending its reach and deepening its scope. A good example here is the approach to policy analysis developed by Carol Bacchi. She asks of policy interventions 'what is the problem represented to be?', arguing that 'what we say we want to do about something indicates what we think needs to change and hence how we constitute the "problem"'. She goes on to suggest that we can look at any policy and 'work backwards' so as to 'deduce how it produces a "problem" ... to explore the terms of reference within which the issue is cast – that is, to study its problematization' (Bacchi 2012: 4). That can be applied to all sorts of policy areas – for example, drug and alcohol usage (Bacchi 2015, 2018). One purpose of such analysis is to show what the state treats as unproblematic, the things about which it is silent, and in so doing to retrieve possibilities for thinking differently (see Bacchi 2009; also Bacchi and Goodwin 2016). Complementary policy research focused on how terms, concepts and the overall rhetoric of policy discourse help to constitute – in unstable and shifting situations – the alliances which make policy formation and implementation possible (Fischer and Gottweis 2012; Turnbull 2013).

Governmentality analyses of the state and politics have proliferated in recent years in response to the emergence of neoliberalism as the dominant rationality of government policy (see Foster, Kerr and Byrne 2014; Teo and Wynne-Hughes 2020). It is important to remember, however, that invocations of 'the state' or 'government' as a name for a unified institution are still frequently made by social and political forces. The inviolable symbolic unity of the state is still invoked to justify the use of organized force against 'enemies' within and without its boundaries (see Poulantzas 1978: 76–86). At key moments, such as in wartime or during a 'social emergency', the state is invested by certain groups with a unity of purpose that legitimates its distinctive repressive functions and articulates its diverse elements around a relatively coherent project. At such times, the state *does* employ 'repressive' sovereign power in deciding who can live and who shall die. We might therefore plausibly combine Foucauldian analyses with the study of 'hegemony' and the formation of identities in international space.

Conclusions

Just as there is no single account of poststructuralism, neither is there any specific political orientation that it endorses. Poststructuralists do take a certain critical attitude towards the world and to 'the political' as such – to the wider, paradigmatic contexts within which politics (in a narrow sense) is conducted and which are constituted through forms of power and exclusion too often hidden by an exclusive focus on politics as negotiation, bargaining and dialogue. For them, the state is positioned, somewhat ambiguously, towards the political understood in this sense. It is a site of politics that nevertheless functions by simultaneously narrowing the parameters of the political.

We have seen this, for instance, in arguments about hegemony as well as in analyses of representation in geopolitics. The state, it is implied, can only secure its management of the wider environment by strategically delimiting politics and subjecting it to forms of reasoning that determine in advance the nature of the 'political game'. The state is therefore both a site of politics and also a source of depoliticization. Whether it be through social and economic policies or action within the international environment, states govern by defining the field in which they act, thus making their environment governable by holding off alternative ways of defining the situation. This paradoxical depoliticization, we suggest, is not simply a vice that we put up with in an uncertain world; it is the ineradicable condition of all efforts to impose order on the world and, hence, the very condition of politics itself.

Further Reading

Dean, M.M. (2013), *The Signature of Power: Sovereignty, Governmentality and Biopolitics*, London: SAGE.

Edkins, J. (1999), *Poststructuralism and International Relations: Bringing the Political Back In*, Boulder, CO: Lynne Rienner.

Finlayson, A. and J. Valentine (eds) (2002), *Politics and Poststructuralism*, Edinburgh: Edinburgh University Press.

Howarth, D.R. (2000), *Discourse*, Milton Keynes: Open University Press.

Howarth, D.R., A. Norval and Y. Stavrakakis (eds) (2000), *Discourse Theory and Political Analysis: Identities, Hegemonies and Social Change*, Manchester: Manchester University Press.

Rose, N. (1999), *Powers of Freedom*, Cambridge: Cambridge University Press.

Walker, R.J.B. (1993), *Inside/Outside: International Relations as Political Theory*, Cambridge: Cambridge University Press.

Part II

Issues

9

The State and Sovereignty

Chris Brown

Introduction

It has become a commonplace for the concepts we employ in the study of politics to be designated 'essentially contested' but, if anything, this term understates the protean nature of the notion of sovereignty. Not only has the meaning of the word changed over time, but in each era the notion has been and is, contested. International relations scholars are given to using the expression 'Westphalian sovereignty' to describe the meanings given to the notion after the Peace of 1648, but, even setting aside the fictional nature of the so-called Westphalian order (Teschke 2009), in the mid-seventeenth century the meaning of sovereignty was as hotly contested as it is at the beginning of the twenty-first century. The 'sovereigns' – usually individuals but sometimes collectives – who emerged in this period had established that they had no internal equals and no external superiors but, beyond that, the nature of their sovereignty was heavily contested. Hobbes, equating the sovereign with the God of the medieval nominalists, held that the sovereign made the law, Pufendorf and Locke that the Law of Nature governed the sovereign as well as his (or her, but usually his) subjects. Move on a couple of centuries and the notion of 'popular sovereignty' comes slowly, more slowly than is often appreciated, to replace the sovereignty of the monarch, but how this happens, and whether the powers of the individual sovereign are transferred intact to the collectivity, and, if so, how, is a matter for dispute, as is the role of the notion of sovereignty in federal systems, or indeed in any system where the actions of the sovereign are constrained by positive law. In the middle of the twentieth century, the establishment of the United Nations fails to clarify the situation; on the one hand the UN Charter sets out a strong doctrine of state sovereignty (albeit a sovereignty where the power to make war has been, in principle, removed), but on the other the promotion of the idea of human rights is potentially subversive of that same doctrine, placing theoretical limits on the ability of states to determine their own systems of government. Later in the century, this contradiction is developed and intensified as some states endorse a new conception of sovereignty – 'sovereignty as responsibility' – and develop international institutions that support this new notion, while other states continue to adhere to what they believe to be the conventional meaning of the term. And the era is replete with examples of the 'pooling' of sovereignty – relatively uncontroversial when it comes to some of the functional agencies of the United Nations, hotly contested when it comes to the deeper integration promised by the European Union.

All told, there is much material for consideration here – understanding the relationship between sovereignty and the state is no simple task. Partly this is because the 'state' as that term came to be understood in the early modern period already entails the idea of sovereignty; it is precisely because the state comes to be understood as sovereign that it can be distinguished from the political entities that existed earlier. It is because of this entanglement that, in order to understand where we are today, we need to explore the origin of the notion of sovereignty and equally we need to understand its evolution over the last few centuries, and in particular the way in which it came to be entangled not just with the state but also with the nation. Accordingly, the first part of this chapter will focus on the emergence of competing ideas of sovereignty from the seventeenth through to the early twentieth centuries. In the second part of the chapter, the various competing notions of sovereignty current today will be examined and, finally, the re-emergence of a strong doctrine of sovereignty as a defining feature of contemporary populism will be explored.

Sovereignty as *dominium*

That the sovereign state emerged in Europe at the end of the 'long' sixteenth century (1492–1648) is a commonplace observation, and, for once, what is commonplace is essentially correct. During this long century, the religious unity of Europe was broken into several pieces, leading to large-scale internal strife in most parts of the continent; Renaissance learning introduced the political thought of the Greeks and, especially, the Romans to a wider audience than ever before; changes in military technology, the increased use of gunpowder and the development of expensive professional infantry, tilted the balance away from smaller political units who could no longer afford the new kit; and changes in the economy generated by the conquest of the Americas, and, later in the century, catastrophic climate change – all these factors created a Europe in 1650 that was dramatically different from that of 1500. Instead of a political order characterized by cross-cutting political allegiances based on an 'empire', territorial polities, cities, universities, the church and its religious orders, the local and the universal had by 1650 both given way to the territorial sovereign state as the key political actor of the new Europe (Nexon 2009; Parker 2013; Tilly 1975; see also Chapter 11). The sovereign state was 'sovereign' in so far as it was ruled by an individual who claimed that title – the small number of significant polities that claimed to be republics hardly undermine this generalization; the Doge in Venice, the Stadtholder in the Netherlands and the Protector in Commonwealth England may not have been sovereigns in the full sense of the term, but their existence supports the general proposition that personal rule was the norm.

These new sovereigns were different from their medieval predecessors. The latter generally had to accept that within their realms there would exist serious competitors – great magnates who were not easily coerced, proud cities with royal charters, monasteries and bishoprics that exercised independent power – and that externally the universal church would claim jurisdiction over matters spiritual while the Holy Roman Empire claimed a hazy overall jurisdiction. Political entities may have possessed territorial names – France, Aragon, Burgundy and so on – but their rulers could not establish effective control over these territories, nor were they believed to have the right to do so. Now, however, the new sovereigns acknowledged no internal equal and no external superior (Hinsley 1966); even in Catholic lands the universal church was tamed and could no longer shape the actions of rulers, and this was, of course, true also of the Lutheran and Calvinist lands. The great magnates were still of considerable political significance in some contexts but gradually lost their capacities to defy the monarch; Louis XIV of France drove the lesson home by requiring the nobility to reside at his new court in Versailles. Chartered cities whose power ultimately rested on their ability to close their gates to all comers found their walls could no longer protect them from rulers with the new cannons.

Sovereigns declared, and in many cases actually believed in, their divine right to rule, but some at least of their subjects wanted a rather more plausible justification for royal power. Hobbes, Pufendorf and Locke offered different accounts of the way in which sovereignty could be reconciled with the idea of natural law, the notion that there are conceptions of right and wrong that are not contingent, although Hobbes's account of the power of the sovereign gave the latter an almost unfettered right to determine the law (Skinner 2008). The idea of natural law could be traced back to medieval times and there is much high-quality contemporary scholarship on how thinkers of the seventeenth century understood the term (Tuck 1979) – but this may not be the best way to get into what sovereignty actually meant in this period. Instead, the notion of sovereignty as *dominium* offers a rather better way into the key issues.

Dominium is the Roman law term for real property, and Fredrich Kratochwil makes a good case for saying that it is the Renaissance rediscovery of this notion that forms the backdrop to the notion of sovereignty in the seventeenth century (Kratochwil 1995). Kratochwil traces the way in which medieval notions of rulership, according to which the prince stood enmeshed in a web of relationships with external and internal actors, came to be replaced by a world in which their sovereignty was understood in terms of *dominium*. Rulers came to think of themselves as owning their realms, and, just as one can dispose of one's own property as one wishes, so they could dispose of their states – this position supports a strong norm of non-intervention; unless rulers behave towards their own people in such a way as to cause a threat to the peace and security of other rulers, they are entitled to the protection of this norm.

This absolutist doctrine of sovereignty is often thought to have been endorsed in the Westphalia settlement of 1648, and later is certainly reflected in the positive international law of the nineteenth century, influenced as it was by the understanding of law as the command of a sovereign. Interestingly, it is also partially represented in the UN Charter of 1945. The Charter is intended to remove one of the traditional powers of sovereign states, the right to wage war, but it actually restates very firmly the doctrine that the state is sovereign in its own territory; Article 2(7): 'Nothing contained in the present Charter shall authorize the United Nations to intervene in matters which are essentially within the domestic jurisdiction of any state or shall require the Members to submit such matters to settlement under the present Charter; but this principle shall not prejudice the application of enforcement measures under Chapter VII.' Chapter VII concerns actions with respect to threats to the peace – the basic idea that states are sovereign within their own territory except in so for as their actions affect other sovereigns is thus preserved.

Still, within a very few years of the signing of the Charter, the 'domestic jurisdiction' clause was under threat; the newly independent Indian government argued that the apartheid system then being established in South Africa constituted a 'threat to international peace and security' under Chapter VII, and therefore overrode Article 2(7). This reinterpretation of 2(7) became the standard way in which domestic issues were raised at the UN, and has been used to justify a number of interventions over the decades (Wheeler 2000); it has become the legal link between the much expanded contemporary international human rights regime and the UN Charter. What is interesting in the current context is that this challenge to the absolutist account of sovereignty can actually be found repeatedly in the history of the states-system, starting at the very point at which the system was coalescing into something recognizable as a genuine international system.

Stephen Krasner has pointed out that the Westphalian treaties which allegedly produced this system actually endorsed intervention in a number of circumstances, mostly to do with protecting religious minorities; he asserts that the principle of non-intervention, though frequently affirmed, was as frequently violated; this is 'sovereignty as organised hypocrisy' (Krasner 1999; see also Teschke 2009). Krasner actually defines 'interventions' very widely to achieve this characterization – for example, by including limitations on sovereignty established by freely entered into treaties – but an important collection of essays put together by the historians Brendan Simms and David Trim establishes that specifically 'humanitarian' interventions have been a feature of the system throughout the period (Simms and Trim 2011). These interventions were sometimes justified by the 'threat to international peace and security' argument but equally were sometimes justified simply by reference to the violation of decent standards of behaviour by the ruler intervened against. The idea that sovereignty was always understood in absolute terms does not pass muster. The state may have been the property of the sovereign but how that property could legitimately be disposed of was always considered contestable.

In any event, in the 250 years after Westphalia, sovereignty gradually came to be understood as vested in the nation or the people, as opposed to an actual sovereign individual, which requires the notion of *dominium* – indeed sovereignty itself – to be understood in a new light (Bourke and Skinner 2016: Tuck 2016: Grimm 2015). If the nation is to be understood as the property of the people, as opposed to the property of an individual or a family, then the key question shifts from being how sovereignty is acquired or justified to being how the people actually govern themselves. Whereas in the seventeenth century the nature of sovereignty is the focus of the work of the leading political theorists of the age, by the nineteenth century sovereignty is no longer front and centre, being displaced by the study of government. There are two important exceptions to this generalization. First, in the new European empires popular sovereignty is explicitly denied and complex notions of suzerainty coexist with direct rule by foreigners; here, in the British case, the king-emperor is the sovereign property-owner in the empire, while at home the people are sovereign via their representation in Parliament (although the fiction of royal sovereignty, that of 'the King in Parliament' lasts longer here than elsewhere). The sovereignty of non-European peoples and states is not generally recognized unless they are able to meet the 'standards of civilization' laid down by Europeans. Second, in federal systems sovereignty is still crucial because it is not necessarily clear where it resides, in the units or in the whole. It took an enormously destructive civil war in America before 'these united states' became 'the United States' and the superiority of the federal centre was recognized – even then identifying the equivalent of 'the King in Parliament' is still problematic.

These complications stem partly from confusion over the difference between sovereignty as a *juridical status* and as a *political concept*. On the one hand, to say of a state that it is sovereign is to make a judgement about its legal position in the world – namely, that it recognizes no legal superior; that it is not, for example, a colony or part of a suzerain system. On the other hand, to say that a state is sovereign generally implies that it possesses certain sorts of capacities; the ability to act in certain ways, to perform certain tasks. One essential difference between these two meanings of sovereignty is that the first is unqualified – states either are, or are not, legally sovereign – while the second clearly involves matters of degree; that is, both the tasks themselves can be added to and subtracted from without losing the basic idea, and the manner in which they are performed can be more or less effective. On the one hand, we have sovereignty as a *status*, which states either possess or do not possess; and on the other, we have sovereignty as a *bundle of powers and capacities* that can become larger or smaller. The significance of these distinctions, incidentally, was inadvertently illustrated during the Brexit referendum in June 2016; those who wished Britain to leave the European Union made much of the idea of 'taking back control', by which they meant increasing Britain's powers and capabilities. Opponents of Brexit argued that, while leaving the EU might change Britain's status in that it would no longer be formally bound by the rules that accompanied EU membership, the actual bundle of powers it could exercise might not be increased, or even might be decreased; more on this below.

In any event, this distinction was of no great significance in the early years of the 'Westphalia System', because the powers that states exercised were limited in scope and range. Tax collection and 'pacification' – the establishment of law and order – were the main domestic activities of states, and warfare and imperialism the main external activities; here, differential capabilities were most striking, but this in no sense undermined the idea of anarchy – indeed, as Kenneth Waltz insists, a key feature of anarchy is that the units in an anarchical system try to perform the same functions with different capabilities (Waltz 1979). However, once it became accepted that among the functions of a sovereign state are the achievement of certain kinds of social goals, and the successful regulation, if not actual management, of the economy, the situation does change quite dramatically, because it is clear that exercising these powers effectively might well, in some circumstances, be impossible without external cooperation and a degree of *pooling* of sovereignty. Thus, to take a very simple example, one of the 'powers' a state has is the power to set up a postal service – but such a service will be of limited value unless it is possible to send and receive letters across state boundaries, and to arrange this effectively states have had to give up certain powers to an international body, originally the Universal Postal Union of 1874. The bundle of powers that a state possesses as a 'sovereign' body is thereby simultaneously diminished *and* enhanced – the state now has the capacity to set up an effective postal system, but it buys this capacity by giving up part of its capacity to regulate this system. Paradoxically, to be truly sovereign it may be necessary to surrender part of one's sovereignty.

Another way of putting the same point is that the 'fit' between state and society/economy has altered since the beginning of the Westphalia System. Initially, social policy was minimal, and economic activity was, for the most part, agricultural, local and small-scale. However, with the coming of manufacturing and the factory system, and recognition that efficiency gains – economies of scale – could be achieved via production for a wider market, the range and scope of economic activity expanded, and with it the possibilities for social policy. The first consequence here was a step up in the optimum size of states; Britain and France created 'single markets' by removing local obstacles to trade, while Germany moved from being a customs union to a single state. However, the needs of the new societies went beyond these steps, and gradually, from the 1860s onwards, regulatory international bodies were established: the International Telegraphic Union of 1865; the establishment of an International Bureau of Weights and Measures in 1875; and the International Labour Office in 1901 (Murphy 1994, 2008). In the twentieth century, the League of Nations and UN systems accelerated the institutionalization of functional cooperation, and institutions such as the IMF, the World Bank and the WTO attempted to regulate ever-wider areas of state activity. Each of these new institutions grew out of the exercise of sovereign powers, but each constituted a diminution of sovereignty, in the sense that here we have powers that can only be exercised effectively by a degree of pooling of sovereignty. This is a major theme of the second half of this chapter.

Sovereignty and the United Nations

The United Nations Charter is central to an understanding of modern notions of sovereignty for two reasons: first, because it removed the distinction between those nations entitled to claim to be sovereign and the rest; and, second, because it set out in black and white what would turn out to be the central contradiction concerning sovereignty for the next 75 years. In effect, the UN Charter resolved one issue by creating another.

In the nineteenth century the European states-system – and with it notions of sovereignty – came to dominate on a world scale. Non-European political systems were either incorporated into the European empires, losing the potential for sovereign status, or, for a small number of significant actors – China, Japan, the Ottoman Empire, Thailand – preserved a degree of independence but under the overall supervision of the Europeans. The basis for this latter supervision was that every state needed to reach the 'standards of civilization' that the Europeans were assumed to have achieved; these countries failed this test and were therefore required to accept that their laws did not apply to Europeans and that they would be supervised by their betters until they could put their houses into what the Europeans described as order (Gong 1984; see also Bull and Watson [1984] 2018). Naturally this inferior status was deeply resented and the countries concerned did their best to leave it; what was particularly iniquitous about the 'standards of civilization' was not their contents – such matters as the establishment of the rule of law and effective government – but the proposition that the European powers by definition met these standards and thus were entitled to sovereign status, while others had to prove their worthiness. The events of the first half of the twentieth century revealed the speciousness of this position, if any such revelation was required – after two World Wars, the Holocaust and the Gulag, claims of European superiority could hardly be sustained.

The regimes of capitulation associated with the standards of civilization had gone by 1945, and the UN Charter regularized the new situation. From now on, all states who were members of the UN would have equal rights (although the five permanent members of the UN Security Council would be more equal than the others). These states would find their war-making powers restricted by the UN Charter, but, as noted above, in other respects the UN Charter promulgates a very strong doctrine of sovereignty. Most founder members of the UN were actually European or of predominantly European descent, but the support the Charter gave to the norm of self-determination, combined with imperial exhaustion meant that soon, over the next 20 years, the old empires would more or less disappear and nearly 150 new UN state members would be able to claim the same sovereign rights as the original 50 signatories.

Doubts about some of these new claimants of sovereign status remained. Robert Jackson, a leading English School theorist of international relations has referred to some of these new states as 'quasi-states' (Jackson 1990). His point is that in the past the claim to be a sovereign state had positive and negative implications – it was a claim to be able to govern itself effectively (the positive side) and a claim that it should be allowed to do so without exterior interference (the negative side). Many of the new states made this negative claim but without the positive capacities required to make sense of it. Indeed, many of the new states required external aid in order to come close to making good their claim to be able to govern themselves. Be that as it may, the new states were able to claim sovereign status at the UN; international law does not recognize the category of 'quasi-state', whatever the political realities may be.

So, 1945 saw the formal end of the idea that non-Western states would be judged in accordance with the 'standards of civilisation' – but, at the same time as one discriminatory code was jettisoned, a new, formally non-discriminatory, code was signalled. The Preamble to the UN Charter states that the peoples of the United Nations 'reaffirm faith in fundamental human rights, in the dignity and worth of the human person, in the equal rights of men and women and of nations large and small'. The use of the term 'reaffirm' indicates that this is a commitment that has always been present, but, although David Boucher has argued in favour of the 'recognition theory of rights', this is actually a contentious claim (Boucher 2011); sovereign states in the past have clearly not believed in the equal rights of men and women, and the very term 'human rights', as opposed to the specific and limited rights that are based on a system of positive law, is innovatory.

The UN Charter itself does little to give flesh to the notion of human rights, but in 1948 the UN General Assembly adopted the Universal Declaration of Human Rights (UDHR) which became the basis upon which a very substantial legal regime has been created. It led directly to the two major Covenants of 1966 (*On Civil and Political Rights* and *On Economic, Social and Cultural Rights*) and to an extraordinary range of additional international and regional treaties and declarations – the authoritative *Brownlie's Documents on Human Rights* (2010) now runs to 1,296 pages – including the *Convention of the Prevention and Punishment of the Crime of Genocide (the Genocide Convention)* 1948, *The Convention on the Elimination of All Forms of Racial Discrimination* 1966, *The Convention on the Elimination of All Forms of Discrimination Against Women (CEDAW)* 1979, *The Convention Against Torture and Other Cruel, Inhuman or Degrading Treatment or Punishment* 1984, the *Convention on the Rights of the Child* 1989, and the *Declaration of the Rights of Indigenous Peoples* 2007, to name some of the most significant. Were all these legal documents to be regarded as authoritative and mandatory, the sovereign capacity of states to determine their own form of government and social and economic policies would obviously be severely limited.

In practice, states have regarded these legal documents as, at best, aspirational, and, in any event, for thirty years after the signing of the UDHR, as Samuel Moyn has documented, human rights were very much on the back burner (Moyn 2012). The Cold War put a damper on any serious politics of human rights, and the drive for self-determination (itself perhaps partially based on human rights) dominated the UN's agenda. More, although the UDHR and the later legal instruments set out the rights of individuals, they took the form of inter-state agreements, and the state was expected to be the deliverer of human rights. It was not until the 1970s that human rights came to be seen as something to be claimed *against* rather than *through* the state; the rise in significance of human rights NGOs such as Amnesty and Helsinki Watch (later the basis for Human Rights Watch) and the explicit espousal of human rights as a goal of US policy by President Carter in 1977 changed the nature of the discourse in significant ways.

The result of these changes was to create a somewhat confused relationship between the state and the notion of sovereignty. On the one hand, as we have seen, the UN Charter formalized in international law a very strong doctrine of state sovereignty, stronger in fact than anything that had come before on the so-called Westphalia System, and applying to all states – at least all states with UN membership. But, on the other hand, there were several ways in which this legal status was being undermined. First, some, indeed many, of the new states that emerged post-1945 were sovereign in name only, lacking the capacities for self-government that previously had been thought necessary for that status. Second, the pressures to pool sovereignty in order to solve practical problems identified above became more compelling as the various capitalist economies recovered from the devastation of the Second World War; formal integration of these economies was limited to Western Europe, but as global markets in trade and finance grew, and production increasingly came to be global in scope, all the industrial capitalist countries found themselves cooperating in ways that limited their capacity for sovereign action. And, third, in the background, the human rights regime posed a potential threat to any attempt to use the state sovereignty apparently guaranteed by the UN in order to protect a way of life that did not meet the required standards – admittedly this threat was potential rather than, in most cases, actual, but nonetheless it was perceived as real by those who marched to a different drummer from the international norm.

Sovereignty as responsibility

The contradictions identified above were present from the 1950s onwards but remained unresolved, and largely undiscussed, during the Cold War years. The theoretical problems posed by 'quasi-states' were concealed by the unwillingness of the major players in the Cold War to upset opinion in the Global South by drawing attention to them. The practical integration of Western capitalist economies was noted and discussed, but sidelined in the interests of anti-communist solidarity. Similarly, the possibility of giving teeth to the notion of human rights by developing a doctrine of humanitarian intervention, although addressed by some of the new rights-based NGOs and by some international theorists, could not be operationalized in a context where intervention by one side in the Cold War was more or less certain to generate a counter-intervention by the other (Wheeler 2000).

All this changed after the end of the Cold War. Setting aside for the moment intra-advanced world issues, the dynamics of human rights protection changed dramatically. On the one hand, now that the possibility of counter-intervention was no longer a consideration, humanitarian crises presented a genuine challenge for the international community, or, to put the matter more accurately, to the one remaining superpower, the United States, and its allies, who were then the only states with the capacity to act. On the other hand, the end of the Cold War actually created humanitarian crises in some areas of the Global South, most obviously in the Horn of Africa. During the Cold War, Ethiopia and Somalia had been client states of the Soviet Union and the United States respectively, preserving a balance of power as far as the important waterways of the Red Sea and the Horn were concerned, and keeping in power governments that, while not in any respect democratic, did at least provide the rudiments of law and order. When the superpowers withdrew (leaving behind a lot of weaponry) chaos followed, especially in Somalia. What followed set a standard for the practical problems and intellectual confusion of the interventions of the 1990s, with a US/UN intervention that failed to respect the sovereignty of Somalia, but also failed to provide the improvement in human rights that it was designed to produce.

There is no space to tell this story here, but the basic point is that, in this crisis, as in the crises generated by the Wars of the Yugoslav Succession, and, most tragically in the case of the Rwandan genocide, the sovereignty regime set up in 1945 was clearly at odds with the human rights regime created as part of the same post-war settlement. To respect the sovereignty of countries descending into chaos was to put in extreme jeopardy any notion of universal human rights, but to act to promote human rights was to violate the very regime of sovereignty that was valued in particular by those countries of the Global South who had only recently achieved independence (Coady et al. 2018; Weiss 2016; Teson and van der Vossen 2017).

Although the characteristic 1990s' response to this situation was pragmatic (and not particularly successful) there was more systematic and principled thinking going on and, at the end of the decade, this thinking bore fruit. The essential point of the new approach, promoted by some international lawyers (for example, Thomas Franck 1992), some governments (mostly Northern European) and some UN officials (in particular Francis Deng (1996) and Kofi Annan), was to argue that there are now new standards of international legitimacy which privilege human rights and democratic government over the traditional norm of non-intervention. Kofi Annan summarized the argument well in an article in *The Economist* on 16 September 1999.

> State sovereignty, in its most basic sense, is being redefined – not least by the forces of globalisation and international co-operation. States are now widely understood to be instruments at the service of their peoples, and not vice versa. At the same time individual sovereignty – by which I mean the fundamental freedom of each individual, enshrined in the charter of the UN and subsequent international treaties – has been enhanced by a renewed and spreading consciousness of individual rights. (Annan 1999)

This was an interesting conceptual move; in effect, the notion of sovereignty was being redefined as the property of individuals rather than, or as well as, that of states – and this time the individuals concerned were not to be the rulers but the ruled.

One important feature of the 1990s was that the crisis in the Balkans was regarded by the major Western countries as more important than crises in central Africa and the Congo, even though the latter were far more destructive in terms of human life. This is why the notion of 'sovereignty as responsibility' attracted substantial African support – a point worth bearing in mind when considering the often-heard claim that this notion is the product of liberal imperialism. In any event, in response to this new approach, the Canadian government sponsored the formation of an *International Commission on Intervention and State Sovereignty* (ICISS) in 2000 to attempt to answer a specific question posed by Annan: 'if humanitarian intervention is, indeed, an unacceptable assault on sovereignty, how should we respond to a Rwanda, to a Srebrenica – to gross and systematic violations of human rights that affect every precept of our common humanity?' The ICISS was co-chaired by former Australian Foreign Minister Gareth Evans, and Algerian and UN diplomat Mohamed Sahnoun – other members included Canadian philosopher Michael Ignatieff, US Congressman Lee Hamilton, South African Trade Union leader (and post-2018, President) Cyril Ramaphosa, Russian human rights activist Vladimir Lukin and Indian/UN civil servant and academic Ramesh Thakur.

Their report, published in December 2001, attempts to shift the emphasis away from a right to undertake humanitarian interventions, towards the idea of a responsibility to protect (sometimes RtP or R2P) (ICISS 2001). In the report, the responsibility to protect rests initially with the state itself; sovereignty is justified in terms of a responsibility to protect populations. But when the state is unwilling or unable to act to end mass atrocities or humanitarian disasters, or when the state is actually perpetrating mass atrocities, the principle of non-intervention must yield to an international responsibility to protect. The responsibilities of the international community are threefold: to do all in its power to prevent mass atrocities in the first place; to react to them if they occur; and to rebuild the society in question post-conflict. In extreme cases (defined by conventional just-war criteria – just cause, last resort, proportionality) it may the duty of the international community to act militarily, as authorized by (another just-war criterion) 'right authority', deemed to be, in the first instance at least, the UN Security Council. The Security Council should establish guidelines to govern its responses to claims for military intervention, and the Permanent Five powers should agree not to cast vetoes when these criteria are met. In the absence of agreement in the Security Council, if there is a clear-cut case, the UN General Assembly and Regional Organizations are mentioned as sources of legitimacy.

The timing of the ICISS report was inauspicious. December 2001 was three months after the terrorist attacks of 9/11 and the subsequent Global War on Terror changed the appetite for reform of the rules on intervention; the UN Security Council was relatively unified in 2001, but oriented towards punishing terrorism rather than the wider issue of intervention. Still, the report regained significance in the context of the UN's 60th Anniversary World Summit in September 2005. The UN Secretary-General's High-Level Panel on Threats, Challenges and Change, established in 2004 preparatory to the World Summit, included Gareth Evans in its membership and adopted much of the language of the ICISS report, which in turn was adopted in the World Summit Outcome final document. The most important section of the latter in this context reads:

> The international community, through the United Nations, also has the responsibility to use appropriate diplomatic, humanitarian and other peaceful means, in accordance with Chapters VI and VIII of the Charter, to help protect populations from genocide, war crimes, ethnic cleansing and crimes against humanity. In this context, we are prepared to take collective action, in a timely and decisive manner, through the Security Council, in accordance with the Charter, including Chapter VII, on a case-by-case basis and in cooperation with relevant regional organizations as appropriate, should peaceful means be inadequate and national authorities manifestly fail to protect their populations from genocide, war crimes, ethnic cleansing and crimes against humanity. (§139)

This formulation is sometimes referred to as 'R2P Lite' because it drops a lot of the detail of the ICISS report, in particular the latter's proposals for curbs of the veto power. This form of words achieved consensus, but on the basis that no new legal obligations were being created. Still, the result was that the idea of a responsibility to protect became 'mainstreamed' in the UN system. The Summit Outcome Document led to the appointment of a Special Adviser on R2P in 2008 and, most importantly, the Secretary-General's report of 2009 on the Implementation of the Responsibility to Protect. In effect, R2P language has become the language of choice for the UN in dealing with mass atrocities – though state discourse has only taken up this language to a limited degree.

In terms of principle, several criticisms of the doctrine of R2P have been made. Protection, it can be argued, is overemphasized as the function of the state and treated as something that can be divorced from politics and interests (Brown 2013); it has been argued by, for example, Anne Orford that, if the UN Security Council were actually capable of acting as the ICISS report intended, it would constitute an undemocratic, bureaucratic 'world government' with powers far beyond those envisaged by the framers of the UN Charter (Orford 2011). In practice, the UN Security Council is rarely united, and for that reason the more serious problems with the notion of responsibility to protect are practical rather than principled.

One of the goals of the ICISS report was to differentiate R2P from humanitarian intervention, disassociating the former from the imperialistic implications of the latter (Evans 2009; Bellamy 2009). In fact, the two notions are indeed very different – humanitarian intervention is based on the idea that the sovereignty norm of non-intervention is generally valid but can sometimes, in extreme circumstances, be overridden, whereas the responsibility to protect denies the validity of the norm of non-intervention, replacing it with a new understanding of sovereignty (Brown 2018). This is, potentially, a radical change. One aim of this chapter is to show that the meaning of sovereignty has always been contested and that an account of the concept that stresses the absolute autonomy of the state – sovereignty as *dominium* in its purest form – has never been widely accepted, but, still, this new understanding of sovereignty, if generally accepted, would be a radical break with the past. In fact, there is little evidence that it is generally accepted. The attempt to persuade states, especially states in the Global South, that the responsibility to protect is genuinely different from humanitarian intervention has been unsuccessful. Many states maintain a principled commitment to a traditional understanding of sovereignty and the non-intervention norm and do not wish to commit to a change in this area of international law, and other states are suspicious of the proposed new norm because they believe it likely that it will be used against their interests.

The politics of R2P and the new meaning of sovereignty in the practice of the UN and other bodies have not been encouraging for those wishing to promote the new norm. The language of R2P has indeed been used with some success in some conflicts in Africa, but elsewhere the record has been poor. Intervention in Libya in 2011 was initially seen as a success for R2P but the unwarranted expansion of the mandate by the interveners from protecting civilians to overthrowing the Gadhafi regime was widely regarded as illegitimate, and the failure to follow through with state-building after the fall of Gadhafi has left the country in a parlous state (*Ethics & International Affairs* 2011; Hehir and Murray 2013). Partly in reaction to this failure, the UN has not been able to employ R2P notions effectively to end the conflict in Syria, or the currently almost equally damaging war in Yemen (Bellamy 2014). In short, while the notion of a responsibility to protect is a genuinely innovative attempt to square the circle of respect for sovereignty and human rights protection, as of now it cannot be described as a success.

Conclusion: 'Taking back control'

The contradiction between the sovereignty and human rights norms has obvious implications for all states, not just those of the Global South, but in the world of advanced capitalist states, most of which are committed in their domestic arrangements to the protection of human rights, this contradiction is of less potential significance than that created by the necessity to pool sovereignty in order to promote economic growth and allow for the expansion of global markets. With the ending of the Cold War, which provided solid practical reasons for the advanced capitalist world to stick together, one might have expected increased tension in intra-capitalist relations, but such tension did not, in fact, materialize. Even after the financial crash of 2008, the political classes of the advanced countries of the West have managed their relations without resolving, or indeed acknowledging, the situation created by the necessity for such high levels of cooperation. The political elites of the European Union perhaps understood the situation rather better than those of the United States, whose size made it easier to maintain the illusion of sovereign independence. After the crisis broke in 2008 many commentators assumed that action would have to be taken to assert some kind of more effective international control of the financial markets, but such action has not, in fact, materialized; instead, we have seen a decade of austerity and a continuing slow-motion crisis (Tooze 2018).

But if the political classes of the advanced industrial world lost contact with the notion of sovereignty, focused as they have been elsewhere, that is on the smooth running of the world economy, there have been other political forces which have been less insouciant about the pooling of sovereignty. The last two decades, and especially the last decade, have seen the rise of populism both of the left and of the right (see Chapter 14). The harsh requirements of the eurozone in Greece after 2008 which led to stratospherically high levels of youth unemployment and general immiseration produced the left-populist Coalition of the Radical Left (Syriza) government in 2015, and similar forces have produced a coalition of left and right populists in Italy in 2018. In Europe as a whole it is now the case that between roughly one-fifth and one-quarter of votes go to populist parties – a higher percentage in France, lower in Germany and Scandinavia. In the United States, populists have actually taken over one of the established parties – especially after the mid-term elections of 2018, the Republican Party is now the Trump Party, with 'Never Trump' Republicans either surrendering or leaving the party. On both sides of the Atlantic, populism has been partly driven by opposition to immigration, and, in particular in Europe, to the waves of refugees and immigrants who have arrived in recent years from Africa, the Middle East and Afghanistan. Still, a wider concern with loss of sovereignty is in some respects more significant than immigration as a driver. The successful campaign to leave the European Union in the UK showed the way here – immigration was clearly a central concern of 'Leave' voters, but the most compelling slogan – one that can serve for all the populist movements – was 'take back control' (Eatwell and Goodwin 2018).

As noted above, campaigners for leaving the EU did not have a clear understanding of the nature of sovereignty. 'Taking back control', on the face of it, understands sovereignty in terms of the powers and capabilities that a state can exercise, and it is by no means clear that changing the status of the UK by leaving the EU would actually increase the capabilities of the British state. The ability to control one's own borders, so important given the concern with immigration, does constitute such an increase, but if it is bought by giving up influence in other areas, the overall balance in terms of 'taking back control' may be negative, leaving a formally independent UK with less control over the life of the nation than before.

But it is clear that for many of the Brexiteers all this is by the by – they place great store on the formal independence of the nation, and are less concerned with the detailed implications of that independence than are the political elites who have largely lost interest in such symbolic matters but who focus precisely on the managerial aspects of contemporary politics. Sovereignty as a status no longer has much meaning for such elites – but it still has significance for large numbers of ordinary people, even if the same ordinary people have only a hazy idea of what the term means (Goodhart 2017). Symbolic issues, such as the colour of British passports, act as place-holders for sovereignty and the values associated with patriotism, values that have little meaning for the elites, Goodhart's 'anywheres', but which are still of great importance for his 'somewheres', those non-elite members of society who feel, largely with justification, that the benefits of globalization have passed them by.

Taking back control of one's life circumstances may not actually be achievable in current conditions, but the strength of the desire to do so is undeniable. This, I suggest, is the true significance of the notion of sovereignty today. For the political theorist, sovereignty is a conundrum, a concept that has too many meanings, too complicated a past to be of much use in understanding the present. For the political classes of the advanced capitalist world, it is either an irrelevance, of no significance for the ways in which they go about their business, or a positive menace, interfering with their freedom of action. But for ordinary people in the West and, indeed, for the peoples of the Global South, it is a concept that, however hazily understood, is still of central, if largely symbolic, importance.

Further Reading

Bourke, R. and Q. Skinner (2016), *Popular Sovereignty in Historical Perspective*, Cambridge: Cambridge University Press.

Eatwell, R. and M. Goodwin (2018), *National Populism: The Revolt against Liberal Democracy*, London: Pelican Books.

Goodhart, D. (2017), *The Road to Somewhere: The Populist Revolt and the Future of Politics*, London: Hurst & Co.

Tuck, R. (2016), *The Sleeping Sovereign* Cambridge: Cambridge University Press.

10

The State and Security

Pinar Bilgin

Introduction

During the 1990s, at a time when critical approaches were making inroads into the study of security, R.B.J. Walker (1997) issued an important caution, reminding us that our thinking about security had, until then, been about the modern state and its relations with other states, and that any rethinking on security would have to also involve rethinking the state. Thinking about (let alone beyond) the state did not, at the time, have that much of a legacy to draw upon in the study of security. Indeed, scholarly elaborations on the state-security relationship had, until then, seldom gone beyond cursory references to Weber, Mann or Tilly. Given that protecting the state has been a central preoccupation in the study of security, such a degree of inattentiveness to understanding statehood comes across as paradoxical.

Critical approaches have come a long way since then, exploring the ways in which the relationship between state and security could be understood differently 'depending on whether one adopts a liberal, Marxist, realist, constructivist, postmodern feminist – or whatever – approach to interpreting the state' (Booth 2007: 188). For realists, states are the basic units of analysis as well as the locus of concentration for political loyalty and scholarly attention (as per the contractarian understanding; see below). For feminists, such understandings of the state-security relationship and the practices that they shape have sustained insecurities experienced by the most vulnerable in society (Peterson 1992b). This is because the state is one of several structures that perpetuate a hegemonic masculinity that allows violence against women to occur (Ling 2002; Shepherd 2007). From a Marxist perspective, security has functioned as a system of 'order-building' by the United States 'domestically via social security and internationally via national security' throughout the twentieth century and beyond (Neocleous 2008: 8). For poststructuralists, security is a 'political technology of the body, the economy and the state simultaneously' (Burke 2008: 11). Accordingly, poststructuralism understands the relationship between security and the state in not (only) functional (as with defence) but (also) productive terms: 'on this view, states, acting as unitary authoritative entities, perform violence, but violences, in the name of security, also perform states', write Laura Shepherd and Jutta Weldes (2008: 535; see also Chapter 8). Finally, from a postcolonial perspective, it is not only the material riches that were transferred from one part of the globe to another but also the very practice of securing colonies that has been constitutive of state institutions of both the colonizers and the colonized. The argument being that 'without addressing the process of colonisation itself as part of state formation' (Bhambra 2018: 200) neither the colonized nor the colonizing states or their insecurities can be understood (Barkawi and Laffey 2006).

What follows lays out the complex relationship between the state and security in three parts. Section 1 is titled 'the state in security' and looks at how the state-security relationship has been understood in the study of world politics. Section 2 ('the state as security?') considers the ways in which state practices do not always fit prevalent assumptions re: state as 'protector'. Section 3 underscores the need for studying 'connected and entangled histories' of the state-security relationship.

The state in security

In familiar (and admittedly Eurocentric) narratives (see section 3), thinking about security and state share a birthday in the seventeenth century. Thomas Hobbes, who wrote in civil war conditions (Koselleck 2000), is accepted as having offered an early articulation of the contractarian approach to the state and security relationship (see section 2 for further discussion). To quote Keith Krause and Michael Williams (1997: 40),

> In a conception most commonly (if somewhat erroneously) identified with Thomas Hobbes, the individual subject as autonomous rational actor is confronted by an environment filled with other similar actors. These others

are a source of insecurity … From this starting point, there can be no security in the absence of authority, the state.[1]

Critical approaches have highlighted two limitations of such an understanding of the state-security relationship: (1) a naturalized notion of state (as prior to social interaction and fixed); (2) an emphasis on the need to maintain the state as the primary referent of security, especially at a time when states' capacity and/or willingness as security provider (agent of security) is put under closer scrutiny.[2]

The first limitation is that security was equated with protecting the state while presuming that it is constituted prior to social interaction, thereby failing to consider the state as work in progress, with political actors (re)shaping their gendered/racial/class-based interests and identities at the same time as mobilizing resources in their defence. As such, the separation of security thinking from 'most basic questions of political theory' (Walker 1997: 63) has impoverished our understanding of statehood. When states and their insecurities are naturalized as such, what is left is 'focusing attention onto the acquisition of security for the state' and very little else (Shepherd and Weldes 2008: 530).

An important exception to those studies that have naturalized the state is David Campbell's 1992 book *Writing Security*, where the author analyses the ways in which US policies of defending against the Soviet Union helped to construct and sustain a particular 'American political identity' that served its domestic and international interests. While such understandings are customarily explained away with reference to American identity as a 'melting pot' and therefore bearing little relevance for understanding other parts of the world, Campbell's study offers insights of relevance beyond the US context. The author writes:

> All states are marked by an inherent tension between the various domains that need to be aligned for an imagined political community to come into being – such as territoriality and the many axes of identity – and the demand that such an alignment is a response to (rather than constitutive of) a prior and stable identity. (Campbell 1992: 11)

Put differently, what is being secured in the United States is constituted and sustained even as policies are formulated in its defence. The implication of

---

[1]For a postcolonial reading of the Hobbesian notion of the 'state of nature', see Beier (2002); Mamdani (2020).
[2]The point that so-called 'state failure' does not take place in a vacuum is taken up in section 3.

Campbell's analysis is that all states are works in progress in so far as 'the tension between the demands of identity and the practices that constitute it can never be fully resolved, because the performative nature of identity can never be fully revealed' (Campbell 1992: 11).

Be that as it may, how was it possible to sustain such inattentiveness to statehood in the study of security? Arguably, this was due to our unacknowledged and unquestioned embrace of realist assumptions regarding statehood: that states already fulfil their contractual obligations and provide security 'inside'; and that they are primarily busy with defending citizens vis-à-vis 'outside'. Section 2 will look at these two assumptions in counterpoint to state practices around the world. Before doing so, let us consider the second issue that the critics highlighted as a limitation in understanding the 'state in security'.

The second limitation has to do with the emphasis put on the state *both* as protector (agent of security) *and* as needing protection (the referent of security). On the one hand, equating security with defending the state can be understood in terms of US Cold War exigencies. Indeed, the study of security was shaped largely in response to Cold War fears and policy incentives in the United States. During these early years, states were treated as the primary unit of analysis in the attempt to introduce some neatness to the complexity of studying world politics. The focus on states was deemed necessary partly because the complex task of dealing with non-state actors would not have produced the neat and tidy analyses a 'scientific' approach to the study of security was presumed to demand. It was also because the apparent urgency of Cold War concerns made it difficult for its students to undertake the kind of complex analyses that the study of non-state actors (in all their diversity) required (Tickner 1997). As assumptions adopted for the reasons of political expediency and/or disciplinary exigency came to be mistaken for 'reality', we began to lose sight of the complexities of world politics. This is how, in Cynthia Enloe's (1996: 189) memorable words, the study of state in world politics 'too often ends up looking like a Superman comic strip, whereas it probably should resemble a Jackson Pollock'.

Yet, on the other hand, we have failed to appreciate how state-centric analyses, however unintendedly, have resulted in the entrenchment of statism. The less complexity our analyses revealed, the less complicated the world seemed to us, and the easier it became to rely on exclusively state-centric analytical frameworks. Consequently, the less naive it seemed to hold on to the assumption that 'inside' the state is a realm of security, and that states deserved our loyalty and protection against threats originating from 'outside'. Let me elaborate.

In the study of security, state-centrism is considered as analytically distinct from statism. State-centrism is viewed as a methodological agreement by those scholars who modelled the study of world politics after the natural sciences by creating a 'closed system' (by identifying states as the actors to focus on, assuming them to be like units and focusing on the military dimension of security). Statism, in turn, is viewed as a normative disposition involving 'the concentration of all loyalty and decision-making power at the level of the sovereign state' (Booth 1998: 52). Understood as such, the analytical distinction between state-centrism and statism comes across as straightforward. It is possible, in theory, to eschew statism but utilize a state-centric research framework (see, for example, Buzan, Waever et al. 1998). Yet, this distinction has proven difficult to sustain in practice. Over the years, state-centric approaches to the study of security have reinforced statism by way of rendering less than visible other referents and agents of security. I will highlight two issues here.

First, if the study of security has been dominated by portrayals of states as primary (if not sole) protectors of citizens, this is not because there are no others who serve as agents of security – military or non-military. The invisibility, in the study of security, of the practices of non-state actors has resulted in their role as protectors of citizens being overlooked, even as some constitute a threat to state monopoly of violence. In recent years, the role played by non-state actors as agents of security has received better recognition by scholars who study 'global security assemblages'. The notion of 'assemblage' allows us to think about the emergence and/or empowerment of new actors beyond the binary of 'retreat of or return to' the state, but approaches the field of security in terms of 'settings where a range of different global and local, public and private security agents and normativities interact, cooperate and compete to produce new institutions, practices, and forms of security governance' (Abrahamsen and Williams 2009: 3).

Second, the state's dominant position as the actor best endowed to provide certain aspects of security does not warrant adopting a state-centred (let alone statist) approach to security. To draw on Ken Booth's (1991: 320) house analogy, 'there is obviously a relationship between the well-being of the sheltered and the state of the shelter, but can there be any question as to whose security is primary?' Indeed, the argument that 'since it is states that act for security, their security should be given primacy in our analyses' indicates a confusion of agents and referents (Bilgin 2002). Over the years such conflation of agents and referents in the study of security has re-entrenched statism, even as individual scholars sought to distance themselves from adopting such a normative position. Certainly, there is no yardstick to help us answer the question: when is a state secure? A staple of anti-nuclear protest movements during the Cold War, this question was raised once again during Hurricane Katrina, when a global power at war in Afghanistan and Iraq for reasons of state security failed to protect its own citizens, thereby presenting an instance of Booth's house analogy (see section 2 for further discussion).

This is not to deny the salience of the role states play in the realm of security; they remain significant actors with crucial roles to play. Rather, it is to argue that our failure to recognize the important roles that are already being played by non-state actors has ended up granting oversized recognition to state agency. It is in this sense that state-centric approaches to security do not simply reflect a field characterized by the centrality of states, but also help constitute statism. Over the years, analytical choices made by analysts (i.e. choosing to focus on the state) have had normative implications (according primacy to the state as agent and referent) even as the very same states have failed to fulfil their protective duties.

To recap: in the study of security, our understanding of state has suffered from two limitations: 1) a naturalized notion of state (as prior to social interaction); 2) an emphasis on the need to protect the state (referent of security). The emergence of constructivist and international political sociological approaches has, to a large extent, remedied the first limitation. However, the second limitation has persisted, even as states' capacity and/or willingness to fulfil their protective duties has come to be questioned – be it under conditions of globalization or the Global War on Terror. This is what we turn to in section 2.

The state as security?

The assumption that states already fulfil their obligations and provide security 'inside' is drawn from a contractarian understanding of the state-security relationship (Krause 1998). States are understood as deserving of our loyalty and protection by virtue of providing security to citizens. Yet, this is what we assume! As feminist students of security have maintained for a long time, and as the Global War on Terror has further exposed, state practices often belie such assumptions (Enloe 1990, 2010; Tickner 1995).

To begin with, some states do not seem to be in the business of providing security to their citizens, let alone to 'outsiders'. Examples include what Booth (1991: 313) referred to as 'protection rackets' that 'resemble mafia neighbourhoods ... rather than the national societies of our text-books'. Here, Booth's reminder is not only about the perils of assuming all states to be the same but also the fact that some states constitute a significant source of insecurity, be it in the form of structural or direct violence.[3] Accordingly, the operative word in the quote above is not 'national' (i.e. absence of a nation-state) but 'societies' (i.e. weak state-society relations).[4] More often than not, what is missing from such states is a lack of openness vis-à-vis the society (mostly but not exclusively) because of 'rentier' economies (Beblawi and Luciani 1987) where a resource-rich state fails to respond to the concerns of its citizenry, due to the particularity of state-society dynamics. The point is that such states channel their resources to bolster regime security via establishing coalitions with key domestic and international actors, thereby turning upside down the aforementioned assumptions regarding security provision. That the international context (be it the Cold War, great power rivalry over resources and/or markets, or the Global War on Terror) has not always been conducive to, and is sometimes outright inhibitive of, building capacity in some such states is a factor that often goes unnoticed, as Siba Grovogui (2002) has underscored.

Even in the case of those states that do provide security to their citizens, this often happens at the expense of 'outsiders' who are rendered less secure, as with citizens of target states who are threatened with annihilation via weapons of mass destruction (WMD). The logic of nuclear deterrence rests on the unavoidability of seeking security 'at home' via threatening others 'abroad' with annihilation (Cohn 1987). During the Cold War, the proponents of 'common security' and 'non-offensive defence' highlighted the unstable nature of 'peace' generated through nuclear deterrence and called for security sought together with others and not against them. Yet, in the post-Cold War period, those nuclear states who acquired their weapons before 1970 have tended to portray others (i.e. proliferators) as the problem, rendering invisible the ways in which security maintained through nuclear

---

[3]On structural vs. direct violence, see Galtung (1969).

[4]Following Mahmood Mamdani (2020), the persistence of so-called 'state failure' could be understood in terms of the prevalence of a particular form of statehood defined in terms of a 'nation' and that it needs decolonizing toward understanding occurrences of violence in the name of building and securing a 'nation', without conflating 'nation' and political community that constitutes the state.

deterrence renders peoples insecure, regardless of whether they abide by the provisions of the Non-Proliferation Treaty or not (Biswas 2014).[5] What is more, it is not only 'outsiders' who are rendered insecure as states resort to nuclear deterrence. Insecurities experienced by 'insiders' in nuclear power states include those who work at nuclear weapons facilities or live next to nuclear test sites (Gusterson 2004), and the human subjects of Cold War radiation studies (Lee 1995).

Granted, the very logic of citizenship rests on providing security for citizens at the expense of 'outsiders'. Hence Barry Hindess's (2000: 1489–1490) characterization of 'citizenship as conspiracy against the rest of the world'. That said, discriminatory measures toward 'outsiders' have varied over the years, becoming particularly acute in the aftermath of 9/11 when immigrants came to be identified by many as a threat to national security, the response being to mobilize statist and militarist practices (Doty 1998, Bilgin 2016c).

A formidable challenge to the first assumption (that states need defending by virtue of security they provide to citizens) has come from those scholars and activists who have laid bare the ways in which citizens may be rendered insecure in the name of 'national security'. Feminist scholars and activists in particular have taken issue with the assumption that states are in the business of providing protection to all their citizens (see Chapter 6). They have done so through highlighting insecurities experienced by women. For instance, 'base women' in the developing world were rendered insecure, wrote Cynthia Enloe (1990), even as they helped to keep those military bases running. That military bases may be a source of insecurity for the broader public was an issue that was highlighted by women who set up Greenham Common Women's Peace Camp to protest the placement of (nuclear-headed) cruise missiles in the UK in the early 1980s. Activists were concerned with not only nuclear contamination but also with Western Europe becoming a theatre in a potential nuclear war (Sylvester 1994). Carol Cohn (1987) highlighted how the nuclear edifice was kept together by gendered security-speak which underemphasized human insecurities and suffering while making it easier for strategists to practise the unthinkable. Taken together, feminist scholars and activists highlighted the ways in which theorists and other practitioners of security overlooked insecurities that states generated for their own citizens – all in the name of 'national security' (see also Chapter 6).

A present-day instance of how citizens may be rendered insecure while practising 'national security' is from August 2005 when Hurricane Katrina

---

[5] On the 'nuclear orientalism' of current thinking about WMD, see Gusterson (1999).

relief efforts fell short of what is expected from a great power, rendering thousands of people homeless while local and federal actors struggled to provide relief. To quote Karin Fierke (2007: 200):

> It is not only that it took more than five days to launch a relief effort. Or that the delay raised serious questions about whether the government would have acted more quickly if primarily white middle-class people were starving and in danger of their lives. The images of New Orleans revealed a stratum of American society that, on a day-to-day basis, and for over a century, has been stranded and imprisoned in a desperate situation, from which they were unable to escape and from which no one would rescue them.

Lest it be thought that no single power would be able to respond to such a 'natural disaster' and that this instance by no means reflects poorly on the United States as a security provider, three issues are worth highlighting.

One, Hurricane Katrina happened at a time when the United States was deeply involved in two wars in another part of the world: in Afghanistan and Iraq. By then the cause of the war on Iraq had already turned out to be less than compelling, due not only to US failure to find an active WMD programme in Iraq but also the revelations regarding the feeble nature of the intelligence reports that were used to justify the war. US involvement in two overseas wars in the name of 'national security', while failing to provide for its citizens' basic security needs at home, turned on its head the Hobbesian contractarian assumption.

Two, as reflexive approaches to the study of risk have laid bare, so-called 'natural disasters' are not natural but human-made in so far as they are the consequences of human decisions and actions (Beck 1992). In this particular instance, such actions included undercutting the Federal Emergency Management Administration (FEMA) which is the institution that would customarily take care of relief efforts. Set up during the Cold War years to address the effects of the potential use of chemical or nuclear weapons, FEMA was given cabinet status in the 1990s and was tasked with a broader range of emergency management duties. Shortly after 2000, FEMA lost not only its cabinet status but also its funding. After September 11, it was subsumed under the Department of Homeland Security. By the time of Hurricane Katrina, FEMA had an inexperienced director and had lost much of its resources to Homeland Security as part of the Global War on Terror. Since the National Guard had left for Iraq and Afghanistan, they were not able to return quickly and/or with the necessary equipment.

Three, when the relief effort arrived in New Orleans, it turned out to have a 'militarized' (and sometimes racialized) face. For one thing, whatever resources were mobilized after Katrina turned out to be more fitting for fighting a nuclear, chemical or terrorist attack and not a civilian emergency (Zunes 2005). For another,

> The white armed men who looked passively down at the black masses in the convention centre became white armed men in armoured vehicles or speed boats, who focused more on stopping black male looters than feeding, comforting or evacuating desperate people or burying the already dead. A militarized and masculine image of control replaced the crying and desperate voices of women begging for food, help and protection. (Fierke 2007: 200– 201)

In case insecurities experienced by US citizens during Hurricane Katrina come across as unique to this particular context, it is worth underscoring that militarization of domestic protection is not particular to any geography or time (Enloe 1983). In the post-Cold War period, domestic security provision in various parts of the world was militarized as both the equipment and experiences of the military were transferred to the police (see Hönke and Müller 2016; Coyne and Hall 2018). Hence Fierke's (2007: 201) conclusion that Katrina 'revealed a global experience, where militarization takes priority over human needs'.

So much for the realist assumption that states already fulfil their contractual obligations and provide security 'inside'. The other realist assumption regarding statehood is that states primarily focus on defending against threats from 'outside' the state boundaries, the corollary being that it is only so-called 'failing' or 'weak' (Bilgin and Morton 2002) states which are outside the 'norm' in that they focus their efforts on fighting internal threats, sometimes targeting their own citizens as they do so. Yet, it is not only 'failing' or 'weak' states that are busy with threats 'inside'. After the September 11 attacks and the onset of the Global War on Terror, multiple states instituted a version of the US Department of Homeland Security, bringing 'internal' and 'external' security agencies under one roof. Furthermore, externalization policies that the European Union have followed have a longer history than the Global War on Terror. Through these practices, the European Union increasingly began to defend against 'external' threats 'at home', while at the same time EU actors sought to address 'internal' concerns beyond borders in collaboration with neighbouring countries. This is what Didier Bigo (2001) referred to as 'the merging of internal and external security' by the European Union. To recapitulate, it is not only 'failing' or 'weak' states that focus their efforts on fighting 'internal' threats; what is more, such focus on the 'internal' is not exceptional to the Global War on Terror but was observed in state practices around the world during the Cold War and beyond.

Indeed, as Campbell's research on the United States showed (see above), during the Cold War, the United States was very much preoccupied with internal threats. Also consider Mark Neocleous's (2006) research where the author laid bare the ways in which both domestic and international interests were served through US security policies in the run-up to and in the aftermath of the Second World War. Neocleous's study points to the material dynamics and interests at work during this period when US policymakers utilized the notions of 'social security' at home and 'national security' abroad to produce a particular 'social order'. The author argued that, from President Roosevelt's New Deal to the Truman Doctrine,

> in the space of 15 years the concept 'economic security' moved from being a key ideological trope for reorienting individuals, classes and corporations around a new form of capitalist order, under the rubric of 'social security', to being a key factor in the US attempt to shape the world in an anti-communist fashion, under the rubric of 'national security'. (Neocleous 2006: 380)

Understood thus, US national security policies were not merely designed to defend 'our way of life' but were also constitutive of that particular way of living which, in turn, was sustained through global political-economic relations.

Finally, state practices of pointing to exigencies of threats 'outside' to explain and justify insecurities generated for citizens ('inside') are not new. During the 1950s, leaders of revolutionary Arab republics such as Egypt's President Nasser asked their citizens to be patient and make sacrifices until the 'Arab world' was secured. While that moment never came, citizens continued to make sacrifices in the name of 'national security'. Women suffered disproportionately in the process, argued Fatima Mernissi (1992), as they felt discouraged from voicing their gendered insecurities for fear that such claims would be viewed as less than patriotic. As recently as the 1991 and 2003 wars on Iraq, the same governments continued to point to threats to 'national security' to explain away their failings in addressing citizens' insecurities.

As part of the Global War on Terror, citizens of the United States and United Kingdom, among others, have found their rights and liberties to be compromised (often without their knowledge) as part of post-9/11 surveillance practices (Bauman et al. 2014). The issue here is not about seeking to 'balance' the needs of the state and citizens; 'balance' is in fact a misleading metaphor, argued Bigo and his co-authors (2010: 210) for, 'balance … presumes that just two values are being evaluated and that these two values are measurable on the same scale, subject to the same calculation'. Yet the 'balance' metaphor is regularly invoked, as if threats emerge independently of policymakers' recognition and interpretation of phenomena, the presumption being that only after 'outside' insecurities have been addressed will the state be able to stop asking citizens to make sacrifices. Contrariwise (and building on discussions above about the state as work in progress) neither states nor the threats that they face are prior to social interaction. Political actors (re)shape their gendered/racial/class-based interests and identities at the same time as mobilizing resources in their defence (Weldes 1999).

Indeed, different citizens have experienced insecurities differently, depending on their gender, race, class and/or geographical location. This is because even apparently 'neutral' surveillance technologies have racialized consequences, to focus on race. The very notion of 'racialising surveillance' refers to 'those moments when enactments of surveillance reify boundaries and borders along racial lines, and where the outcome is often discriminatory treatment' (Browne 2012: 72). A case in point are second- and third-generation immigrants and/or minorities in North America and Western Europe, who are 'insiders' by virtue of citizenship, but have nevertheless found themselves 'outside' by virtue of their cultural identity (Balibar 2005).

'Intertwined and overlapping histories' of the state-security relationship

Amidst post-Cold War discussions on globalization and the so-called 'retreat' of the state, and post-September 11 debates on the Global War on Terror and the so-called 'return' to the state, it is easy to lose sight of the ways in which state and security have historically had a mutually constitutive relationship. This is what section 3 focuses on: 'connected and entangled histories' of the state-security relationship in world politics. In this telling, the history of the state-security relationship does not begin in the seventeenth century (see section 1) but extends to the age of colonization, when not only material riches but also ideas and practices were transferred from one part of the world to another (Mamdani 2020). The very practice of securing and sustaining colonies has been constitutive of state institutions of both the colonizers and the colonized (Barkawi 2005). In the absence of insight into 'intertwined and overlapping histories' (Said 1993) of the state-security relationship, our understanding of both the so-called 'First' and 'Third' worlds has suffered.[6]

To begin with the 'Third World', scholarship on 'security in the Third World' has approached these states as if their insecurities had developed in a vacuum (i.e. autonomously from the rest of the world) (but see Grovogui 2002). In consequence, these studies did not allow deeper insight into the very phenomenon they sought to understand. To elaborate: on the one hand, scholarship on 'security in the Third World' approached these states as works in progress, in so far as they are understood to be in search of security through building state capacity as well as development (Al-Mashat 1985, Thomas 1987, Ayoob 1995). On the other hand, this qualifier comes across as a distinction without a difference. This is because states in the 'Third World' were considered to be an aberration, a deviation from the 'norm'. So, when Brian Job (1992) wrote about the 'insecurity dilemma' of those states that face internal challenges but do not (always) need defending from the outside (thanks to UN safeguarding the sovereignty principle; see also Chapter 9), the author failed to reflect on the underdeveloped understanding of statehood in the study of security (see section 1). Accordingly, students of 'security in the Third World', even as they explicitly focused on the relationship between state capacity and security, nevertheless implicitly persisted in making use of benchmarks regarding what a 'normal' state is/does. The point is that, while students of 'security in the Third World' did not bracket the 'state' in the way that some others did, they still failed to consider constitutive relations between what is taken as the 'norm' and what is treated as an 'aberration'. This is because they failed to reflect on the 'connected and entangled histories' of the state-security relationship around the world (Grovogui 2002; Bilgin and Morton 2002). Indeed, the very fact that students of 'security in the Third World' insisted on the need for time and space to be given to states in the developing world so that they could become 'normal' (see, for example, Ayoob 1995, Ayoob 1998) betrayed their inattentiveness to discussions on statehood in other fields (Shilliam 2021).

To have a sense of what is overlooked in the study of security, consider Sandra Halperin's (1997) argument that the 'normal' state (to which the students of 'security in the Third World' aspire) became the 'norm' in Western

---

[6]The terms, 'First' and 'Third' world are Cold War relics. I utilize them here, because the discussion related to the Cold War period. On the origins and history of these terms, see Pletsch 1981.

Europe much later than popularly presumed. 'When the national idea was promulgated', wrote Halperin (2017: 33), 'the states to which it was applied resembled far more closely the city state polities of the past 5,000 years than the national integrated state form of national cultural imaginaries and nation state ideology'. The transformative period, according to Halperin, was the first half of the twentieth century when the World Wars brought about a 'decisive shift in the balance of class power throughout Europe'. In the 'Third World', noted Halperin, a similar transition did not take place, as many went through decolonization without undergoing 'any social revolutionary transformation' (Halperin 2013: 173–188). What is more, the post-Second World War period in the 'Third World' witnessed efforts to block the kind of socioeconomic change that could, potentially, have brought about such transformation. The agents of such change (or its absence) were not only international but also local 'elites and ruling groups' (see also Mitchell 2002b; Halperin 2013). The implication of Halperin's argument is that the 'normal' state that has become a yardstick for measuring the success/failure in security acquisition is more a myth than the 'norm' (see also Milliken and Krause 2002). As myths go, this is not a harmless one in that it has shaped our understanding of the emergence of a security community in the 'First World' (be it defined as the EU or NATO) and the absence of similar communities of security elsewhere (Adler and Barnett 1998; cf. Barkawi and Laffey 2001). Let me elaborate.

Writing soon after the end of the Cold War, Barry Buzan (1991a) responded to the question 'is international security possible?' in the following manner: since it is 'mature states' that allowed the creation of a security community in Western Europe, argued Buzan, their absence in other parts of the world would limit the chances of achieving international security. This is because, Buzan argued, less than 'mature' states experiencing problems 'inside' were less likely to be able to sustain security collaboration with other states. By articulating this argument, Buzan issued an important corrective to those analyses that inquired into international security without paying due attention to statehood. That said, in so far as Buzan (1991b) defined 'maturity' in terms of the absence of threats 'inside' the state, he allowed a definition of 'normal' statehood in through the back door.

The point is that, in the absence of insight into the 'connected and entangled histories' of the security community in the First World, studies focusing on the possibility of its replication in the 'Third World' are bound to remain wanting. Hence the need for '[attending] to the multiple relations between liberalism and other social processes' in the making of the said security community (Barkawi and Laffey 1999: 423). Fatima Mernissi

(1996) expressed it more compellingly when she insisted on the need for studying the ways in which 'liberal' actors have contributed to the rise of political Islam across the Middle East as a means of maintaining stability and ensuring the flow of oil at reasonable prices, her argument being that the current state of prevalence of political Islam in the Middle East needs to be understood by inquiring into the relationships that helped keep one part of the world secure while subjecting another to 'Palace fundamentalism' (Mernissi 1996; see also Mitchell 2002a).

To recap: studying the 'intertwined and overlapping histories' of the state-security relationship in the 'First' and 'Third' Worlds is not about us, as students, making these connections; it is about uncovering already existing connections through adopting Edward Said's (1975, 1993) method of 'contrapuntal reading' (Bilgin 2016a). Several scholars have already illustrated multiple dimensions of the significance of studying 'intertwined and overlapping histories' of humankind as they reconsidered the history of development in Europe as reflected in 'the mirror of the Third World' (Halperin 1997) or the history of the nineteenth century as 'the global transformation' (Buzan and Lawson 2015; cf. Bilgin 2016b). Other scholars have explicitly drawn upon Said to read contrapuntally the voices of the postcolonial and the global (Duvall and Varadarajan 2007) toward 'understanding our contemporary international relations as a product of a history of cultural encounters (in which colonialism played a key part)' (Biswas 2007: 117) including war (Barkawi 2005; Barkawi and Laffey 2006) and terrorism (Barnard-Wills and Moore 2010). Our insight into the state-security relationship around the world can only flourish by drawing on such 'contrapuntal readings' that do *not* look at the past through 1) state-centric lenses; 2) often without being aware of the particularity of the notion of state that is used; and 3) overlooking relationships of mutual constitution between myriad actors around the world.

Conclusion

In the late 1980s, Fred Halliday (1987) famously called for 'bringing back in' the state to the study of world politics. Soon after, Spike Peterson (1992a: 3) declared that the state was 'back in', highlighting the following three factors:

> intellectual reorientations (greater attention to cross-disciplinary research; disillusion with behaviouralism; and expansion of critical, institutional,

and interpretative approaches), empirical transformations (postcolonial increase in the number and 'types' of states and the state's increasing role in macroeconomic management), and political realities (declining US hegemony; the search for powerful steering mechanisms in the face of systemic crises; and the blurring of distinctions between the state and civil society divisions).

Since then, the study of security has come a long way, exploring statehood, referents of security other than the state and gendered and/or racialized structural insecurities that such referents face; the mutually constitutive relationship between states and insecurities against which they seek protection; and non-state actors whose agency cannot be understood in terms of the binary of 'retreat of or return to' the state and that need to be explored as part of 'global security assemblages' (Abrahamsen and Williams 2009).

Further Reading

Abrahamsen, R. and M.C. Williams (2009), 'Security beyond the state: Global security assemblages in international politics', *International Political Sociology*, 3(1), 1–17.

Bilgin, P. (2020), 'Security', in A. Tickner and K. Smith (eds), *International Relations from the Global South: Worlds of Difference*, London: Routledge.

Booth, K. (2007), *Theory of World Security*, Cambridge: Cambridge University Press.

Jabri, V. (2006), 'War, security and the liberal state', *Security Dialogue*, 37(1), 47–64.

11

The State and Territory

Rhys Jones

Introduction

Various authors, writing from a range of disciplinary perspectives, have contended that one of the distinctive features of the state as an organization is the way in which it seeks to govern a defined territory. Weber, for instance, argued that a state is a 'human community that (successfully) claims the monopoly of the legitimate use of physical force within a given territory' (Weber in Gerth and Mills 1970: 78). Giddens (1981), too, describes the state as a 'bordered power container'. Indeed, for some, it is the idea of territory that lies at the heart of the 'autonomous power of the state' (Mann 1984). In effect, it is impossible for some authors to conceive of the state without also considering its connection with territorial forms of control (Gottmann 1973). The essence of this argument is that a number of different organizations – whether it be the established church or a club or whatever – seek to use the idea of a territory as a way of helping them govern a particular set of people (Sack 1986). It is only the state, however, according to authors such as Mann (1984), that seeks to govern a particular territory and, as a result of doing so, is able to govern a population in more effective ways. The territory of a state, from this viewpoint, is deemed to be an essential prerequisite for the state's sovereignty or of its capacity to govern effectively. And it is because of this association between state sovereignty and state territories that the functional and territorial restructuring linked with the processes of globalization is so significant. A number of authors have argued that the processes associated with economic, political and cultural globalization (along with increased emphases on multi-level forms of governance) are increasingly undermining the territoriality of the state and, by extension, its sovereignty (e.g. Brenner et al. 2003; Sassen 2006). While so-called 'boosterist' accounts of globalization – ones which posit an 'end of geography' (O'Brien 1992) and a political reality in which 'traditional nation states have become unnatural, even impossible business units in a global economy' (Ohmae 1996a: 5) – have been shown to be somewhat misguided, their work points to the essential territorial qualities of state sovereignty and to the potential challenges facing it.

Nor are these merely academic issues. At the time of writing this chapter, political debates are raging on both sides of the Atlantic about the need for the United States and the UK to reassert their sovereignty, in relation to Donald Trump's attempts to 'make America great again' and with respect to Brexit. What is apparent in both cases is the significance of debates about territories and borders. In the United States, attention has been focused by Donald Trump on the need to stop illegal immigration, with the erection of a wall or fence along the border being touted as the key means of achieving this aim. Similarly, the border has become a crucial source of discord in the Brexit process, with specific concerns being raised about the implications of Brexit for the land border between the UK and the EU in Northern Ireland. One key issue identified, in this respect, has been the need to protect the EU's customs union and single market from potential encroachment by an independent UK. With the creation of two divergent economies in the offing, attention has centred on the need to create some kind of infrastructure to manage the relationship between them. The Covid-19 pandemic, similarly, has been associated with a series of debates concerning the ability of states to manage the flow of people – ultimately, the movement of a virus – across territorial boundaries. Covid-19, in this respect, can be viewed as something that is contributing to the reinforcement of state boundaries and, potentially, of more vigorous forms of nationalism.

The above discussion shows that a state's territory and its borders are critical issues, both in academic and more policy-related contexts. And yet, what is the exact role played by a territory in bolstering the power of a state? What are the mechanisms and processes that enable a state to govern a territory? How are people and different kinds of 'things' enrolled into such a process? In short, how should we understand the conceptual and empirical significance of territories for states? The discussion of current political debates in the United States and the UK, as well as the pressing concerns that have arisen in relation to Covid-19, I believe, points to certain ways in which we can approach this issue. It is these different kinds of approach that structure the remaining sections of this chapter.

First and foremost, a state territory, as Elden (2010: 799; see also 2005) has argued, must be 'understood as a political technology: it comprises techniques for measuring land and controlling terrain'. Any understanding of territory, therefore, needs to highlight different mechanisms for measurement or, in other words, for knowing what is happening within a defined and demarcated space. It must also focus on the way in which such measurements allow a degree of control by state bureaucracies of those processes occurring within a defined territory. Clearly, such concerns lie at the heart of debates surrounding Brexit. With proposals afoot for the UK to exit the Customs Union and the Single Market, new forms of measurement and control will exist in the UK as opposed to the rest of the EU, leading, therefore, to an evident need to measure and control what is happening on one side of the Northern Ireland border as opposed to the other.

Second, the short discussion of current border debates in the United States and the UK, as well as debates that have arisen in relation to Covid-19, illustrates the practised, embodied and affective qualities of state territories (Merriman and Jones 2017). There is clearly a recognition in recent debates in both the United States and the UK about the significance of peopled interactions with state territories. It is individuals crossing the border between Mexico and the United States, for instance, that has led to calls in some quarters for the erection of a wall or fence – one that would be difficult for individuals, in an embodied sense, to cross. Meanwhile, similar embodied engagements with a potentially reconfigured border between the Republic of Ireland and Northern Ireland – with individuals, in a worst-case scenario, having to negotiate border checks on a daily basis – have raised the spectre of a return to political violence in the north. And Covid-19 has illustrated the need for states to understand the flows of people across state boundaries and within state territories. Embodied experiences are crucial to understanding state territories.

Third, current debates demonstrate the material and infrastructural aspects of state territories (Bouzarovski et al. 2015). There has been considerable debate, for instance, concerning Donald Trump's reliance on very conventional infrastructures – walls and fences – to demarcate more effectively a boundary between the United States and Mexico. The re-emergence of once-familiar border infrastructures of checkpoints and guard towers has also featured as part of the political and popular debates surrounding the potential re-emergence of a hard border between the

Republic of Ireland and Northern Ireland. The success or otherwise of digital infrastructures has featured heavily in relation to states' response to the Covid-19 crisis, most notably in relation to states' efforts to monitor the everyday practices of their citizens. There is, in consequence, a need to understand the more material and infrastructural contexts within which state territories are reproduced.

It is these three themes that will structure the remaining sections of this chapter. In section 2, I discuss the significance of territory as a political technology, which allows a more effective governance of people, places, processes and things. I build on this theme in the following section, where I use the idea of networked territories to examine the practised, material and affective aspects of state territories. Brief conclusions follow.

Territory as a 'space of calculation'

A sustained attempt has been made to grapple with the conceptual and historical understanding of territory and territoriality in recent years. Eschewing biological understandings of the term – where territory is conceived almost as a 'natural' and ahistorical feature of animal and human behaviour – authors such as Elden (2010) and Painter (2010) have attempted to unpack its conceptual underpinnings. Territory, when viewed in these terms becomes an important technique of government; one that encompasses ways of thinking as well as ways of doing. Indeed, it is only by doing – by measuring land and all that occurs within it in more effective and more detailed ways – that space can assume the status of territory and, thus, be used to control the people and processes that occur within it. It is in these twin contexts of measurement and control that territory, moreover, becomes a 'political technology' and a space of calculation (Elden 2010: 799).

Some of the most obvious instances of territorial measurement and control – and the creation of a space of calculation – occur in relation to national censuses. Hannah (1999) discusses the development of a national census in the United States during the late nineteenth century; a space of calculation for measuring the distribution and characteristics of the population. Hannah describes how the US census was an essential element in the emerging US state's ability to 'see' (Scott 1998) its population more clearly and, in seeing it, to govern it more effectively. What facilitated this exercise, moreover, was the subdivision of the US federal state as a territorial entity. It was only by creating a geographical framework of precisely defined enumeration districts that the territory could be charted fully and without overlap (Hannah 1999).

There are other, perhaps less obvious, examples of the role of territory as a political technology based on measurement and control. Ogborn (1998) has explored the significant role played by the Excise in England and Wales during the seventeenth century. Excise duties on alcohol were a key way of enabling the English state to collect revenue from its people, resources and land, but this whole process was dependent on the creation of effective and territorial means of measurement and control. A series of new practices and technologies was developed in order to facilitate this process and to ensure its efficiency and consistency. At one level, this meant employing a range of officers to survey how and where beer was brewed. Officers travelled throughout the country to ensure consistency in the way in which beer was produced and sold. Measurement and control also took place at another, totally different, scale, with sustained attempts being made to comprehend and measure the internal geometry of barrels and casks. It was by 'mapping' the internal 'geographies' of barrels, according to Ogborn (1998), that the English state could raise as much revenue as possible, could do so in ways that were as consistent and fair as possible, and could thus legitimize the whole process to its citizens.

While the above two historical examples demonstrate the importance of low-tech and embodied forms of measurement and control – whether in relation to paper-based census returns or in the context of actual visits by excise officers to breweries the length and breadth of England and Wales – we have entered a world in which forms of measurement and control are far more automated and high-tech. A great deal of work has been done, for instance, on the significance of biometrics as ways of measuring and controlling the flow of people in and out of state territories. Amoore (2006), for instance, draws attention to the role of biometrics in places like the United States – through its Visitor and Immigrant Status Indicator Technology (VISIT) programme – in governing mobility in the context of the so-called 'war on terror'. Through the use of retinal eye scanning and fingerprinting, certain kinds of mobility and certain kinds of person become acceptable and admissible to US territory, while others are excluded. Moreover, there is an automation inherent in the use of such technologies, as data about migrants and visitors are collected and circulated, are subject to algorithmic processing, and are stored in a range of governmental organizations.

The impression given by the above discussion is of a state territory that is perfectly constructed and perfectly practises political technology. And yet, many authors, writing from different perspectives, have emphasized that state territories are actually characterized by many flaws and blind spots. Scott (1998), writing about a state that seeks to make its territory, along with all that happens within it, more 'legible', spends considerable time explaining how such attempts are doomed to failure. The processes of abstraction and simplification that are a fundamental part of a state's attempt to create a territory as a space of calculation lead to a situation in which the many complexities of life within that territory cannot be computed or 'fall off the radar'. In a different context, Painter (2010: 1090; see also 2006) draws on anthropological understandings of the state to conceive of state territories as 'the outcome of networked socio-technical practices'. And, by extension, one has to accept that these sociotechnical practices are inherently contested and imperfect. Painter draws on the example of the economic measure of Gross Value Added as an attempt to make state territories calculable in an economic sense but concludes quickly enough that the measure is an imperfect one, particularly when it is used to measure economic performance at regional scales within territories.

Of course, such statements should not surprise us. We are all aware of the imperfect vision of the state and of the cracks that exist in relation to state territories; blind spots in the state's attempt to use territories to measure and control. To return to one of the examples discussed already, those attending to the development and improvement of the US census during the nineteenth century bemoaned some of the practical difficulties associated with collecting accurate data about the population. The US Superintendent of Censuses, Francis A. Walker, was at the forefront of these efforts, particularly in relation to his efforts to create a territorial framework of subdivisions within the United States, which could act as the basis of the collection and collation of information (Hannah 1999). Walker used the template of reference grids, which had already subdivided the United States into a series of smaller territorial units, as the basis of the census's enumeration districts. Yet doing so presented its own difficulties. In certain parts of the United States, enumeration districts were too large, being the same size as counties. In other more populous regions, enumeration districts could contain over 20,000 people. In both these cases, the collection of data could be arduous, with concerns being raised about the accuracy of the data being collected. And there are more extreme examples of the limitations of the census as a territorial form of political technology. Hannah (2009), for instance, has examined the census boycott movement that took place in West Germany during the 1980s and has viewed it as an attempt to contest some of the more sinister aspects of the state's attempt to collect information about its population and to govern its territory more effectively. One can also consider how more banal acts of contestation – where, for instance, nearly 400,000 people self-identified their religion as being 'Jedi' (from the Star Wars film franchise) – as examples, ultimately, of the state's inability to make its population and territory fully legible (http://news.bbc.co.uk/1/hi/uk/2757067.stm, accessed 11 April 2019).

And if such statements are true of the census, then they are equally relevant to other territorial forms of political technology. Part of the significance of Ogborn's (1998) work in relation to the Excise is that it illustrates the many blind spots that existed during the seventeenth century in relation to the state's ability to measure and control the production of beer. There are numerous instances in which beer and other forms of alcohol were produced in illegal stills, examples of beer being siphoned off from barrels prior to them being measured by excise officers and '[o]n the Isle of Wight, casks [being] spirited away to nearby ships before they could be assessed' (ibid.: 302). Further complications arose in the context of the smuggling of beer and other forms of alcohol across state borders (Donnan and Wilson 1999; Mountz et al. 2012).

While the above examples of contestation illustrate the way in which the ideal of the political technology of territory can be challenged and undermined by others, it is also worth noting that states themselves sometimes either: 1) recognize the limits to their territorial authority; or 2) seek to subvert it. Some of the more interesting examples of the former are the islands' policies that have been adopted by a number of states. Islands, in a number of cases, represent some of the most remote and inaccessible parts of a state's territory and, as such, are in need of special measures in order to incorporate them fully into the body politic. The document produced to support the UK's three most isolated island communities – Shetland, Orkney and the Western Isles – for instance, explicitly describes some of the challenges associated with island life, most notably those arising from their geographic location (Scotland Office 2015: 3). Furthermore, the document also signals the commitment of the UK government to an '"Islands proofing" principle' or, in other words, to 'ensure that policy and legislation take account of islands' circumstances, where practicable' (ibid.). The significance of such statements, I contend, is that they show the sometimes tenuous claims to authority that states have over some of the more remote parts of their territory. While states claim that their territory is an essential form of political calculation and one that enables them to measure and control land and people in a consistent way, the reality is, in certain cases, more ambiguous.

States can also attempt to subvert their own control of territory for their own political gain. Among the most notorious examples in recent times have been the detention and rendition centres located outside a given state's territory; examples include Guantanamo Bay and the CIA 'black sites' dotted around the territories of many US allies. The significance of such places, as authors such as Gregory (2006) have noted, is that they lie outside of a state's sovereign territory and can therefore escape from the forms of measurement and control associated with a state's legal system. The act of extraordinary rendition creates individuals and practices that exist beyond any state's jurisdiction. But, of course, the unusual character of such 'spaces of exception'(ibid.) – ones that lie beyond official forms of measurement and control exercised by the state – merely serves to emphasize the close relationship that exists, as a rule, between state territories and practices of measurement and control.

Beyond such conceptual challenges to the notion of state territoriality, more empirical challenges have also emerged over the past fifty or so years. Social scientists of different hues have studied the emergence of multi-level governance or, in other words, a reconfiguration of political power and territoriality vertically between different scales of governance and horizontally across a range of non-governmental actors (Bache et al. 2016; Hooghe and Marks 2003). As part of this process, the state becomes merely one institution seeking to exercise sovereignty through its control of territory. Territoriality takes on a fractured and overlapping quality through multi-level forms of governance. Territoriality in the states of the European Union, for instance, exists in plural forms. In certain contexts, it is the laws of the European Union that hold sway; in others it is the laws of individual states. And of course, the decentralization or devolution of power to sub-state regions has only served to complicate matters further (e.g. Bulmer et al. 2002). Multi-level governance and processes of devolution have not solely affected state territoriality in legal or constitutional contexts. They have also been implicated in the emergence of multiple and overlapping forms of territorial identity. Keating (1998) has examined the relationship between the territorial restructuring associated with multi-level governance and the (re)emergence of new kinds of territorial identity in Europe – a theme that is also explored by

McEwen and Cetrà in this volume. Once again, such tendencies pose fundamental challenges to the territoriality of the state, in terms of identity and ideology.

Networked territories

The above discussion begins to highlight how state territories represent contingent and contested 'geographical accomplishments' (cf. Parr and Philo 2000). Rather than being homogeneous and 'flat' spaces, state territories are fractured, uneven and incomplete. A useful way of further developing such an understanding of state territories exists in relation to networked and relational ways of thinking.

Conventional approaches to networked and relational ways of thinking tend to be positioned in opposition to more territorial understandings of social and spatial life. Arguably beginning with Massey's (1994) work on networked understandings of place and Castells' (1996) discussion of a network society linked to a space of flows, academics have questioned the significance of bounded understandings of space and place, preferring instead to approach places as open, dynamic, relational entities that are always in connection – through flows of people, ideas and material things – with other places across the world (Allen 2003; Amin 2004). Networked ways of thinking, thus, tend to be connected with discourses of deterritorialization or, in other words, with a perception that, in an increasingly globalized world, territories and bounded space do not matter any more (cf. Elden 2005). In O'Brien's words (1992), we are supposed to be witnessing 'the end of geography' or, in effect, the emergence of an era when state territories, and their associated boundaries, do not matter.

One obvious comeback to such an argument is to point to the growth of nationalism and populist politics in many parts of the world in recent years (Mudde 2007). While there are clear empirical grounds for contesting the alleged demise of territories and borders, it is perhaps more interesting to seek to develop a dialogue between territorial and relational/networked understandings of social and spatial life. Important work in this area has increasingly attempted to think about territories in networked and relational ways. Painter (2010: 1090), for instance, has maintained that 'far from refuting or falsifying network theories of spatiality, the current resurgence of territory can be seen as itself a product of relational networks'. This is not a case of just tagging on networks to more conventional understandings of territory. Rather, it requires a fundamental rethinking of what we understand by territory. According to Painter (2010: 1094),

> from this viewpoint territory is necessarily porous, historical, mutable, uneven and perishable. It is a laborious work in progress, prone to failure and permeated by tension and contradiction. Territory is never complete, but always becoming. It is also a promise the state cannot fulfil.

There are serious implications, therefore, arising from thinking about state territories in relational and networked ways. Doing so helps to underline the fact that state territories are 'geographical accomplishments' (cf. Philo and Parr 2000) but, importantly, they are not ones that are static or guaranteed to succeed. They are, in effect, state aspirations – sometimes realized, sometimes not. And crucially, this is not just a feature of state territories in southern states, lacking in 'infrastructural power' (Mann 1984). All states, to varying degrees, struggle to make their use of territory – as a form of measurement, calculation and control – meaningful and real.

Thinking about state territories in relational and networked ways opens up a series of new conceptual vistas for all social scientists interested in the state, and its control of people and space. I discuss three different issues in the remaining paragraphs of this section, which highlight some key areas of academic inquiry that have been informed by relational and networked understandings of state territories.

Practising state territories

One of the key implications of thinking about state territories in relational and networked terms is the need to consider the role of people – as individuals and groups – in reinforcing and contesting territory. Some of the discussion in this chapter has already hinted at the significance of such issues. The name of Francis A. Walker, the US Superintendent of Censuses, has already been mentioned. He played a key role in bringing order to the territorial administration of the census in the United States during the late nineteenth century (Hannah 1999). In a similar vein, Ogborn's (1998) work on the development of the Excise in England and Wales during the late seventeenth century draws attention to the role played by Charles Davenant in systematizing the collection of information about brewing practices. It was he, for instance, who developed a new kind of political arithmetic in order to calculate the internal volume of casks and barrels. He also travelled extensively throughout England and Wales to monitor the production of beer. In this way, we witness how state formation – whether thought of in relation to organizational development or in specifically territorial contexts – comes about as a result of the agency of a range of actors. While their motives and their interactions with the state as an organization may be varied, they are all involved in reproducing the state as an organizational and territorial entity (Ballvé 2012).

Two contrasting examples can help us to appreciate the role of individuals both in making sense of state territories and in making them 'real'; or, in other words, making them effective influencers of different aspects of social and spatial life. The first example is drawn from the nineteenth century and relates to the attempts being made in the UK at this time to open up new spheres of activity to state territorial control. Authors such as MacDonagh (1958: 53) have argued that the 'function and structure of executive government changed profoundly in the course of the nineteenth century' and that the growing extent and character of government were underpinned by an increasing measurement, calculation and monitoring of different kinds of activity (e.g. Driver 1989: 272). A key aspect of this process was the role played by state agents in bringing the legislative process 'into life' (MacDonagh 1958: 59). Some of the most important figures in this process were the so-called government inspectors. Indeed, the significance of inspectors for the fundamental changes affecting the British state of this period was such that the nineteenth century has been described as the 'age of the inspector' (Burn 1964: 17). While historians have charted the critical role played by government inspectors in shaping new state organizations, laws and policies during this period, there is also a need to attend to the equally great contributions they made to the evolving territorial form of the state.

One key set of individuals were those charged with inspecting factory production. The social conditions of factory production had been a key issue of debate for much of the early nineteenth century and, in many ways, provided the precedent for subsequent legislation and inspection in other spheres of socioeconomic activity. It has been argued, moreover, that '[t]he Factory Act, 1833 … contained the most detailed and far-reaching exposition of inspectorial powers ever produced in Britain' (Bartrip 1982: 612) and, as such, it provides an invaluable insight into the role played by government inspectors in producing new kinds of state territory. As well as seeking to implement the Factory Act in procedural and organizational ways, the four inspectors appointed as a result of the Act also contributed much to its territorial form. It was the territory of the North of England, with its numerous factories, that proved to be most problematic in this respect. In the period immediately after the promulgation of the Act, Inspector Robert Rickards was responsible for a large and highly industrial area that included Yorkshire, Lancashire, Cheshire, north-west Derbyshire and north Staffordshire, as well as the northern Welsh counties of Caernarfonshire, Denbighshire, Flintshire and Anglesey. His responsibilities were nigh on impossible to discharge since his district covered a large area and comprised approximately 2,700 factories that employed more than 250,000 workers. It should come as no surprise that Rickards literally collapsed under the strain of coordinating the inspection duties within this district and subsequently resigned from his post (Jones 2008: 130). It is significant that the inspectors, themselves, decided to rearrange the territorial boundaries of their districts in 1837, with some of the responsibilities of the Inspector for the North of England being transferred to others. According to the inspectors, the new territorial arrangement worked well, enabling them to discharge their responsibilities more effectively (quoted in Thomas 1948: 99–100). We witness here a clear instance of the inspectors, as a result of their administrative experience, actively producing the new state territories of factory inspection in England and Wales.

Jump ahead nearly 200 years and witness the attempts being made to monitor the UK state's borders in the face of heightened immigration. While the increasing role of immigration has been the source of much political and public debate, it has also led to a sustained academic inquiry into its peopled and practised characteristics. Some of the more interesting work in this area has examined the agency of those individuals charged with policing – in a literal and more figurative sense – the state's borders. Research by Gill (2009, 2010), for instance, has examined the role played by asylum-sector decision-makers in reproducing the UK state's boundaries. The agency displayed by a range of individuals – those employed directly by the UK state, those working for private companies providing a service for the UK state, and those employed by NGOs seeking to act as advocates of the rights of asylum seekers – demonstrates that the state, along with its boundary and territory, are not stable organizational and spatial entities. Instead, they are continuously produced and questioned in active and varying ways by a range of individuals. State territories, when viewed in this way, are not unitary or homogeneous but are rather constantly shifting and evolving. They are, as Painter (2010: 1094) puts it, 'never complete, but always becoming'.

Territory, infrastructures and materialities

The second conceptual consequence of thinking about state territories in relational and networked ways is that there is a need to consider the role of infrastructures and material objects in bringing a degree of permanence and durability to those territories. Work that attends to the infrastructural and material aspects of state territories has been informed, either implicitly or more explicitly, by insights from actor-network theory (ANT) and/or assemblage theory (DeLanda 2016). ANT highlights the significance of what Law (1992) has described as a 'relational materialism' or, in other words, the way in which different aspects of social and spatial life are created on the basis of networks, which comprise a range of individuals and a great many things. For advocates of such an approach, it is the incorporation of material things or non-human actants into these networks (Latour 2005) that enables social and spatial formations to be 'stretched' over time and space (Murdoch 1997: 327). Such work has received an additional fillip in recent years as a result of an academic engagement with notions of assemblage (Deleuze and Guattari 1987; DeLanda 2016). The concept of assemblage has been posited as a 'materialist social ontology' that can be used to decipher the networks of people and things that constitute 'communities and organisations, cities and countries' (DeLanda 2016: 3). We also need to realize the 'force' that resides in objects of different kinds. Building on work within anthropology and archaeology, many authors argue for the need to take seriously the vitality of objects and material things. Rather than seeing objects as items that merely reflect pre-existing meaning that resides elsewhere, Meehan et al. (2013: 3) have argued that they should be 'repatriate[d] … with the ontological force they themselves generate'. In other words, we need to see a focus on materiality as something that allows us to move beyond 'the textual and symbolic realm' in which 'objects are often containers or reflections of power'. Instead, we should conceive of objects as things that generate power and hold agency in their own right (ibid.: 8; Merriman and Jones 2017: 602).

What are the implications of such ways of thinking for our understanding of state territories? It is clear that state territories can be conceived of as networks that are constituted, in far-reaching ways, on the basis of materials, objects and things (Barry 2013). Some of the more obvious material infrastructures that bring meaning or 'ontological force' to state territories reside at the borders of states. Various physical demarcations of a state's boundaries – such as walls, fences and barbed wire – reinforce in a literal sense the notion, however illusory, that a state's territory possesses a degree of permanence and stability. Immigration processing and detention centres, too, have also played a significant role in marking the existence of a state's boundaries in a physical and, of course, embodied sense. Angel Island and Ellis Island, for instance, helped reinforce the significance of the US western and eastern boundaries respectively in the past (Hoskins and Maddern 2011). Nowadays in the United States, detention centres process hundreds of thousands of people in a migrant detention system comprising 350 facilities and operating at an annual cost of more than US $1.7 billion (Mountz et al. 2012). And, of course, additional technologies and material infrastructures have been developed in recent years to monitor and limit the flow of people across state borders, with the development of new biometric infrastructures being the most notable examples (Amoore 2006).

But it is worth appreciating that material infrastructures permeate and reproduce state territories in additional, more far-reaching, ways. Nearly forty years ago, Williams and Smith (1983) emphasized the need to examine the role played by different infrastructures in a process of nation- and state-building: infrastructures such as railways, road networks and other public services, such as those associated with health services and education systems. Others, following in their wake, have studied material infrastructures in a range of empirical contexts. Usher (2018), for instance, has examined the impact of the engineering of new kinds of drainage systems on a process of state organizational and territorial reconfiguration in Singapore. Similar work has focused on the infrastructures linking hydro-politics and state transformation in Spain, particularly in the period of sustained 'modernization' that took place during the twentieth century (Swyngedouw 2015). Railway networks have been another source of empirical inquiry into the material and infrastructural qualities of state territories. Martí-Henneberg (2017: 160), for instance, highlights the significance of railways as conduits of nation- and state-building from the mid-nineteenth century onwards. The territorial aspect of this process was paramount. He maintains that 'the railway network interconnected the states of Europe and helped to integrate their individual national territories and this also had an enormous political impact'. Even today – in an age when the significance of rail travel has been in many cases supplanted by road networks and air travel – railways still play a key role in providing a material and infrastructural underpinning to state territory. Railway transit systems, therefore, are more than about 'moving people'. They represent political and territorial projects possessing significant symbolic power (Siemiatycki 2005: 23).

Admittedly, talk of the material and symbolic significance of infrastructures may seem quaint and old-fashioned in an age of digital communication and virtual living. After all, one might assume that those infrastructures that undergird lives that are increasingly lived online might be disconnected from state territories. And yet, some work has begun to examine the continued significance of such digital infrastructures in entrenching – in ways that are hidden and often unquestioned – state territories and forms of national socio-spatial consciousness that, arguably, lie beyond banality (cf. Billig 1995). Work in this area has examined the extent to which the digital or 'coded infrastructures' (Kitchin and Dodge 2011: 6; see also Thrift and French 2002) that increasingly underpin our everyday existence have the potential to reproduce state territories. Examples of such digital infrastructures include digital maps and automated address information on websites and other digital interfaces. A recent project undertaken on behalf of the Welsh Language Commissioner in Wales, for instance, has shown that digital maps and automated address data, perhaps inadvertently but almost inevitably, privilege the English versions of place names and addresses (Griffiths et al. 2015). Welsh versions of place names and addresses are either ignored or corrupted. Moreover, given the often automated reproduction of digital data (Thrift and French 2002), there is a real sense in which errors and omissions – once they have entered digital or coded infrastructures – are incredibly difficult to correct or remove. The upshot of this whole process is a privileging of the English language and, by implication, of the national territory of the UK state, rather than the Welsh language and Wales as a devolved territory of the UK. Digital infrastructures, in this sense, have the potential to accentuate an age-old connection between material infrastructures and state territories.

Affective state territories

In the above two sub-sections, I have been guilty perhaps of separating human agents from material infrastructures. Both play a significant role in reproducing state territories in their own right but there is clearly a need to examine the important interplay between the two. After all, ANT emphasizes the interplay between human agents and non-human actants in the reproduction of networks of different kinds (Latour 2005). Similar concerns animate assemblage theory (DeLanda 2016). One way in which the connections between humans and material things can be examined in more detail is through recourse to work on affect.

Recent research on emotions and affect have, at heart, been concerned with the subconscious and embodied interactions between individuals, the environment they inhabit and the material things that they engage with in their lives (Thrift 2000). The embodied practices of individuals, in this sense, cannot be considered in isolation; a body is always 'imbricated in a set of relations that extend beyond it and constitute it' (Anderson 2014: 9). Another important insight of this work is that the affective engagements between individuals and spaces, infrastructures and things sustain power relationships of different kinds. Space can be manipulated for political ends, such as the use that is often made of public space within many authoritarian regimes in order to engender a sense of loyalty towards the state or towards political parties (Thrift 2004). And, of course, an increased sensitivity to affective forms of power can open up new forms of political engagement and contestation. Amin and Thrift (2013: 156), for instance, have maintained that politics is 'shot through with emotion from start to finish'.

What are the implications of such ways of thinking for national territories? Certainly, for much of modern history, nation-states have attempted to use affect as a way of promoting their own political agenda in discursive and more territorial contexts (Deleuze and Guattari 1987: 101–102). So, for instance, the communal practices of members of a nation-state on a day of remembrance or celebration can help to mark out the national territory in embodied and affective ways (Edensor 2002: 69–70). One can think, for instance, of the acts of remembrance associated with war monuments and, in particular, the affective qualities of these public displays of national unity (Heffernan 1995). Closs Stephens (2016: 181) has described these embodied, affective and material aspects of nationalism as things that are akin to national atmospheres – ones which 'congeal around particular objects and bodies and echo as part of an assemblage'. She uses the example of the London Olympics of 2012 as a way of illustrating the significance of these national atmospheres, as a particular place was transformed into a generator of object/body/emotion relations. The Olympic Stadium, in particular, became a significant node in the generation of positive emotions, such as happiness, pride and togetherness. In a very real sense, therefore, a nation – and, we would argue, a national territory – 'becomes materialized through … sets of social practices' (Kingsbury 2008: 53).

But is also clear that certain groups have had tangled and ambivalent relationships with these affective infrastructures. Recent work by Merriman and Jones (2017) has focused on the affective qualities associated with two different road infrastructures in Wales – namely, the A470 trunk road that connects North and South Wales, and the Severn Bridge, which connects South Wales with South-West England. Ever since it was designated as a new trunk road in 1972, the A470 has played a significant role in enabling embodied connections between North and South Wales, and in instilling a series of emotional responses among its many travellers, including excitement and boredom in equal measure. It has, thus, become a linear infrastructure that has influenced individuals' sense of belonging to Wales and Welsh identity. It is, in effect, 'a road that ... provide[s] an affective and relational glue' for the Welsh nation (ibid.: 611). The Severn Bridge, on the other hand, has played more of an ambivalent affective role as an infrastructure that defines the border between Wales and England. When it was first proposed, it was deemed by many Welsh nationalists to be something that would connect Wales more closely with England, with negative cultural, linguistic and political consequences arising as a result. Today, the picture is more complicated. For some Welsh people, crossing the Bridge from England into Wales provides an opportunity to enjoy and celebrate the fact that they are 'coming home'. A journey in the opposite direction engenders other sentiments, most notably the sense of loss and dislocation associated with leaving one's own territory and nation (Merriman and Jones 2017).

Another example from Wales illustrates more starkly the affective aspects of nationalist infrastructures (Jones and Merriman 2012). I refer to the campaign in favour of bilingual road signs in Wales, which ran from the mid-1960s through to the mid-1980s. During the 1960s and 1970s, many British politicians described the campaigners as vandals because of their tendency to either deface or destroy monolingual English road signs. The response of the campaigners to these accusations is significant. They maintained that the English road signs themselves, rather than the defaced signs, were the real eyesores, being acts of cultural vandalism in their own right:

> If our road-signs fulfil the demands of aesthetic standards, they also destroy completely the standards of Welshness. In the eyes of the Welshman [sic], they are ugly, unbearably ugly. And the only way ... to convince everyone of this, is by offending other standards, the standards of superficial aesthetics, i.e. by painting English road-signs and leaving them – for all to see – untidy and illegible. (Iwan quoted in Jones and Merriman 2009)

Members of the Welsh nationalist movement possessed a totally different set of affective relationships with these monolingual road signs (Jones and

Merriman 2009), conceiving of them as objects that served to exclude Welsh speakers from their own national territory (cf. McEwen and Cetrà in Chapter 13 of the current volume). Defacing road signs was a necessary evil, therefore, in order to foreground the linguistic and cultural defilement associated with English-language infrastructures located within an emerging Welsh national territory. Moreover, the violent destruction of such signs enabled a new set of affective relationships to be developed: ones of anger, frustration and a sense of linguistic and national injustice.

Conclusions

My aim in this chapter has been to examine different ways of approaching state territories in conceptual and empirical contexts. Territories are fundamentally important political technologies for states, allowing states to measure and control all aspects of social and spatial life taking place within their borders. The examples of censuses and the Excise illustrate the saliency of such claims. Subdividing territory into smaller spatial units and using these as the basis for the collection and analysis of all kinds of information become key mechanisms for state bureaucracies to govern more effectively. But, of course, even in the most centralized and sophisticated of states, the territorial control of land and people is always a tentative and incomplete 'geographical accomplishment'. People contest this territorial form of control, and states themselves are also aware of their limitations in this area. Similarly, processes of devolution and the existence of multi-level forms of governance further serve to undermine notions of a singular and unproblematic state territoriality. Territory, when viewed in these ways, is merely one among many 'state effects' or, in other words, a set of discourses and practices that gives the illusion of stability and consistency to the state (Mitchell 1991).

One important way of highlighting this more tentative take on territory is by using the emerging literature that views state territories as relational and networked entities. Thinking about state territories in such ways helps to foreground the practised, the material and affective aspects of state territories. State agents and 'ordinary' subjects reproduce and contest the state through their everyday actions. Material infrastructures bring a degree of permanence to state territories but also highlight their uneven character; some places are connected, while others are not. And, finally, a focus on affect illustrates the variegated impact of infrastructures on individuals and groups. Taken together, such work reinforces the notion that state territories are heterogeneous entities. Their ability to enable measurement and control, and the meaning ascribed to them by different actors, is highly variable.

And, of course, such a viewpoint possesses considerable political implications. If state territories are fractured and tentative, the state, by extension, is also replete with similar internal inconsistencies. Rather than being an all-powerful and 'all-seeing' organization (Scott 1998), and one that possesses a perfect territorial mechanism for measurement and control, the state (and a state territory) is a 'laborious work in progress, prone to failure and permeated by tension and contradiction' (Painter 2010: 1094). The 'blind spots' that exist within state territories inevitably open up new possibilities for those seeking to contest the state and – from a more explicitly geographical perspective – potentially new locations from which to conduct this resistance.

Further Reading

Amoore, L. (2006), 'Biometric borders: Governing mobilities in the war on terror', *Political Geography*, 25(3), 336–351.

Balivé, T. (2012), 'Everyday state formation: Territory, decentralization, and the Narco Landgrab in Colombia', *Environment and Planning D: Society and Space*, 30(4), 603–622.

Elden, S. (2010), ' Land, terrain, territory', *Progress in Human Geography*, 34(6), 799–817.

Jones, R. (2008), *People/States/Territories: The Political Geographies of British State Transformation*, Oxford: Blackwell.

Mann, M. (1984), 'The autonomous power of the state: Its origins, mechanisms and results', *European Journal of Sociology*, 25(5), 185–213.

Painter, J. (2010). 'Rethinking territory', *Antipode*, 42, 1090–1117.

12

The State and Capital

David Marsh

Introduction

The relationship between capital and the state, or business and government, has always been a topic of concern for those interested in the operation of democracy. This first sentence itself reflects two of the dominant views of that relationship, and the nomenclature is revealing. Marxism, historically, focused upon the relationship between capital and the state, seeing the state as serving the interests of capital. Here, there was relatively little attention given to the divisions within the state, or within capital. Pluralism, in contrast, highlighted these divisions, often arguing that conflicts between different departments within government, and between different business sectors, increased the plurality of the system, ensuring that business, at best, had limited influence within some policy areas. Here, I discuss the relationship between business and government, not because I am convinced by the pluralist argument, but, rather, because, first, this is the terminology now most commonly used, and, secondly, not even Marxists would these days see capital, or the state, as undifferentiated institutions/processes.

This is a large topic which I address in three substantive sections. First, I briefly examine developments in the two main theories of the relationship, Marxism and pluralism, arguing that there has been some convergence between them, with Marxism recognizing that class and economic relations are not the only basis of social division and shaper of state action, while pluralism has acknowledged that business may enjoy a particularly important role, although that role is still significantly limited by other constraints on government. Second, I briefly highlight the significantly reduced focus on the role of business within democratic politics at the end of the twentieth and beginning of the twenty-first century – a focus which re-emerged after the Global Financial Crisis (GFC). Finally, I examine empirical evidence about the power of business, showing the contestation that exists between the different sides of the argument, while concluding that we underestimate the power of business in democracy at our peril.

The theoretical debate on the power of business

Here, I briefly examine the changes in the Marxist theory of the state, an issue dealt with at more length by Hay in Chapter 3. Subsequently, I explore the pluralist position in more detail, covered by Smith in Chapter 1, because it is the position which has dominated on this question. Finally, I briefly consider the structure/agency problem, which is rightly emphasized by Hay, in the context of the faces of power debate.

Marxist views on the power of business

Given Hay's thorough review of the Marxist position, I merely reinforce a few points here. Over time, most Marxist scholarship has relaxed the emphasis on determinism, structuralism and essentialism in much traditional Marxism. To put it another way, Marxism has changed, as a result both of changes in the nature of the world it examines, particularly within the capitalist system, but also in gender relations, the environment and so on, and of critiques of traditional Marxism from both within and outwith the position. In consequence, most Marxist state theorists have accepted that the state is not an undifferentiated whole; that there are fractions of capital which often compete; that the state does not inevitably, or always, act in the interest of capital; and that class is not the only, or always the most important, basis of social division within capitalist societies.

All this means that Marxists are no longer committed to the view that business power is omnipotent in capitalist societies, or even that business always wins when it is faced by what pluralists term countervailing forces. Probably the most it is fair to say is that Marxists believe that business – perhaps, on different occasions, separate fractions/sectors of capital/business – is the dominant political force in contemporary capitalism. At the same time, the implication of authors like Jessop (1982) or Hay is that the extent to which it does so is, in large part, an empirical question.

Pluralism and the power of business

The first thing to emphasize here is that, again, nomenclature is important. Pluralists talk of influence, not power, which they see as associated with coercion, and that, as I emphasize, has clear methodological implications.

As Smith shows in Chapter 1, classical pluralism, associated with Bentley (1908), later Truman (1951) and even, for the most part, Dahl (1961), argued that power was diffused, not concentrated; that government did not promote any particular interest; and that the outcome was slowly evolving policy which served the general interest, rather than a particular interest. The focus of pluralism was thus on interest groups and their role vis-à-vis government; they acted both as a channel of representation and a check on the power of the state.

Lindblom (1977) broke with this view, arguing that business enjoyed a privileged position in capitalist democracies. He argued that there were two major reasons for this privilege: first, business controls the key decisions about the economy, thus very clearly affecting a government's re-election chances, so they enjoy significant structural power; and, second, business has the resources and contacts to manipulate volitions, shaping the ideas of citizens so they think that, in a dated phrase, 'what is good for General Motors is good for America'. On the other hand, government has key resources that business needs, particularly legitimacy/authority; it can provide grants and has the capacity to invest in expensive infrastructure which benefits business. For Lindblom, because each has resources that the other needs, the core of democratic politics ('the grand issues'), which involves those things that most affect business, economic policy, labour policy, taxation and so on, revolves around negotiations between government and business.

However, to Lindblom, pluralism is broadly retained because much of business's power is negotiated away by government. At the same time, other groups may have crucial, even veto, power in other fields (for example, doctors in health policy). Crucially, for Lindblom, but even more so for pluralists who followed, a government always has to be concerned about re-election and therefore about the views of voters, so it will not make too many obvious concessions to business.

Lindblom was heavily criticized by fellow pluralists, and I spend some time on this more recent material which deals specifically with the role of business and does not feature in Smith's review in Chapter 1. Vogel (1989), in particular, defended a more traditional view of pluralism, playing down the power of business in democracy, arguing three points that are at the core of modern pluralism: business is just one interest among many; it is also crucially a divided one; and its power fluctuates. More recently, Vogel (2005: 16–17) has revived a focus upon the role of citizens in constraining the influence of business, in particular arguing that the increased importance, as he sees it, for business of concerns about Corporate Social Responsibility (CSR) can force it to respond to the public's demands. As with many of the criticisms of Lindblom, this avoids his focus on business's capacity to manipulate volitions.

In broader terms, Lindblom's work has been criticized for being too structuralist – a view strongly developed by Culpepper (2010) and Bell (2011). Culpepper (2010) argues that, while business has structural power, it varies over time, and between policy sectors. In particular, in his view this power is mediated by the role of the media and public opinion. In this vein, Culpepper distinguishes between issues of high and low salience, depending upon their 'importance to the average voter, relative to other political issues' (Culpepper 2010: 4). For him, corporate issues are low salience issues, kept off the political agenda by lobbying and influence, and because legislators and reporters have limited corporate expertise. It is in this area of 'quiet politics' where business exercises most influence. It is the noisier, high salience, issues of 'jobs and protection of wages' (Culpepper 2010: 5), which are reported in the media and are at the fore during elections, but it is in the quiet arenas that business exercises its power. Culpepper also follows Vogel and others in arguing that business is usually divided, indeed suggesting that it is only united on high-profile issues. Here, the main point for Culpepper is that these issues are also the ones in which public interest is greatest; so business's power is reduced by the glare of publicity.

In my view, a key problem with Culpepper's, and indeed Vogel's, argument, is that it ends up placing too much emphasis on agency, and this is a charge I would also level at Bell, one of the key authors in the recent resurgence of interest in the power of business. Bell takes particular issue with Lindblom's view that the structural power of business means that it is automatically advantaged. Instead, he emphasizes the ideas and perspectives of leaders/ agents, which are formed within the broader political and economic context in which they operate, and which then shape the decisions that they make (Bell, 2012: 663). In consequence, in keeping with much of the contemporary political science literature (Blyth 2003), Bell privileges the role of ideas, arguing that it is 'how agents (politicians) develop and use ideas' that drives their decision-making, a factor he sees as inadequately considered within the business power literature (Bell, 2012: 661; see also Chapter 5). In essence, he reverses Lindblom's, and indeed Culpepper's (Culpepper 2015; Culpepper and Reinke 2014: 427), claim that business, and business leaders, manipulate volitions, rather suggesting it is ideas that shape policy outcomes (Bell 2012: 662). Bell and Hindmoor (2014c: 470) pursued these arguments through a case study on the Australian Mining Tax, his treatment of which I have critiqued elsewhere (Marsh et al. 2014).

The overall point here is that, like Marxism, the pluralist position on the role of business in democracy has changed significantly. Lindblom's argument about the privileged position of business had considerable influence, although, as we have seen, it has been heavily criticized from within pluralism itself. Nevertheless, there is an acknowledgement that the power of business needs particular attention as a potential constraint on democracy, although all agree that the question is, in large part, an empirical one and, as Hay emphasized about Marxism, one which places the structure/agency problem centre stage.

The structure/agency problem and the faces of power debate in relation to positions on the power of business

Here, I examine two separate, but related, issues: first, the structure/agency problem, a perennial one in social science; and, second, the question of how we assess/measure the power of business, which immediately raises the 'faces of power' argument.

I have written before on the structure/agency problem (Marsh 2018) emphasizing that the debate has moved beyond the dualism between structure and agency. I identify three dialectical approaches which see the relationship as a duality, rather than a dualism: Giddens' (1979) structuration theory; Archer's (2003) morphogenesis approach; and Jessop's (1982) strategic-relational approach. This is not the place to discuss those positions; instead, I merely assert that the best of both Marxist and pluralist positions adopt a dialectical approach, either the strategic-relational approach in the case of Jessop and Hay, or Archer's approach for Bell.

In fact, the main issue here is not a theoretical, or even a conceptual, one; rather, it is methodological, which brings us to the 'faces of power' debate. This debate originates in the work of Lukes (1974), who identified three faces of power: the first face involves decision-making, so the focus is on which interest (group) 'wins' on each policy issue; the second face involves agenda-setting, so groups can exercise power by keeping issues off the agenda, as well as by more directly shaping policy; and the third face involves preference shaping, so groups can have an effect on the broad value-system/ideology within which policy is made.

Three points are crucial here. First, I would argue that these faces are 'nested', so each reflects an aspect of the power of an interest, in this case business. Second, while Marxism has always emphasized the role of the third face, it has not neglected the two other faces; for example, these two were the major focus of Miliband's (1965) analysis of the capitalist state, as Hay shows in Chapter 3. In contrast, pluralism has generally neglected the third face, although here Lindblom's focus on the manipulation of volitions provides a partial exception. Third, and relatedly, this means that the different positions, to a significant extent, look at different 'evidence' when trying to assess the power of business. In consequence, they are in danger of talking past one another.

The declining focus on the role of business within democratic politics

I first wrote on the power of business almost fifty years ago and then it was a key topic of concern for all analysts of the operation of democracy, whether Marxists (see Chapter 3), elitists (see Chapter 2) or pluralists (see Chapter 1). The simple, brief, point I want to make here is that this focus became much less prominent in the decades that spanned the millennium (with some notable exceptions, see especially Vogel 2003). In this vein, Culpepper argues (2015: 392) that this concern was phased out of political science following the end of Keynesianism and the rise of neoliberalism. Neoliberalism focuses on the deregulation of markets and downplays the role of government, with the mantra becoming: 'markets good, state bad'. This view was reflected in the policies of Thatcher in the UK and Reagan in the United States, with both governments cutting taxes for business, limiting government intervention and loosening legislation on environmental, safety and labour regulation.

My argument here is straightforward. First, neoliberalism became the dominant value-system/ideology in liberal democracies after 1980, although there were clear variations between different systems, with alternative policies receiving little, if any, consideration (see also Culpepper and Reinke 2014: 429). Second, in broad terms, neoliberalism reflected the interests of business. Third, this clearly reflects the third face of power in operation.

The 2008 GFC stimulated renewed interest, particularly in the United States and the UK, in the role of business and led many scholars to question interpretations of that role. Put simply, the 2008 GFC occurred, in large part, due to big banks making risky financial decisions, which led to large amounts of accumulated debt. Governments subsequently bailed out many large banks and institutions because, in many observers' views, the banks were 'too big to fail', with government relying on them for their survival and the stability of the economy.

Developed countries spent huge amounts of economic resources supporting these banks and institutions. In response, the Organisation for Economic Cooperation and Development (OECD 2009) advised that these banks and financial institutions should be tightly regulated, brought together under the umbrella of a single regulator, with legislation introduced to restrict and supervise them. Nonetheless, many governments struggled to repair the damage caused by these financial decisions, as was clear from the pain and impact caused by the austerity reforms that were subsequently introduced in the United States and throughout the Western world.

So, the GFC revived interest in the role of business, but the response of government hardly suggested the state was standing up to business, an issue I return to in the next section, when considering the work of Bell and Hindmoor (2014), Culpepper and Reinke (2014) and Johal, Moran and Williams (2014).

Empirical analyses of the power of business

Assessing the 'power' of business is difficult in large part because of the methodological issues already discussed. Pluralists focus on the first, and to an extent the second, face of power, while Marxists and other critics of pluralism place more emphasis on the second and particularly the third face. Here, I shall look briefly at a variety of 'evidence', while recognizing these contestations and acknowledging the limitations of the brief space available. However, it seems fair to say that there is an emerging agreement that business is becoming more powerful in contemporary polities.

I start, drawing on the discussion of structure/agency, by examining the structural changes there have been in business, in government and in the relationship between government and business over the last few decades, as that provides the structural context within which government and business interact. Subsequently, I turn to evidence of the extent to which, and the way in which, business influences government policy, using work which adopts different methodological approaches. Here, I look in turn at the work of Vogel, Culpepper, Edwards and Sass, and then Bell and Hindmoor, Culpepper and Reinke. and Johal et al. on the GFC.

Beetham: The changing structure of business and government

Beetham (2011) argues very forcefully that the power of business is greater than it has ever been. Importantly, the evidence he adduces relies heavily on a structuralist position, but it is telling. Beetham (2011) identifies four changes which have significantly increased the power of business in relation to the contemporary state in the UK, although the argument has much broader resonance:

- The triumph of market fundamentalism (Beetham 201: 5–6). The rise of neoliberalism both strengthens the position of big business and weakens the position of the state, given the prevalent mantra is 'markets good, states bad'; this is an argument about the second/third face of power and shares something with Lindblom's focus upon the manipulation of volitions.
- Globalization and financialization. Although the extent, nature and consequences of globalization can be contested (see, for example, Hirst et al. 2009; Hay 2006), there is little doubt that the mobility of financial capital in particular makes regulation by individual states more problematic, and threats of capital strikes more believable (Beetham 2011: 6–7). Beetham doesn't make the point, but the large IT/social media companies avoid state control and particularly taxation, in similar ways to the financial sector.

- Tax avoidance schemes (Beetham 2011: 7–9). Large corporations pay relatively little tax, which leads to significantly reduced government revenues. Transnational corporations declare profits in low tax countries, and pressurize states to make policy concessions or provide infrastructure support as a condition of locating in a particular country.
- Decline in government expertise and organizational capacity. Beetham (2011: 9–10) argues that lower revenue has led to a reduction in capacity, with the increased use of consultancies meaning that the corporate sector is filling the gaps. Here, there is ample evidence that large corporations have many more specialists in policy areas than even a rich state like the United States (**Sass forthcoming**).

Beetham (2011: 10–20) subsequently focuses on the ways in which the corporate sector influences government, emphasizing how that has developed recently, although he doesn't provide detailed examples of influence of the type a pluralist would demand. Rather, he points to the increased influence of the wealthy in policymaking; the financial sector's control of money which is used actively to 'continually reshape the corporate world' (Beetham 2011: 11); the way in which the corporate sector buys informal influence through financing political parties, think tanks and lobbying activities; and the significant increase in the use of revolving doors, with ministers and civil servants moving into corporate jobs when they leave government, while people from the corporate sector are appointed to government posts, advisory committees and departmental boards. He goes further arguing that, concomitantly, there has been a weakening of the position of countervailing forces, notably, but not exclusively, of trade unions, which offered a challenge to the position and arguments of business. In addition, he contends that, rather than weakening the position of business, which might have been expected given that the banks and other financial institutions were particularly heavily implicated in its causes, the GFC has weakened the state, given the almost universal response to it was to cut public expenditure.

Vogel and Culpepper: The fluctuating power of business

'Fluctuating fortunes' is Vogel's (1989) term, and Culpepper's (2010) work certainly suggests business is significantly more powerful than Vogel suggests, but both see significant constraints upon business when issues come clearly into the political arena.

Vogel is probably the most cited of the contemporary political scientists defending a pluralist position on the power of business. He contends that the political power of American corporations fluctuates (for a similar view in relation to US welfare policy see J.S. Hacker and Pierson 2002), but is greatest when their economic power is threatened, particularly in periods of high-level economic growth, when their position in the economy is almost taken for granted. To substantiate this contention, he compares government/ business relations in the 1960s and 1970s.

More specifically, Vogel argues that, in the 1960s, the developing environmental and consumer movements, represented by groups like the Sierra Club and the Friends of the Earth, with Ralph Nader as the key figurehead, were very successful in influencing the US Congress, which passed the Highway Safety Act, the National Environmental Policy Act, the Toxic Substances Control Act, the Occupational Safety and Health Act, the Clean Air Act and a series of Water Acts. Indeed, Vogel (2003: 90) emphasizes: 'Ironically, the period of industry's greatest political vulnerability – at least in the areas of social regulation and tax policy – coincided with the presidency of Republican Richard Nixon.'

Subsequently, Vogel contends, the 1973 oil embargo led to a period of economic stagnation, which actually increased the influence of business in Washington. In large part, this was because corporations established political-action committees and hired a large number of lobbyists, so increasing their instrumental reach and having greater influence in Congress, leading to a relaxation of environmental and auto-safety legislation under Carter and Reagan. While Vogel acknowledges that the business community had increased influence in the 1980s, he still argues that it 'is likely to remain highly divided and fragmented' and that the 'adversarial relationship between government and business' will continue (Vogel 2003: 299). In addition, Vogel argues that interest-group mobilization, linked to media influence, remains the lifeblood of social movements, which still directly limit business power.

Culpepper's view on the power of business is more sanguine. His empirical work examines the role of business in four countries, Germany, France, the Netherlands and Japan, focusing on how the political salience of issues affected the extent to which business had influence. He emphasized that, although there were different 'socio political, cultural and economic contexts in which those businesses operate' (Culpepper 2010: 4), all the managers of large corporations in the different systems possessed the power that they needed to achieve their goals (Culpepper 2010: 4) – a position Edwards (2020) would endorse.

For Culpepper, these managers exercised power because, for the most part, they operated in 'quiet' areas of politics, where ministers and public servants knew much less about a policy than did business executives, and where citizens had little, if any, knowledge or interest. However, Culpepper argues that issues of low salience can become issues of high political salience under two circumstances: if a political scandal is revealed; or as a result of 'the mobilisation efforts of political entrepreneurs' (Culpepper 2010: 6).

Culpepper emphasizes that the media plays a central role in determining the political salience of an issue: 'When governing parties and their opponents know that political issues are debated in the media – and that the people are watching – they have powerful electoral incentives to respond to the dictates of public opinion' (Culpepper 2010: xv). He contends that political scandals are more effective at raising the political salience of an issue because they are less complex to understand than corporate governance issues, which are 'boring and technical' (Culpepper 2010: 147). For example, 'it is much easier to grasp a $165 million individual annual compensation package than it is to understand the implications of hostile takeover rules ' (Culpepper 2010: 147).

The difference between Culpepper and Vogel is that the latter sees such social movements as a continuous constraint on business power, while Culpepper views this as a constraint only when politics moves out of the arena of quiet politics.

Edwards: The growing instrumental power of business

Beetham (2011) forcefully defends an anti-pluralist position, stressing the structural, ideational and instrumental power of business, but does not look at detailed examples of its influence. In contrast, Edwards (2020) provides a more detailed examination of the conflict between Australia's largest companies and government over seven key issues between 2008 and 2018 – so covering the Labor (Rudd–Gillard) and Coalition (Abbott–Turnbull) governments. Edwards emphasizes that the large companies use their enormous size to squeeze their suppliers, distributors and consumers. So, she argues: 'in each of these case studies the corporations were battling with government over laws that shape where profits sit in the supply chain' (xi). However, she also contends that: 'The differing contexts, the complex swirl of countervailing forces, competing forms of power, random events, and a hundred hands on every decision, are awesome in their complexity' (xxiii–xxiv).

Edwards would accept a number of Beetham's claims, particularly that the rise of the mega-corporations has gone hand in hand with a more professionalized approach to political lobbying (Halpin and Warhurst 2016), while the benefits of the economic growth of the last forty years have disproportionately gone to the extremely wealthy. However, she also recognizes that, at least since Dahl, modern pluralists have argued that business is much more diverse and divided than critics recognized, with business interests often on both sides of an issue, so competition between business interests significantly reduce the power of any one of them.

Edwards assesses the extent of business power and the relative importance of the structural, ideational and instrumental aspects of its role, using what in large part is a decision-making approach (see also Culpepper and Reinke 2014: 5–6, although their conclusion is different). Her conclusion is clear:

> In three of the five sectors we looked at, our democracy was not able to rein in the mega-corporations and defend the public interest … For the most part, the miners, the banks, the media moguls and Coles and Woolworths (the largest Australian supermarkets) all circumvented attempts to rein them in. (Edwards 2020: 197)

When turning to the factors which explain the power of business, Edwards plays down the role of its structural position:

> We saw mega-corporations attempt to claim structural power in some cases, but the arguments didn't stand up to scrutiny. The economic policy community overwhelmingly rejected arguments that delivering on corporations' preferences served the wider community. (Edwards 2020: 198)

She also downplays the role of neoliberal ideas:

> In six of these seven case studies Australia's neoliberal institutions didn't back the corporate preferences. They generally advocated reining in the corporations and exposing them to more competitive pressure. Neoliberal ideas were not the definitive factor. (Edwards 2020:199)

In contrast, she emphasizes the role of the instrumental power which business enjoys and, in particular, the reluctance of the Australian governments, both Labor and Coalition, to stand up to it:

> Politicians are legislating policy outcomes that are difficult to justify as being in the national interest. They are doing so because they believe that

> their political interests rely upon it … the mega-corporations have so much influence – through the soft-power network of mates, through donations, marginal seats campaigns, and public media campaigns – that our politicians feel beholden to them. (Edwards 2020:199)

Edwards identifies a limited difference between the parties, with Labor marginally more willing to stand up to business, and she recognizes that agents can make a difference. However, her message is clear: business, or rather large corporations, dominate Australian politics in large part because governments will not stand up to them. In addition, although she doesn't directly consider Culpepper's argument that most of business's influence occurs in the 'quiet' areas of politics, her evidence contradicts it, given all the issues she considers played out in a heated political arena.

In my view, Edwards's argument is convincing and my only reservation is that her method, in essence a decision-making approach, fails to do justice to arguments about structural power and the manipulation of volitions. Indeed, her conclusion immediately suggests a question: *why* do governments think their re-election chances depend on keeping business onside? Any answer to this question would surely lead us to consider the second and third faces of power.

These contributions to the debate clearly raise a number of questions, which are not exclusively empirical. What factors influence whether an issue is kept off, or placed at the forefront of, the political agenda? What role does interest-group mobilization play in shaping policy outcomes? What role does the media play in shaping political opinion? Overall, the most fundamental questions concern Lindblom's view that there is a continuing, and largely stable, 'exchange relationship' between business and government. Beetham and Edwards would say no, because business has more, and increasing, power vis-à-vis government; Vogel would say yes, because business power fluctuates over time and between issues, but is constrained by other actors and by the electoral concerns of governments; while Culpepper would say that business's power does fluctuate, but that in 'quiet' areas of politics it has privileged access and significant influence. It is also interesting here, that in the aftermath of the GFC, Culpepper (2010: 198) argued: 'Many indicators suggest that we are living through a period of radical renegotiation of the political status quo, and that organised business sits in a weakened bargaining position.' This is a view that would enjoy no support from Beetham, Edwards or Johal, Moran and Williams (2014).

Sass: Monsanto usually wins

Sass (2020) uses a detailed analysis of Monsanto's company reports and business correspondence, together with interviews with the most active members of the company's steering committee to examine the relations between Monsanto and the US government since the 1970s. He argues that Monsanto changed its public affairs ethos in the 1970s and early 1980s, becoming much more proactive (Sass 2020: 136). Using this material, Sass (2020: 136) claims:

> What emerges is an image of a firm with enormous political ambition. To transform itself from a bulk chemical to a biotechnology firm, Monsanto's leaders knew they would first need to transform their institutional environment, and they did.

Monsanto began its efforts to change the US regulatory context in 1983 in discussions within the OECD about principles that would guide safety and ecological regulations for the development of genetically modified crops. In this context, Sass argues (2020: 140) that: 'by its second year of operation, Monsanto's Steering Committee claimed a series of victories with respect to its influence over the policy formation process at the OECD. By mid-1984, the Steering Committee had worked its way from the Environmental Protection Agency to the White House' (Sass 2020: 146). As a result of this access and influence, Sass (2020: 152) shows that in the United States, unlike in the UK and Germany, 'the safety of agricultural biotechnologies was given the benefit of the doubt'.

Monsanto's aim was to prevent

> biotechnology becoming the kind of issue that would evoke strong public opinion because this would entail arbitrary regulatory decisions. The object of the Steering Committee's public opinion campaign, then, was nothing less than reshaping the public language surrounding biotechnology. (Sass 2020: 154)

In other words, the aim was to shape preferences, control the agenda and keep the issue in what Culpepper calls the 'quiet' arena of politics.

Sass (2020: 155) shows that Monsanto was very active in the PR field. attempting to bring any external actors who were not strongly opposed to genetically modified crops closer to their position, while isolating their opponents. At the same time, 'the Steering Committee sought to shape the opinions of influential politicians and government officials' (Sass 2020: 162).

Perhaps most crucially, Monsanto conducted a very broad survey to discover citizens' attitudes to biotechnology and published scores of newspaper articles, while also running TV and radio ads. The aim was to project itself as a leading biotechnology firm. Subsequent surveys revealed a substantial shift in the increase in support for biotechnology experimentation and a more positive view of Monsanto. In this context, Sass (2020: 167) quotes Gary Barton, the director of this programme, as claiming that Monsanto found it could 'move the needle of public opinion'.

So, Monsanto had privileged access to decision-makers and was able to manipulate volitions, but did they have influence? Sass's conclusion is stark:

> Incredibly, this group of executives achieved all of their aims. They drafted the federal regulations adopted in the United States – regulations that, needless to say, were entirely consistent with Monsanto's strategic needs. With help from the State Department, Monsanto shaped the regulatory guidelines for biotechnology promoted around the world by the OECD. Monsanto shaped American public opinion about biotechnology, creating nation-wide educational campaigns for schools, producing documentaries for popular use, and engaging intensively with groups most likely to influence policy, as well as individuals and communities that had shown resistance.

Bell and Hindmoor, Culpepper and Reinke, and Johal, Moran and Williams: The GFC and its aftermath

In the final section on empirical evidence, I focus on work by Bell and Hindmoor (2014a,b,c,d) (and Hindmoor and McGeechan (2013)), Culpepper and Reinke (2014) and Johal, Moran and Williams (2014)[1] on governments' response to the GFC. In setting the context, Bell and Hindmoor argue that governments face major problems in negotiating with the financial centre because of large inequities in capacity. They contend: 'Both the City and Wall Street have historically been one jump ahead of regulators in the game of regulatory arbitrage' (2014a: 356). Overall, their argument is essentially that state authorities are unlikely to have 'the administrative or regulatory capacity to tame finance' (2014a: 357), an argument which resonates with Beetham's and Edwards' arguments about business more generally.

---

[1] With co-authors I have dealt at more length with this work in Marsh, Akram and Birkett, 2015.

Both Bell and Hindmoor and Hindmoor and McGeechan adopt a dialectical approach to the structure/agency problem, although, in my view, they downplay the importance of structure and emphasize the role of ideas and agency, because of both their rejection of the view that structures can have independent causal power (on this see Marsh 2018) and their use of a bounded rationality model.

In focusing on the banking sector, Hindmoor and McGeechan (2013: 842–846) show how, over time, the lobbying activities (agency) of US banks resulted in legislative and regulative changes that led to the widespread idea that the banks were 'too big to fail'. Here, the point for Hindmoor and McGeechan is that the 'systematic luck' of banks, getting what they want without trying (a very different picture than in the Monsanto case considered above), had its origins in prior lobbying activity.

Dealing with the GFC, Bell and Hindmoor (2014b,) argue:

> It is ironic that the institutional and structural pressures that were to have such a devastating impact were largely created prior to the crisis by bankers (and supportive state elites) in the heartland financial markets of the US and UK. The key changes were part of a wider process of 'financialisation' and a revolution in banking in the core economies in the decades prior to the crisis: a period in which bankers were widely seen as Masters of the Universe. Once the crisis was triggered however, bankers were quickly overwhelmed by forces they had not anticipated and were revealed as almost Slaves of the Markets they had helped create.

Bell and Hindmoor, like Edwards, identify and discuss the structural, ideational and instrumental aspects; however, in contrast to Edwards, who stresses the instrumental power of business, they see the relationship between the three as interactive, and often cumulative. For Bell and Hindmoor (2014b: 16), ideas mediate the effects of structural power, either increasing or decreasing it. At first, they contend, the dominant ideas about the efficacy of the market benefited the bankers, but, subsequently: 'The ideas held by agents about the safety of the system blinded them to mounting systemic risk prior to the crisis. Prevailing ideas and assumptions concealed the true nature of the structural dynamics confronting agents.' Here, ideas are seen as a resource which can facilitate or constrain agents; structure is given a limited role.

Like Lindblom, Bell and Hindmoor (2014b:16) see the structural power of business as deriving from the firms' positions within the economy and how that position constrains governments' actions. In contrast, for them, instrumental power derives from 'the various means, unrelated to the core functions of the firm, through which business influences politics: donations for campaigns, privileged access to policymakers, and lobbyists and organizations that defend business interests'.

For Culpepper and Reinke (2014: 5–6), both structural and instrumental power can be automatic or strategic. In developing this position, they are taking issue, although not directly, with Ward (1987) who contended that structures cannot exercise power, only agents can, and who would also argue, like Bell and Hindmoor, that agents do not act automatically, but strategically, bearing in mind their preferences (interests) and the decision-making scheme with which they are faced. Instead, Culpepper and Reinke see structure and agency as both playing a role and contend that instrumental action is shaped by the structural context within which it occurs – some way towards a dialectical view.

Culpepper and Reinke suggest that the relationship between the structural position of business and the instrumental action of business agents, both individual and collective, is, in some sense, interactive – a point amply demonstrated by their comparative case study of the government bailout of the banks in the United States and the UK during the GFC (Culpepper and Reinke 2014: 6–7).

In both the United States and the UK, the governments 'intervened on a sector-wide scale and provided liquidity, debt guarantees and recapitalizations' (Culpepper and Reinke 2014: 8). However, they show that, in the UK, the outcome was better for the banks, and worse for the government, while the reverse was the case in the United States. Culpepper and Reinke (2014: 9–10) suggest that the most important reason for this outcome was structural. Most of the business of US banks was within the jurisdiction of the US regulator – so, for example, 75 per cent of Wells Fargo's business came from the United States, while in the UK that was not the case for HSBC, which generated only 20 per cent of its profits from the UK (Culpepper and Reinke 2014: 12–13). In the UK, while Barclays relied heavily on the domestic market, it was able to borrow funds from Qatar and Abu Dhabi. In this context, HSBC refused to be involved in the UK government's recapitalization plan and Barclays quickly followed their lead. In contrast, US regulators made Wells Fargo and JP Morgan 'an offer they could not refuse' (Culpepper and Reinke 2014: 14). Culpepper and Reinke (2014: 15) conclude: 'HSBC's action was intentional, but it was a product of its structural position in the market, not the result of its lobbying access.' It is interesting here that in none of their articles on the banking crisis do Bell and Hindmoor point to this 'structural difference' between the UK and US banking sectors, so they do not assess its effect on policy outcomes.

Johal, Moran and Williams take a different approach, framed by an interesting take on Lukes' (1975) faces of power arguments discussed above. They add a fourth face of power, capillary power, which is derived from Foucault's work. This fourth face 'consciously dispenses with the language of either domination or agency ... It entails the internalisation of values in such a way as to ensure that discipline becomes something not imposed externally but the product of restraints learnt and then followed voluntarily' (Johal et al. 2014: 402).

They examine the development of City power in the UK and argue that, before the establishment of democracy, City power was based on agenda-setting, while post-1918 it depended on 'the creation of a hegemonic narrative which fused constitutional, regulatory and economic policy elements' (Johal et al. 2014: 409). However, they contend that cultural change, regulatory failure and economic policy changes weakened this hegemonic narrative. The response during the long market boom involved a process of governmentality, in which

> the project was to make markets and their operation highly visible as policymakers, financial elites and populations were supposed to perform behaviours and internalize a whole series of normative constraints that were market sensitive. (Ibid.)

A key point for Johal, Moran and Williams is that this was a process of which agents were unaware. It was also a process/project in which little agency was involved on the part of the financial sector.

Johal, Moran and Williams (2014: 410–414) identify six elements of this capillary power: structural changes, like privatization of nationalized industries and social housing, which exposed the population to the risks and rewards of the financial markets; the development of new financial products to 'protect' the population against increased risk/uncertainty; the increased role of the market as a mode of governance, particularly in relation to the setting of interest rates; the 'celebration of the superior intelligence of markets in the management of risk' (Johal et al. 2014: 411); the emergence of authority figures, 'economic analysts', who spread the message about the superiority of markets; and the development of a narrative emphasizing that 'the deregulation of London as a financial sector had created an alternative economic dynamic, had given the UK a comparative advantage in building a post-industrial service economy' (Johal et al. 2014: 412).

However, Johal, Moran and Williams (2014: 413) argue that it was a failed project, emphasizing that 'Dominance and ubiquity is not the same as stability or sustainability of power.' It failed because 'the reach of governmentality exceeded its growth both when appropriate norms were not internalised by the population and when the widely accepted complacent account of the workings of financial markets was controverted by events such as the great crash of 2007-8' (Johal, Moran and Williams 2014: 409).

In more detail, they contend that the failure resulted from a number of factors. First, they emphasize the GFC, arguing that 'when events falsify the terms of a legitimating narrative, that narrative is in trouble' (2014: 414). This directly raises the issue of the relationship between structure and the ideational realm. One way to see this issue, as Marsh (2010) argues when discussing the relationship between the 'reality' of globalization and narratives about it, is to evoke a concept of 'resonance'. Here, the argument would be that, while any notion of how the financial market operates is possible, the realities of how it operates will constrain the effectiveness and longevity of that narrative.

Johal, Moran and Williams (2014: 415) also emphasize that the GFC had important structural and policy consequences, particularly the transfer of banks to public ownership, which weakened the governmentality project. This was exacerbated by a series of scandals – for example, around the mis-selling of endowment mortgages and personal pensions. For Johal, Moran and Williams (2014: 416), one consequence was 'an electorate of suspicious customers', with rising antipathy towards banks. Together with the widespread financial illiteracy of the population, this meant that there was no 'government of the self', which is crucial for the success of capillary power.

In the light of their analysis of the changes in the power of the City of London over time, Johal, Moran and Williams develop an interesting take on the faces of power argument. They contend that the City used different forms of power at different times. For much of the twentieth century it used hegemonic power, but, as a result of cultural change, regulatory failure and economic policy changes, it came to rely on capillary power. This was an unsuccessful project, so, in a period where policy towards the banking sector is more contested, they have increasingly had to use the first face (Johal et al. 2014: 416). So, it is not so much the power of the financial sector that fluctuates, as Vogel would suggest, but rather the means they use to exercise that power that changes.

Johal, Moran and Williams emphasize the importance of what they term capillary power through which the views and actions of agents can be shaped in ways of which they are unaware. However, they also show that such power is not automatic; the project involved is not necessarily successful. It can be thrown off course by structural change and 'events'. What is perhaps less successful is their treatment of agency – a common criticism of Foucauldian-inspired work (see Chapter 8). They see the failed establishment of governmentality as a process/project more or less without agents, although they do briefly discuss the role of agents in the period post-crisis.

Conclusion

In this brief survey, I first reviewed the developments within Marxist and pluralist thought about the power of business in contemporary capitalism, before briefly examining the reasons for the decline of interest in the power of business over the two decades spanning the millennium. However, my main concern has been to examine more recent empirical material on this issue. Although this is a contested area, in part because of the use of different methodologies to assess the issue, there is a clear pattern.

My argument is certainly not that business always wins, or that there are not significant differences between the power of different companies/financial institutions on different policies. I also acknowledge that, at one level, the question of the power of a particular company/financial institution is an empirical one. However, the work of authors such as Edwards, Sass, and Johal, Moran and Williams, suggest there is a clear pattern. Business is clearly a powerful interest in contemporary capitalism – I would suggest the most powerful interest, although no comparative data is presented here. In addition, in my view, its power has also increased over the last period, in part because of structural and ideational changes which have strengthened its position, as Beetham convincingly shows.

One other conclusion seems important here. Although Edwards makes a strong case that business is very powerful in contemporary Australian policymaking, I am less convinced by her conclusion that it is largely instrumental power that explains business's influence. Rather, in my view, the three forms of power, four if we consider capillary power, are nested. So, my answer to the question I posed to Edwards above is that government fails to stand up to business in large part because they are operating within a context inscribed by the operation of the second and third faces of power.

Further Reading

Bell, S. and A. Hindmoor (2014), 'The ideational shaping of state power and capacity: Winning battles but losing the war over bank reform in the US and UK', *Government and Opposition*, 49(3), 342–368.

Culpepper, P.D. (2010), *Quiet Politics and Business Power*, Cambridge: Cambridge University Press.

Culpepper, P. and R. Reinke (2014), 'Structural power and bank bailouts in the United Kingdom and the United States', *Politics and Society*, 42(4), 1–28.

Lindblom, C. (1977), *Politics and Markets*, New York: Basic Books.

Vogel, D. (1989), *Fluctuating Fortunes: The Political Power of Business in America*, New York: Basic Books.

13

The State and Nationalism

Nicola McEwen and Daniel Cetrà

Introduction

The preceding chapters in this section have examined different aspects of statehood. Each reaffirms the importance of the state to political organization, despite pressures of global financial interdependence and supra-national governance. The state also remains the primary unit of analysis in political science research. The field of comparative politics is dominated by studies that compare and contrast political phenomena across states, while the field of international relations focuses upon the interactions between states in the international community.

Implicit within discussions of the state is the concept of the nation-state. In the modern era, the boundaries of the state are often presented as the boundaries of the nation. This is not accidental. Whereas statehood is associated with formal institutions, laws and functions, nationhood taps into emotional bonds of solidarity and mutual belonging. A shared sense of nationhood serves to reinforce the legitimacy of the state as a system of rule. Nationhood and the collective identity of 'the people' are invoked to legitimize the sharing of risks and resources among citizens of the state, and to defend the actions of the state in the international community.

Nationhood is especially important in sustaining legitimacy in democratic states. Democratic governance requires enough of a shared identity between citizens to ensure that the decisions they reach collectively as the *demos* (the people), and those made by elected representatives in their name, will be accepted. Citizens in a democratic state must be prepared to make the necessary contributions to ensure the functioning and defence of the state – for example, to support a system of taxation that redistributes income and resources from some citizens to others, or to risk the sacrifice of loss of life or loved ones in defence of the state's authority and territory. Charles Taylor remarked that 'the modern democratic state needs a healthy degree of what used to be called patriotism, a strong sense of identification with the polity, and a willingness to give of oneself for its sake'. In the context of the modern state, 'nationalism has become the most readily available motor of patriotism' (Taylor 1996: 201–202).

Yet, students of politics should guard against assuming that 'the state' is a coherent unit. Many states are marked by internal territorial diversity such that the boundaries of the state and the boundaries of the nation may not be aligned. It is often in these cases that the politics of nationalism is most visible.

Nationalism is understood in this chapter as both a political doctrine and a form of politics. As a doctrine, it holds that nations have the right to self-determination. The doctrine finds expression in the UN Covenant as the right of 'peoples' to 'freely determine their political status and freely pursue their economic, social and cultural development' (UN 1976: Part 1, Article 1). This has long been recognized, at least among scholars, as an 'idealistic element of state formation' (Danspeckgruber 2002: 2) rather than a sound organizing principle. Moreover, the doctrine gives rise to the question: who are the 'peoples' – the 'self' – who are to be permitted the right to freely determine their political status? The answer to that question is political. Nationalism is also a form of political behaviour. It may be manifest in subtle nation-building initiatives intended to develop narratives of nationhood, nurture national identity and reinforce attachment to the nation. Or it may be evident in political mobilization intended to strengthen territorial demands or pursue goals in the people's name.

In this chapter, we place emphasis on the relationship between nationalism and the state. The state can be an agent of nationalism, seeking to reinforce bonds of nationhood across the whole country. Those states that include more than one nation sometimes engage in nationalist behaviour to marginalize or even repress minority nations. Conversely, their multinational character may be acknowledged and celebrated in the symbols, narratives, customs and laws that represent the state to its citizens and the wider world. The state is also the object of nationalists from minority or 'sub-state' nations within states, who aim to increase the status and power of the nation in whose name they act. That may involve trying to change the way the state is governed to introduce devolution or federalism. More radical sub-state nationalists aim to leave one state and set up (or join) another.

This chapter will explore these different manifestations of nationalism. It will first consider different scholarly perspectives on nationalism and the state. It will then explore nationalism on the part of states and nations within states. In the final section, we will examine state and sub-state nationalism in the UK/Scotland and Spain/Catalonia, as these are among the most prominent cases in Europe.

Theoretical perspectives on nationalism and the state

Three main approaches have dominated the study of nationalism: primordialism, modernism and ethnosymbolism. The role of the state features to varying degrees in each of these.

Primordialism is an umbrella term to describe the view that nations are natural and have existed for all time. This approach pays little heed to the role of the state. Instead, it emphasizes common bonds of ancestry, kinship and ethnicity which, it is suggested, endure across time (van den Berghe 1994: 98–99; Geertz 1994: 30–31). Scholars who stress the antiquity of nations while conceding that they are not natural entities are sometimes labelled perennialists (Hastings 1997: 3–4; see also Smith 2002: 12–14). While primordialism may reflect the view of many nationalists themselves, it has become a very marginal position in nationalism studies.

The overwhelmingly dominant approach is modernism. The state is a central feature of modernist accounts of nationalism. Rather than seeing them as natural entities, nations are viewed as modern phenomena linked to the emergence of the modern state. For modernists, nations are historically situated entities constructed by nationalism, and nationalism is a product of the demands of the social, political and economic transformations of the modern world. Modernist perspectives on nationalism point to the importance of communication networks and the standardization of language as central to the generation of shared customs and narratives of political community (Deutsch 1966; Anderson 2006). Benedict Anderson famously argued that the spread of standardized language, combined with capitalism and print technology, created the conditions that allowed us to 'imagine' nations. According to Anderson, capitalism assembled vernacular languages to be disseminated through the market, and this produced an association between linguistic distinctiveness and national culture. A unified field of exchange and communication emerged below Latin and above the spoken languages; this was the 'embryo' of the nationally imagined community (Anderson 2006: 37–46).

One of the most influential contributions within the modernist tradition was provided by Ernest Gellner (1983). He argued that states engaged in nation-building to achieve and sustain linguistic and cultural homogeneity. This, in turn, supported the territorial and political integration of the population. For Gellner, modern industrial societies required cultural homogeneity because they demanded high levels of social and geographic mobility in the labour market. Nationalism, understood by Gellner as the political principle which holds that the political and the national unit should be congruent (ibid.: 5), transformed a 'folk culture' into a high national culture and imposed it on society. Some languages developed to become the *national* language of the state while others did not. This has normative consequences as those languages elevated to the status of national languages come to be associated with modernity and progress, while others are often considered anachronistic and backward (May 2001). According to Gellner, the motor of this process of cultural homogenization was the state education system, which provided generic training and a standardized, shared language and culture that allowed people to communicate and move from one occupational position and location to another. Thus, in Gellner's work, nationalism is a unifying process that seeks political integration through full-scale cultural assimilation, generating and sustaining shared ideas of the nation.

Other scholars who adopt a modernist interpretation of nationalism have placed even greater emphasis on the state and the politics that surround it. While acknowledging the importance of a standardized culture, advanced communication and print capitalism in supporting the spread of nationalist ideas, for John Breuilly, these did not *explain* nationalism. Instead, he noted, the key to the emergence of nationalism was the development of the modern state, which set the context in which nationalism emerged and also represented the prize over which nationalists compete. 'To focus upon culture, ideology, identity, class or modernization is to neglect the fundamental point that nationalism is, above and beyond all else, about politics and politics is about power. Power, in the modern world, is principally about control of the state' (Breuilly 1993: 1–2). Michael Mann (1993) also saw nationalism as closely related to the emergence of the state, identifying three distinct phases. The first was the militarist phase, when eighteenth-century warfare turned the state into a key actor in people's lives. State taxes raised revenues, conscription recruited soldiers, and the population was mobilized around state goals. In the second industrial phase, from the mid-nineteenth century to the First World War, the notion of popular sovereignty took hold and state functions gradually expanded (see also Chapter 9). This increased the state's ability to permeate social life and implement its decisions throughout the territory it claimed to govern. The third, modernist, phase saw popular sovereignty become firmly embedded in newly democratized national states, while authoritarian regimes used nationalism as an aggressive way of extending state power.

Modernists often place emphasis on instrumentalism, that is, the strategic use of cultural factors and national identities by political elites for generating mass support and political legitimacy (Brass 1994: 87–88). Eric Hobsbawm and Terence Ranger (1986) spoke of nationalism as 'the invention of tradition', whereby national customs and beliefs are constructed and mobilized for political ends. They suggested that elites forge a sense of historical continuity through the modification and creation of songs, languages and traditions. For example, Hobsbawm observed that the Flemish taught in Belgium today is the product of standardization and mass schooling, and it is very different from the language that the mothers and grandmothers of Flanders spoke to their children. As such, it is only metaphorically, but not literally, a 'mother-tongue'. Hobsbawm also highlighted the invention of public ceremonies. In France, Bastille Day was invented in 1880 to transform the heritage of the Revolution into a combined expression of state pomp and power (1994: 76–78).

The third approach to the study of nationalism, ethnosymbolism, emerged as a critique of modernism, with less focus on nationalism as an instrumental tool of the state. In contrast to ideas of invented traditions, ethnosymbolism emphasizes that modern nations are often founded on pre-existing collective cultural identities, or *ethnies*. Anthony D. Smith (1986, 1998) is the leading proponent of this approach, with others following in his wake (see also Armstrong 1982; Hutchinson 1994; Grosby 2005). Ethnosymbolists have emphasized the relevance of myths, symbols, memories, values and traditions as key components of national identity. While they recognize the transformations brought about by modernity, they argue that modern states did not create a blank slate upon which a nation's traditions were invented. On the contrary, they argued that there is a great deal of continuity between 'traditional' and 'modern' societies and therefore scholars must adopt a *longue durée* approach, exploring the differences and similarities between the 'content' of contemporary nations and pre-modern ethnic communities.

The debate between primordialists, modernists and ethnosymbolists is essentially about the origins of nations and nationalism. Wherever scholars of nationalism position themselves in that debate, there is more agreement on the enduring significance of nationalism in the world today. Nationalism establishes the ultimate source of political legitimacy – 'the people' – and remains the fundamental organizing principle of the political order – national sovereignty.

Varieties of nationalism: Inclusion and exclusion

Combined with other 'thicker' ideologies, nationalism may be a weapon of exclusion and repression, or it can be a source of liberation, empowerment and inclusion. Its inclusivity or exclusivity depends upon the uses to which it is put by those pursuing political goals in the name of the nation, in defence of, or against the actions of, the state. There is thus nothing inherently liberal or illiberal about nationalism.

How may we make sense of the variety of nationalisms in the world? A common analytical distinction is between those nationalisms that are deemed to be 'civic' and those characterized as 'ethnic'. Hans Kohn (1944) developed the most influential articulation of the civic–ethnic distinction. Although he couched this difference in terms of 'Western' and 'Eastern' forms of nationalism in Europe, the distinction was understood to have implications beyond Europe and has become a universal category of analysis. Civic, 'Western-style', nationalism is characterized as primarily territorial, rooted in common citizenship, and liberal, voluntarist, universalist and inclusive. In determining who constitutes 'the people', civic nationalism bases belonging to the nation on living in a country, irrespective of place of birth. By contrast, ethnic, 'Eastern-style', nationalism rests on members of the nation sharing a common ethnicity and often common ancestry. It is usually characterized as illiberal, ascriptive, particularist and exclusive; you cannot join an ethnic nation, you must be born into it.

Various nationalism scholars have drawn on the civic–ethnic distinction, sometimes interpreting it in slightly different ways (Smith 1986: 134–152; 1991: 13–16; Greenfeld 1992: 10–11; Ignatieff 1993: 3–6). For example, Rogers Brubaker (1992: 3) famously distinguished between the French civic understanding of nationhood as state-centred and assimilationist, and the German understanding of nationhood as *Volk*-centred and differentialist. In the French tradition, the dominant conception of the nation is political, tied closely to the institutional and territorial frame of the state. In Germany, ideas of nation are deemed pre-political as they developed before the state and are grounded in cultural and linguistic aspects. As a result, French citizenship came to be defined as a territorial community based on *ius soli* (the law of the soil) while in Germany, citizenship was formed on the basis of a community of descent, on *ius sanguinis* (the law of blood). These two cases highlight the problems in equating civic–ethnic with liberal–illiberal traits. While Germany has clearly had periods of illiberal nationalism, post-war Germany has combined liberalism with an ethnic conception of nationhood. Conversely, civic nations can be exclusive – in France, loyalty to the values of *la République* and the equality of all French citizens can appear less tolerant to minorities, and less accommodating of ethnic, religious or linguistic diversity.

While the civic–ethnic dichotomy has greatly shaped the literature on nationalism, it has also faced convincing criticisms. Nationalism scholars and liberal theorists have persuasively argued that civic forms of nationalism also have a cultural dimension – they evolve out of particular cultures and histories which they seek to protect and promote (Brown 1999: 297–300; Kymlicka 1999). Bernard Yack identified 'the myth of the civic nation' to underline that civic nations are not only based on political notions such as choice and consent but also include cultural elements and connections with pre-political identities. He stressed that the vast majority of people are born into and inherit national and cultural traditions they have not chosen (Yack 2012: 23–43). This puts into question notions such as 'constitutional patriotism' (Habermas 1992) which propose that people feel attachment to liberal democratic values rather than nations. The audience for constitutionally focused patriotism is not a random association of individuals united only by allegiance to universal principles, but rather a specific national community with its own inherited cultural and historical features.

Perhaps more useful than the civic–ethnic distinction is an understanding of nationalism as spanning liberal to illiberal forms. The key issue is the degree of openness and tolerance displayed by nationalism. All nations are defined by the boundaries that separate one nation from another; indeed, we often define and understand 'our' nation in relation to 'the other' (Jenkins 1996). Liberal nationalists recognize the importance of national groups to individuals but, crucially, create a set of constraints to mitigate the illiberal, exclusionary potential of nationalist policies (Kymlicka 1995; Miller 1995; Moore 2001; Tamir 1993, 2019). Will Kymlicka argued that, in liberal nations, individual members can opt out and non-members can opt in, diversity and dissent are permitted in the public sphere, and minorities are able to express and cherish their own identity (Kymlicka 2001: 39–41). This requires a 'thin' and inclusive definition of the national community. Given that, from a liberal perspective, membership of the nation should not be restricted to those of a particular race or ethnicity, the terms of admission should be relatively accessible, such as participating in common public institutions or learning the language.

Indeed, language is a relevant aspect in discussions of inclusion and exclusion in national projects. Many nationalisms devote special attention to linguistic distinctiveness, presenting their language as a national identity marker demarcating 'the people' from 'the others' and using it as a tool to foster a sense of common identity. The interesting point here is that national leaders may use language either as an instrument of inclusion or as a tool for exclusion. Language policies may be used by dominant groups to elevate the language of their nation to the state as a whole, marginalizing speakers of minority languages. Conversely, a common language – which need not require linguistic homogeneity – may also be an important element in fostering civic community, political equality and mass participation, and can be used as a mechanism for integration rather than exclusion (Cetrà, 2019). Learning a language is demanding but it is a relatively thin criterion of admission, and therefore it can fit with liberal accounts of nationalism that permit new entrants to opt in to the national community.

Discussions of inclusion and exclusion in national projects should also take account of the importance of gender (see also Chapter 6). Mainstream theories of nationalism are often gender-blind, overlooking what some scholars have suggested is a close connection between nationalism and masculinity (Nagel 1998). The beliefs and practices of nationalist ideology emphasize and resonate with masculine cultural themes, such as honour, duty and bravery. Male intellectuals have been the relevant actors in nation-building while women have rarely been permitted active participation. Yet narratives of the nation and national struggles are often told as if experienced identically by men and women, and as if they had the same role in defining the nation (Enloe, 2014).

While stressing that there is no unitary, unproblematic category of women, Nira Yuval-Davis identified five major ways in which women have participated in national projects (1997). First, nationalism often defines women as biological reproducers of the nation, with pressures to have, or not to have, children in the national interest. Second, women are characterized as reproducers of the boundaries of national groups, acting in many national projects as symbolic border guards which classify people as members and non-members through specific cultural codes – for instance, in relation to styles of dress, behaviour and religion. Third, women are often constructed as 'mothers of the nation', reproducing the nation not only biologically but culturally, socializing the new generation and instilling them with national values and culture. Fourth, nationhood is often characterized in the female form, the 'motherland', embodying the nation's respectability and purity. From the French Marianne to the British Britannia and the American Statue of Liberty, or more generically, Mother Russia and Mother India, the nation is gendered as a motherland, constructing for both women and nations the idealized traits of a nurturer and care-giver. Finally, Yuval-Davis has critiqued the 'sexual division of labour' observed in nationalist struggles, where women are more often afforded the role as carers of the wounded and dying than as 'freedom fighters'. Indeed, the construction of women as symbols of national honour makes them the most vulnerable to sexual crimes when violence erupts between national or ethnic groups (Alison 2009). Some brutal recent examples of sexual violence used as a weapon of war were seen in the ethnic conflicts of the Bosnian War (1992–95) and the Rwandan genocide (1994). Rape was meant to humiliate and destroy the enemy by targeting the 'mothers of the nation', and to biologically attack the enemy group's reproduction, bloodline purity and, ultimately, its survival (Hamel, 2016).

While nationalism may adopt more liberal or reactionary forms in different places at different times, there can be little doubt that it is a pervasive force in our contemporary world. But nationalism is, at most, a 'thin' ideology. As Bernard Yack points out, 'nationalist principles tell us who should have the final say over a state's instruments of authority, not what tunes to play on them. That is one reason why nationalism combines so easily with other ideologies, from liberalism and conservatism to fascism and even socialism' (2012: 129).

This helps to explain why nationalism is sometimes confused with another 'thin-centred' ideology: populism. However, the two are conceptually distinctive. As discussed in Chapter 14, populism emphasizes that the politics of the modern state are built around a conflict between two homogeneous and antagonistic groups, the 'people' and the 'elite'. Mudde (2004: 546) suggested that 'the people of the populists are an "imagined community", much like the nation of the nationalists'. In drawing boundaries around 'the people', both populist and nationalist narratives engage in a process of 'othering', to identify who belongs and who does not. But, with populism, the key distinction is less in/out and more up/down, with a downtrodden 'people' differentiated from a corrupt and powerful elite. Populists thus claim to speak for 'the ordinary people' – the 'man in the street' – and rail against a self-serving 'establishment' (De Cleen 2017). Nationalism, by contrast, demarcates a national community of citizens extending from the past to the future, with a shared history, shared purpose and a mutual sense of belonging. Populism and nationalism sometimes come together; radical-right populism, for example, often relies on 'nativist' ideology that targets external others (usually immigrants or asylum seekers) as well as the establishment (Mudde 2007: 19). But this is only one manifestation of nationalism among many others. Nationalism is a much broader phenomenon, used sometimes to include, sometimes to exclude, and can be a tool of the political elite as much as of those railing against it.

State and sub-state nationalism

Nationalism is often most visible when associated with 'hot' manifestations, such as independence movements like those in Scotland, Catalonia or Kurdistan; right-wing, anti-EU, and anti-multicultural politics of UKIP or the Front national; or ethnic conflicts like those that accompanied the break-up of the former Yugoslavia. Yet, recalling the centrality of nationalism to maintaining the legitimacy of the state as a system of rule, less visible forms of nationalism also merit our attention. Michael Billig (1995) coined the influential notion of 'banal nationalism' to draw attention to the subtle daily reminders of nationhood surrounding us in our normal life. From coins, bank notes and stamps with national figures, to flags flying over public buildings, politicians and journalists evoking a national 'we', or weather maps placing 'us' within 'our' homeland, these reminders are so integrated into our lives and so familiar to us that we do not register them consciously (ibid.: 106–109, 119). Banal nationalism is associated with all forms of nationalism. In powerful, well-established 'nation-states', nationalist symbols are so pervasive that they become camouflaged against the backdrop of the ordinary. In addition to the physical symbols of nationhood, Calhoun (1997: 4–5) discussed nationalism as a form of discourse which reinforces the boundaries of territory and population (see Chapter 11), the assumption of (or aspiration to) sovereignty (see Chapter 10), and the 'ascending' notion of legitimacy that sees popular support as a requirement for just government.

The nation is at the heart of the legitimacy of the state. A shared national identity supports the collective understandings, commitments, contributions and sacrifices necessary to the functioning of the state and supports the legitimacy of the state as a system of rule. Yet there are many more nations in the world – many more territories and communities identifying themselves as *national* communities – than there are states. The lack of congruence between the boundaries of the nation and the boundaries of the state underlies the politics of nationalism.

State nationalism

State nationalism aims to sustain the view of the state as a *nation-state*. All states engage in the politics of nationalism, building and reinforcing the boundaries of the nation to support the legitimacy of the state and state actions (Gagnon et al. 2011; see also Chapter 11). State nationalism is implicit in the 'constant reproduction and promotion of the nation by state elites and institutions' (Cetrà and Brown Swan 2020: 3). Often, this takes the form of banal nationalism, with the subtle use of discourse, policies, institutions and cultural practices to construct and reproduce conceptions of 'the nation'. State-wide actors can also readily access the institutional apparatus of the state, in both positive and negative ways, to manage and respond to territorial challenges from minority nations within the state.

States containing more than one nation may project what and who they represent in more or less pluralistic ways. Majority groups may seek to dominate the state by elevating the symbols, narratives, customs, laws or policies of their nation to the state as a whole. For example, in India, the Bharatiya Janata Party (BJP)'s electoral victories of 2014 and especially 2019 emboldened the Indian government to redefine citizenship and reimagine the state to reflect the majority Hindu nationalist perspective. Conversely, the state may explicitly recognize its cultural diversity and/or its plurinational character in law, narratives, customs or policies, even if at times the majority group remains dominant. For example, the Spanish constitution, introduced in 1978 after almost forty years of unitarist dictatorship under Franco's regime, celebrates linguistic diversity and granted autonomy to 'nationalities and regions' while enshrining 'the indissoluble unity of the Spanish Nation'. Under Evo Morales's administration (2005–19), Bolivia was 'refounded' and declared a plurinational state, developing a national project that drew from the repertoire of indigenous groups' history, values and practice, but in a state-controlled process aimed at legitimizing state authority and unity.

Sub-state nationalism

States' claims to nationhood are often challenged by members of territorially based communities who consider themselves as belonging to a distinctive nation within the state, with an inherent right to self-determination. Sub-state nationalist movements are associated with all forms of nationalism. They may be more or less liberal, open to new entrants or see membership as rooted in the myth of common ancestry. They may be violent and bloody like the aforementioned Bosnian and Rwandan examples, or they may be peaceful and democratic, as in Scotland or Catalonia, with many shades in between. Even where nationalist leaders can be identified as conforming to liberal or illiberal forms of nationalism, the movements themselves may include a more diverse range of views about who belongs to the nation, and where the boundaries of nationhood lie.

Like all forms of nationalism, sub-state nationalism is a thin ideology that can be combined easily with other ideologies across the left-right spectrum. Scottish nationalism, for example, has often been associated with territorially based social democratic goals. By contrast, sub-state nationalism in South Tyrol and Flanders tends to be more conservative socially and economically. Common to sub-state nationalist movements and parties, though, is the 'core business' of defending the interests of their nation and advancing its right to self-determination (Brancati 2006; Hepburn 2009). Recognition of the right to self-determination need not imply independent statehood. Not all parties and movements exercising the right to self-determination and making political demands in the name of the nation are seeking to separate from the state to create a new independent state; indeed, the pursuit of political independence remains a minority sport among sub-state nationalist parties. Rather, the doctrine of self-determination concerns a nation's right to determine its constitutional future, whatever that may be (Keating 2001: 28).

There are several typologies within the literature which demonstrate varying degrees of self-government to which sub-state nationalist movements and parties aspire. Rudolph and Thompson classified territorially based demands into four categories: (i) 'output demands', which refer to favourable cultural or economic policies directed towards the sub-state national community; (ii) enhanced representation within the institutions of the state – government, parliament and/or the bureaucracy – so as to enhance the nation's influence and 'voice' amongst the centres of power; (iii) a change in the constitutional structure of the existing state, for example, through the introduction of decentralization or federalization, or to enhance the nation's political autonomy and self-government within the state; and (iv) political independence, enabling the nation to secede from, or dissolve, the existing state to establish a new state of its own (Rudolph and Thompson 1985: 293–294). Others have used similar classifications to distinguish between the territorial demands of sub-state nationalist movements and parties, ranging from cultural, autonomist, federalist to secessionist, or 'independentist' goals (Sorens 2008; Lluch 2014).

What these typologies share is a sense of progression, from modest to more radical demands. Sub-state nationalists may seek some or all of these goals simultaneously. Others may be content with more modest territorial ambitions. There is no necessary progression from one goal to the next. Independence – often used synonymously with separatism or secessionism – has been considered to be 'the culmination of national development, the peak manifestation of nationalism, reflecting a nation's collective desire to establish or protect its own state in the international arena, one that is equal or superior in status to all other states' (Hale 2008: 3). Yet pro-independence movements may also vary between those seeking 'full sovereignty' and those who see value in sharing and pooling sovereignty transnationally. For many European sub-state nationalists, there is no contradiction between political independence and political interdependence where sovereignty is pooled and shared between states (see also Chapter 9). McEwen and Brown Swan characterized the goals of such movements as 'embedded independence', embedded not only in the project of European integration but with a vision of institutional cooperation and governing 'partnerships' with the state from which they want to secede (McEwen and Brown Swan).

Sub-state nationalists also engage in more banal nation-building, to reinforce their claims to represent a nation with a collective identity and distinctive interests. Though they may not have access to the apparatus or resources of the state, sub-state nationalists use discursive tools and symbols to generate and reinforce a shared sense of nationhood among those they claim to represent, to bolster and legitimize demands made in the name of the nation. States with federal structures, devolution or other forms of multi-level government provide greater opportunities for sub-state nationalists to enter government, enabling them to access and use public institutions or pursue policy goals which support nationalist objectives.

State responses to sub-state nationalism

When faced with demands from sub-state nationalism, state-wide actors may try to ignore, accommodate or repress them (Rudolph and Thompson 1985; Guibernau 1999: 35–39). Ignoring the demands altogether may be politically risky, especially when there is evidence of strong popular support for sub-state nationalism. Using the forces of law and order to repress demands may also backfire. Even if it leads to a diminution of support for secession in the short term, coercion and repression are unlikely to sustain the popular consent necessary to maintain attachment to the nation-state. Moreover, as Rudolph and Thompson pointed out (1985: 296), repression of sub-state nationalist demands tends to generate further escalation, increasing the risk of violence in return.

Most democratic states respond to sub-state nationalist challenges by adopting strategies to 'manage' or accommodate territorial demands (Keating 1988). There are four main approaches to territorial management. First, states may engage in elite accommodation to try to contain the conflict within the centralized structures of the state. This might include co-opting sub-state nationalist elites within state-wide political parties, or enhanced representation within state-wide institutions such as the parliament or government bureaucracy.

Second, state institutions may be used to prevent or address the socioeconomic grievances that are often associated with sub-state nationalism. The 'people' may be more inclined to feel a sense of belonging and attachment to a nation-state that secures their social and economic well-being. Karl Deutsch recognized the relationship between national interests and class politics when he noted that:

if they (the workers) find not merely factories and slums but schools, parks, hospitals and better housing; where they have a political and economic 'stake in the country' and are accorded security and prestige, there the ties to their own people, to its folkways and living standards, education and tradition, will be strong in fact. (Deutsch 1966: 99)

Deutsch's concern then was the state's response to the threat of international socialism, but the observation is just as valid in states facing internal threats to their legitimacy and their integrity (McEwen, 2006). If securing the economic and social security of citizens helps to reinforce the ties that bind them to the existing state, economic turmoil, fiscal austerity or welfare retrenchment may weaken those ties and bolster the claims of sub-state nationalist parties to alternative constitutional futures (Béland and Lecours 2008).

Third, giving symbolic recognition to minority nations or celebrating territorial and cultural diversity might help national minorities feel at home in the state. For example, in Canada, one of the ways federal political elites sought to respond to the nationalist challenge from the predominantly French-speaking province of Quebec was to promote Canada as a bilingual nation, where francophones and anglophones could share a sense of belonging together (Taylor 1993; McRoberts 1997). Symbolic recognition of *national* distinctiveness has proven to be politically difficult, however. The UK remains unusual when compared to many countries around the world in the extent to which it recognizes that it is made up of more than one nation, allowing dual national identity (being Scottish and British, Irish and British, etc.) to flourish. Reluctance to recognize Quebec's status as a nation or even a distinct society derailed successive attempts at constitutional reform in Canada in the 1980s and 1990s. The ambiguity of the constitutional recognition of Spain's 'historic nationalities' alongside the indissoluble Spanish nation reflects unresolved disagreement about whether Spain contains one or more nations. The view that sovereignty belongs to the Spanish people as a whole, and the implicit lack of recognition of any distinct nations besides the Spanish nation, has shaped the state's resistance to sub-state nationalist demands in Catalonia and the Basque country.

Fourth, accommodating sub-state nationalism can involve changing the constitution to give political authority to national minorities in federal or decentralized political institutions (Rudolph and Thompson 1985: 297; Keating, 1988: 66). There are many varieties of multi-level government. In federal systems, sovereignty is divided between the federal level and the federated units. In decentralized systems, sovereignty rests with the central parliament, with powers devolved to some or all territories across the state. Either way, such constitutional structures represent a means of balancing territorial diversity with the unity of the state. Of course, there is the risk that, rather than containing the challenge of sub-state nationalism, decentralization or federalism may strengthen it, either by offering too little and thus creating new grievances, or by creating institutions that create new symbols of sub-state nationhood and new institutional opportunities for sub-state nationalists to pursue their goals. Political decentralization as a response to nationalist demands gives institutional recognition to the idea that the state is made up of more than one nation, and more than one *demos* (Burgess and Gagnon 2010: 16; Requejo 2005: 11). Such plurinational democracies can function effectively so long as there is broad compatibility between the preferences of state-wide and sub-state actors. However, they can also create conditions for increased territorial divergence, by perpetuating territorially based divisions. Erk and Anderson described these effects as 'the paradox of federalism', noting that its features could be both secession-preventing and secession-inducing (Erk and Anderson 2009).

Breaking up states? Nationalism and independence

The most radical demand of sub-state nationalists – to secede from the state and create a new independent state – is almost always resisted. The loss of part of the state's territory can have economic and political effects that undermine its legitimacy to govern the successor state, and risks weakening its reputation and authority in the international community. In authoritarian states, secessionist challenges may lead to violent repression or war. But, even democratic states can face such demands in contrasting ways. Recent experiences in the UK and Spain are illuminating.

Once again, the UK has been unusual when compared to other countries. In the case of Northern Ireland, the Good Friday Agreement explicitly put the decision about its constitutional future in the hands of the people, with provision for a border poll if there is sufficient evidence of demand that Northern Ireland be reunited with the rest of Ireland. In the case of Scotland, the UK government facilitated the 2014 independence referendum by agreeing a temporary transfer of power to the Scottish Parliament, to enable it to pass the necessary legislation setting out the rules for the vote. The UK government also gave a commitment to negotiate Scotland's independence if more than half of the voters chose to vote Yes to the question: 'Should Scotland be an independent country?' (Keating and McEwen, 2017). This was a political calculation and negotiated agreement. There are very few countries in the world that provide for a constitutional right to secession; the UK is not one of them.[1] But nor does the UK constitution pose any barriers to secession. Rather, the then prime minister, David Cameron, chose to recognize that Scots represented a nation with a right to self-determination, and recognized the mandate of the Scottish National Party to fulfil its manifesto pledge to hold an independence referendum following its election victory in 2011. His government's confidence that independence would be defeated in the referendum likely contributed to the prime minister's response. The altered political context, with higher levels of support for independence, may explain why his successors have resisted similar referendum demands.

Nonetheless, the UK role in facilitating the Scottish independence referendum of 2014, while championing the case for union, stood in sharp contrast to the Spanish state's response to Catalan nationalism. Once a textbook case of non-secessionist nationalism, Catalonia has recently experienced an unprecedented social and political mobilization for independence. In part, this more radical manifestation of nationalism emerged from both Spain's economic crisis and the rejection of more modest reforms to Catalonia's statute of autonomy, suggesting that the failure of socio-economic and constitutional forms of accommodation led to the escalation of secessionist demands. The election of pro-independence parties, with the central objective of promoting Catalonia's 'right to decide' its future, led ultimately to a unilateral referendum and subsequent declaration of independence by the Catalan government in 2017 (Cetrà and Harvey, 2019). The Constitutional Court declared the vote to be unconstitutional and, in an effort to stop it, the Spanish government mounted an intervention that included police charges against voters and removal of ballot boxes. Soon after, it suspended autonomous government in Catalonia for seven months. Twelve leaders of the independence movement, including the former vice-president of the Catalan government, and the former president (speaker) of the parliament, were found guilty of sedition and misuse of public funds and

---

[1] Those countries that do recognize the often conditional right to secession include Ethiopia, Canada, Moldova, Saint Kitts and Nevis, Liechtenstein and Denmark (vis-à-vis Greenland).

were sentenced to between nine and thirteen years in prison. Other leaders fled into exile in Belgium, Switzerland and Scotland.

Conclusion

Nationalism is both a political doctrine establishing that nations have a right to self-determination, and a form of politics that sees political actors nurture and mobilize a national community and make claims in their name. Nationalism identifies a 'people' presumed to share a sense of mutual belonging and tells us that they should have the right to decide their political future. As such, it is a 'thin' ideology which may be combined with ideological claims from the far left to the far right and all points in between. A useful way to distinguish between the great variety of nationalisms in the world is to place them on a continuum from liberal (tolerant to internal dissent and open to outsiders) to illiberal (where, for example, sharing the same ethnicity is essential 'to membership of the nation'), moving beyond the traditional civic–ethnic distinction that has dominated much of the literature.

The state is central in forging nationalism. Modernist scholars have explained how the development of the modern state set the context in which nationalism emerged and nationalist ideas spread. States engaged in cultural standardization and nation-building in order to make the political unit (the state) and the national unit (the people) congruent. But there are many more nations in the world than there are states – that is to say, many more communities within and across states that consider themselves to represent distinctive nations with legitimate claims to self-determination. That incongruence between nation and state is at the root of nationalist conflict and contestation. To counteract the challenge from sub-state nationalism, states continuously foster attachment to the nation to reinforce the boundaries of the nation and to reinforce the legitimacy of the state. They often do so in 'banal' ways, through the subtle use of discourse, rituals, institutions and cultural practices.

The presence of more than one nation in a state need not necessarily result in nationalist conflict. As citizens, we generally have multiple identities anyway, some linked to a sense of belonging to territorial communities at different scales. However, plurinational states can sometimes generate competition between state and sub-state nationalists over where the boundaries of nationhood lie and who speaks for 'the people'. In the context of multi-level government, where sub-state national boundaries are congruent with sub-state political institutions, competitive nationalism can spill into the relations between governments, leading to disputes over resources, policy competence and narratives of nationhood. Competing nationalist claims introduce a territorial dynamic to government and party competition that, when backed by popular mobilization, usually prompts a policy or institutional response from central government actors. Such nationalist disputes are rarely solved but they ebb and flow, depending on the strength and popular support for nationalist parties and movements.

To date, no advanced liberal democracy has disintegrated as a result of the secession of part of its territory. This may reflect the variety of mechanisms that states can use to manage such challenges in ways that accommodate nations within the existing state, as well as judgements about the relative risk and uncertainty processes of secession may entail. But, at least in some countries, there is a potential route to independence that is peaceful and democratic. Even in democracies, conceding secession is a last resort, given the political, economic and reputational risks it would entail. However, the enduring strength of nationalist challenges faced by states in the contemporary world, including in democracies like the UK and Spain, suggests that it may be a prospect that has to be confronted sooner or later.

Further Reading

Anderson, B. (1995), *Imagined Communities*, London: Verso.

Billig, M. (1995), *Banal Nationalism*, SAGE Publications.

Hutchinson, J. and A. Smith (eds) (1995), *Nationalism*, Oxford: Oxford University Press.

Lecours, A. (2021), *Nationalism, Secessionism, and Autonomy*, Oxford: Oxford University Press.

Tamir, Y. (2020), *Why Nationalism*, Princeton, NJ: Princeton University Press.

Yuval-Davis, N. (1997), *Gender and Nation*, London: SAGE.

14

The State and Populism

Mikko Kuisma

Introduction

The academic and popular debates of the 2010s were dominated by populism. In 2017 it was Cambridge Dictionary's word of the year (Mudde 2017). The electoral success of parties and politicians associated with populism across the world has certainly contributed to this. Events such as the election of Donald Trump as the 45th president of the United States in 2015, and the United Kingdom's European Union membership referendum less than a year later certainly made people talk more about populism. It has also proven to have a global appeal. The election of Narendra Modi as the prime minister of India in 2014, Jair Bolsonaro as the president of Brazil in 2018, and the increasing power grip of President Recep Tayyip Erdoğan in Turkey have been discussed as examples of the success of populism as a global phenomenon.

The popularity of populism as a political concept may be related to its nebulous definitions. Cas Mudde, a leading scholar of populism and far-right politics, argues that part of the reason why populism has become such a popular buzzword is that it is often so poorly defined and vaguely used (2017). In this chapter, I will, first, define populism and discuss the different approaches to populism in the academic literature. While I advocate here for a definition of populism that builds on populism as a 'thin ideology' (Mudde 2007; Stanley 2008), I will also discuss populism as a discourse and as a political style. More importantly for the overall focus of this book, I will also discuss populism's relationship to the state, an issue that is often largely under-investigated. Even though populism is at least implicitly entangled in the politics and administration of the state, the emphasis, at least the public discourse, has often been on its sociopolitical and economic origins and effects. Indeed, populist parties and movements are considered to represent an anti-establishment approach to politics, characterized by values that also stand in opposition to those of the liberal democratic state. The state is primarily interested in long-term stability and reproducing itself, while populism is more about identifying problems that the current regime and the elites that control the state have either caused or been unable to solve. Populism is, in that sense, a movement that advocates for political change. However, populism, as opposed to movements that would advocate for a revolutionary transformation of the system, such as anarchism or communism, tends to advocate for law and order. In that sense, it is not necessarily opposition to the state as such but a particular form of the state or specific politics of the state that it stands in direct opposition to. The assumption is that politics will improve once power has been returned to the people.

The chapter will proceed in three steps. First, I will define populism, what it is – and what it is not – about. Secondly, I will ask to what extent populism can be considered a challenge or even a threat to democracy and the state. I argue here that populism could be understood not as a direct challenge to the state itself but rather to the current established understanding of democracy, especially its liberal democratic variant. It is more about access to and ownership of the state than about overthrowing or transforming its structures altogether. In this sense, it is more illiberal than undemocratic, albeit its understanding of democracy differs from the current mainstream moderate centre-left and centre-right political definitions of it. As such, it represents a challenge to the current liberal order. Thirdly, I will anchor the debate on populism and the state to the historical development of populism and discuss the changing demand of populist politics in the twenty-first century.

Defining populism

It is almost a cliché to begin a conceptual discussion by saying that the concept under discussion is an essentially contested one. In this case, however, it is true. Populism is a 'many-headed monster' (Canovan 2004) that 'refers in different contexts to a bewildering variety of phenomena' (Canovan 1981: 3). There have been many attempts over the years to come to an agreement on a definition. As early as 1967, a conference was organized at the London School of Economics where over forty leading political theorists and political scientists met in order to define populism. While a seminal contribution was published in the form of an edited book a couple of years after the conference (Ionescu and Gellner 1969), during the event the participants were unable to agree on one single definition of populism (Ionescu 1968). The long conceptual debate that has followed reflects not only the academic disputes within the field but also the very nature of populism itself. As Ernesto Laclau famously argued, studying populism is often an exercise in circular arguments (1977). The starting point for many is the assumption that there is such a thing as populism. This is then defined, examples of it are identified and studied, after which the definition of populism is refined to fit the concrete cases studied. This process is a reflection of how populism 'tricks' its students. The more you zoom into the detail of populist politics, the less clearly you see.

Laclau's ideas of the elusiveness of the concept, especially at closer scrutiny, would support a more sceptical approach to defining populism as a concept. Indeed, some commentators claim that the term has now been overused and abused to such an extent that it has lost its analytical value and become meaningless (Moffitt and Tormey 2014). However, while some academic commentators remain cautious about the term, it has increased in popularity and made its way into popular discourses across the world. Indeed, Mudde famously argued that our time is characterized by a 'populist Zeitgeist' (2004). Since the publication of Mudde's article, the appeal of populist politics has, if anything, become even stronger. However, despite its contemporary ubiquity, populism is not a new concept. It is as old as modern democracy itself. For that reason, it is useful to begin by discussing what populism is and is not about.

What is populism?

In the literature, populism has been defined in a number of ways. Mudde and Kaltwasser (2017) mention five approaches to populism that all approach the concept from different perspectives. First, the popular agency approach understands populism as a positive force in mobilizing people and that is a part of the development of a communitarian model of democracy. This approach has been used especially by historians in the United States, in particular to describe the first wave of populism in America in the nineteenth century. Second, the Laclauan approach understands populism not only as the essence of politics but also as an emancipatory force (Laclau 2007). This approach is essentially a critique of liberal democracy and the underlying power relations – expressed and reproduced through discourse – to which radical democracy is the solution (Laclau and Mouffe 2014; Mouffe 2018). Third, the socioeconomic approach, particularly popular in studies of Latin American populism in the 1980s and 1990s, focuses on economic corruption and mismanagement of Latin American countries. Fourth, populism has been understood as a specific political strategy deployed by leaders who want to make a direct connection to their supporters. Here, there is often an underlying critique of the failures of representative democracy, to which a more direct form of democracy is seen as a solution. Donald Trump could be a good example of this in action. The fifth approach mentioned by Mudde and Kaltwasser approaches populism as a political style. In addition to a particular communication style, this approach also highlights a particular aesthetic expression of this. Examples of this include drawing attention to oneself with outrageous behaviour or 'trademark clothing' but it is also about using style as a way of highlighting that they stand with the 'common people'.

> Morales never wears a regular suit, instead donning his traditional Bolivian chompa or sweater, even at meetings of world leaders; Chávez wore tracksuits, sang and danced to traditional Venezuelan songs, and took calls from 'the people' on his television show; while Thaksin swapped his suit-and-tie attire and technocratic style for unbuttoned shirts, sleeping in tents on his reality television show, and talking about his sex life on radio to prove his everyday credentials with 'the people'. (Moffitt 2016, 143)

Jagers and Walgrave concentrate on the performative aspects of populism and define it 'as a political communication style of political actors that refers to the people' (Jagers and Walgrave 2007: 322). This is an important distinction, as in populism the way in which the message is delivered is at least as important as the message itself.

However, while these definitions and various approaches to populism summarize the existing scholarly attempts to understand populism as a political phenomenon, they actually say very little about the content of populism and what, if anything, unifies populists. The so-called ideational approach to populism is essentially an attempt to get closer to the content and the very meaning of populism. Even in the 1967 conference it was agreed that populism could be viewed as an ideology. However, it is not like other ideologies. It has 'many of the attributes of an ideology, but not all of them' (Taggart 2000: 1). As such, it has been suggested that populism could be defined as a thin ideology (Mudde 2004: 543; Stanley 2008). Unlike 'thick ideologies', such as liberalism or socialism, thin ideologies such as populism have a 'restricted morphology, which necessarily appears attached to – and sometimes even assimilated into – other ideologies' (Mudde and Kaltwasser 2017: 6). This means that populism alone, while representing a certain interpretation of the world, cannot produce clear-cut and coherent explanations as to how political life ought to be organized. In finding these answers, it needs to attach itself to many other ideologies and political worldviews.

This approach to populism is based on two core assumptions. Firstly, populists assume that our societies are made up of two homogeneous and antagonistic groups, the pure people and the corrupt elite. Secondly, they argue that politics ought to be based on 'volonté générale' (the will of the people) (Mudde 2004). Beyond these core characteristics, it populism can also attach itself to a number of other ideologies (Stanley 2008). This explains how both left and right, nationalist and Eurosceptic populists can coexist. The exact nature of the elite/people division varies but the core message is the same. And often the means are also overlapping. Populist radical-right parties are marked by an anti-elitist/anti-establishment impulse that leads them to emphasize the direct rather than representative aspects of democracy (Mudde 2007: 65–69). One characteristic of this is also the way in which these parties and movements often appeal to common victimization – small people in front of big corporations or normal people governed by elites who live in a parallel universe (Gerbaudo 2014: 72).

Populism and the people

Apart from common-sensical claims about the will of the people that clearly seem to resonate with many voters, talking about the people is not as straightforward as it may originally seem. Indeed, suggesting that 'the people' can be approached as a sovereign unitary body, a singular monolith, is highly problematic (Canovan 2005). Indeed, there are times when we think about people in a collective singular sense, while at other times we see them as a plurality of individuals. To be certain which definition of the people we are talking about, we can ask 'how many people are involved'. Weale (2018: 30–46) gives a great example of this. We can find a clear answer to the question of how many people in the United States like watching courtroom dramas. However, we cannot say how many US citizens are involved in court cases like the one depicted in the 2015 courtroom drama *The People vs Fritz Bauer*, since in these court cases the public authorities bring the action on behalf of the people as a collective. The problem here is, of course, that if, as some populists would claim, the democratic institutions and the authorities of the state have lost their legitimacy in representing 'the people', we need to either change the public authorities or reform democracy. In this, however, the challenge for the populists is that, despite their claims of representing 'the people', theirs may not be the majority view. Indeed, even if we were to introduce direct democracy, the 'status quo' might still win.

If populism is thought of as a movement, then one core message is in the idea of returning to the 'heartland' (Taggart 2000). Taggart argues that the idea of the 'heartland' that the populists identify themselves with 'represents an idealised conception of the community they serve. It is from this territory of the imagination, that populists construct the "people" as the object of their politics' (Taggart 2004: 274). It is through using the imagery of the heartland in their discourse and political style that the clear boundaries of who is and who is not a member of the community are also generated. Indeed, the 'heartland' is not necessarily fully compatible with the idea of the nation (see Chapter 13). Appealing to national imagery can be a straightforward method through which 'the other' can be excluded. It still does not mean, for example, that all members of the Swedish nation would be seen to belong to the 'pure Swedish people'.

What populism is not

In order to achieve conceptual clarity and be 'precise, distinctive and consistent' with our usage of the term, as pleaded by Rooduijn (2019), we should perhaps also think about what populism *is not*. For, if there is already a valid term or concept describing a phenomenon, there should not then be a need to reinvent it or wrongly use another term in its stead. One way in which populism has been discussed, especially in the wider societal discourses, has been through using it as a 'battle term'. If anything, this has increased after Trump's election and the Brexit vote. In other words, many politicians and political commentators tend to use the term as a derogatory term to describe their own enemies and the politics they represent. Obviously, this approach does not help if we are trying to define the contents of populism. Describing populists, and especially those who vote for them, as 'angry', 'frustrated' and suffering from 'resentment' (Müller 2016: 1) does not help in understanding the phenomenon itself. These descriptions are perhaps symptomatic of some of the polarization we witness in our twenty-first-century societies but they are unsatisfactory explanations for a complex political phenomenon, as they pay no attention to the actual content of populism and the political motivations behind it. Surely being angry, frustrated and resentful is in any case not a unique characteristic of one political movement or ideology.

A second rather common feature in the literature and societal debates is to conflate populism with other related concepts and terms. However, in most cases, generally accepted terminology exists to describe these phenomena and, therefore, to call them populism is neither correct nor necessary. As Giovanni Sartori famously reminded us, as scholars we should exercise caution against 'conceptual stretching' (Sartori 1970). For the danger of conceptual stretching is that we 'cover more ... by saying less, and by saying less in a far less precise manner' (Sartori 1970: 1035). The danger is that the words we use begin to lose meaning if we are not consistent and precise with our use of them. Furthermore, especially in comparative politics, it becomes difficult to know what we are comparing if our conceptual definitions are imprecise and inconsistent.

One example of this is how populism has been often conflated with nationalism or nativism (see Chapter 13). Smith refers to the 'nation' as a 'named human population occupying a historic territory or homeland and sharing common myths and memories; a mass, public culture; a single economy; and common rights and duties for all members'. 'Nationalism', however, is the 'ideological movement for the attainment and maintenance of autonomy, unity, and identity on behalf of a population deemed by some of its members to constitute an actual or potential "nation"' (Smith 2000: 3). It is understandable how some casual commentaries on populism might conflate it with nationalism. They are clearly related to each other and many populists are sympathetic to the core tenets of nationalism and nativism. At the same time, this conceptual stretching can lead to flawed conclusions. Indeed, many populists may also be nationalists but not all nationalists are, by definition, populists. As with using concepts to describe any phenomenon, it is not necessary to find another one if there is an existing one that 'does the job'.

Another conceptual flaw in the debate on populism is to use terms like 'far right', 'radical right', or 'extreme right' as working synonyms for populism. This is understandable, as the 'thin ideology' of populism blends in and overlaps with other ideologies. The marriage of populism and the radical right is known as 'populist radical right' (Mudde 2007). At the heart of the radical right, there is often an ethnonationalist belief rooted in the myths of the past (Rydgren 2018: 2) and this has certainly been shared by some of the European populist radical right parties. They also tend to emphasize sociocultural authoritarianism that rests upon traditional themes, such as family values and law and order. They also tend to see external threats to the national community. These are predominantly cultural but also in some cases economic. In any case, in terms of their economics, some populist radical-right parties have also been associated with neoliberal economic positions that are obviously generally seen as right-wing (Kitschelt and McGann 1995). What separates the radical right from populism is that one of their aims is a total and radical transformation of the political system and also often the closing down of opposing views and arguments (Rydgren 2018: 2). Hence, only some, not all, populists also belong to the radical right. There are far-right parties like Golden Dawn in Greece or Hungary's Jobbik who, according to many commentators (see for instance Golder 2016; Mudde 2007; Pappas and Aslanidis 2016), are not populists even though they are considered to belong to the far right.

Related to the idea of transforming the current political status quo, some have equated populism with anti-establishment or challenger politics (De Vries and Hobolt 2020). With this we could consider parties that are outside of the current established mainstream and that have not been in government. While many populist parties are considered to be 'natural parties of opposition', to be a populist does not necessarily overlap with being a challenger party. This also relates to more specific political projects, such as European integration and, indeed, some populist parties are also openly Eurosceptic. However, while some, not all, challenger parties are Eurosceptic, not all populist parties are Eurosceptic or there are various degrees to their Euroscepticism. There are also established mainstream parties that are Eurosceptic, such as the British Conservative Party.

Populism and the modern state

Much of the literature on populism has concentrated on populist political parties and their electoral performance rather than on the relationship of populism to the state and its institutions. However, populism's relationship to the state is an increasingly valid question, especially as we have more and more examples of populist parties moving from the fringes of opposition politics into government power (Albertazzi and McDonnell 2015). While research into populism is about understanding new political movements and making sense of their increasing electoral success, it is also about the failures of the old mainstream parties, the centre-left and centre-right parties that have dominated post-war politics in Europe and beyond. Should populism be considered a challenge or, worse still, a threat to the state? If we follow the established theories of populism, most of them are essentially not about the object of politics or its core institutions and structures. Hence, the critique of the current political situation that is at the heart of populist (thin) ideology is not primarily about the structures of the state or the institutions of democracy but about how the current custodians of these institutions are essentially abusing them.

At the heart of the populist worldview is a set of grievances constructed against a backdrop of a utopian nostalgia. A 'golden age' approach in this sense appeals to populists and their supporters. 'Our country was great when we had no immigrants.' 'Everything was good during the golden age of the welfare state.' They want to turn the clock back and, essentially, return the state to its rightful owners. At the same time, they are critical of what the state has become, voicing their dissatisfaction at the bureaucracy and, perhaps even more importantly, the bureaucrats at the heart of the institutions of the state. Indeed, if populism and especially its nationalist variants are seen as, at least in part, a reaction against globalization and Europeanization, in that case we could easily argue that, instead of a threat to the state, populism can be seen as an advocate of the state. The state according to populism might be less about the institutions that can be seen to define it than about the people to whom the state belongs. However, the classical state theories have always been concerned more about power than about institutions. Certainly, in this sense, populism in its relationship to the state is a kindred spirit of elitism (see Chapter 2) and also Marxism (see Chapter 3). Though even if we accept the basic premise that populism is essentially not an existential threat to the state, the question remains as to what kind of a state populists would like to achieve. Instead of a threat to the state per se, populism can be considered a threat to the modern liberal democratic state. Some have suggested that some populist movements, especially through their authoritarian leanings, can be considered undemocratic (Weyland 2013). Equally, some have claimed that populism can be grounded in illiberal politics (Berezin 2009; Pappas 2019). However, first of all, populism is not unambiguously either undemocratic or illiberal or both. And, even if it was either of these two, it might not be anti-state.

Important here is also how we conceptualize the state. Pierson compares the process of defining the state to an obscenity case in the US Supreme Court. During the proceedings a judge, when asked about his definition of 'pornography', said: 'I know it when I see it' (Pierson 2011: 4). However, as with the conceptual treatment of 'populism', we should use caution over how we define 'the state'. As will have become clear from various chapters of this volume, there is a plurality of understandings and conceptualizations of the term itself. As Pierson points out, behind the nuances and interpretations, there are common themes and 'at least "a cluster" of characteristic ideas, institutions and practices around which many commentators isolate their working definitions of the modern state' (Pierson 2011: 2). He later defines nine of the most important features: monopoly control of the means of violence; territoriality; sovereignty; constitutionality; impersonal power; the public bureaucracy; authority/legitimacy; citizenship; and taxation. It is unlikely that many populists would disagree with many or most of these core elements of the state, or reject them as problematic for their political aims. However, compared with many other theories and approaches, their position is one that, first, emphasizes the role of the people; more importantly, that the politics of the modern state are built around a fundamental conflict between two antagonistic groups – the pure people and the corrupt elite. Secondly, especially for many populists, their approach is grounded in a particularist ontology (Kuisma 2013), as opposed to the universalism of many Marxists and liberals. What follows from this is a populist approach to the state that is perhaps sceptical of some of the institutions of the state but, more than anything else, questions the existing power structures in terms of access to and control of those institutions. We can understand the state as 'the simultaneous combination of, on the one hand, its claim to act as a public power responsible for the governance of a tightly delineated geographical territory and, on the other, its separation from those in whose name it claims to govern' (Hay and Lister 2006: 5). A populist interpretation of this would, first of all, emphasize that there is too much separation between the state and those who have access to its institutions and those who are governed by it. Populist nationalist and radical-right parties, for instance, would also have strong claims about the need to re-emphasize and reclaim the boundaries of the political communities in a response to the borderless world advocated by the hyperglobalists.

What I argue here is that, while some populists locate their politics in opposition to both the economic logic of the market that dominates the liberal right wing of the political mainstream and the political logic of the system that dominates the progressive centre-left, it is still difficult to argue that populism is anti-state in principle. Populism as a thin-centred ideology is actually more about observing what is going wrong with the contemporary state. Here, the idea of pivoting corrupt elites against the pure people is primarily about saying that the people should have more access to the state, that the elites have taken the state away from its rightful owners. The argument that is often constructed is that the masters have become servants in their own house. An example of this in action is the Capitol Hill rioters in January 2021 shouting: 'Whose house? Our house!'

When contrasted with the other mainstream state theories, a populist theory of the state is a kindred spirit to elitism (see Chapter 2), as it buys its Manichean and monist worldview. However, if elite theory is based on the idea of the elites as civilized, educated and virtuous and the people as dangerous, dishonest and vulgar, this is completely upside down in populism (Mudde and Kaltwasser 2017: 7). The centrality of the struggle of power is also shared between populism and Marxism, and some populists, especially those on the left, share the Marxist suspicion of capitalism. However, populism does not give a privileged position to capitalism and social class in its Manichean struggle. It is obvious that pluralism (see Chapter 1) is the one of the mainstream state theories that shares the least with populism. If pluralism sees diversity as a strength, for populists it is a source of antagonisms and conflict.

However, it is in relation to the question about the relationship between populism and the state where the matter of clarity of definition becomes absolutely crucial again. If we follow the ideational definition of populism, it is not so much a matter of populism representing a threat to the state as a set of political institutions. Specifically, it is more about ownership and access. In contrast to this, the far right and the far left would represent a more dramatic shift and transformation, whereas populism itself at its core is essentially about the conflict and struggle of power between the pure people and the corrupt elite.

Illiberal, yet democratic?

The modern state, certainly since the latter half of the twentieth century in Europe, has been associated with the liberal democratic state. It is this variant of the state that is also most often the target against which European populists set their politics. This is especially the case if we consider liberalism as a set of institutional arrangements and governance practices rather than just a broad political ideology or set of values and ideas. However, it is not very straightforward to assess liberalism, even its institutional expressions, from a populist perspective. Certainly, many populists would find it difficult to agree with some of the political and cultural expressions of liberalism but, at the same time, might find it entirely acceptable to advocate its economic expressions. There is an apparent contradiction in this but, again, if examined through the principles of populism as a 'thin ideology', the contradictions tend to disappear.

For populists, political liberalism, especially if considered in its historical context, entails elements that they might not disagree with. We can, for instance, consider that those nineteenth-century developments in the democratization of predominantly Western Europe that were constructed on liberal principles motivated 'the early-modern resistance to tyranny and absolutism and to specific doctrines such as the divine right of kings, which opened up a path to constitutional and restricted government' (Freeden and Stears 2013: 331).

However, populism is sometimes confused with democracy. This is an outcome of conceptual stretching or lack of precision with understanding democracy itself. Canovan, for instance, has argued that this happens because, like democracy, populism promotes popular sovereignty (Canovan 1996; 1999). However, rather than stating that populism is democracy, we could approach it as 'pathology' of democracy, as it is also associated with a lack of toleration (Taggart 2002).

Obviously, democracy means many things to many people and there is no such thing as a perfect model of democracy. Indeed, in democracy, there is always a tension between representative and direct democracy (Dalton, Bürklin and Drummond 2001). One of the populist claims is that representative democracy is in crisis and one way out of this is through introducing more direct democracy. Referendums, for instance, are one way of getting the people's voice heard.

There is a way of thinking about populism as a corrective force for democracy. Following the work of Laclau (2007) and Mouffe (2018) whose approach, anchored in critical political theory, is based on the argument that populism is an emancipatory force and that the problems of liberal democracy can be overcome through radical democracy. Here, the populism that is advocated arises from the political left. It is still founded upon the same thin-centred ideology as other forms of populism, where it is seen 'as a discursive strategy of construction of the political frontier between "the people" and "the oligarchy"' and its promise is to generate politics that can recover and deepen democracy (Mouffe 2018: 5). The key difference between right and left variants of populism is here. The populist radical right understands popular sovereignty as national sovereignty (see Chapter 9) and aims at restoring social order for the national community that it sees as damaged by globalization. Left populism shares the critique related to the excesses of twenty-first-century global capitalism and advocates a restoration of popular sovereignty but wants to commit to a process of recovering and deepening democracy that is essentially based on an inclusive conception of the people at the heart of democracy.

While the liberal democratic state and the elites that currently dominate the access to it might consider populism – both left and right – a challenge to the state, populism could also be seen as the exact opposite. It could be considered a saviour for the state against the excesses of global finance and capitalism. When put into the context of the ongoing worldwide corruption as exposed in the Paradise Papers or via movements like Wikileaks, the nature of populism as an enemy of the state becomes questioned.

However, what becomes clear is that some of the core elements of state theory appear also in populism. Indeed, rather than questioning the existence of the state or seeing it as a fundamental problem, populism is also an intervention into the debate about the role of the state and the struggle of access and ownership. It revisits familiar themes from both elitism and Marxism but at the same time approaches the question from its own perspective. It is essentially built upon a series of fundamental questions about the relationship between people and the state and, as suggested by authors like Pappas, could be seen essentially as illiberal democracy (Pappas 2019).

Changing demand – populists in power

The backdrop against which the rise of populism is analysed and discussed is the broad idea of a transformation that refers directly to a fundamental change in late capitalism and mature representative democracy. As early as the 1970s, the transition from an industrial society into a post-industrial age was being discussed (Bell 1973). The whole state-market nexus that had very much come to define twentieth-century European societies, associated with established agreements and practices relating, for instance, to wages, employment legislation, pensions, welfare state and education policy, was about to face challenges. The changing of old to new risks of welfare (Taylor-Gooby 2004) came with significant challenges for governance and pressures for the institutions of the state. More importantly, though, this has placed democratic institutions under a considerable strain, as political elites have found it increasingly difficult to manage expectations and govern in a system that is increasingly fluid and based on more blurred boundaries of identity and authority. This change in politics and society was referred to by Peter Mair as a task of 'ruling the void' (Mair 2013). Instead of the stability they enjoyed at the height of the industrial age, when even the party-political system was seen to have become frozen and predictable (Lipset and Rokkan 1967), political leaders are experiencing considerable difficulties in convincing the electorate that they govern in the national interest and that their voters should remain loyal to them.

Much of the broad economic context against which these new political challenges have emerged can be classified under the broad concept or phenomenon of globalization. It has been argued that globalization has divided societies into two groups: the winners and losers of globalization (Glyn 2007; Kriesi et al. 2008). For example, the world of work has changed so much during the last couple of decades that keeping up with it now requires a skills and knowledge base that may be beyond the reach of the unskilled and low-skilled workers who were previously employed in the industrial sector. Reversing and further preventing this polarization of life chances and outcomes is a real challenge to our twenty-first-century leaders. Furthermore, globalization and post-industrialization have caused policy problems for European countries and other developed economies, which have, in turn, created sociocultural concerns on immigration, integration and law and order (Akkerman, De Lange and Rooduijn 2015: 52–53). In Europe, while the process has had different trajectories and different political outcomes, it is argued that by the early 2000s the 'increasing pace of European integration coupled with shifting demographics had fueled a new political culture of legitimate populism' (Berezin 2009: 25).

While the change is possibly more political and cultural than economic, the economic and financial crises since 2008 have certainly fed Euroscepticism that has, in turn, been one of the catalysts of European populism, especially its left-wing variants (Glencross 2014). Indeed, some have highlighted the deepening European integration as a critical juncture for European populism (Berezin 2009). European integration was 'an instance of enforced transnationalism' that challenged 'the standard prerogatives of the territorially defined nation-state' (Berezin 2009: 6). Hence, the populist movements could be considered as an identitarian backlash against European integration. This is perhaps also slightly counterintuitive, since the European project has clearly also made Europe more open and liberal, diverse and multicultural. Many have benefited from the freedom of movement and, it might be added, those who have are not only highly skilled and academically educated EU citizens. 'In a multicultural Europe of acknowledged social and political integration and increased cultural contact, rightwing populism represents a recidivist contraction and turning inward that is puzzling' (Berezin 2009: 11).

Waves of populism

However, it is worth pointing out that populism is not a new, or exclusively European, phenomenon. Populism is as old as representative democracy itself. Populism has emerged in waves, and these waves have varied in terms of content, time and space since the beginning of modern democracy (Taggart 2000; Pauwels 2013: 13–17). Putting populism into its wider historical context also reveals that, despite the current Eurocentrism of the debate, populism has never been an exclusively European phenomenon. The first wave of populism dates to the end of the nineteenth century when Russian *narodniki* and the US People's Party gained support, especially among the agrarian populations. The two parties represented the interests of deprived farmers to fight the dominance of the economic elites of bankers and industrialists (Pauwels 2013: 13–14). The second wave has been associated with the growth of more authoritarian and even state-led populist movements in Latin America during the twentieth century. A prime example of this is Peronism in Argentina. One of the characteristics that sets the second wave of populism apart from predecessors and successors is that one of its core foci was on fighting economic corruption. A third wave is often identified in the breakthrough of European populist radical-right parties like the Front National in France, Vlaams Belang in Belgium or the Danish People's Party. While some elements of the earlier waves are shared, the third, mostly European, wave of populism tends to be more focused on nativist nationalism than the first two variants. However, in all three, shared general characteristics of populism have been accompanied by particular local and regional articulations.

We might now be witnessing a fourth wave of populism emerging in many corners of the world. Syriza in Greece and Podemos in Spain are European examples that certainly suggest that even the most recent wave of populist politics is not the exclusive property of the radical right. Similarly, Hugo Chávez in Venezuela and Evo Morales in Bolivia are examples of this trend in Latin America. To some extent, this perspective has been used in explaining the popularity of former Labour Party leader Jeremy Corbyn in the UK and Bernie Sanders in the US through related phenomena. The critique of global capitalism that populist left parties often build on, with policy solutions that call for a renationalization of industries, is but one example of how some of them fit into this picture.

The wave analogy reminds us of the importance of the contextual factors, in both a temporal and a spatial sense, in our analysis of populist politics. In her analysis of the rise of the radical right in France and Italy, Mabel Berezin emphasizes the role of key events and turning points. She links Italian and French populist movements to the fascist history of the countries in question. In the opposite corner of Europe, in Finland, on the other hand, the populist movement arises from the Centre Party's agrarian politics and in social and economic policies that are very much anchored in the social democratic tradition (Kuisma 2013). In South Africa, the turning point that defines much of the new populist politics expressed by Julius Malema and his Economic Freedom Fighters (EFF) is the end of apartheid and the rise of the African National Congress into its hegemonic position (Hurt and Kuisma 2016). Malema's EFF is a very useful example of populism as a political style; it highlights how 'populism is *done*' rather than concentrating on it as an ideology (Mbete 2020). However, while context matters, and populism is diverse, there are common denominators between the temporally and spatially specific populist movements. Some can be found in the (thin) ideology of populism, some in populist political style, but also in their approach to the state.

Conclusion

In many ways, the answer to the question of the challenge of populism to the modern state lies very much in how we approach the nature of the relationship between the elites and the state. Or, to put it differently, it is about how the role of the state is understood. This, in many ways, could resemble the key questions in the Miliband–Poulantzas debate. To what extent is the state involved in the power struggle between the corrupt elite and the pure people? Is it a neutral arbiter in between or essentially a vehicle of the corrupt elite? If our answer is an instrumentalist one and we consider this being essentially about a struggle of power and access to the state, we could consider populism as a very specific kind of a challenge that is more a threat to the status quo than to the structures of the state? However, if our reading of the situation leans more towards a structuralist reading then also the populist challenge to the state becomes qualitatively different. According to that interpretation, the state is inherently involved in the current struggles. Therefore, it follows that the populist threat is also rather different in nature.

However, as Mudde has argued, the populist radical right is no longer an anomaly. It has gone from normal pathology to 'pathological normalcy' (Mudde 2007: 296–297). It is about a radicalization of mainstream views. This is also where populism becomes a very peculiar challenge to the modern state and what makes trying to respond to it so complex. It is not simply an undemocratic challenge for the institutions of democracy that could be responded to with more or better democracy. It is also not merely an illiberal challenge that could be tackled by more liberalism, pluralism and tolerance. Populism itself is also not essentially about regime change or radical transformations, though it can offer a discursive toolbox for radical-right and radical-left movements that attach populism to their political repertoires of contention (Tarrow 2011). As 'pathological normalcy', populism in its various forms might be here to stay and, depending on our perspective, we might continue to consider it either an unwanted challenge to our existing political structures or a positive opportunity for the revitalization of politics and radicalization of democracy.

Further Reading

Canovan, M. (1999), 'Trust the people! Populism and the two faces of democracy', *Political Studies*, 47(1), 2–16.
Laclau, E. (2007), *On Populist Reason*, London: Verso.
Moffitt, B. (2020), *Populism*, Cambridge: Polity.

Mudde, C. and C.R. Kaltwasser (2017), *Populism: A Very Short Introduction*, Oxford: Oxford University Press.

Müller, J.-W. (2016), *What Is Populism?* Philadelphia, PA: University of Pennsylvania Press.

Pappas, T.S. (2019), *Populism and Liberal Democracy: A Comparative and Theoretical Analysis*, Oxford: Oxford University Press.

Conclusion

Michael Lister and David Marsh

This book, across fourteen different chapters, provides an overview both of the diverse theorizations of the state and the role that the state plays in relation to other institutions and interests, within a variety of policy areas. No conclusion could summarize all of the arguments and positions covered in these diverse chapters. Indeed, one of the key arguments of the book is that there is no one set way of thinking about the state. Continuing a theme of the first edition of this book, scholarship around the state is vibrant and diverse.

Instead, we aim in this conclusion to mainly focus on the impacts of the Covid-19 pandemic on the state. The chapters in this book were written in a period which spanned the beginning of the pandemic. At the time of writing (summer 2021) vaccines appear to have reduced the intensity of the pandemic in many Western countries, but the pandemic is ongoing. In some cases, where appropriate, chapter authors have made explicit reference to the pandemic and its significance for that theory or issue of the state. In this conclusion, we wish to address the pandemic in an explicit and focused way. We examine two particular questions. The first is – what issues does the pandemic pose for thinking about the state? We argue that the pandemic largely confirms the centrality and importance of the state (as argued in the Introduction to this volume and across the chapters). At the same time, the pandemic has thrown into relief a number of key questions and challenges for the state, such as inequality and environmental governance and change. The second question we address concerns the ways in which the pandemic is likely to change or influence the state. Here, we survey a range of arguments made during the pandemic about the likely future shape of the state. These debates oscillate between two poles, one of which argues that broad continuity is likely to shape the post-pandemic state; the other which argues that radical change (understood in different ways) is a more likely outcome. We argue that present trends seem to suggest that the former view is more likely to represent the post-pandemic future of the state. As in the Introduction, we point to the state as a factor which selects for, but does not determine, continuity in understanding political, social and economic outcomes.

Finally, the conclusion finishes with some brief thoughts about the second major global political event of 2020, the wave of Black Lives Matter protests inspired by the murder of George Floyd in May 2020. Reflecting on these events highlights the relative absence of theorizing about race within state theory and therefore highlights potential future directions for state theory. As a step towards addressing this, the conclusion points to work, ideas and themes with which this absence could be addressed.

The Covid-19 pandemic and the state

The pandemic is a useful prism through which to think about the state. Whilst in many ways the Covid-19 pandemic is a global event, it is at the same time one that is deeply mediated by states, for a number of reasons. One is that it is states which have led and directed the response to Covid-19. Organizations like the WHO have sought to provide global and international leadership, but states have developed their own ways of seeking to address the issues and challenges that the pandemic has created. We shall return to this point below.

A second reason is that the pandemic has been experienced in a series of geographically different 'waves'. The virus first emerged in China at the end of 2019, before appearing in Western Europe and the eastern states of the United States in early 2020. Later in 2020, the pandemic spread across North and South America, before resurging in parts of Europe and, in mid-2021, reaching horrific levels in India. Of course, it should also be noted that some states, such as New Zealand, and to an extent Australia, have managed to significantly limit cases and deaths, and not really experience a 'wave', or at least not one of the same magnitude as other states. Crucially, a number of states have experienced multiple waves, with perhaps more to come. The precise explanations for these variations are not our concern here (some of them relate to things like the emergence of new variants of the virus, while others relate to the consequence of governments' attempts at containment), but they point to the fact that, whilst Covid-19 is a global pandemic, it has been experienced differently by different states at different times. In consequence, the focus at any given time during the pandemic has been on particular states; first China, then Italy and so on.

This highlights the third reason why the pandemic has been experienced through the perspective of states. The pandemic has been marked by the emergence of a kind of league table of states, to highlight which states are doing 'best' and which 'worst' during the pandemic. Media organizations like Bloomberg have produced 'Covid Resilience Rankings' which designate the 'best and worst places to be' (Bloomberg 2021). The *Financial Times* has also produced graphics and data to help people compare the experiences and performances of different states as the pandemic has progressed (Financial Times 2021). These kinds of league tables, using data such as deaths per million people, attempt to assess and rank which states have been most, and least, affected by Covid-19.

(Re)return of the state?

Therefore, taken together, these elements point to the centrality of the state during the pandemic. In the first edition of this book, published in 2005, many (although by no means all) of the debates and discussions concerned whether we were witnessing the end of the (nation) state, as argued by commentators such as Ohmae (1996b). The volume concluded that such assertions were overblown and overstated and that the state remained a crucial and central part of political, economic and social dynamics. It would seem even more difficult to make an argument about the end of the state today. Empirically, even prior to the pandemic, events such as Brexit and the election of populist leaders such as Trump, Orbán and Bolsonaro, point to the resurgence of national state projects (if, indeed, such things ever went away). In addition, in theoretical terms, the chapters in this book attest to the continued significance and vibrancy of the state in political analysis. The experiences of the pandemic thus far further support the idea that the state is, and is likely to remain, a (if not the) central political entity.

As noted above, it is the state that has taken on the responsibility for dealing with the pandemic through a wide range of initiatives which show the power of the state. At a time of crisis and emergency, the state became the central actor. States have imposed a range of restrictions on movement, ordering people to stay at home, closing businesses and imposing widespread travel restrictions. In response to the economic dislocation and fallout from the pandemic, central banks have cut interest rates and governments have spent heavily. In the UK, the Covid Job Retention Scheme has paid up to 80 per cent of workers' wages who have been furloughed. In the United States, loans and direct payments to households have been used to support people. *The Economist* (2020) estimates that the overall effect of this on the size of the state will be to lift state spending as a proportion of GDP from an average of 38 per cent for rich countries in 2019, to 'well above 40%, perhaps to its highest-ever level'. They go on to speculate that the effects of such increases in state spending may be long-lasting, noting that, following other significant increases in state spending, such as those which occurred around the World Wars in the twentieth century, states did not return to their earlier, more limited roles and functions. They also note that, given that states have supported businesses and wages in this downturn, they might be expected to perform similar roles again: 'If politicians are able to preserve jobs and incomes during this crisis, many people will see little reason why they should not try again in the next one' (*The Economist* 2020).

The state has also been a central actor in both developing and distributing vaccines. Despite Boris Johnson's assertion that private-sector greed was the formative factor in successful vaccine development, a study suggested that 97 per cent of the funding for the Astra Zeneca vaccine had come from public bodies (Guardian 2021). Similarly, reports suggest that the Pfizer-Biontech vaccine was significantly supported by the German government and, latterly, by US government funding (Bloomberg 2020).

The centrality of the state during the pandemic is mirrored in what is widely seen to be the failure of international governance and cooperation. The UN Secretary-General, in September 2020, claimed that '[t]he pandemic is a clear test of international cooperation – a test we have essentially failed' (UN 2020). Similarly, Gordon Brown (2020), the former British prime minister, decried the ineffectiveness of international governance regimes:

> If coronavirus crosses all boundaries, so too must the war to vanquish it. But the G20, which calls itself the world's premier international forum for international economic cooperation and should be at the centre of waging that war, has gone AWOL.

Others have referred to a 'near-total lack of global policy coherence' (Patrick 2020). It appears that international institutions like the WHO and UN have largely been ineffective, whilst states have pursued their own interests with a lack of effective cooperation. The reasons for this are diverse, but include the presence of populist/nationalist leaders in key positions, such as Trump and Bolsonaro. As detailed by Chris Brown in Chapter 9, nationalist/populist leaders have particular conceptions of sovereignty which render pooling of authority and international cooperation more difficult (see also Pevehouse 2020), while the influence of populist leaders and their antagonism to global institutions is also a theme of Mikko Kuisma in Chapter 14. Patrick (2020: 50) argues that another reason for the failure of international institutions is that they lack sufficient power and authority, as states, populist and others, remain reluctant to compromise their own (national) sovereignty:

> [T]he reason for the haphazard global response, was the persistent ambivalence that all countries, particularly great powers, feel toward global health governance. All governments share a fundamental interest in a multilateral system that can respond quickly and effectively to stop potential pandemics in their tracks. They are less enthusiastic about delegating any of their sovereignty to the WHO, allowing it to circumscribe their freedom of action, or granting it the authorities and capabilities it needs to coordinate a pandemic response.

Thus, not only has the state been an important, central, actor during the pandemic, but international cooperation has failed to deliver, *in part due to the centrality and continued dominance of states*. Yet, arguing that the state has been a central actor during the pandemic is not the same as arguing that the state has been strengthened by the pandemic, or that all states have acted successfully in the roles discussed. In terms of the former point, in ways which invoke the points McEwen and Cetrà raised in Chapter 13, the pandemic has exposed, or accentuated, subnational pressures on the state. As Eric Taylor Woods (Woods et al. 2020) notes, in some cases, such as the UK, the subnational entities may use the pandemic to push for greater autonomy and even independence. That Scotland, Wales and Northern Ireland, given devolved powers, have followed their own routes through the pandemic in some, although not all, areas, along with the greater media and public attention which the devolved administrations have received when so doing, has enabled nationalist parties and leaders to portray themselves as potential viable national governments. Yet, whilst certain states such as the UK may emerge from the pandemic weakened (although this is by no means a certainty), this is not, as Wood notes, a challenge to the state system per se, as these subnational entities want to *become* states.

Another way in which states have been challenged by the pandemic, whilst being at the centre of it, lies in the question of 'success' and/or 'failure'. The league tables noted above have highlighted that certain states appear to have managed the pandemic better than others. This links to a number of issues raised across the chapters. For those states seen to have 'failed' in their response to Covid-19, the discussions in Chapter 4 about public choice debates on state failure may be relevant. The extent to which such failures might be explicable in ways related to Taylor and Bosworth's discussion of the distorting effects of special interest politics is one interesting avenue for exploration. Prima facie, the way in which the UK government sought to outsource many of the key tools to address the pandemic (such as track and trace), ignoring established state expertise in the process, appears to display many of the features Taylor and Bosworth identify.

A different way of analysing this issue is to examine the bureaucratic competence and capacity of states. This is pointed to by Jones and Hameiri (2021) who argue that states which have progressively been 'hollowed out' through neoliberal governance reforms lacked a range of capacities to successfully deal with the pandemic, and that states which were not structured thus (such as South Korea) performed better. This points to the issues raised across many chapters, not least by David Marsh in Chapter 12, about the ways in which the interests of capital and elites have distorted state structures and priorities. Thus, Jones and Hameiri point to the ways in which in the UK, at least in part because the state had divested itself of key public administration capabilities, private business was able to capitalize on a bonanza of Covid-related contracts, whilst delivering inefficient and sub-optimal outcomes, all the while shielded from accountability. They conclude:

> As the COVID-19 pandemic demonstrates, neoliberal states may be highly functional for large-scale, internationally-oriented capital, but they have clearly become dysfunctional for solving very basic social problems. Importantly, this is a feature, not a bug. (Jones and Hameiri 2021: 21)

In making this argument, Jones and Hameiri echo the claims made by a number of state theorists presented in this book that the power of capital and business has systematically distorted the state and its priorities.

This also points towards questions about the efficiency and competence of public bureaucracies, and the extent to which certain state formations are (better) able to deliver these. A debate has arisen during the pandemic as to whether authoritarian states have been better able to manage and cope with the pandemic, with the performance of states such as China and Vietnam being held up as examples of the delivery of more effective outcomes than those of Western liberal democratic states (see Hamid 2020; Kleinfeld 2020). The precise outcome of such debates – and any implications for both liberal democratic and authoritarian states – are unclear (plus, at the time of writing, Vietnam is experiencing its most serious outbreak of the virus with the Delta variant, reminding us that the pandemic is not yet over and so firm conclusions must be reserved). In addition, states which have proved to be effective in certain aspects of management of the pandemic on occasions have been less so with regard to others. Australia is an example of a country which managed to largely contain the virus effectively, but which has struggled to deliver an efficient vaccination programme. The UK is almost the reverse, with poor performance during the early stages of the pandemic and one of the highest mortality rates in the world, being contrasted with an effective vaccination programme. How such varying performances are rated and understood by state managers and citizens will go a long way toward shaping some of the longer-term impacts of the pandemic on the state and its form (see below).

Covid-19 and (in)equality

A related aspect of the debate around state success/failure links to issues around gender, connecting to arguments raised by Johanna Kantola in Chapter 6. Countries who had female leaders, such as Germany (Angela Merkel), New Zealand (Jacinda Ardern), Denmark (Mette Frederiksen), Taiwan (Tsai Ing-wen) and Finland (Sanna Marin), all experienced better Covid-19-related outcomes, even controlling for other factors such as geography and demography. Some, rather essentialist, explanations for this seek to point to inherent gender differences in attitudes to risk and leadership (see Garikipati and Kambhampati 2021). Set against this increased prominence of some female leaders (although female premiers remain a minority, with only around 10 per cent of states being led by a woman), the pandemic has also, some argue, exacerbated the broader social and economic inequality of women. From women experiencing a greater likelihood than men of losing jobs, to increased risk of domestic violence caused by lockdowns, to increased burdens of care and home-schooling and difficulties accessing healthcare, a number of reports point to the ways in which the pandemic – and the response to it by states – have created conditions which are deleterious for women and gender equality (Fawcett Society 2020; Azcona et al. 2020). The view that the pandemic has potentially led to divergent gender outcomes is perhaps reflective of the wider feminist unease about the state (in its ability to promote gender equality for some women, whilst contributing to the reproduction of wider gender inequality) that Kantola describes in Chapter 6.

A number of the chapters in the book noted the ways in which power is concentrated in the hands of an elite. Martin Smith's chapter on pluralism argues that, despite the arguments of pluralists that power is not concentrated in the hands of dominant groups, pluralist theory struggles to explain outcomes which are frequently consistent with such concentration. Such a focus on the concentration of power comes within the natural remit of both elite theory (Mark Evans, Chapter 2) and Marxism (Colin Hay, Chapter 3), although they differ on the nature and basis of such elite preeminence. Also in this vein, David Marsh in Chapter 12 characterizes at some length the ways in which business is privileged by and within the state.

The experience of the pandemic does little to dispel the notion that the state is an institution which privileges and is dominated by elites. Some initial commentary on Covid-19 sought to emphasize the universal nature of the virus and the pandemic. It was, some argued, a virus that could affect anyone and that had no respect for national borders. That high-profile individuals like Donald Trump, Jair Bolsonaro and Boris Johnson all contracted Covid-19 may have reinforced the idea that 'we are all in this together'. Yet such a point does not withstand much scrutiny, and deep experiences and manifestations of inequalities are one of the hallmarks of the pandemic.

Nowhere is this more starkly illustrated than in the data about mortality from the virus. Studies from the first wave of the pandemic to hit the United States found stark disparities in who was dying from the virus. By April 2020 in Louisiana 70 per cent of the people who have died were Black, despite African Americans comprising only 32 per cent of the state's population. In Chicago, Black residents have died at a rate six times that of White residents (*Washington Post* 2020). This pattern was reinforced across the globe. In the UK, the Office for National Statistics found that, controlling for age, self-reported health and disability, and other sociodemographic characteristics, Black people were nearly twice as likely as White people to die as a result of Covid-19. Similar disparities were noted for those of South Asian backgrounds (ONS 2020a). This pattern of the increased risk of dying from Covid-19 for ethnic minorities has also been noted in less affluent countries like Brazil (Martins-Filho et al. 2021). Explanations for these outcomes are complex, with a range of factors intersecting. In terms of socioeconomic factors, ethnic minorities are more likely to work in less secure jobs which generally involve more close contact and make working from home, or social distancing, more difficult. Similarly, ethnic minorities are more likely to live in multigenerational households, which again makes virus transmission more likely. In a broader sense, research has found that deprivation is a significant factor in explaining the noted disparities between ethnic groups (Razieh et al. 2021).

As well as disparities in mortality rates amongst ethnic groups, there are also socioeconomic disparities. The Office for National Statistics calculated that for the first wave of the pandemic in early 2020 in the UK, controlling for age, deaths from Covid-19 were twice as high in the poorest areas as in the wealthiest ones (ONS 2020b). Similarly, men in low-skilled jobs were found to be more likely to die than men in professional jobs (ONS 2020c). As Whitehead et al. (2020) note: 'It is clear that we are not "all in it together" and the less privileged in society are suffering the brunt of the damage.'

Whilst some studies have suggested that economic inequality may have been attenuated through government economic stabilization packages, such as the UK's Coronavirus Job Retention Scheme, and welfare state efforts (Aspachs et al. 2020; Brewer 2020; Clark 2020), poverty has increased during the pandemic in a number of countries. Parolin et al. (2020) identify an increase of the poverty rate in the United States from 15 to 16.7 per cent in 2020. In the UK it is estimated that the poverty rate had climbed from 22 to 23 per cent by the end of 2020 (Legatum Institute 2020). Poverty increases have also been noted beyond the Anglosphere, such as in Germany (Bertelsmann Foundation 2020). Other studies point to the differential impact of school closures on poorer families, which will have long-term effects on educational attainment and future labour market performance (Blundell et al. 2021). Early assessments also suggest a significant increase in global poverty as a result of the pandemic (Kharas 2020).

It will take some time for the full effects of the pandemic to be clear. However, there is evidence, both in terms of health impacts and wider economic impacts, that the state has struggled to protect all citizens equally from the worst of the pandemic, pointing to the ongoing inequalities in economic and political power. This discussion of the inequalities apparent in the pandemic is, in many ways, redolent of the critique of the state's capacity to ensure the security of its own citizens presented by Pinar Bilgin in Chapter 10. Such inequality is also evident between states, with, for instance, high levels of vaccination in affluent states contrasting with much lower rates of vaccination in less affluent states. The chapters in this book and the analyses of the state which they present offer a range of tools to help us understand how and why such inequalities have become manifest.

Covid-19 and the environment

In the initial waves of the pandemic, optimism grew that, awful though its effects were on human life, the pandemic offered an opportunity for environmental renewal. In early 2020, as many states and cities were in lockdown, reports emerged of better air quality and lower pollution, with some estimates that CO_2 emissions would be reduced by 7 per cent for 2020 (Le Quéré et al. 2020). Yet it became apparent as 2020 wore on that any such effects would be temporary. More recently, climate scientists have both identified that emissions are rising again and posited that the pandemic and lockdowns would have a fairly insignificant long-term effect on climate change:

> In both the short and long term, the pandemic will have less effect on efforts to tackle climate change than many people had hoped … Looking further ahead to 2030, simple climate models have estimated that global temperatures will only be around 0.01C lower as a result of Covid-19. (Forster 2021)

It seems therefore that, *in and of itself*, the pandemic and associated responses are unlikely to directly contribute to a greener state and/or society. Yet there remains the possibility that the pandemic can indirectly contribute to greater attention on environmental issues, whether through the experience of things like increased home-working (and localism in consumption patterns), or simply because of people being forced to behave in different ways due to the pandemic, demonstrating that different ways of working, living and being are possible. In other words, might the pandemic result in ideational change? Here, we might usefully invoke the tools of discursive institutionalism as outlined by Vivien Schmidt in Chapter 5. The pandemic arguably creates a discursive space into which environmental concerns can be articulated to create the kind of paradigm shift that many green theorists would wish to see, and perhaps offers a way to analyse the issue, raised by Annica Kronsell and Roger Hildingsson in Chapter 7, of how transitions to a greener state can be stimulated. Such processes of ideational change may also be analysed and understood through the lens of rationalities as outlined by James Martin and Alan Finlayson in Chapter 8. Whether the pandemic will destabilize established ways of doing and being, or whether hitherto dominant rationalities will reassert themselves is, as yet, unclear (although see discussion below). Poststructuralism would also invite us to think about the complex and dispersed ways in which such rationalities might be defended or challenged, and to see the state as both site and outcome of such struggles.

The state after Covid-19

It might be argued that much of the above discussion of the impacts of the pandemic is nothing new; that in one sense, whilst the pandemic has changed everything, in other senses not much has changed at all. A new virus has swept the globe, leaving in its wake a toll in human life and a wealth of suffering. Yet the experience of the pandemic has been, as noted above and as historical institutionalists would be quick to point out, heavily mediated by the pre-existing social, political and economic structures. In the early twenty-first century, significant power disparities exist within, and across, the state and these have shaped the way in which the pandemic has been experienced across the globe.

For some, the pandemic represents a crisis moment, and crises represent opportunities and moments of significant change (Hay 1996). Larry Summers, for example, believes that '[t]he COVID-19 crisis is the third major shock to the global system in the 21st Century, following the 2001 terror attacks and the 2008 financial crisis. I suspect it is by far the most significant ... We are living through not just dramatic events but what may well be a hinge in history' (cited in Drezner 2020: E19). As noted above, *The Economist* believes that state capacity and expectations about what politicians do with it may be fundamentally altered by the pandemic. Set against this, Drezner argues that the pandemic is likely to produce rather less change than some might expect, particularly in international relations:

> In the far past, pandemics transformed international politics. In the recent past, the effect of infectious diseases has been more muted. I argue that while the aftershocks of COVID-19 will be real, the pandemic's lasting effects may be minimal. If one examines the distribution of power and the distribution of interests, the effect of COVID-19 has been to mildly reinforce the status quo. (Drezner 2020: E31)

It is tempting to argue that it is too soon to tell. At the time of writing, the pandemic is ongoing and it is unclear exactly how or when it will end. Yet such tentativeness is perhaps insufficient, although, of course, considering the effect that Covid-19 is likely to have on the role of the state in future and trying to predict the future is fraught with difficulties. We address the issue by first focusing on the commentaries/predictions about the future that emerged from observers, some of whom were major social theorists, during the first year of the pandemic. Many of these discussed the likelihood of fundamental changes in the role of the state, seeing, like Summers above, the pandemic as a crisis which might undermine the existing order, variously leading to a further 'collapse' of US hegemony, the break-up of the European Union, a significant decline in the influence of neoliberalism, or a widespread lurch towards authoritarianism. Of course, not all observers predicted such broad dislocation, focusing instead, like Drezner above, upon important, but more limited, changes. Here, it is interesting, and we are sure many would say revealing, that the talk of crisis and fundamental change has been reeled back more recently, with greater focus upon how the existing order has survived or will survive. Our intention here is not to adjudicate between these positions; predicting the future is always fraught. Rather, we suggest that the issues we consider briefly here are ones that anyone interested in the future of state/civil society relations needs to consider. In addressing these issues, this section is divided into three parts: first, we examine some of the contributions which emphasized crisis and fundamental change; second, we consider some of the less radical readings of the future; before finally looking at why the latter, less radical, scenarios, seem to have come more to the fore.

Crisis, dislocation and fundamental change

The contributions from those who see Covid-19 as a crisis which will lead to fundamental change are varied, but many are well-reflected in the interviews which Adil Najam (2021) and colleagues conducted with ninety-nine thinkers on how Covid-19 will impact our future. Their interviews focused on the fundamental questions Covid-19 has raised about the rise of populist nationalism, the 'end' of hyperglobalism, the decline of multilateralism and the future of neoliberalism and, indeed, of liberal democracy itself. Certainly, none of their experts expected politics anywhere to become less turbulent than it was pre-pandemic. These interviewees focus on what they see as 'likely' future scenarios. However, there is also a series of radical analyses which have much stronger normative underpinnings and here we touch on the analyses of Yanis Varoufakis, John Gray and Slavoy Žižek (this section has greatly benefited from the work and contribution of Michael Chisnall).

a) The rise of nationalism

This is an argument that clearly pre-dates the pandemic and has received a great deal of attention (see Chapters 13 and 14). A key element in this literature is the argument that the cosmopolitanism which has marked the last few decades, characterized by freer trade, increased travel, the growth of international organizations and so on, has been increasingly challenged by the rise of a populism rooted in nationalism. From this perspective, the pandemic has accentuated this trend by restricting travel and face-to-face interaction, provoking national responses, particularly in relation to the production and supply of vaccines and economic stimulation packages.

b) The end of hyperglobalization

The UK political philosopher John Gray, like many others, sees the crisis as a historic economic turning point with no way back to an old hyperglobal neoliberal normal, but dismisses the idea of an effective coordinated response to the economic problems post-Covid as 'magical thinking' (Gray 2020). Gray (2020) contends: 'Governments everywhere (are) struggling through the narrow passage between suppressing the virus and crashing the economy. Many will stumble and fall.' He rejects the rise of what he refers to as 'small-scale' localism, a bottom-up communitarianism because it couldn't be compatible with the planet's huge population, but, at the same time, he is adamant that the hyperglobalization of the previous few decades is not coming back. This is a view echoed by many, including Dani Rodrik, a leading expert in international trade, although he emphasizes that this is a development which pre-dates Covid (see Najam 2021). Gray further argues that the dependence of countries like the UK on 'foreign countries' such as China is a risk that can no longer be accepted, hence the nationalistic lurch.

In this context, Gray asks the question: 'what will replace rising material living standards as the basis of society?' As emphasized, he rejects the idea of the world adopting a steady-state, 'zero-growth', sustainable economic model, still capable of innovation, on the basis of the lack of any collaborative 'world authority' and the continuing 'highly uneven living standards' between the First World and developing countries.[1] In this context, he foresees the collapse of the EU, the end of 'hyperglobalization' and the creation of domestic industries to secure essential goods and services. Clearly, any move in such a direction would mean significant changes in patterns of governance, involving increased nationalism and much greater market regulation.

c) The end of neoliberalism

This line of argument has been fairly common, although it is not addressed very directly in Najam's interviews. However, the point is made forcefully in the work of Yanis Varoufakis, the former Greek finance minister, economist and social theorist, and the pan-European DiEM25 (n.d.) (Democracy in Europe Movement 2025) which emerged in 2015. Varoufakis, like others, locates his discussion of the need for reform against the background of the unresolved and continuing fallout from the Global Financial Crisis in 2008. The core argument is that the neoliberalism which has dominated over the past forty years has damaged democracy and de-legitimized political authority (and thus trust in politicians) to the point that the EU will either reform or disintegrate. More specifically, Varoufakis claimed in late 2020 that financial capitalism was decoupling from the capitalist economy, with the stock market flourishing while the broader economy faltered. More broadly, DiEM25 argue that Europe is currently suffering from five crises, debt, banks, poverty, low investment and migration, all of which have been worsened by Covid-19. However, they see the pandemic as an opportunity to promote more radical, progressive policies, arguing for fundamental change: 'EU institutions, which were initially designed to serve the industry, need to become fully transparent and accountable to European citizens. Our long-term vision is for Europeans to write a democratic constitution for the EU' (DiEM25 n.d.). In essence, both Varoufakis and Gray argue that the economic system, patched up after the 2008 financial crisis, has unravelled to the point that 'liberal capitalism is bust'.

---

[1] Cf. arguments between developed and developing nations at the Paris Climate Change convention in 2015 (Saran 2015).

d) A different geopolitical future

Here again, observers see Covid-19 as exacerbating an existing trend: China's geopolitical rise over the last three decades in the making. This has led to what Graham Allison (2020) calls an 'underlying, fundamental, structural, Thucydidean rivalry', with China threatening to displace the established power, the United States. However, Allison also argues that 'while China has successfully transformed itself into an economic and technological superpower, no one expected it to become a "soft power" superpower'. He contends that China's crisis diplomacy has been much more successful than that of the United States, and that a perception endures that Beijing has been far more effective than the rest of the world in its response to the outbreak of Covid-19 – perhaps unsurprisingly, given Trump's role in the initial period of the pandemic. More broadly, rather than increasing international cooperation and coordination in the face of a dangerous common threat, Covid-19 has increased Great Power rivalry in Asia, Europe, Africa, Latin America and the Middle East.

e) The decline of liberal democracy and a move towards authoritarianism

For Slovenian philosopher Slavoy Žižek (2021), the dislocatory nature of the problem, which has been building for a long time but is greatly exacerbated by Covid-19, leaves humanity with a stark choice. Given 'whole countries (are) in lockdown' and we are facing an 'economic mega-crisis', he suggests we can either continue with an increasingly barbaric and self-defeating market capitalism or embrace a new form of collective governance. Žižek (2021: s4-s5) is concerned that what the future holds is 'barbarism with a human face – ruthless survivalist measures enforced with regret and even sympathy, but legitimized by expert opinions'; the emphasis is upon 'the survival of the fittest'. More specifically, he argues that governments need to directly control areas of health, welfare and production. In his view, responses cannot simply be left to markets or involve temporary stimulus packages – the common response across richer countries. Žižek emphasizes the need to move away from the dominant 'top-down' form of governance rooted in hierarchy, which has undermined trust in government, towards a more participatory form. Given the pandemic is, by definition, global, Žižek (2021: s5) also contends that we need 'some kind of effective international cooperation ... to produce and allocate the necessary resources'. However, he acknowledges the 'impossibility' of the radical changes he sees as necessary, while seeing 'no alternative to it except new barbarism'. So, for Žižek, the pandemic needs to transform economic organization and governance, but may not do so. Certainly, from this perspective, as Perry Mehrling (2020) puts it less colourfully, 'society will be transformed permanently ... and returning to status quo ante is, I think, not possible'.

Change, but with underlying continuity

Of course, not all observers who look into the future see fundamental change, involving the end of neoliberalism and major changes in the pattern of governance and the role of the state. Indeed, much of the focus has been on how long it is likely to take for life to return to 'normal'. Here, the focus is on the economy, generally, and GDP growth, jobs, tourism and unrestricted movement, in particular. The basic assumption is that the economy can, and will, return to its pre-Covid state; the only question is how long it will take. However, even among those who do not see the future as involving a move away from neoliberalism and/or towards authoritarianism, many authors see less fundamental changes in the organization/operation of broad aspects of life as we know it. This section is divided into two sub-sections: first, we briefly consider two examples of work/arguments that emphasize the return to normality; then we highlight some of the areas where change is most likely, largely using Najam's interviews.

A return to normality

Fivethirtyeight is an online, US-based, opinion survey aggregator that, among many other things, undertakes a 'regular survey of quantitative macroeconomic economists'. In late 2020, the economists they surveyed believed that: 'It could take six months or more before our economy is back to where it was before the pandemic hit. And if a smaller share of the population became immune ... returning to economic normalcy would likely take more than a year' (Wolfe and DeVeaux 2020). To support this view, they argued that the US economy had made significant progress, with unemployment falling steadily from the highest level it had reached since the Great Depression in April 2020. In subsequent surveys, the economists revised their predictions a little, with their long-term estimate now that there was a 67 per cent chance that GDP would return to pre-pandemic levels by the first half of 2022. They do, however, acknowledge that the recovery is not affecting all workers equally, with Black and Hispanic workers bearing the brunt of high unemployment and economic insecurity.

The second, Australian, example comes from a September 2020 report by the influential and highly respected Commonwealth Scientific and Industrial Research Organisation (CSIRO 2020). The report, which, understandably, is largely a pitch for increased investment in science and technology research, supports a similar mainstream understanding of post-pandemic economic recovery:

> Today more than ever, science and technology are vital to drive our recovery from the pandemic-led recession and build our future resilience. Crucially, investment in innovation can deliver both short-term shots in the arm from commercialisation of market-ready technologies, and longer-term job creation and growth from burgeoning breakthroughs and nascent new industries ... We have all the foundations to accelerate critical Australian industries by building on our world-class scientific expertise, high-value workforce, and national advantages if we make the right investments now. (CSIRO 2020)

While the commitment of CSIRO to sustainability and resilience is undeniable and evident in much of its research output, the message underlying the report is that science and technology will champion the return to economic growth, albeit a growth that is more sustainable. Increased investment in science and technology then holds the promise of mitigation of Covid-19's dislocatory challenge to the economic order.

These are just two examples of the assumptions upon which the actions of conservative governments around the world are based and, tautologically, where 'a return to normal' implies that governance continues to occur and develop in the pre-Covid-19 way. This is the dominant mainstream position, but, as we saw, it is a position that is heavily challenged by those who see Covid-19 as heralding the need for more fundamental change in governance which can respond to bigger existential challenges than academic economists and most of those within the system are willing to contemplate.

Change within the existing system

Of course, many observers resist the temptation to discuss the possibility of broad changes in the nature of the economic and governance systems, instead focusing on likely changes within their particular areas of expertise, although some of these would have a substantial effect. The interviews with experts referred to throughout this section provide many examples. We only have space to list them here, but the list, which is far from exhaustive, does indicate the scale of possible/likely changes. We start with those who predict, or in some cases hope for, more significant, and importantly, positive changes:

- Science journalist Laurie Garrett (2020) sees the pandemic as an opportunity to address the injustices of our economic and societal systems, while Thomas Piketty (2020) emphasizes the dangers of growing nationalism and inequality, but hopes we can learn 'to invest more in the welfare state'; both these contributions return us to the broader putative changes discussed earlier.
- Environmentalists Bill McKibben (2020) and Yolanda Kakabadse (2020) see the pandemic as having a possibly positive influence on views toward climate change. So, McKibben views the pandemic as a wake-up call that may make citizens realize that, while 'crisis and disaster are real possibilities', they can be addressed and averted. Similarly, Kakabadse argues that Covid-19 may lead to a recognition that 'ecosystem health equals human health', focusing greater attention on the environment, strengthening the legitimacy of public investments in health.

On a narrower stage, some authors predict other important changes, some positive:

- Ian Bremmer (2020), Eurasia Group President, suggests that the pandemic will lead to a decade or more of disruption in national and international health systems.
- Phil Baty (2020) from Times Higher Education warns that universities will change 'profoundly [and] forever', with changes in the nature of teaching and, perhaps, a move away from the increasing focus on generating funding which has dominated the last decades.
- Atif Mian (2020) emphasizes the deleterious consequences of increased structural global debt.

- All experts were agreed that habits developed during the pandemic would persist, with particular emphasis on the use of Zoom, etc., working from home and telemedicine.

An overview: Towards an explanation

As we have emphasized, predicting the future is a dangerous exercise. However, we want to finish here with one observation, which we then attempt to explain. Our reading of what has happened over the pandemic period is that there has been a move away from the more apocalyptic views of the future, although this development may not last. In our view, the decline in apocalyptic thinking has come about in large part because, as we showed earlier in this chapter, many of the world economies have bounced back more quickly than many/most predicted, and partly as a result of large stimulus packages (as detailed above). As regards politics, the picture is more mixed. Certainly, the popularity of some governments, and particularly some leaders, has been boosted by the perception that they have dealt effectively with the challenges posed by the pandemic, as noted above. At the same time, other leaders have been widely viewed as unsuccessful and this has affected their popularity. Indeed, Donald Trump's defeat in the 2020 US Election surely owes a great deal to the pandemic and his failure to deal with it. In addition, in some countries (Australia is a good example), trust in government increased in response to its handling of the initial stages of the pandemic crisis, although it has fallen as a result of their mishandling of the vaccination programme.

All this means that there have been ebbs and flows which have played out differently in different countries. So, any attempt to explain future trends is likely to be even more difficult than predicting outcomes. In our view, a useful way to look at the issue is through a historical institutionalist (HI) lens. The future is likely to be marked by both stability and change; they are a duality, not a dualism. Here, the concept of path-dependency is important. Many critics conflate path-dependency with path-determinacy, and there has been a long-standing critique that HI can only explain stability, not change (on this see Peters, Pierre and King 2005), which in our view is a big mistake. Rather, the argument is that stability, underpinned by path-dependency, is the context within which change occurs; it constrains, and perhaps sometimes facilitates, change, but it does not determine it. In addition, we would argue that there are three separate path-dependencies, institutional, discursive and socioeconomic (see Marsh, Hall and Fawcett 2014). They all affect, without determining, outcomes, but it is the interaction between them which is very important.

We also need to introduce one other distinction before we proceed, that between endogenous and exogenous causes of change. It is common to argue that, if one utilizes an HI approach, then the cause of any change has to be exogenous, from outside the HI structure. We reject that argument because it equates HI with path-determinism. Rather, we suggest again that the relationship between endogenous and exogenous causes of change is dialectical – that is, interactive and iterative. So, as an example, exogenous change will change the endogenous institutional relationships, which, in turn, are likely to change the endogenous relationships; although the extent of such change is always an empirical question.

Covid-19 is clearly a major exogenous shock to all political and economic systems. But, equally clearly, the way that this shock plays out in different systems is mediated by the social, economic and political features of each individual system; in a system with strong path-dependencies the extent of change is likely to be less. In this context, we would argue that a system like that of the UK is characterized by three strong path-dependencies:

- an institutional path-dependency characterized by strong, long-lasting, political institutions, which in the more recent period have been affected by the growth of new public management (NPM) and the replacement of hierarchy by a symbiotic relationship between hierarchy, markets and networks as the dominant mode of governance;
- a discursive or ideational path-dependency, with neoliberalism underpinning both economic policy and the mode of governance;
- a socioeconomic path-dependency characterized by deep-seated structural inequality, close links between the social, political and economic elites and policies which consistently favour these elites.

In the context of these strong path-dependencies, it is likely that the transformative role of Covid-19 will be less radical than many initially claimed. What we have seen consistently in the UK, and elsewhere, is the prioritizing of the economy over increased control of the pandemic. Most rich countries have either increased the generosity of existing unemployment benefits or introduced temporary coronavirus-related programmes in order to support those without work – a group which has increased substantially everywhere. The Institute for Government (2021) compared support for workers in nine countries: the UK, Denmark, Australia, the United States,

Canada, France, Germany, Ireland and Sweden. Pre-Covid, these countries provided significantly different types of unemployment benefit, with the UK, Ireland and Australia having a flat-rate, means-tested, payment for the unemployed, while other countries offer unemployment benefits which aim to replace some part of previous earnings. In essence, payments in the former countries are lower than in the latter, and this is reflected in the level of support for workers in the pandemic. In particular, the payments in the UK are lower, often significantly lower, than in the other countries (excluding the United States).

In our view, the focus on the economy and the lower level of Covid-19 support in the UK reflect the existing path-dependencies. The policies have been clearly directed towards the interests of business and reflect the dominance of neoliberalism and the view, long-established, that what is in the interest of business is in the interest of the country. We therefore argue that the chances of the type of radical change suggested by the authors in the initial part of this section are significantly constrained by the role of the three path-dependencies. This does not mean that fundamental change is impossible, but such change is constrained by the continued dominance, to date, of neoliberalism in societies like the UK which are marked by structured inequality and have a very limited participatory political tradition.

Race and the state

To end this concluding chapter, we turn from analysis of the ways in which the Covid-19 pandemic has, and may, shape (and be shaped by) states, to consider a different global shock. On 25 May 2020 a Minneapolis police officer, Derek Chauvin, while seeking to arrest George Floyd, an African American man, knelt on George Floyd's neck for 9 minutes and 29 seconds, killing him. Images of the murder were captured on a mobile phone and broadcast around the world. Chauvin was later convicted of second-degree murder. The death sparked worldwide protests about police brutality and racial inequalities. The murder occurred during the Covid-19 pandemic, which itself had already been identified (as noted above) as disproportionately affecting ethnic minorities. These evident health inequalities had already prompted discussions and debates around race and inequality. George Floyd's murder and the subsequent protests (sometimes under the umbrella of the Black Lives Matter movement) fused with the racial inequalities of the pandemic to stimulate a debate and conversation about race, racial justice and inequalities which thrust these issues to a prominence, many argued, not seen since the Civil Rights Movement of the 1960s.

Yet, in contrast to the earlier discussions in this chapter about how the Covid-19 pandemic has impacted states and how state theory can inform our analyses of the present (and future) situation, on the surface, it appears that state theory has very little to contribute to the conversation about race. Issues of race do appear in this book, not least in Johanna Kantola's discussion of how feminist scholars have used intersectional analyses to probe the complex ways in which gender interacts with other axes of different and (in)equality in Chapter 6. Yet mainstream theorizing about the state has remarkably little to say about race. Goldberg argues that this silence occurs in *both* state theory *and* the literature on race/racism:

> One of the most telling evasions in these past two decades of thinking about race has concerned the almost complete theoretical silence concerning the state. Not just the way the state is implicated in reproducing more or less local conditions of racist exclusion, but how the *modern* state has always conceived of itself as racially configured. The modern state, in short, is nothing less than a racial state … The history of the modern state and racial definition are intimately related. So it is surprising perhaps that the theoretical literature on state formation is virtually silent about the racial dimensions of the modern state. And the theoretical literature on race and racism, given the culturalist turn of the past two decades, has largely avoided in any comprehensive fashion the implication of the state in racial formation and racist exclusion. (Goldberg 2001a: 233)

Perhaps surprisingly, some twenty years later, this is still, by and large, the case. Jung and Kwon (2013: 928) refer to a 'rather diminutive literature' on race and the state (see also James and Redding 2005). To end this concluding chapter, we consider this absence and point to some ways in which this might be remedied.

Goldberg's (2001a, 2001b) own work has sought to develop theorizing around the 'racial state'. Interestingly, in this work, he uses Marxist state theory in exactly the way in which Hay, in Chapter 3, suggests will be useful for non-Marxist approaches, which is to avoid entirely the instrumentalism/structuralism debate which figured in Marxist state theory. Thus, while Hay urges feminist scholars to avoid the question of whether the state was essentially patriarchal or a state in a patriarchal society, we might add that scholars of race and the state need not ask themselves: 'Is the contemporary state essentially racist or merely a state in a racist society?' And Goldberg, taking on board the insights from debates about Marxist state theory, does just that, avoiding what Hay might refer to as the 'fatuous' question, moving the debate towards a position akin to Jessop's formulation of the issue. After discussing the Marxist tradition, including Jessop, Goldberg argues for a view of the state as both the site and outcome of social struggles. 'The (racial) state, in its institutional sense, must be seen thus not as a static thing but as a *political force* fashioning and fashioned by *economic, legal,* and *cultural forces* (forces of production, of sociolegality, and of cultural representation)' (Goldberg 2001a: 239, original emphasis). This links to a view of the racial state as plural and heterogeneous, such that 'it is more accurate to speak of racial states, for the forms and manifest expressions are multiple and multiplicitous, diverse and diffuse' (ibid.: 236).

In drawing a distinction between *racial* states and *racist* states, Goldberg seeks to advance the position that all (modern) states are *racial*, in that all states play crucial, central roles in the categorization and reproduction of race. A state is *racist* to the extent that such processes entail the systematic preference of certain categories over others. Despite this openness and contingency as regards whether states are (inherently) *racist*, Goldberg argues that race is integral to the modern state, in that the modern state is inherently imbued with aspects of race. 'Race is integral to the emergence, development and transformations (conceptually, philosophically, materially) of the modern nation-state' (ibid.: 234). This co-constitution of race and the state is heightened through a reading of the state as performance. If, following Jessop and Butler, the state lacks an essence or a permanence, it acquires its institutional force and materiality through performance and iteration. Similarly, Goldberg argues, if we see race as discursive and socially reproduced, it too requires reassertion and rearticulation to maintain its significance and force – and this rearticulation requires the state: 'it cannot reproduce and replicate sans the state' (ibid.: 248).

States, Goldberg argues, are deeply implicated in the reproduction of race in a range of ways: they define – bureaucratically and administratively – populations into different racial groups (this argument perhaps echoes Jones's claim that it is the state which makes territory – see Chapter 12); they regulate relations between different racial groups; they govern populations in explicitly racial terms; and they structure, primarily through the openness or otherwise of labour markets, the racial nature of economic engagement (ibid.: 242). As to the effects of these and other activities, Goldberg invokes Balibar's distinction between '(official) State racism' and 'racism within the State', with the former represented by states like Nazi

Germany and South Africa where racism becomes a state project. For the latter (racism within the state), states 'license racist expression within its jurisdiction simply by turning a blind eye, by doing nothing or little to prevent or contest it' (ibid.: 244).

This links to a further central claim that Goldberg wishes to advance: that racial states function and exercise power not only through formal state institutions but through capillary power and the governance (and formation) of subjects. Drawing on Gramsci and Foucault, Goldberg argues that the racial state seeks to create subjects who self-govern, such that racial subjugation might be less imposed from without than assumed from within, by subjects themselves. In turn, Goldberg argues that such a view (as pointed to by Martin and Finlayson in Chapter 8) destabilizes many assumptions about the boundaries of the state. Racism, it is argued, functions in and through a wide and diverse array of institutions but also social practices, rendering the racial state 'everywhere – and simultaneously seen nowhere' (ibid.: 236). The racial state, Goldberg wants to argue, is (re)produced through capillary power relations which transverse public/private, formal/informal. Therefore, thinking about race and the state requires attention to the everyday and decentred nature of rationalities which are constitutive of the experience and (re)production of race within and without the state.

This short summary of Goldberg's work outlines a theory of race and the state. The relative silence of scholars of race and state theory is all the more surprising given, for Goldberg, the central and (co)constitutive nature of the relationship between the state and race. The issue of race and the state is, in many ways, parallel (although not without differences) to that of Marxists and feminists, particularly in terms of the instrumentalist/structuralist question. Goldberg's work, influenced by Marxists, feminists, poststructuralists and others, argues that the outcomes of the state are contingent on the contestation and sedimentation of social forces within and without the state. Yet he argues that the modern state is fundamentally imbued with the language of race. It is therefore a view of the state which is cognate with a wide range of the ideas and concepts within this volume, while at the same time marking out new (and important) territory and debates. It is a potent area for future exploration.

It is our contention that understanding and conceptualizing the state remains a central task for political analysts. This conclusion has focused on two discussions/debates. In terms of the first – how the Covid-19 pandemic has been experienced and mediated by states, and the likely legacies from the pandemic for states – the conclusion has emphasized two points. The first is that states have been a crucial actor, if not *the* central actor, during the pandemic; indeed, the pandemic has demonstrated the continued significance and importance of the state. Whether through exerting significant powers over populations, administering vaccines or intervening to protect economies and livelihoods, the state has been a hugely important actor. The second argument developed here is that, whilst initial prognoses about the likely impact of the pandemic leaned into forecasts or predications of radical change, more limited change, or even continuity, is a more likely outcome. The state as an institution is one which selects for path-dependency. Whilst this is not the same as path-determinacy, things like the long-term legacies of the structural power of capital are likely to continue to exert significant influence. Such arguments are ones derived from theorizing about the state and we contend that thinking and theorizing about the state is a vital project for understanding contemporary social, political and economic processes and outcomes. By contrast, the final discussion in the conclusion, about race and the state, marks out territory that state theory has not yet fully explored. This is an area which state theory might fruitfully seek to develop in the coming years.

References

Abrahamsen, R. and M.C. Williams (2009), 'Security beyond the state: Global security assemblages in international politics', *International Political Sociology*, 3(1), 1–17.

Abrams, P. A. (1988), 'Notes on the difficulty of studying the state', *Journal of Historical Sociology*, 1 (1), 58–89.

Acker, J. (1989), 'The problem with patriarchy', *Sociology*, 23 (2), 235–240.

Adler, E. and M.N. Barnett (1998), *Security Communities*, Cambridge; New York: Cambridge University Press.

Adler-Nissen, R. (2016), 'Towards a practice turn in EU studies: The Everyday of european integration', *Journal of Common Market Studies*, 54 (1), 87–103.

Adorno, T.W. and Horkheimer, M. ([1944] 1973), *Dialectic of Enlightenment*, London: Allen Lane.

Afshar, H. (ed.) (1996), *Women and Politics in the Third World*, London: Routledge.

Agamben, G. (1998), *Homo Sacer: Sovereign Power and Bare Life*, trans. D. Heller-Roazen, Stanford, CA: Stanford University Press.

Agamben, G. (2005), *State of Exception*, trans. K. Attell, London: University of Chicago Press.

Aglietta, M. (1979), *A Theory of Capitalist Regulation*, London: New Left Books.

Agnew, J. and S. Corbridge (1995), *Mastering Space: Hegemony, Territory and International Political Economy*, London: Routledge.

Agnew, J. and G.Ó Tuathail (1992), 'Geopolitics and discourse: Practical geopolitical reasoning in American foreign policy', *Political Geography*, 11, 190–204.

Ahmed, S. (2004), *The Cultural Politics of Emotion*, London: Routledge.

Ahmed, S. (2008), 'Open Forum. Imaginary prohibitions. Some preliminary remarks on the founding gesture of the "new materialism"', *European Journal of Women's Studies* 15 (1), 23–39.

Akerlof, G.A. and R.J. Shiller (2009), *Animal Spirits*, Princeton, NJ: Princeton University Press.

Akkerman, T., S. De Lange and M. Rooduijn (eds) (2015), *Radical Right in Western-Europe: Up to the Mainstream?* London: Routledge.

Albertazzi, D. and D. McDonnell (2015), *Populists in Power*, Routledge Studies in Extremism and Democracy, Abingdon: Routledge.

Alison, M. (2009), *Women and Political Violence: Female Combatants in Ethnonational Conflict*, London: Routledge.

Allen, J. (2003), *Lost Geographies of Power*, Oxford: Blackwell.

Allen, J. (1990), 'Does Feminism Need a Theory of "The State"?' in S. Watson (ed.), *Playing the State: Australian Feminist Interventions*, 21–37, London: Verso.

Allison, G.T. (2020), 'The world after coronavirus: The future of Thucydides', available online: https://www.youtube.com/watch?v=n8yHZIQj-uI (accessed 17 March 2022).

Al-Mashat, A.M. (1985), *National Security in the Third World*, Boulder, CO: Westview.

Althusser, L. (1969), *For Marx*, London: Allen Lane.

Althusser, L. (1974), *Essays in Self-Criticism*, London: New Left Books.

Altvater, E. (1973), 'Notes on some problems of state interventionalism', *Kapitalistate*, 1, 97–108 and 2, 76–83.

Alvarez, S.E. (1990), *Engendering Democracy in Brazil: Women's Movements in Transition Politics*, Princeton, NJ: Princeton University Press.

Amin, A. (2004), 'Regions unbound: Towards a new politics of place', *Geografiska Annaler*, 86B: 33–44.

Amin, A. and N. Thrift (2013), *Arts of the Political: New Openings for the Left*, Durham, NC: Duke University Press.

Amoore, L. (2006), 'Biometric borders: Governing mobilities in the war on terror', *Political Geography*, 25: 336–351.

Andersen, M. and D. Liefferink (1997), *European Environmental Policy: The Pioneers*, New York: Manchester University Press.

Anderson, B. (2006), *Imagined Communities: Reflections on the Origin and Spread of Nationalism*, London: Verso.

Anderson, B. (2014), *Encountering Affect*, Farnham: Ashgate.

Annan, K. (1999), 'Two Concepts of Sovereignty', *The Economist*, 26 September, available online: www.economist.com/international/1999/09/16/two-concepts-of-sovereignty (accessed 17 March 2022).

Aradau, C. (2010), 'Articulations of Sovereignty', in R.A. Denemark (ed.), *The International Studies Encyclopedia*, Oxford: Blackwell.

Archer, M. (2003), *Structure, Agency and the Internal Conversation*, Cambridge: Cambridge University Press.

Armstrong, J.A. (1982), *Nations before Nationalism*, Chapel Hill: University of North Carolina Press.

Ashford, N. and S. Davies (eds) (2012), *A Dictionary of Conservative and Libertarian Thought*, London: Routledge Revivals.

Ashley, R.K. (1988), 'Untying the sovereign state: A double reading of the anarchy problematique', *Millennium*, 17 (2), 227–262.

Aspachs, O., R. Durante, J. García-Montalvo, A. Graziano, J. Mestres and M. Reynal-Querol (2020), 'Measuring income inequality and the impact of the welfare state during COVID-19: Evidence from bank data', available online: https://voxeu.org/article/income-inequality-and-welfare-state-during-covid-19 (accessed 17 March 2022).

Avelino, F. and J. Rotmans (2009), 'Power in transition: An interdisciplinary framework to study power in relation to structural change', *European Journal of Social Theory*, 12(4), 543–569.

Avineri, S. (1968), *The Social and Political Thought of Karl Marx*, Cambridge: Cambridge University Press.

Ayoob, M. (1995), *The Third World Security Predicament: State Making, Regional Conflict, and the International System*, Boulder, CO: Lynne Rienner.

Ayoob, M. (1998), 'Subaltern Realism: International Relations Theory Meets the Third World', in S.G. Neuman (ed.), *International Relations Theory and the Third World*, 31–54, London: Macmillan.

Ayoub, P.M. and D. Paternotte (eds) (2014), *LGBT Activism and the Making of Europe: A Rainbow Europe?* Basingstoke: Palgrave.

Azcona, G., A. Bhatt, J. Encarnacion, J. Plazaola-Castaño, P. Seck, S. Staab and L. Turquet (2020), 'From insights to action: Gender equality in the wake of COVID-19', available online: https://www.unwomen.org/en/digital-library/publications/2020/09/gender-equality-in-the-wake-of-covid-19 (accessed 17 March 2022).

Baber, W. and R. Bartlett (2005), *Deliberative Environmental Politics*, Cambridge, MA: MIT Press.

Bacchi, C. (2009), *Analysing Policy: What's the Problem Represented to Be?* London: Pearson.

Bacchi, C. (2012), 'Why study problematisations? Making politics visible', *Open Journal of Political Science*, 2(1), 1–8.

Bacchi, C. (2015), 'Problematizations in alcohol policy: WHO's "alcohol problems"', *Contemporary Drug Problems*, 42(2), 130–147.

Bacchi, C. (2018), 'Drug problematizations and politics: Deploying a poststructural analytic strategy', *Contemporary Drug Problems*, 45(1), 3–14.

Bacchi, C. and S. Goodwin (2016), *Poststructuralist Policy Analysis: A Guide to Practice*, Basingstoke: Palgrave.

Bache, I., I. Bartly and M. Flinders (2016), 'Multi-level governance', in C. Ansell and J. Torfing (eds), *Handbook on Theories of Governance*, 486–498, Cheltenham: Edward Elgar.

Bachrach, P. and M.S. Baratz (1962), 'Two faces of power', *American Political Science Review*, 56(4), 947–952.

Bäckstrand, K. and A. Kronsell (eds) (2015), *Rethinking the Green State: Environmental Governance towards Climate and Sustainability Transitions*, London: Routledge.

Bäckstrand, K., J. Khan, A. Kronsell and E. Lövbrand (eds) (2010), *Environmental Politics and Deliberative Democracy: Examining the Promise of New Modes of Governance*, Cheltenham: Edward Elgar.

Bailey, D. (2015), 'The environmental paradox of the Welfare State: The dynamics of sustainability', *New Political Economy*, 20(6), 793–811.

Bailey, D. (2020), 'Re-thinking the fiscal and monetary political economy of the green state', *New Political Economy*, 25 (1): 5–17.

Bakker, I. (2003), 'Neo-liberal governance and the privatization of social reproduction: Social provisioning and shifting gender orders', in I. Bakker and S. Gill (eds), *Power, Production and Social Reproduction*, 66–82, Basingstoke: Palgrave Macmillan.

Balibar, É. (2005), 'Difference, otherness, exclusion', *Parallax*, 11(1), 19–34.

Balivé, T. (2012), 'Everyday state formation: Territory, decentralization, and the Narco Landgrab in Colombia', *Environment and Planning D: Society and Space*, 30, 603–622.

Banaszak, L.A. (2010), *The Women's Movement: Inside and Outside the State*, Cambridge: Cambridge University Press.

Banaszak, L.A., K. Beckwith and D. Rucht (2003), 'When Power Relocates: Interactive Changes in Women's Movements and States', in L.A. Banaszak, K. Beckwith and D. Rucht (eds), *Women's Movements Facing the Reconfigured State*, 1–29, Cambridge: Cambridge University Press.

Barkawi, T. (ed.) (2001), *Democracy, Liberalism, and War: Rethinking the Democratic Peace Debate*, Boulder, CO: Lynne Rienner.

Barkawi, T. (2005), *Globalization and War*, Lanham, MD: Rowman & Littlefield.

Barkawi, T. (2006), 'The postcolonial moment in security studies', *Review of International Studies*, 32(2), 329–352.

Barkawi, T. and M. Laffey (1999), 'The imperial peace: Democracy, force and globalization', *European Journal of International Relations*, 5(4), 403–434.

Barkawi, T. and M. Laffey (eds) (2001), *Democracy, Liberalism, and War: Rethinking the Democratic Peace Debate*, Boulder, CO: Lynne Rienner.

Barkawi, T. and M. Laffey (2006), 'The postcolonial moment in security studies' *Review of International Studies*, 32(2), 329–352.

Barnard-Wills, D. and C. Moore (2010), 'The terrorism of the other: Towards a contrapuntal reading of terrorism in India', *Critical Studies on Terrorism*, 3(3), 383–402.

Barrett, M. (1980), *Women's Oppression Today: Problems in Marxist Feminist Analysis*, London: Verso.

Barrow, C.W. (1993), *Critical Theories of the State: Marxist, Neo-Marxist, Post-Marxist*, Madison: University of Wisconsin Press.

Barry, A. (2013), *Material Politics: Disputes Along the Pipeline*, Oxford: Wiley-Blackwell.

Barry, J. (2012), 'Climate change, the cancer stage of capitalism and the return of limits to growth' in M. Pelling, D. Manuel-Navarrete and M. Redclift (eds), *Climate Change and the Crisis of Capitalism*, 129–142, New York: Routledge.

Barry, J. and R. Eckersley (eds) (2005), *The State and the Global Ecological Crisis*, Cambridge, MA: MIT Press.

Bartrip, P.W.J. (1982), 'British government inspection, 1832–75: Some observations', *Historical Journal*, 25, 605–626.

Bastow, S. and J. Martin (2003), *Third Way Discourse: European Ideologies in the Twentieth Century*, Edinburgh: Edinburgh University Press.

Bateman, J. ([1883] 2014), *The Great Landowners of Great Britain and Ireland*, Cambridge: Cambridge University Press.

Bates, R. (1987), 'Contra contractarianism: Some reflections on the new institutionalism', *Politics and Society*, 16, 387–401.

Baty, P. (2020), 'The world after coronavirus: The future of global higher education', available online: https://www.youtube.com/watch?v=qjTLOPtoyfk (accessed 17 March 2022).

Bauman, Z., D. Bigo, P. Esteves, E. Guild, V. Jabri, D. Lyon and R.B. Walker (2014), 'After Snowden: Rethinking the impact of surveillance', *International Political Sociology*, 8(2), 121–144.

Beblawi, H. and G. Luciani (1987), *The Rentier State*, London: Croom Helm.

Beck, U. (1992), *Risk Society: Towards a New Modernity*, London, SAGE.

Beck, U., A. Giddens and S. Lash (1994), *Reflexive Modernisation*, Cambridge: Polity.

Beetham, D. (2011), 'Unelected oligarchy: Corporate and financial dominance in Britain's democracy', available online: https://democraticaudituk.files.wordpress.com/2013/06/oligarchy-1.pdf (accessed 17 March 2022).

Beier, M. (2002), 'Beyond Hegemonic State(ment)s of Nature: Indigenous Knowledge and on-State Possibilities in International Relations', in G. Chowdhry and S. Nair (eds), *Power, Postcolonialism, and International Relations: Reading Race, Gender, and Class*, 82–114, London: Routledge.

Béland, D. and A. Lecours (2008), *Nationalism and Social Policy*, Oxford: Oxford University Press.

Bell, D. (1973), *The Coming of Post-Industrial Society: A Venture in Social Forecasting*, New York: Basic Books.

Bell, D. (1987), 'The World and the United States in 2013', *Daedalus*, 116 (3), 1–31.

Bell, S. (2011), 'Do we really need a new "Constructivist Institutionalism" to explain institutional change?' *British Journal of Political Science*, 41(4), 883–906.

Bell, S. (2012), 'The power of ideas: The ideational mediation of the structural power of business', *International Studies Quarterly*, 56, 661–673.

Bell, S. and A. Hindmoor (2009), *Rethinking Governance: The Centrality of the State in Modern Society*, Cambridge: Cambridge University Press.

Bell, S. and A. Hindmoor (2014a), 'The ideational shaping of state power and capacity: Winning battles but losing the war over bank reform in the US and UK', *Government and Opposition*, 49(3), 342–368.

Bell, S. and A. Hindmoor (2014b), 'Masters of the universe but slaves of the market: Bankers and the great financial meltdown', *British Journal of Politics and International Relations*, 17(1), 1–22.

Bell, S. and A. Hindmoor (2014c), 'The structural power of business and the power of ideas: The strange case of the Australian mining tax', *New Political Economy*, 19(3), 470–486.

Bell, S. and A. Hindmoor (2014d), 'Taming the City? Ideas, structural power and the evolution of British banking policy amidst the great financial meltdown', *New Political Economy*, 20(3), 454–474.

Bellamy, A. (2009), *Responsibility to Protect: The Global Effort to End Mass Atrocities*, Cambridge: Polity Press.

Bellamy, A.J. (2014), 'From Tripoli to Damascus? Lesson learning and the implementation of the responsibility to protect', *International Politics*, (51) 1, 23–44.

Bentley, A.F. (1908), *The Process of Government: A Study of Social Pressures*, London: Routledge.

Berezin, M. (2009), *Illiberal Politics in Neoliberal Times: Culture, Security and Populism in the New Europe*, Cambridge: Cambridge University Press.

Berger, T.U. (1998), *Cultures of Antimilitarism: National Security in Germany and Japan*, Baltimore, MD: Johns Hopkins University Press.

Berman, S. (1998), *The Social Democratic Moment: Ideas and Politics in the Making of Interwar Europe*, Cambridge, MA: Harvard University Press.

Bernstein, S. and M. Hoffmann (2019), 'Climate politics, metaphors and the fractal carbon trap', *Nature Climate Change*, 9, 919–925.

Bertelsmann Foundation (2020), 'Kinderarmut: Eine unbearbeitete Großbaustelle', available online: https://www.bertelsmann-stiftung.de/de/themen/aktuelle-meldungen/2020/juli/kinderarmut-eine-unbearbeitete-grossbaustelle (accessed 17 March 2022).

Bertramsen, R.B., J.P.F. Thomsen and J. Torfing (1991), *State, Economy and Society*, London: Unwin Hyman.

Bevir, M. (2002), 'A decentered theory of governance', *Journal des Économistes et des Études Humaines*, 12(4), available online: https://www.degruyter.com/view/journals/jeeh/12/4/article-jeeh.2002.12.4.1073.xml.xml (accessed 24 September 2020).

Bevir, M. and J. Blakely (2018), *Interpretive Social Science: An Anti-Naturalist Approach*, Oxford: Oxford University Press.

Bevir, M. and R.A.W. Rhodes (2003), *Interpreting British Governance*, London: Routledge.

Bevir, M. and R.A.W. Rhodes (2010), *The State as Cultural Practice*, Oxford: Oxford University Press.

Bevir, M. and R.A.W. Rhodes (eds) (2015), *Routledge Handbook of Interpretive Political Science*, London: Routledge.

Bevir, M., K. Dowding, A. Finlayson, C. Hay and R. Rhodes (2004), 'The interpretive approach in political science: A symposium', *British Journal of Politics and International Relations*, 6(2), 129–164.

Bhambra, G.K. (2018), 'The State: Postcolonial Histories of the Concept', in O.U. Rutazibwa and R. Shilliam (eds), *Routledge Handbook of Postcolonial Politics*, 200–209, London: Routledge.

Biedenkopf, K. and C.A. Dupont (2013), 'Toolbox Approach to the EU's External Climate Governance', in A. Boening et al. (eds), *Global Power Europe*, Vol. 1, 181–199, Berlin: Springer.

Biermann, F. (2014), *Earth System Governance: World Politics in the Anthropocene*, Cambridge, MA: MIT Press.

Biermann, F. and P. Pattberg (eds) (2012), *Global Environmental Governance Reconsidered*, Cambridge, MA: MIT Press.

Biersteker, T.J. and C. Weber (eds) (1996), *State Sovereignty as Social Construct*, Cambridge: Cambridge University Press.

Bigo, D. (2001), 'The Möbius Ribbon of Internal and External Securit(ies)', in M.E.A. Albert (ed.), *Identities Borders Orders: Rethinking International Relations Theory*, 91–116, Minnesota: University of Minnesota Press.

Bigo, D., E. Guild and R. Walker (2010), 'The Changing Landscape of European Liberty and Security', in D. Bigo, E. Guild, R. Walker and S. Carrera (eds), *Europe's 21st Century Challenge: Delivering Liberty*, 1–27, London: Routledge.

Bilgin, P. (2002), 'Beyond statism in security studies? Human agency and security in the Middle East', *Review of International Affairs*, 2(1), 100–118.

Bilgin, P. (2016a), 'Edward Said's "contrapuntal reading" as a method, an ethos and a metaphor for Global IR', *International Studies Review*, 18(1), 134–146.

Bilgin, P. (2016b), 'How to remedy Eurocentrism in IR? A complement and a challenge for The Global Transformation', *International Theory*, 8(3), 492–501.

Bilgin, P. (2016c), 'Temporalizing Security: Securing the Citizen, Insecuring the Immigrant in the Mediterranean', in A.M. Agathangelou and K.D.

Killian (eds), *Time, Temporality and Violence in International Relations: (De)Fatalizing the Present, Forging Radical Alternatives*, 221–232, London: Routledge.

Bilgin, P. and A.D. Morton (2002), 'Historicising representations of "Failed States": Beyond the Cold-War annexation of the social sciences?' *Third World Quarterly*, 23(1), 55–80.

Billig, M. (1995), *Banal Nationalism*, London: SAGE.

Bina, O. (2013), 'The green economy and sustainable development: An uneasy balance?' *Environment and Planning C: Government and Policy*, 31, 1023–1047.

Birch, A. (1993), *The Concepts and Theories of Modern Democracy*, London: Routledge.

Biswas, S. (2007), 'Empire and global public intellectuals: Reading Edward Said as an international relations theorist', *Millennium – Journal of International Studies*, 36(1), 117–133.

Biswas, S. (2014), *Nuclear Desire: Power and the Postcolonial Nuclear Order*, Minneapolis: University of Minnesota Press.

Block, F.L. (1987),*Revising State Theory: Essays in Politics and Postindustrialism*, Philadelphia, PA: Temple University Press.

Block, F.L. (1990), *Postindustrial Possibilities*, Los Angeles: University of California Press.

Bloomberg (2020), 'Pfizer vaccine's funding came from Berlin, not Washington', available online: https://www.bloomberg.com/news/articles/2020-11-09/pfizer-vaccine-s-funding-came-from-berlin-not-washington (accessed 17 March 2022).

Bloomberg (2021), 'The Covid resilience ranking', available online: https://www.bloomberg.com/graphics/covid-resilience-ranking/ (accessed 17 March 2022).

Blühdorn, I. (2020), 'The legitimation crisis of democracy: Emancipatory politics, the environmental state and the glass ceiling to socio-ecological transformation', *Environmental Politics*, 29(1), 38–57.

Blühdorn, I. and M. Deflorian (2019), 'The collaborative management of sustained unsustainability', *Sustainability*, 11(4), 1189.

Blundell, R., J. Cribb, S. McNally, R. Warwick and X. Xu (2021), 'Inequalities in education, skills, and incomes in the UK: The implications of the COVID-19 pandemic', available online: https://www.ifs.org.uk/inequality/wp-content/uploads/2021/03/BN-Inequalities-in-education-skills-and-incomes-in-the-UK-the-implications-of-the-COVID-19-pandemic.pdf (accessed 17 March 2022).

Blyth, M. (2002), *Great Transformations: Economic Ideas and Institutional Change in the Twentieth Century*, New York: Cambridge University Press.

Blyth, M. (2003), 'Structures do not come with an instruction sheet: Interests, ideas, and progress in political science', *Perspectives on Politics*, 1 (4), 695–706.

Blyth, M. (2013), *Austerity: The History of a Dangerous Idea*, Oxford: Oxford University Press.

Blyth, M. and R. Vargwese (1999), 'The state of the discipline in American political science: Be careful what you wish for?' *British Journal of Politics and International Relations*, 1 (3), 345–365.

Blyth, M., O. Helgadottir and W. Kring (2016), 'Ideas and Historical Institutionalism', in O. Fioretos, T.G. Falleti and A. Sheingate (eds), *The Oxford Handbook of Historical Institutionalism*, 142–164, Oxford: Oxford University Press.

Blyth, M.M. (1997), '"Any more bright ideas?" The ideational turn in comparative political economy', *Comparative Politics*, 29(2), 229–250.

Boettke, P.J. and E.E. Piano (2019), 'Public Choice and Libertarianism', *The Oxford Handbook of Public Choice*, Vol. 1, available online: https://www. oxfordhandbooks.com/view/10.1093/oxfordhb/9780190469733.001.0001/ oxfordhb-9780190469733-e-42 (accessed 24 September 2020).

Bomberg, E. (2015), 'Greening the State, American Style', in A. Bäckstrand and K. Kronsell (eds), *Rethinking the Green State: Environmental Governance towards Climate and Sustainability Transitions*, 122–137, London: Routledge.

Bonefeld, W. (1993), 'Crisis of theory: Bob Jessop's theory of capitalist reproduction', *Capital & Class*, 50, 25–48.

Booth, K. (1991), 'Security and emancipation', *Review of International Studies*, 17(4), 313–326.

Booth, K. (1998), 'Cold Wars of the Mind', in K. Booth (ed.), *Statecraft and Security: The Cold War and Beyond*, 29–55, Cambridge: Cambridge University Press.

Booth, K. (2007), *Theory of World Security*, Cambridge: Cambridge University Press.

Börzel, T.A. (2003), *Environmental Leaders and Laggards in Europe: Why there is (not) a 'Southern Problem'*, London: Routledge.

Boucher, D. (2011), 'The recognition theory of rights: Customary international law and human rights', *Political Studies*, 59(3), 753–771.

Bourdieu, P. (1990), *In Other Words: Essays towards a Reflexive Sociology*, Stanford, CA: Stanford University Press.

Bourke, R. and Q. Skinner (2016), *Popular Sovereignty in Historical Perspective*, Cambridge: Cambridge University Press.

Bouzarovski, S., M. Bradshaw and A. Wochnik (2015), 'Making territory through infrastructure: The governance of natural gas transit in Europe', *Geoforum* 64: 217–228.

Brancati, D. (2006), 'Decentralization: Fuelling the fire or dampening the flames of ethnic conflict and secessionism?', *International Organization*, 60 (3), 651–685.

Brass, P. (1994), 'Élite Competition and Nation-Formation', in A.D. Smith and J. Hutchinson (eds), *Nationalism*, 83–88, Oxford: Oxford Readers.

Bremmer, I. (2020), 'The world after Coronavirus: The future of geopolitics', available online: https://www.youtube.com/watch?v=tWtVhgljmwc (accessed 17 March 2022).

Brennan, G. and J.M. Buchanan (1983), 'Predictive power and the choice among regimes', *The Economic Journal*, 93(369), 89–105.

Brennan, G. and J.M. Buchanan (2000), *The Reason of Rules: Constitutional Political Economy*, Indianapolis, IN: Liberty Fund.

Brenner, N., B. Jessop, M. Jones and G. MacLeod (2003), 'State Space in Question', in N. Brenner, B. Jessop, M. Jones and G. MacLeod (eds), *State-Space: A Reader*, 1–26, Oxford: Blackwell.

Breuilly, J. (1993), *Nationalism and the State*, Manchester: Manchester University Press.

Brewer, M. (2020), 'What are the effects of Covid-19 on poverty and inequality?', available online: https://www.economicsobservatory.com/what-are-effects-covid-19-poverty-and-inequality (accessed 17 March 2022).

Broome, A. (2010), *The Currency of Power: The IMF and Monetary Reform in Central Asia*, Basingstoke: Palgrave Macmillan.

Brown, C. (2013), 'The antipolitical theory of responsibility to protect', *Global Responsibility to Protect*, (5)4, 423–442.

Brown, C. (2018), 'Intervention', in T. Allen, A. Macdonald and H.Radice (eds), *Humanitarianism: A Dictionary of Concepts*, 181–190, London: Routledge.

Brown, D. (1999), 'Are there good and bad nationalisms?' *Nations and Nationalism*, 5(2), 281–302.

Brown, G. (2020), 'The G20 should be leading the world out of the coronavirus crisis – but it's gone awol', *The Guardian,* available online: https://www.theguardian.com/commentisfree/2020/jun/02/g20-leading-world-out-of-coronavirus-crisis-gordon-brown (accessed 17 March 2022).

Brown, W. (1992), 'Finding the man in the state', *Feminist Studies*, 18(1), 7–34.

Brown, W. (1995), *States of Injury: Power and Freedom in the Late Modernity* Princeton, NJ: Princeton University Press.

Brown, W. (2010), *Walled States, Waning Sovereignty*, Brooklyn, NY: Zone Books.

Brown, W. (2015), *Undoing the Demos: Neoliberalism's Stealth Revolution*, Brooklyn, NY: Zone Books.

Browne, R. (2018), 'Elon Musk warns A.I. could create an "immortal dictator from which we can never escape", CNBC Tech, 6 April 2018, available online: https://www.cnbc.com/2018/04/06/elon-musk-warns-ai-could-create-immortal-dictator-in-documentary.html (accessed 13 September 2020).

Browne, S. (2012), 'Race and Surveillance', in K. Ball, D. Lyon and K.D. Haggerty (eds), *Routledge Handbook of Surveillance Studies*, 72–79, London: Routledge.

Brownlie's Documents on Human Rights (2010), 6th edn, by Ian Brownlie and G. S. Goodwin-Gill, Oxford: Oxford University Press.

Brubaker, R. (1992), *Citizenship and Nationhood in France and Germany*, Cambridge, MA: Harvard University Press.

Bruno, J. (1989), 'The normative frameworks of public policy', *Political Studies*, 37, 376–386.

Bryson, V. (1992), *Feminist Political Theory*, London: Macmillan.

Buchanan, J.M. (1975), 'Public finance and public choice', *National Tax Journal*, 28(4), 383–394.

Buchanan, J.M. (1984), 'Politics without Romance: A Sketch of Positive Public Choice Theory and Its Normative Implications', in J.M. Buchanan and R.D. Tollison (eds), *The Theory of Public Choice II*, 11–22, Ann Arbor: University of Michigan Press.

Buchanan, J.M. (1995), 'Federalism as an ideal political order and an objective for constitutional reform', *Publius* 25(2), 19–27.

Buchanan, J.M. (2000), *The Limits of Liberty: Between Anarchy and Leviathan*, Indianapolis, IN: Liberty Fund.

Buchanan, J.M. (2005), *Why I, Too, Am Not a Conservative: The Normative Vision of Classical Liberalism*, Cheltenham: Edward Elgar.

Buchanan, J.M. and G. Tullock (1999), *The Calculus of Consent: Logical Foundations of Constitutional Democracy*, Indianapolis, IN: Liberty Fund.

Büchs, M. and M. Koch (2017), *Postgrowth and Wellbeing: Challenges to Sustainable Welfare*, Basingstoke: Palgrave Macmillan.

Bukharin, N.I. ([1921]1926), *Historical Materialism: A System of Sociology*, London: Allen & Unwin.

Bulkeley, H., V.C. Broto and A. Maassen (2010), 'Governing Urban Low Carbon Transitions', in H. Bulkeley, V.C. Broto, M. Hodson and S. Marvin (eds), *Cities and Low Carbon Transitions*, 45–57, London: Routledge.

Bulkeley, H., L. Andonova, M. Betsill, D. Compagnon, T. Hale, M. Hoffmann, P. Newell, M. Paterson, C. Roger and S. VanDeveer (2014), *Transnational Climate Change Governance*, New York: Cambridge University Press.

Bull, H. and A. Watson (eds) ([1984] 2018), *The Expansion of International Society*, Oxford: Clarendon Press.

Buller, J. (1999), 'A critical appraisal of the statecraft interpretation', *Public Administration*, 77(4), 691–712.

Buller, J. (2000), *National Statecraft and European Integration*, London: Pinter.

Buller, J. and T. James (2011), 'Statecraft and the assessment of national political leaders: The case of New Labour and Tony Blair', *British Journal of Politics and International Relations*, 14(4), 534–555.

Bulmer, S., M. Burch, C. Carter, P. Hogwood and A. Scott (2002), *British Devolution and European Policy-Making: Transforming Britain into Multi-Level Governance*, London: Palgrave Macmillan.

Bulmer, S., D. Dolowitz, P. Humphreys and S. Padgett (2007), *Policy Transfer in the European Union*, London: Routledge.

Bulpitt, J. (1986), 'The Discipline of the New Democracy: Mrs Thatcher's Domestic Statecraft', *Political Studies*, 34, 19–39.

Bumiller, K. (2008), *In an Abusive State: How Neoliberalism Appropriated the Feminist Movement against Sexual Violence*, Durham, London: Duke University Press.

Burgess, M. and A.-G. Gagnon (2010), 'Introduction: Federalism and Democracy', in M. Burgess and A.-G. Gagnon (eds), *Federal Democracies*, 1–25, London; New York: Routledge.

Burke, A. (2008), *Fear of Security: Australia's Invasion Anxiety*, Cambridge: Cambridge University Press.

Burn, W.L. (1964), *The Age of Equipoise: A Study of the Mid-Victorian Generation*, London: Allen and Unwin.

Burnham, J. (1943), *The Managerial Revolution*, London: Putnam & Co.

Butler, J. (1990), *Gender Trouble: Feminism and the Subversion of Identity*, New York: Routledge.

Butler, J. (1997), *The Psychic Life of Power*, Stanford, CA: Stanford University Press.

Butler, J. (2002), 'Is kinship always already heterosexual?' *A Journal of Feminist Cultural Studies*, 13(1), 14–44.

Buzan, B. (1991a), 'Is International Security Possible?' in K. Booth (ed.) *New Thinking about Strategy and International Security*, 31–35, London: Harper Collins.

Buzan, B. (1991b), *People, States, and Fear: An Agenda for International Security Studies in the post-Cold War Era*, New York: Harvester Wheatsheaf.

Buzan, B. and G. Lawson (2015), *The Global Transformation: History, Modernity and the Making of International Relations*, Cambridge: Cambridge University Press.

Buzan, B., O. Waever and J. De Wilde (1998), *Security: A New Framework of Analysis*, Boulder, CO: Lynne Rienner.

Cagaptay, S. (2017), *The New Sultan. Erdoğan and the Crisis of Modern Turkey*, London: Bloomsbury I.B. Tauris.

Cairney, P., T. Heikkila and M. Wood (2019), *Making Policy in a Complex World*, Cambridge: Cambridge University Press.

Calhoun, C. (1997), *Nationalism*, Buckingham: Open University Press.

Campbell, D. (1992), *Writing Security: United States Foreign Policy and the Politics of Identity*, Manchester: Manchester University Press.

Campbell, J.L. (2004), *Institutional Change and Globalization*, Princeton, NJ: Princeton University Press.

Campbell, J.L. (2018), *American Discontent: The Rise of Donald Trump and Decline of the Golden Age*, Oxford: Oxford University Press.

Campbell, J.L. and O. Pedersen (2001), *The Rise of NeoLiberalism and Institutional Analysis*, Princeton, NJ: Princeton University Press.

Canovan, M. (1981), *Populism*, London: Junction Books.

Canovan, M. (1996), *Nationhood and Political Theory*, Cheltenham: Edward Elgar.

Canovan, M. (1999), 'Trust the people! Populism and the two faces of democracy', *Political Studies*, 47(1), 2–16.

Canovan, M. (2004), 'Populism for political theorists?' *Journal of Political Ideologies*, 9(3), 241–252, doi:10.1080/1356931042000263500.

Capoccia, G. (2016), 'When do institutions "bite"? Historical institutionalism and the politics of institutional change', *Comparative Political Studies*, 49(8), 1095–1127.

Carnoy, M. (1984), *The State and Political Theory*, Princeton, NJ: Princeton University Press.

Castells, M. (1996), *The Rise of the Network Society*, Oxford: Wiley-Blackwell.

Celis, K. S. Childs, J. Kantola and M.L. Krook (2008), 'Rethinking women's substantive representation', *Representation: The Journal of Representative Democracy*, 44(2), 99–110.

Cetrà, D. (2019), *Nationalism, Liberalism and Language in Catalonia and Flanders*, London: Palgrave Macmillan.

Cetrà, D. and C. Brown Swan (2020), 'State and majority nationalism in plurinational states: Responding to challenges from below', *Nationalism and Ethnic Politics*, 26(1), 1–7.

Cetrà, D. and M. Harvey (2019), 'Explaining accommodation and resistance to demands for independence referendums in the UK and Spain', *Nations and Nationalism*, 25(1), 607–629.

CGTN (2020), 'Sudan ends 30 year rule of Islamic rule separating religion and state', available online: https://newsaf.cgtn.com/news/2020-09-05/ Sudan-ends-30-year-rule-of-Islamic-rule-separating-religion-and-state-Twkirn8kZq/index.html (accessed 13 September 2020).

Chandrashekeran, S., B. Morgan, K. Coetzee and P. Christoff (2017), 'Rethinking the green state beyond the Global North: A South African climate change case study', *WIREs Climate Change*, 8, e473, doi.org/10.1002/wcc.473.

Chappell, L. (2000), 'Interacting with the state', *International Feminist Journal of Politics* 2(2), 244–275.

Chappell, L. (2002), *Gendering Government: Feminist Engagement with the State in Australia and Canada*, Vancouver: University of British Columbia Press.

Chappell, L. (2003), *Gendering Government: Feminist Engagement with the State in Australia and Canada*, Vancouver: University of British Columbia Press.

Chappell, L. (2013), 'State and Governance', in G. Waylen, K. Celis, J. Kantola and L. Weldon (eds), *The Oxford Handbook on Gender and Politics*, 603–626, New York: Oxford University Press.

Checkel, J. (1998), 'The constructivist turn in international relations theory', *World Politics*, 50, 324–348.

Christoff, P. (1996), 'Ecological modernization, ecological modernities', *Environmental Politics*, 5(3), 476–500.

Christoff, P. (2005), 'Out of Chaos, a Shining Star? Towards a Typology of Green States', in Barry and Eckersley (eds), *The State and the Global Ecological Crisis*, 25–51, Cambridge, MA: MIT Press.

Clark, A.E., C. D'Ambrosio and A. Lepinteur (2020), 'The fall in income inequality during COVID-19 in five European countries', Working Papers 565, ECINEQ, Society for the Study of Income Inequality, available online: http://www.ecineq.org/2020/12/21/the-fall-in-income-inequality-during-covid-19-in-five-european-countries/ (accessed 17 March 2022).

Clemenson, H. (1982), *English Country Houses and Landed Estates*, London: Croom Helm.

Closs, S.A. (2016), 'The affective atmospheres of nationalism', *Cultural Geographies*, 23, 181–198.

Coady, C.A.J., N. Dubos and S. Sanyal (2018), *Challenges for Humanitarian Intervention*, Oxford: Oxford University Press.

Coates, D. (1980), *Labour in Power? A Study of the Labour Government 1974–79*, London: Routledge.

Cohn, C. (1987), 'Sex and death in the rational world of defense intellectuals', *Signs: Journal of Women in Culture and Society*, 12(4), 687–718.

Colletti, L. (1972), *From Rousseau to Lenin: Studies in Ideology and Society*, New York: Monthly Review Press.

Colletti, L. (1975), 'Introduction', in L. Colletti (ed.), *Karl Marx: Early Writings*, 7–56, London: Pelican.

Collier, D. and R. Collier (1991), *Shaping the Political Arena*, Princeton, NJ: Princeton University Press.

Connell, R.W. (1987), *Gender and Power*, Cambridge: Polity Press.

Connell, R.W. (1990), 'The state, gender and sexual politics: Theory and appraisal', *Theory and Society*, 19, 507–544.

Coole, D. and S. Frost (2010), 'Introducing New Materialisms', in D. Coole and S. Frost (eds), *New Materialisms: Ontology, Agency and Politics*, 1–43, Durham, NC; London: Duke University Press.

Cooper, D. (2019), *Feeling Like a State: Desire, Denial and the Recasting of Authority*, Durham, NC: Duke University Press.

Cowen, Tyler and Daniel Sutter (1999), 'The costs of cooperation', *Review of Austrian Economics*, 12(2), 161–173.

Coyne C.J. and R. Hall (2018), *Tyranny Comes Home: The Domestic Fate of U.S. Militarism*, Stanford, CA: Stanford University Press.

Craig, M. (2018), 'Greening the state for a sustainable political economy', *New Political Economy*, 25(1), 1–4, doi:10.1080/13563467.2018.1526266.

Credit Suisse (2019), *Global Wealth Report*, available online: https://www.credit-suisse.com/about-us/en/reports-research/global-wealth-report.html (accessed 17 March 2022).

Crenshaw, K. (1991), 'Mapping the margins: Intersectionality, identity politics, and violence against women of color', *Stanford Law Review*, 43 (6), 1241–1299.

Crone, P. (1989), *Pre-Industrial Societies: New Perspectives on the Past*, Oxford: Blackwell.

CSIRO (2020), *CSIRO Annual Report 2019–20*, available online: https://www.csiro.au/en/about/Corporate-governance/annual-reports/19-20-annual-report (accessed 17 March 2022).

Culpepper, P.D. (2010), *Quiet Politics and Business Power: Corporate control in Europe and Japan*, Cambridge: Cambridge University Press.

Culpepper, P.D. (2015), 'Structural power and political science in the post-crisis era', *Business and Politics*, 17, 391–409.

Culpepper, P.D. and R. Reinke (2014), 'Structural power and bank bailouts in the United Kingdom and the United States', *Politics and Society*, 42(4), 1–28.

D'Alisa, G., F. Demaria and G. Kallis (2015), *Degrowth: A Vocabulary for a New Era*, New York: Routledge.

D'Alisa, G. and G. Kallis (2020), 'Degrowth and the state', *Ecological Economics*, 169, 106486.

Dahl, R.A. (1957), 'The concept of power', *Behavioral Science*, 2(3), 201–215.

Dahl, R.A. (1961), *Who Governs?* New Haven, CT: Yale University Press.

Dahl, R.A. (1966), 'Further reflections on "the elitist theory of democracy"', *American Political Science Review*, 60(2), 296–305.

Dahl, R.A. (1967), *Pluralist Democracy in the United States*, Chicago, IL: Rand McNally.

Dahl, R.A. (1973), *Polyarchy: Participation and Opposition*, New Haven, CT: Yale University Press.

Dahlerup, D. (1987), 'Confusing Concepts – Confusing Reality: A Theoretical Discussion of the Patriarchal State', in A.S. Sassoon (ed.), *Women and the State*, 93–127, London: Routledge.

Dalton, R.J., W.P. Bürklin and A. Drummond (2001), 'Public Opinion and Direct Democracy', *Journal of Democracy*, 12(4): 141–153.

Danspeckgruber, W.F. (2002), 'Introduction', in W.F. Danspeckgruber, *The Self-determination of Peoples: Community, Nation and State in an Interdependent World*, 1–12, Boulder, CO: Lynne Rienner.

Darwell, Stephen (ed.) (2002), *Contractarianism/Contractualism*, Oxford: Blackwell.

Davies, J.S. (2011), *Challenging Governance Theory: From Networks to Hegemony*, Bristol: Policy Press.

De Cleen, B. (2017), 'Populism and Nationalism', in C.R. Kaltwasser, P. Taggart, P. Ochoa Espejo and P. Ostiguy (eds), *The Oxford Handbook of Populism*, 342–362, Oxford: Oxford University Press.

De Vries, C.E. and S.B. Hobolt (2020), 'Challenger parties and populism', *LSE Public Policy Review*, 1(1), 3, doi:10.31389/lseppr.3.

Dean, M.M. (2009), *Governmentality: Power and Rule in Modern Society*, London: SAGE.

Dean, M.M. (2013), *The Signature of Power: Sovereignty, Governmentality and Biopolitics*, London: SAGE.

Death, C. (2016), 'Green states in Africa: Beyond the usual suspects', *Environmental Politics*, 25(1), 116–135.

DeFilippis, J. (2001), 'The myth of social capital in community development', *Housing Policy Debate*, 12(4), 781–806.

DeLanda, M. (2016), *Assemblage Theory*, Edinburgh: Edinburgh University Press.

Deleuze, G. and F. Guattari (1987), *A Thousand Plateaus: Capitalism and Schizophrenia*, London: Athlone Press.

Demsetz, H. (1969), 'Information and efficiency: Another viewpoint', *Journal of Law and Economics* 12(1), 1–22.

Deng, F.M. et al. (1996), *Sovereignty as Responsibility: Conflict Management in Africa*, Washington, DC: Brookings Institute.

Derrida, J. (1978), 'Structure, Sign, and Play in the Discourse of the Human Sciences', in J. Derrida, *Writing and Difference*, trans. A. Bass, 351–370, London: Routledge.

Deutsch, K.W. (1966), *Nationalism and Social Communication: An Inquiry into the Foundations of Nationality*, Cambridge, MA: MIT Press.

DiEM25 (n.d.), 'Democracy in Europe Movement', available online: https://diem25.org/en/ (accessed 17 March 2022).

DiMaggio, P.J. and W.W. Powell (1991), 'Introduction', in Powell and DiMaggio (eds), *The New Institutionalism in Organizational Analysis*, 1–39, Chicago, IL: University of Chicago Press.

Dobbin, F. (1994), *Forging Industrial Policy*, Cambridge: Cambridge University Press.

Dobson, A. (2010), 'Democracy and nature: Speaking and listening', *Political Studies*, 58(4), 752–768.

Dobson, A. and D. Bell (eds) (2006), *Environmental Citizenship*, Cambridge, MA: MIT Press.

Domhoff, G.W. (1967), *Who Rules America?* Englewood Cliff, NJ: Prentice Hall.

Domhoff, G.W. (1970), *The Higher Circles: The Governing Class in America*, New York: Vintage Books.

Domhoff, G.W. (1979), *The Powers That Be: Processes of Ruling Class Domination in America*, New York: Vintage Books.

Domhoff, G.W. (1980), *Power Structure Research*, Beverley Hills, CA: SAGE.

Domhoff, G.W. (1990), *The Power Elite and the State*, New York: Aldine de Gruyter.

Domhoff, G.W. (2014), 'Is the corporate elite fractured, or is there continuing corporate dominance? Two contrasting views', *Class, Race and Corporate Power*, 3(1), 1–42.

Domhoff, G.W. (2017), *Studying the Power Elite: Fifty Years of Who Rules America?* New York: Routledge.

Donnan, H. and T.M. Wilson (1999), *Borders: Frontiers of Identity, Nation and State*, Oxford: Berg.

Dore, E. and M. Molyneux (eds) (2000), *Hidden Stories of Gender and the State in Latin America*, Durham, NC, and London: Duke University Press.

Dorling, D. (2019), *Inequality and the 1%*, London: Verso.

Doty, R.L. (1998), 'Immigration and the politics of security', *Security Studies*, 8(2): 71–93.

Dowding, K. (2001), 'There must be end to confusion: Policy networks, intellectual fatigue, and the need for political science methods courses in British universities', *Political Studies*, 49, 89–105.

Dowding, K. (2016), *The Philosophy and Methods of Political Science*, London: Palgrave.

Dowding, K. and A. Hindmoor (1997), 'The usual suspects: Rational choice, socialism and political theory', *New Political Economy* 2(3), 451–463.

Dowding, K. and B.R. Taylor (2020), *Economic Approaches to Government*, London: Palgrave Pivot.

Draper, H. (1977), *Karl Marx's Theory of Revolution. Volume 1: State and Bureaucracy*, New York: Monthly Review Press.

Drezner, D. (2020), 'The song remains the same: International relations after COVID-19', *International Organization*, 74(s), E18–E35.

Driver, F. (1989), 'The historical geography of the workhouse system in England and Wales, 1834–1883', *Journal of Historical Geography*, 15, 269–286.

Druckman, J.N. (2004), 'Political preference formation: Competition, deliberation, and the (ir)relevance of framing effects', *American Political Science Review*, 98(4), 671–686.

Dryzek, J.S. (1996), 'Political inclusion and the dynamics of democratization', *American Political Science Review*, 90(3), 475–487.

Dryzek, J.S. (2005), *The Politics of the Earth: Environmental Discourses*, Oxford: Oxford University Press.

Dryzek, J.S. (2010), *Foundations and Frontiers of Deliberative Governance*, Oxford: Oxford University Press.

Dryzek, J.S., D. Downies, C. Hunold, D. Schlosberg and H. Hernes (2003), *Green States and Social Movements: Environmentalism in the United States, United Kingdom, Germany and Norway*, Oxford: Oxford University Press.

Duit, A. (2012), 'Adaptive Capacity and the Ecostate', in C. Boyd and E. Folke (eds), *Adapting Institutions, Governance, Complexity and Social-Ecological Resilience*, 127–147, Cambridge: Cambridge University Press.

Duit, A. (ed.) (2014), *The State and the Environment: A Comparative Study of Environmental Governance*, Cambridge, MA: MIT Press.

Duit, A. (2016), 'The four faces of the environmental state: Environmental governance regimes in 28 countries', *Environmental Politics*, 25(1), 69–91.

Duit, A., P.H. Feindt and J. Meadowcroft (2016), 'Greening Leviathan: The rise of the environmental state?' *Environmental Politics*, 25(1), 1–23.

Dunleavy, P. (1991), *Democracy, Bureaucracy and Public Choice: Economic Explanations in Political Science*, London: Harvester Wheatsheaf.

Dunleavy, P. and B. O'Leary (1987), *Theories of the State: The Politics of Liberal Democracy*, London: Macmillan.

Duvall, R. and L. Varadarajan (2007), 'Traveling in paradox: Edward Said and critical international relations', *Millennium – Journal of International Studies*, 36(1), 83–99.

Easton, D.S. (1965), *A Framework for Political Analysis*, Englewood Cliffs, NJ: Prentice Hall.

Easton, D.S. (1967), *A Framework for Political Analysis*, Englewood Cliffs, NJ: Prentice Hall.

Eatwell, R. and M. Goodwin (2018), *National Populism: The Revolt against Liberal Democracy*, London: Pelican Books.

Eckersley, R. (2004), *The Green State: Rethinking Democracy and Sovereignty*, Cambridge, MA: MIT Press.

Eckersley, R. (2016), 'National identities, international roles, and the legitimation of climate leadership: Germany and Norway compared', *Environmental Politics*, 25(1), 180–201.

Eckersley, R. (2018), 'The green state in transition: Reply to Bailey, Barry and Craig', *New Political Economy*, 25(1), 46–56, doi:10.1080/13563467.2018.1 526270.

Eckersley, R. (2019), 'Ecological democracy and the rise and decline of liberal democracy: Looking back, looking forward', *Environmental Politics*, 29(2), 214–234.

Economist, The (2020), 'Rich countries try radical economic policies to counter covid-19', available online: https://www.economist.com/ briefing/2020/03/26/rich-countries-try-radical-economic-policies-to- counter-covid-19 (accessed 17 March 2022).

Edelman (2019), *2019 Edelman Trust Barometer*, available online: https://www. afr.com/leadership/australians-show-surprise-leap-of-faith-in-edelman- trust-survey-20190122-h1abwv (accessed 21 May 2019).

Edensor, T. (2002), *National Identity, Popular Culture and Everyday Life*, Oxford: Berg.

Edkins, J. (1999), *Poststructuralism and International Relations: Bringing the Political Back In*, Boulder, CO: Lynne Rienner.

Edwards, L. (2020), *Corporate Power in Australia: Do the 1% Rule?* Clayton, VIC: Monash University Publishing.

Eisenstein, Z. (1979), 'Developing a Theory of Capitalist Patriarchy and Socialist Feminism', in Z. Eisenstein (ed.), *Capitalist Patriarchy and the Case for Socialist Feminism*, 5–40, New York: London: Monthly Review Press.

Eisenstein, Z. (1986), *The Radical Future of Liberal Feminism*, Boston, MA: Northeastern University Press.

Elden, S. (2005), 'Missing the point: Globalization, deterritorialization and the space of the world', *Transactions of the Institute of British Geographers*, 30, 8–19.

Elden, S. (2010), 'Land, terrain, territory', *Progress in Human Geography*, 34, 799–817.

Elomäki, A. and J. Kantola (2018), 'Theorizing feminist struggles in the triangle of neoliberalism, conservatism, and nationalism', *Social Politics*, 25(3), 337–360.

Elomäki, A. and P.K. Sandberg (2020), 'Feminist perspectives on the economy within transforming Nordic welfare states', *NORA – Nordic Journal of Feminist and Gender Research*, 28(2), 81–85.

Elomäki, A., J. Kantola and P.K. Sandberg (eds) (2022), *Social Partners and Gender Equality: Change and Continuity in Gendered Corporatism in Europe*, Basingstoke: Palgrave.

Elomäki, A., A. Mustosmäki and P.K. Sandberg (2021), 'The sidelining of gender equality in a corporatist and knowledge-oriented regime: The case of failed family leave reform in Finland', *Critical Social Policy*, 41(2), 294–314.

Elster, J. (1985), *Making Sense of Marx*, Cambridge: Cambridge University Press.

Elster, J. and A. Hylland (eds) (1986), *Foundations of Social Choice Theory*, Cambridge: Cambridge University Press.

Engels, F. ([1844] 1975), 'Outline of a Critique of Political Economy', in K. Marx and F. Engels, *Collected Works. Volume 3*, 418–443, London: Lawrence & Wishart.

Engels, F. ([1878] 1947), *Anti-Dühring*, Moscow: Progress Publishers.

Engels, F. ([1884] 1978), *The Origin of the Family, Private Property and the State*, Peking: Foreign Language Press.

Enloe, C. (1983), *Does Khaki Become You?: The Militarisation of Women's Lives*, Boston, MA: South End Press.

Enloe, C. (1989), *Bananas, Beaches and Bases: Making Feminist Sense of International Politics*, Berkeley: University of California Press.

Enloe, C. (1990), *Bananas, Beaches and Bases: Making Feminist Sense of International Politics*, Berkeley: University of California Press.

Enloe, C. (1996), 'Margins, Silences and Bottom Rungs: How to Overcome the Underestimation of Power in the Study of International Relations' in K. Booth, S. Smith and M. Zalewski (eds), *International Theory: Positivism and Beyond*, 186–202, Cambridge: Cambridge University Press.

Enloe, C. (2010), *Nimo's War, Emma's War: Making Feminist Sense of the Iraq War*, Berkeley: University of California Press.

Enloe, C. (2014), *Bananas, Beaches and Bases: Making Feminist Sense of International Politics*, Berkeley: University of California Press.

Epstein, C. (2008), *The Power of Words in International Relations: Birth of an Anti-Whaling Discourse*, Cambridge, MA: MIT Press

Erk, J. and L. Anderson (2009), 'The Paradox of Federalism: Does Self-Rule Accommodate or Exacerbate Ethnic Divisions?' *Regional and Federal Studies*, 19(2), 191–202.

Ethics & International Affairs (2011), 'Roundtable: Libya, Responsibility to Protect and Humanitarian Intervention', 25(3).

Evans, G. (2009), *The Responsibility to Protect: Ending Mass Atrocity Crimes Once and For All*, Washington, DC: Brookings Institution.

Evans, M. (2010), 'The Rise and Fall of the Magic Kingdom: Understanding Kevin Rudd's Domestic Statecraft', in C. Aulich, and M. Evans (eds), *The Rudd Government*, 261–278, Canberra: ANU Press.

Evans, M. (2019), 'International Policy Transfer. Between the Global and Sovereign and between the Global and Local', in D. Stone and K. Maloney (eds), *The Oxford Handbook of Global Policy and Administration*, 94–110, Oxford: Oxford University Press.

Evans, M. and B. McCaffrie (2014), 'Rudderless' – Perceptions of Julia Gillard's Domestic Statecraft', in C. Aulich (ed.), *The Gillard Governments*, 303–321, Melbourne: Melbourne University Press.

Evans, M. and B. McCaffrie (2016), 'From Austerity to the New Economy: Prime Ministerial Leadership in a Time of Mistrust', in C. Aulich (ed.), *From Abbott to Turnbull. A New Direction?* 345–368, West Geelong: Echo Books.

Evans, P.B., D. Rueschemeyer and T. Skocpol (eds) (1985), *Bringing the State Back In*, Cambridge: Cambridge University Press.

Farrall, S., C. Hay and E. Gray (2020) *Exploring Political Legacies*, Basingstoke: Palgrave Macmillan.

Fawcett, P., M.V. Flinders, C. Hay and M. Wood (eds) (2017), *Anti-Politics, Depoliticization, and Governance*, Oxford: Oxford University Press.

Fawcett Society (2020), 'The Coronavirus crossroads: Equal Pay Day 2020 report', available online: https://www.fawcettsociety.org.uk/Handlers/Download.ashx?IDMF=dbe15227-4c02-4102-bbf2-dce0b415e729 (accessed 17 March 2022).

Femia, J.V. (1981), *Gramsci's Political Thought: Hegemony, Consciousness, and the Revolutionary Process*, Oxford: Clarendon Press.

Ferguson, A. (1782), *An Essay on the History of Civil Society*, 5th edn, London: T. Cadell.

Fierke, K.M. (2007), *Critical Approaches to International Security*, Oxford: Polity.

Financial Times (2021), 'Coronavirus tracked: See how your country compares', available online: https://ig.ft.com/coronavirus-chart/ (accessed 17 March 2022).

Finegold, K. and T. Skocpol (1995), 'Marxist Approaches to Politics and the State', in K. Finegold and T. Skocpol, *State and Party in America's New Deal*, 175–199, Madison: University of Wisconsin Press.

Finlayson, A. and J. Valentine (eds) (2002), *Politics and Poststructuralism*, Edinburgh: Edinburgh University Press.

Finnemore, M. (1996a), 'Norms, culture, and world politics: Insights from sociology's institutionalism', *International Organization*, 50(2), 325–347.

Finnemore, M. (1996b), 'Constructing Norms of Humanitarian Intervention', in P. Katzenstein (ed.), *The Culture of National Security: Norms and Identity in World Politics*, 153–185, Ithaca, NY: Cornell University Press.

Finnemore, M. and K. Sikkink (1998), 'International norm dynamics and political change', *International Organization*, 52, 887–917.

Fiore, G. (1970), *Antonio Gramsci: Life of a Revolutionary*, London: New Left Books.

Fiorino, D. (2017), 'Green Economy: Reframing Ecology, Economics, and Equity', in J. Meadowcroft and D. Fiorino (eds), *Conceptual Innovation in Environmental Policy*, 281–306, Cambridge, MA: MIT Press.

Fischer, F. and J. Forester (eds) (1993), *The Argumentative Turn in Policy Analysis and Planning*, Durham, NC: Duke University Press.

Fischer, F. and H. Gottweis (2012), *The Argumentative Turn Revisited: Public Policy as Communicative Practice*, Durham, NC: Duke University Press.

Fischer, R. (2018), 'Environmental Democracy: Participation, Deliberation and Citizenship', in M. Boström and D. Davidson (eds), *Environment and Society*, 257–279, Basingstoke: Palgrave Macmillan.

Fligstein, N. (1990), *The Transformation of Corporate Control*, Cambridge, MA: Harvard University Press.

Fligstein, N. and I. Mara-Drita (1996), 'How to make a market: Reflections on the attempt to create a single market in the European Union', *American Journal of Sociology*, 102, 1–32.

Flinders, M. (2017), 'A new kind of democracy: Anti-politics and the funneling of frustration', *The Conversation*, 12 June 2017, available online: https://theconversation.com/a-new-kind-of-democracy-anti-politics-and-the-funnelling-of-frustration-79128 (accessed 17 March 2022).

Follet, M.P. (1918), *The New State*, London: Longmans.

Forster, P. (2021), 'Covid-19 paused climate emissions – but they're rising again', available online: https://www.bbc.com/future/article/20210312-covid-19-paused-climate-emissions-but-theyre-rising-again (accessed 17 March 2022).

Foster, E.A., P. Kerr and C. Byrne (2014), 'Rolling back to roll forward: Depoliticisation and the extension of government', *Policy & Politics*, 42(2), 225–241.

Foucault, M. (1977), *Discipline and Punish*, London: Penguin.

Foucault, M. (1980), 'Truth and Power', in M. Foucault, *Power-Knowledge: Selected Interviews and Other Writings 1972–1977*, ed. C. Gordon, 109–133, London: Harvester Wheatsheaf.

Foucault, M. (1991), 'Governmentality', in G. Burchell et al. (eds), *The Foucault Effect: Studies in Governmentality*, 87–104, London: Harvester Wheatsheaf.

Foucault, M. (2000), *Power: Essential Works of Foucault, 1954–1984*, vol. 3, ed. J.D. Faubion, New York: New Press.

Foucault, M. (2003), *Society Must Be Defended,* London: Penguin.

Franck, T.G. (1992), 'The emerging right to democratic governance', *American Journal of International Law*, 86(1), 46–91.

Frantzeskaki, N., D. Loorbach and J. Meadowcroft (2012), 'Governing societal transitions to sustainability', *International Journal of Sustainable Development*, 15(1–2), 19–36.

Freeden, M. (2003), *Ideology: A Very Short Introduction*, Oxford: Oxford University Press.

Freeden, M. and M. Stears (2013), 'Liberalism', in M. Freeden and M. Stears (eds), *The Oxford Handbook of Political Ideologies*, 329–348, Oxford: Oxford University Press.

Frey, B.S. and R. Eichenberger (1999), *The New Democratic Federalism for Europe: Functional, Overlapping and Competing Jurisdictions*, Cheltenham: Edward Elgar.

Friedan, B. (1962), *The Feminine Mystique*, New York: Dell Publishing.

Friedman, P. and B.R. Taylor (2012), 'Seasteading: Competitive governments on the ocean', *Kyklos*, 65(2), 218–235.

Fritz, M. and M. Koch (2016), 'Economic development and prosperity patterns around the world: Structural challenges for a global steady-state economy', *Global Environmental Change*, 38, 41–48.

Fuenfschilling, L. and B. Truffer (2014), 'The structuration of socio-technical regimes: Conceptual foundations from institutional theory', *Research Policy*, 43, 772–791.

Gagnon, A.-G., A. Lecours and G. Nootens (eds) (2011), *Contemporary Majority Nationalism*, Montreal: McGill-Queen's University Press.

Gais, T.L., M.A. Peterson and J.L. Walker (1984), 'Interest groups, iron triangles and representative institutions in American national government', *British Journal of Political Science*, 14(2), 161–185.

Galbraith, J. (1952), *American Capitalism: The Concept of Countervailing Power*, London: Routledge.

Galston, W.A. (2017), *Anti-Pluralism: The Populist Threat to Liberal Democracy*, New Haven: CT: Yale University Press.

Galtung, J. (1969), 'Violence, peace, and peace research', *Journal of Peace Research*, 6(3), 167–191.

Gamble, A. (2000), *Politics and Fate*, Cambridge: Polity.

Garikipati, S. and U. Kambhampati (2021), 'Leading the fight against the pandemic: Does gender "really" matter?', available online: https://papers.ssrn.com/sol3/papers.cfm?abstract_id=3617953 (accessed 17 March 2022).

Garrett, L. (2020), 'The world after Coronavirus: The future of pandemics', available online: https://www.youtube.com/watch?v=TU1vwEIYcLg (accessed 17 March 2022).

Geels, F. (2010), 'Ontologies, socio-technical transitions (to sustainability), and the multi-level perspective', *Research Policy*, 39, 495–510.

Geels, F. (2014), 'Regime resistance against low-carbon transitions: Introducing politics and power into the multi-level perspective', *Theory, Culture & Society*, 31(5), 21–40.

Geels, F. and J. Schot (2007), 'Typology of sociotechnical transition pathways', *Research Policy*, 36, 399–417.

Geertz, C. (1994), 'Primordial and Civic Ties', in A.D. Smith and J. Hutchinson (eds), *Nationalism*, 29–33, Oxford: Oxford Readers.

Geist, E. (2015), 'Political fallout: The failure of emergency management at Chernobyl', *Slavic Review*, 74(1), 104–126.

Gellner, E. (1983), *Nations and Nationalism*, Oxford: Blackwell.

Gerbaudo, P. (2014), 'Populism 2.0: Social Media Activism, the Generic Internet User and Interactive Democracy', in D. Trottier and C. Fuchs (eds), *Social Media, Politics and the State: Protests, Revolutions, Riots, Crime and Policing in the Age of Facebook, Twitter and YouTube*, 67–87, New York: Routledge.

Gershtenson, J. and D.L. Plane (2015), 'In government we distrust: Citizen skepticism and democracy in the United States', *The Forum*, 13(3), 481–505.

Gerth, H.H. and C.W. Mills (1970), 'Introduction', in H.H. Gerth and C.W. Mills (eds), *From Max Weber: Essays in Sociology*, 1–83, London: Routledge and Kegan Paul.

Gerth, H.H. and C.W. Mills (1991), 'Introduction: The Man and his Work', in H.H. Gerth and C.W. Mills (eds), *From Max Weber: Essays in Sociology*, 1–74, London: Routledge.

Gibb, R., D.W. Redding, K.Qing Chin, C.A. Donnelly, T.M. Blackburn, T. Newbold, and K.E. Jones (2020), 'Zoonotic host diversity increases in human-dominated ecosystems', *Nature*, 584, 398–402, doi:10.1038/s41586-020-2562-8.

Giddens, A. (1979), *Central Problems in Social Theory*, London: Macmillan.

Giddens, A. (1981), *A Contemporary Critique of Historical Materialism. Volume 1: Power, Property and the State*, London: Macmillan.

Giddens, A. (1984), *The Constitution of Society*, Cambridge: Polity.

Giddens, A. (1991), *The Consequences of Modernity*, Cambridge: Polity.

Gilding, M., E. Merlot, S. Leitch and M. Alexander (2013), 'Business collective action and the Australian mining industry's tax revolt: A comment on McKnight and Hobbs', *Australian Journal of Political Science*, 48(4), 501–506.

Gilens, M. and B.I. Page (2014), 'Testing Theories of American politics: Elites, interest groups, and average citizens', *Perspectives on Politics*, 12(3), 564–581.

Gill, N. (2009), 'Presentational state power: Temporal and spatial influences over asylum sector decision makers', *Transactions of the Institute of British Geographers*, 34, 215–233.

Gill, N. (2010), 'New state-theoretic approaches to asylum and refugee geographies', *Progress in Human Geography*, 34, 626–645.

Glasberg, D.S., A.S. Willis and D. Shannon (2017), *The State of State Theory: State Projects, Repression, and Multi-sites of Power*, Lanham, MD: Lexington Books.

Glencross, A. (2014), 'Bleak prospects? Varieties of Europessimism and their application to the Eurozone debt crisis and the future of integration', *Journal of European Integration* 36(4), 393–408, doi:10.1080/07036337.20 13.846338.

Glyn, A. (2007), *Capitalism Unleashed: Finance, Globalization, and Welfare*, Oxford: Oxford University Press.

Glynos, J. and D.R. Howarth (2007), *Logics of Critical Explanation in Social and Political Theory*, London: Routledge.

Gold, D.A. et al. (1975a), 'Recent developments in Marxist theories of the capitalist state: Part I', *Monthly Review*, 27(5), 29–43.

Gold, D.A. et al. (1975b), 'Recent developments in Marxist theories of the capitalist state: Part II', *Monthly Review*, 27(6), 36–51.

Goldberg, D.T. (2001a), 'Racial States', in J. Solomos and D.T. Goldberg (eds), *Companion to Racial and Ethnic Studies*, 233–258, Oxford: Blackwell.

Goldberg, D.T. (2001b), *The Racial State*, Oxford: Blackwell.

Golder, M. (2016), 'Far right parties in Europe', *Annual Review of Political Science*, 19(1), 477–497, doi:10.1146/annurev-polisci-042814-012441.

Goldstein, J. and R. Keohane (1993), *Ideas and Foreign Policy: Beliefs, Institutions and Political Change*, Ithaca, NY: Cornell University Press.

Gong, G.C. (1984), *The Standard of 'Civilisation' in International Society*, Oxford: Oxford University Press.

Goodhart, D. (2017), *The Road to Somewhere: The Populist Revolt and the Future of Politics*, London: Hurst.

Goodin, R. (1992), *Green Political Theory*, Cambridge: Polity Press.

Gordon, C. (1991), 'Governmental Rationality: An Introduction', in G. Burchell et al. (eds), *The Foucault Effect: Studies in Governmentality*, 1–52, London: Harvester Wheatsheaf.

Gottmann, J. (1973), *The Significance of Territory*, Charlottesville: University Press of Virginia.

Gough, I. (2017), *Heat, Greed and Human Need: Climate Change, Capitalism and Sustainable Wellbeing*, Cheltenham: Edward Elgar.

Gough, I. and J. Meadowcroft (2011), 'Decarbonizing the Welfare State' in J. Dryzek, R. Norgaard and D. Schlosberg (eds), *The Oxford Handbook on Climate Change and Society*, 490–503, Oxford: Oxford University Press.

Gourevitch, P. (1986), *Politics in Hard Times: Comparative Responses to International Economic Crises*, Ithaca, NY: Cornell University Press.

Gramsci, A. ([1929–1937] 1996), *Prison Notebooks*, New York: Colombia University Press.

Gramsci, A. (1971), *Selections from the Prison Notebooks*, ed. Q. Hoare and G. Nowell-Smith, London: Lawrence & Wishart.

Gray, J. (2020), 'Why this crisis is a turning point in history', *New Statesman*, available online: https://www.newstatesman.com/international/2020/04/why-crisis-turning-point-history (accessed 17 March 2022).

Green, D. and I. Shapiro (1994), *The Pathologies of Rational Choice*, New Haven, CT: Yale University Press.

Greenfeld, L. (1992), *Nationalism: Five Roads to Modernity*, Cambridge, MA: Harvard University Press.

Greenhill, B. (2010), 'The company you keep: International socialisation and the diffusion of human rights norms', *International Studies Quarterly*, 54, 127–145.

Gregory, D. (2006) 'The black flag: Guantánamo Bay and the space of exception', *Geografiska Annaler Series B: Human Geography*, 88, 405–427.

Greif, A. and D.D. Laitin (2004), 'A theory of endogenous institutional change', *American Political Science Review*, 98(4), 633–652.

Griffiths, H., R. Jones and P. Merriman (2015), 'Final report on the use of the Welsh language in digital maps and automated address data', copy available from Rhys Jones.

Grimm, D. (2015), *Sovereignty: The Origins and Future of a Political and Legal Concept*, New York: Columbia University Press.

Grin, J., J. Rotmans and J. Schot (2010), *Transitions to Sustainable Development: New Directions in the Study of Long Term Transformative Change*, London: Routledge.

Grosby, S. (2005), *Nationalism: A Very Short Introduction*, Oxford: Oxford University Press.

Grovogui, S.N. (2002), 'Regimes of sovereignty: International morality and the African condition', *European Journal of International Relations*, 8(3), 315–338.

Guardian, The (2021), 'Oxford/AstraZeneca Covid vaccine research "was 97% publicly funded"', available online: https://www.theguardian.com/science/2021/apr/15/oxfordastrazeneca-covid-vaccine-research-was-97-publicly-funded (accessed 17 March 2022).

Guibernau, M. (1999), *Nations without States: Political Communities in a Global Age*, London: Wiley.

Gusterson, H. (1999), 'Nuclear weapons and the other in the Western imagination', *Cultural Anthropology*, 14(1), 111–143.

Gusterson, H. (2004), *People of the Bomb: Portraits of America's Nuclear Complex*, Minneapolis: University of Minnesota Press.

Gwartney, J.D. and R.E. Wagner (1988), 'Public Choice and the Conduct of Representative Government', in J.D. Gwartney and R.E. Wagner (eds), *Public Choice and Constitutional Economics*, 3–28, New York: JAI Press.

Haas, P.M. (1992), 'Introduction: Epistemic communities and international policy coordination', *International Organization*, 46, 1–35.

Habermas, J. (1975), *Legitimation Crisis*, London: Heinemann.

Habermas, J. (1992), 'Citizenship and national identity: Some reflections on the future of Europe', *Citizenship: Critical Concepts*, 2, 341–358.

Habermas, J. (1996), *Between Facts and Norms: Contributions to a Discourse Theory*, London: Polity Press.

Hacker, J.S. and P. Pierson (2002), 'Business power and social policy: employers and the formation of the American welfare state', *Politics and Society*, 30 (2), 277–325.

Hajer, M. (1993), 'Discourse Coalitions in Practice: The Case of Acid Rain in Great Britain', in F. Fischer and J. Forester (eds), *The Argumentative Turn in Policy Analysis and Planning*, 43–76, Durham, NC: Duke University Press.

Hajer, M. (1995), *The Politics of Environmental Discourse: Ecological Modernisation and the Policy Process*, Oxford: Oxford University Press.

Hale, H. (2008), *The Foundations of Ethnic Politics: Separatism of States and Nations in Eurasia and the World*, Cambridge: Cambridge University Press.

Hale, T. and C. Roger (2014), 'Orchestration and transnational climate governance', *Review of International Organizations*, 9(1), 59–82.

Hall, J.A. and G. John Ikenberry (1989), *The State*, Milton Keynes: Open University Press.

Hall, P. (1986), *Governing the Economy: The Politics of State Intervention in Britain and France*, New York: Oxford University Press.

Hall, P. (1993), 'Policy paradigms, social learning and the state: The case of economic policy-making in Britain', *Comparative Politics*, 25, 275–296.

Hall, P. (2010), 'Historical Institutionalism in Rationalist and Sociological Perspective', in J. Mahoney and K. Thelen (eds), *Explaining Institutional Change: Ambiguity, Agency, and Power*, 204–224, Cambridge: Cambridge University Press.

Hall, P. and D. Soskice (2001), 'Introduction', in P.A. Hall and D. Soskice (eds), *Varieties of Capitalism: The Institutional Foundations of Comparative Advantage*, 1–68, Oxford: Oxford University Press.

Hall, P. and R. Taylor (1996), 'Political science and the three new institutionalisms', *Political Studies*, 44(5), 952–973.

Hall, P. and K. Thelen (2009), 'Institutional change in varieties of capitalism', *Socio-Economic Review*, 7(1), 7–34.

Hall, S. and M. Jacques (1983), *The Politics of Thatcherism*, London: Lawrence & Wishart.

Halliday, F. (1987), 'State and society in international relations: A second agenda', *Millennium – Journal of International Studies*, 16(2), 215–229.

Halperin, S. (1997), *In the Mirror of the Third World: Capitalist Development in Modern Europe*, Ithaca, NY: Cornell University Press.

Halperin, S. (2013), *Re-envisioning Global Development: A Horizontal Perspective*, London: Routledge.

Halperin, S. (2017), 'Historical Sociology', in X. Guillaume and P. Bilgin (eds), *The Routledge Handbook of International Political Sociology*, 26–35, London: Routledge.

Halpin, D. and J. Warhurst (2016), 'Commercial lobbying in Australia: Exploring the Australian lobby register', *Australian Journal of Public Administration*, 75(1), 100–111.

Hamel, M.E. (2016), 'Ethnic belonging of the children born out of rape in postconflict Bosnia-Herzegovina and Rwanda', *Nations and Nationalism*, 22 (2), 287–304.

Hamid, S. (2020), 'Reopening the world: How the pandemic is reinforcing authoritarianism', available online: https://www.brookings.edu/blog/order-from-chaos/2020/06/16/reopening-the-world-how-the-pandemic-is-reinforcing-authoritarianism/ (accessed 17 March 2022).

Hammond, M. (2020), 'Sustainability as a cultural transformation: The role of deliberative democracy', *Environmental Politics*, 29(1), 173–192.

Haney, L.A. (2000), 'Feminist state theory: Applications to jurisprudence, criminology, and the welfare state', *Annual Review of Sociology*, 26(1), 641–666.

Hannah, M. (1999), *Governmentality and the Mastery of Territory in Nineteenth Century America*, Cambridge: Cambridge University Press.

Hannah, M. (2009), 'Calculable territory and the West German census boycott movements of the 1980s', *Political Geography*, 28, 66–75.

Hansen, L. (2017), 'Poststructuralism and Security', in *Oxford Research Encyclopedia of International Studies*, available online: https://oxfordre. com/internationalstudies/view/10.1093/acrefore/9780190846626.001.0001/ acrefore-9780190846626-e-278 (accessed 17 March 2022).

Hardin, R. (1991), 'Hobbesian political order', *Political Theory*, 19(2), 156–180.

Hargreaves-Heap, S. et al. (1992), *The Theory of Choice: A Critical Guide*, Oxford: Blackwell.

Harvey, D. (2010), *The Enigma of Capital: And the Crises of Capitalism*, London: Profile Books.

Hastings, A. (1997), *The Construction of Nationhood: Ethnicity, Religion and Nationalism*, Cambridge: Cambridge University Press.

Hay, C. (1994), 'Werner in Wunderland: Bob Jessop's Strategic-Relational Approach', in F. Sebäi and C. Vercellone (eds), *École de la régulation et critique de la raison économique*, 331–355, Paris: Editions L'Harmattan (Futur Antérieur).

Hay, C. (1996a), 'Narrating crisis: The discursive construction of the winter of discontent', *Sociology*, 30(2), 253–277.

Hay, C. (1996b), *Re-Stating Social and Political Change*, Buckingham: Open University Press.

Hay, C. (2001), 'The "Crisis" of Keynesianism and the Rise of NeoLiberalism in Britain: An Ideational Institutionalist Approach', in J.L. Campbell and O. Pedersen (eds), *The Rise of NeoLiberalism and Institutional Analysis*, 193–218, Princeton, NJ: Princeton University Press.

Hay, C. (2002), *Political Analysis: A Critical Introduction*, New York: Palgrave Macmillan.

Hay, C. (2004), 'Re-stating politics, re-politicising the state: Neoliberalism, economic imperatives and the rise of the competition state', *Political Quarterly*, 75(5), 38–50.

Hay, C. (2006), 'Constructivist Institutionalism', in R.A.W. Rhodes, S. Binder and B. Rockman (eds), *The Oxford Handbook of Political Institutions*, 56–74, Oxford: Oxford University Press.

Hay, C. (2007), *Why We Hate Politics*, Cambridge: Polity.

Hay, C. (2013), *The Failure of Anglo-Liberal Capitalism*, Basingstoke: Palgrave Macmillan.

Hay, C. (2014), 'Neither real nor fictitious but "as if real"? A political ontology of the state', *The British Journal of Sociology*, 65 (3), 459–480.

Hay, C. (2021), 'Globalisation's Impact on States', in J. Ravenhill (ed.), *Global Political Economy*, 6th edn, 287–316, Oxford: Oxford University Press.

Hay, C. and M. Lister (2006), 'Introduction: Theories of the State', in C. Hay, M. Lister and D. Marsh (eds), *The State: Theories and Issues*, 98–117, Basingstoke: Palgrave.

Hayward, J. (1996), *Elitism, Populism and European Politics*, Oxford: Oxford University Press.

Heath, J. (2020), 'Methodological Individualism', in E.N. Zalta (ed.), *The Stanford Encyclopedia of Philosophy*, available online: https://plato.stanford.edu/archives/sum2020/entries/methodological-individualism/ (accessed 15 September2020).

Heclo, H. (1978), 'Issue Networks and the Executive Establishment', in A. King (ed), *The New American Political System*, 87–124, Washington, DC: American Enterprise Institute for Public Policy Research.

Heffernan, M. (1995), 'For ever England: The Western Front and the politics of remembrance in Britain', *Ecumene*, 2, 293–323.

Hehir, A. and R. Murray (2013), *Libya, the Responsibility to Protect and the Future of Humanitarian Intervention*, London: Palgrave Macmillan.

Held, D. (1980), *Introduction to Critical Theory: Horkheimer to Habermas*, London: Hutchinson.

Helm, D. (2010), 'Government failure, rent-seeking, and capture: The design of climate change policy', *Oxford Review of Economic Policy*, 26(2), 182–196.

Hepburn, E. (2009), *New Challenges for Stateless Nationalist and Regionalist Parties*, London: Routledge.

Hernes, H.M. (1987), *Welfare State and Woman Power*, Oslo: Norwegian University Press.

Hetherington, M. (2005), *Why Trust Matters: Declining Political Trust and the Demise of American Liberalism*, Princeton, NJ: Princeton University Press.

Hewitt, C.J. (1974), 'Elites and the Distribution of Power in British Society', in A. Giddens and M. Stanworth (eds), *Elites and power in British society*, 45–64, Cambridge: Cambridge University Press.

Hildingsson, R. and J. Khan (2015), 'Towards a Decarbonised Green State? The Politics of Low-carbon Governance in Sweden', in K. Bäckstrand and A. Kronsell (eds), *Rethinking the Green State: Environmental Governance towards Climate and Sustainability Transitions*, 156–173, London: Routledge.

Hildingsson, R., A. Kronsell and J. Khan (2019), 'The green state and industrial decarbonisation', *Environmental Politics*, 28(5), 909–928.

Hill Collins, P. (1991), *Black Feminist Thought: Knowledge, Consciousness and the Politics of Empowerment*, New York: Routledge.

Hindess, B. (2000), 'Citizenship in the international management of populations', *American Behavioral Scientist*, 43(9), 1486–1497.

Hindmoor, A. and J. McGeechan (2013), 'Luck, systematic luck and business power: Lucky all the way down or trying hard to get what it wants without trying', *Political Studies*, 61, 834–849.

Hindmoor, A. and B. Taylor (2015), *Rational Choice*, London: Palgrave Macmillan.

Hinsley, F.H. (1966), *Sovereignty*, London: Hutchinson.

Hirsch, J. (1978), 'The State Apparatus and Social Reproduction: Elements of a Theory of the Bourgeois State', in J. Holloway and S. Picciotto (eds), *State and Capital: A Marxist Debate*, 57–107, London: Arnold.

Hirst, P., G. Thompson and S. Bromley (2009), *Globalization in Question*, 3rd edn, Cambridge: Polity.

Hobbes, T. (1651), *Leviathan*, Oxford: Oxford University Press.

Hobbes, T. (1968), *Leviathan*, ed. C. Macpherson, Harmondsworth: Penguin.

Hobsbawm, E.J. (1994), 'The Nation as Invented Tradition', in A.D. Smith and J. Hutchinson (eds), *Nationalism*, 76–82, Oxford: Oxford Readers.

Hoffman, M. (2011), *Climate Governance at the Crossroads: Experimenting with a Global Response after Kyoto*, Oxford: Oxford University Press.

Hoffmann, E.P. (1986), 'Nuclear deception: Soviet information policy', *Bulletin of the Atomic Scientists*, 42(7), 32–37.

Hönke, J. and M.-M. Müller (eds) (2016), *The Global Making of Policing: Postcolonial Perspectives*, London: Routledge.

Hooghe, L. and G. Marks (2003), 'Unraveling the central state, but how? Types of multi-level governance', *American Political Science Review*, 97, 233–243.

Hooghe, M., S. Marien and J. Oser (2017), 'Great expectations: The effect of democratic ideals on political trust in European democracies', *Contemporary Politics*, 23 (2), 214–230.

hooks, b. (1984), *Feminist Theory: From Margin to Center*, Boston, MA: South End Press.

Hoskins, G. and J.F. Maddern (2011), 'Immigration Stations: The Regulation and Commemoration of Mobility at Angel Island, San Francisco and Ellis Island, New York', in T. Cresswell and P. Merriman (eds), *Geographies of Mobilities: Practices, Spaces, Subjects*, 151–165, Ashgate: Farnham.

Howarth, D.R. (2000), *Discourse*, Milton Keynes: Open University Press.

Howarth, D.R. (2013), *Poststructuralism and After: Structure, Subjectivity and Power*, Basingstoke: Palgrave Macmillan.

Howarth, D.R. and J. Torfing (2005), *Discourse Theory in European Politics: Identity, Policy and Governance*, Basingstoke: Palgrave.

Howarth, D.R., A. Norval and Y. Stavrakakis (2000), *Discourse Theory and Political Analysis: Identities, Hegemonies and Social Change*, Manchester: Manchester University Press.

Huh, T., Y. Kim and J.H. Kim (2018), 'Towards a green state: A comparative study on OECD countries through fuzzy-set analysis', *Sustainability*, 10, 3181.

Hurt, S.R. and M. Kuisma (2016), 'Undermining the "Rainbow Nation"? The Economic Freedom Fighters and Left-Wing Populism in South Africa', in *66th Annual International Conference of the Political Studies Association (PSA)*, Brighton.

Hutchinson, J. (1994), *Modern Nationalism*, London: Fontana.

Hysing, E. (2015), 'Lost in Transition? The Green State in Governance for Sustainable Development', in K. Bäckstrand and A. Kronsell (eds), *Rethinking the Green State: Environmental Governance towards Climate and Sustainability Transitions*, 27–42, London: Routledge.

Ignatieff, M. (1993), *Blood and Belonging: Journeys into the New Nationalism*, New York: Farrar, Straus and Giroux.

Immergut, E. (1998), 'The theoretical core of the new institutionalism', *Politics and Society*, 26 (1), 5–34.

Innes, A. (2015), *Migration, Citizenship and the Challenge for Security: An Ethnographic Approach*, Basingstoke: Palgrave.

Institute for Government (2021), 'Coronavirus: What economic support is the government currently providing for businesses?', available online: https://www.instituteforgovernment.org.uk/explainers/coronavirus-economic-support-businesses (accessed 17 March 2022).

International Commission on Intervention and State Sovereignty (2001), *The Responsibility to Protect*, available online: https://www.globalr2p.org/wp-content/uploads/2019/10/2001-ICISS-Report.pdf (accessed 17 March 2022).

Ionescu, G. (1968), 'To define populism', *Government and Opposition*, 3(2), 137–180, doi:10.1111/j.1477-7053.1968.tb01332.x.

Ionescu, G. and E. Gellner (eds) (1969), *Populism: Its Meanings and National Characteristics*, London: Weidenfeld & Nicolson.

IPBES (2019), *Draft 7th Global Assessment: Nature's Dangerous Decline*, available online: https://www.ipbes.net (accessed 17 March 2022).

IPCC (2014), *Fifth Assessment Report*, Geneva: Intergovernmental Panel on Climate Change.

IPCC (2018), *Special Report on the Impacts of Global Warming of 1.5 Degrees*, Geneva: Intergovernmental Panel on Climate Change.

Iversen, T. and D. Soskice (2006), 'Electoral institutions and the politics of coalitions: Why some democracies redistribute more than others', *American Political Science Review*, 100, 165–181.

Jackson, R. (1990), *Quasi-States: Sovereignty, International Relations and the Third World*, Cambridge: Cambridge University Press.

Jackson, T. (2009), *Prosperity without Growth? Economics for a Future Planet*, London: Earthscan.

Jagers, J. and S. Walgrave (2007), 'Populism as Political Communication Style: An Empirical Study of Political Parties' Discourse in Belgium', *European Journal of Political Research*, 46 (3), 319–345, doi:10.1111/j.1475-6765.2006.00690.x.

James, D.R. and K. Redding (2005), 'Theories of Race and State', in T. Janoski, R.R. Alford, A.M. Hicks and M.A. Schwartz (eds), *The Handbook of Political Sociology: States, Civil Societies, and Globalization*, 187–198, Cambridge: Cambridge University Press.

James, T. (2012), *Elite Statecraft and Election Administration: Bending the Rules of the Game?* Basingstoke: Macmillan.

Jänicke, M. (1990), *State Failure: The Impotence of Politics in Industrial Society*, Cambridge: Polity.

Jänicke, M. (2012), 'Dynamic governance of clean-energy markets: How technical innovation could accelerate climate policies', *Journal of Cleaner Production*, 22, 50–59.

Jenkins, R. (1996), *Social Identity*, London: Routledge.

Jessop, B. (1977), 'Recent theories of the capitalist state', *Cambridge Journal of Economics*, 1(4), 353–372.

Jessop, B. (1978a), 'Capitalism and Democracy: The Best Possible Political Shell?' in G. Littlejohn, B. Smart, J. Wakeford and N. Yuval-Davies (eds), *Power and the State*, 10–51, London: Croom Helm.

Jessop, B. (1978b), 'Marx and Engels on the State', in S. Hibbin et al. (eds), *Politics, Ideology and the State*, 40–68, London: Lawrence & Wishart.

Jessop, B. (1982), *The Capitalist State*, Oxford: Martin Robertson.

Jessop, B. (1985), *Nicos Poulantzas: Marxist Theory and Political Strategy*, London: Macmillan.

Jessop, B. (1990), *State Theory: Putting Capitalist States in Their Place*, Cambridge: Polity.

Jessop, B. (2002), *The Future of the Capitalist State*, Cambridge: Polity.

Jessop, B. (2007), *State Power: A Strategic-Relational Approach*, Cambridge: Polity.

Jessop, B. (2016), *The State: Past, Present, Future*, Cambridge: Polity.

Job, B.L. (1992), 'The Insecurity Dilemma: National, Regime and State Securities in the Third World', in B.L. Job (ed.), *The Insecurity Dilemma: National Security of Third World States*, 11–35, Boulder, CO; London: Lynne Rienner.

Jobert, B. (1992), 'Représentations sociales, controverses et débats dans la conduite des politiques publiques', *Revue Française de Science Politique*, 42, 219–234.

Johal, S., M. Moran and K. Williams (2014), 'Power, politics and the City of London after the great financial crisis', *Government and Opposition*, 49, 400–425.

Johnson, N.D. and M. Koyama (2017), 'States and economic growth: Capacity and constraints', *Explorations in Economic History* 64, 1–20.

Johnstone, P. and P. Newell (2018), 'Sustainability transitions and the state', *Environmental Innovation and Societal Transitions*, 27, 72–82.

Jones, L. and S. Hameiri (2021), 'COVID-19 and the failure of the neoliberal regulatory state', *Review of International Political Economy*, doi:10.1080/0969 2290.2021.1892798.

Jones, R. (2008), *People/States/Territories: The Political Geographies of British State Transformation*, Oxford: Blackwell.

Jones, R. and P. Merriman (2009), 'Hot, banal and everyday nationalism: Bilingual road signs in Wales', *Political Geography*, 28, 164–173.

Jones, R. and P. Merriman (2012), 'Network nation', *Environment and Planning A*, 44, 937–953.

Jordan, A.G. (1981), 'Iron triangles, woolly corporatism and elastic nets: Images of the policy process', *Journal of Public Policy*, 1(1), 95–123.

Jordan, A.G. and J.J. Richardson (1987a), *Government and Pressure Groups in Britain*, Oxford: Oxford University Press.

Jordan, A.G. and J.J. Richardson (1987b), *British Politics and the Policy Process: An Arena Approach*, London: Taylor & Francis.

Jordan, G. (1990), 'The pluralism of pluralism: An anti-theory?' *Political Studies*, 38(2), 286–301.

Joyce, P.D. (2003), *The Rule of Freedom: Liberalism and the Modern City*, London: Verso.

Jung, M.-K. and Y. Kwon (2013), 'Theorizing the US racial state: Sociology Since Racial Formation', *Sociology Compass*, 7 (11), 927–940.

Kaijser, A. and A. Kronsell (2013), 'Climate change through the lens of intersectionality', *Environmental Politics*, 23(3): 417–433.

Kakabadse, Y. (2020), 'The World After Coronavirus: The Future of Sustainable Development', available online: https://www.youtube.com/watch?v=Yn7trRdXND4 (accessed 17 March 2022).

Kantola, J. (2006), *Feminists Theorize the State*, New York; London: Palgrave Macmillan.

Kantola, J. (2007), 'The gendered reproduction of the state in international relations', *British Journal of Politics and International Relations* 9(4), 270–283.

Kantola, J. (2010), *Gender and the European Union*, New York; London: Palgrave Macmillan.

Kantola, J. (2016), 'State/Nation', in M. Hawkesworth and L. Disch (eds), *Oxford Handbook on Feminist Theory*, 915–933, Oxford: Oxford University Press.

Kantola, J. and H.M. Dahl (2005), 'Gender and the State: From differences between to differences within', *International Feminist Journal of Politics*, 7(1), 49–70.

Kantola, J. and E. Lombardo (2017a), *Gender and Political Analysis*, Basingstoke: Palgrave.

Kantola, J. and E. Lombardo (eds) (2017b), *Gender and the Economic Crisis in Europe: Politics, Institutions and Intersectionality*, Basingstoke: Palgrave.

Kantola, J. and E. Lombardo (2019), 'Populism and feminist politics: The cases of Finland and Spain', *European Journal of Political Research*, 58(4), 1108–1128.

Kantola, J. and E. Lombardo (2021), 'Strategies of right populists in opposing gender equality in a polarized European Parliament', *International Political Science Review*, 42(5), 565–579.

Kantola, J. and J. Squires (2012), 'From state feminism to market feminism', *International Political Science Review*, 13(3), 382–400.

Kantola, J., C. Norocel and J. Repo (2011), 'Gendering school shootings in Finland', *European Journal of Women's Studies*, 18(2), 183–198.

Karlsson, C., C. Parker, M. Hjerpe and B.-O. Linnér (2011), 'Looking for leaders: Perceptions of climate change leadership among climate change negotiation participants', *Global Environmental Politics* 11(1), 89–107.

Katzenstein, P.J. (ed.) (1978), *Between Power and Plenty*, Madison: University of Wisconsin Press.

Katzenstein, P.J. (ed.) (1996a), *The Culture of National Security: Norms and Identity in World Politics*, New York: Columbia University Press.

Katzenstein, P.J. (1996b), *Cultural Norms and National Security: Policy and Military in Postwar Japan*, Ithaca, NY: Cornell University Press.

Katznelson, I. and B.R. Weingast (eds) (2005), *Preferences and Situations: Points of Intersection between Historical and Rational Choice Institutionalism*, New York: Russell SAGE Foundation.

Kavka, G.S. (1983), 'Hobbes's War of All against All', *Ethics*, 93, 291–310.

Keating, M. (1988), *State and Regional Nationalism: Territorial Politics and the European State*, Brighton: Harvester Wheatsheaf.

Keating, M. (1998), *The New Regionalism in Western Europe: Territorial Restructuring and Political Change*, Cheltenham: Edward Elgar.

Keating, M. (2001), *Plurinational Democracy: Stateless Nations in a Post-Sovereignty Era*, Oxford: Oxford University Press.

Keating, M. and N. McEwen (2017), 'The Scottish Independence Debate', in M. Keating (ed.), *Debating Scotland: Issues of Independence and Union in the 2014 Referendum*, 1–26, Oxford: Oxford University Press.

Keck, M.E. and K. Sikkink (1998), *Activists beyond Borders: Advocacy Networks in International Politics*, Ithaca, NY: Cornell University Press.

Keech, W.R. and M.C. Munger (2015), 'The anatomy of government failure', *Public Choice*, 164(1–2), 1–42.

Kelso, W.A. (1978), *American Democratic Theory: Pluralism and its Critics*, Vol. 1, Wesport, CT: Greenwood.

Kemp, R., J. Rotmans and D. Loorbach (2007), 'Assessing the Dutch energy transition policy: How does it deal with dilemmas of managing transitions?' *Journal of Environmental Policy & Planning*, 9(3–4), 315–331.

Kharas, H. (2020), 'The impact of COVID-19 on global extreme poverty', available online: https://www.brookings.edu/blog/future-development/2020/10/21/the-impact-of-covid-19-on-global-extreme-poverty/ (accessed 17 March 2022).

King, D. (1999), *In the Name of Liberalism: Illiberal Social Policy in the United States and Britain*, Oxford: Oxford University Press.

King, D. and R.M. Smith (2014), '"Without regard to race": Critical ideational development in modern America', *Journal of Politics*, 76(4), 958–971.

Kingdon, J. (1984), *Agendas, Alternatives and Public Policies*, New York: Longman.

Kingsbury, P. (2008), 'Did somebody say jouissance? On Slavoj Žižek, consumption, and nationalism', *Emotion, Space and Society*, 1, 48–55.

Kitchin, R. and M. Dodge (2011), *Code/Space: Software and Everyday Life*, Cambridge, MA: MIT Press.

Kitschelt, H. and A.J. McGann (1995), *The Radical Right in Western Europe: A Comparative Analysis*, Ann Arbor: University of Michigan Press.

Klein, N. (2014), *This Changes Everything: Capitalism vs. the Climate*, London: Penguin Books.

Kleinfeld, R. (2020), 'Do authoritarian or democratic countries handle pandemics better?' available online: https://carnegieendowment. org/2020/03/31/do-authoritarian-or-democratic-countries-handle-pandemics-better-pub-81404 (accessed 17 March 2022).

Koch, M. (2011), *Capitalism and Climate Change: Theoretical Discussion, Historical Development and Policy Responses*, Basingstoke: Palgrave Macmillan.

Koch, M. (2020), 'The state in the transformation to a sustainable postgrowth economy', *Environmental Politics*, 29(1), 115–133.

Koch, M. and M. Fritz (2014), 'Building the eco-social state: Do welfare regimes matter?' *Journal of Social Policy*, 43(4), 679–703.

Koch, M. and M. Fritz (2015), 'Green States in Europe: A Comparative View', in K. Bäckstrand and A. Kronsell (eds), *Rethinking the Green State: Environmental Governance towards Climate and Sustainability Transitions*, 83–103, London: Routledge.

Kohn, H. (1944), *The Idea of Nationalism: A Study in its Origins and Background*, New York: Macmillan.

Koselleck, R. (2000), *Critique and Crisis: Enlightenment and the pathogenesis of modern society*, Cambridge, MA: MIT Press.

Kostka, G. and C. Zhang (2018), 'Tightening the grip: Environmental governance under Xi Jinping', *Environmental Politics*, 27(5), 769–781.

Krasner, S.D. (1999), *Sovereignty: Organized Hypocrisy*, Princeton, NJ: Princeton University Press).

Krasner, S. (1980), *Defending the National Interest*, Princeton, NJ: Princeton University Press.

Krasner, S. (1988), 'Sovereignty: An Institutional Perspective', *Comparative Political Studies*, 21, 66–94.

Kratochwil, F. (1995), 'Sovereignty as *Dominium*: Is There a Right of Humanitarian Intervention?' in G.M. Lyons and M. Mastanduno (eds), *Beyond Westphalia?* 21–42, Baltimore, MD: Johns Hopkins University Press.

Krause, K. (1998), 'Theorizing security, state formation and the "Third World" in the post-Cold War world', *Review of International Studies*, 24(1), 125–136.

Krause, K. and M.C. Williams (1997), 'From Strategy to Security: Foundations of Critical Security Studies', in K. Krause and C.W. Michael (eds), *Critical Security Studies: Concepts and Cases*, 33–60, London,: University of Minnesota Press.

Kriesi, H., E. Grande, R. Lachat, M. Dolezal, S. Bonschier and T. Frey (2008), *West European Politics in the Age of Globalization*, Cambridge: Cambridge University Press.

Krizsán, A. and C. Roggeband (2018), 'Reversing gender policy progress: Patterns of backsliding in Central and Eastern European new democracies', *European Journal of Politics and Gender*, 1(3), 367–385.

Krizsán, A., H. Skjeie and J. Squires (eds) (2012), *Institutionalizing Intersectionality? Comparative Analyses*, Basingstoke: Palgrave Macmillan.

Kronsell, A. and K. Bäckstrand (2010), 'Rationalities and Forms of Governance: A Framework for Analyzing the Legitimacy of New Modes of Governance', in K. Bäckstrand, J. Khan, A. Kronsell and E. Lövbrand (eds), *Environmental Politics and Deliberative Democracy: Examining the Promise of New Modes of Governance*, 28–46, Cheltenham: Edward Elgar.

Kronsell, A. and H. Olofsdotter Stensöta (2015), 'The Green State and Empathic Rationality', in K. Bäckstrand and A. Kronsell (eds), *Rethinking the Green State: Environmental Governance towards Climate and Sustainability Transitions*, 225–240, London: Routledge.

Kronsell, A., J. Khan and R. Hildingsson (2019), 'Actor relations in climate policy-making: Governing decarbonisation in a corporatist green state', *Environmental Policy and Governance*, 29(6), 399–408.

Krueger, A.O. (1974), 'The political economy of the rent-seeking society', *The American Economic Review*, 64(3), 291–303.

Kuhar, R. and D. Paternotte (eds) (2017), *Anti-gender Campaigns in Europe: Mobilizing against Equality*, Lanham, MD: Rowman & Littlefield.

Kuisma, M. (2013), '"Good" and "Bad" Immigrants: The Economic Nationalism of the True Finns' Immigration Discourse', in U. Korkut, G. Bucken-Knapp, A. McGarry, J. Hinnfors and H. Drake (eds), *The Discourses and Politics of Migration in Europe*, 93–108, New York: Palgrave Macmillan.

Kulawik, T. (2009), 'Staking the frame of a feminist discursive institutionalism', *Politics and Gender*, 5(2), 262–271.

Kuper, L. (1969), 'Plural Societies: Perspectives and Problems', in L. Kuper and M.G. Smith (eds), *Pluralism in Africa*, 7–26, Berkeley and Los Angeles: University of California Press.

Kymlicka, W. (1995), *Multicultural Citizenship: A Liberal Theory of Minority Rights*, Oxford: Oxford University Press.

Kymlicka, W. (1999), 'Misunderstanding Nationalism', in R. Beiner (ed.), *Theorizing Nationalism*, 131–140, Albany, NY: SUNY Press.

Kymlicka, W. (2001), 'Western Political Theory and Ethnic Relations in Europe', in W. Kymlicka and M. Opalski (eds), *Can Liberal Pluralism be Exported?* 13–106, Oxford: Oxford University Press.

Laborde, C. (2000), *Pluralist Thought and the State in Britain and France, 1900–25*, Basingstoke: Palgrave Macmillan.

Laclau, Ernesto (1975), 'The specificity of the political', *Economy & Society*, 4(1), 87–110, reprinted in E. Laclau (1977) *Politics and Ideology in Marxist Theory: Capitalism, Fascism, Populism*, London: New Left Books.

Laclau, E. (1977), *Politics and Ideology in Marxist Theory: Capitalism, Fascism, Populism*, London: New Left Books.

Laclau, E. (1996), *Emancipation(s)*, London: Verso.

Laclau, E. (2007), *On Populist Reason*, London: Verso.

Laclau, E. and C. Mouffe (1985), *Hegemony and Socialist Strategy: Towards a Radical Democratic Politics*, London: Verso.

Laclau, E. and C. Mouffe (2014), *Hegemony and Socialist Strategy: Towards a Radical Democratic Politics*, London: Verso.

Laffont, J.-J. and D. Martimort (2009), *The Theory of Incentives: The Principal-Agent Model*, Princeton, NJ: Princeton University Press.

Latouche, S. (2010), *Farewell to Growth*, Cambridge: Polity Press.

Latour, B. (2005), *Reassembling the Social: An Introduction to Actor-Network-Theory*, Oxford: Oxford University Press.

Laumann, E. (1976), *Networks of Collective Action: A Perspective on Community Influence Systems*, New York: Academic.

Law, J. (1992), 'Notes on the theory of the actor-network: Ordering, strategy, and heterogeneity', *Systems Practice*, 5, 379–393.

Le Quéré, C., R.B. Jackson, M.W. Jones, A.J.P. Smith, S. Abernethy, R.M. Andrew, A.J. De-Gol, D.R. Willis, Y. Shan, J.G. Canadell, P. Friedlingstein, F. Creutzig and G.P. Peters (2020), 'Temporary reduction in daily global CO2 emissions during the COVID-19 forced confinement', *Nature Climate Change*, 10, 647–653.

Lee, G. (1995), 'Clinton apologises for U.S. radiation tests, praises panel report', *Washington Post*, available online: https://www.washingtonpost.com/archive/politics/1995/10/04/clinton-apologizes-for-us-radiation-tests-praises-panel-report/6b6c8ecc-3319-42bb-8097-7a7275c24ebf/ (accessed 17 March 2022).

Lefebvre, H. (1972), *The Sociology of Marx*, Harmondsworth: Penguin.

Le Grand, J. (1991), 'The theory of government failure', *British Journal of Political Science*, 21(4), 423–442.

Legatum Institute (2020), 'Poverty during the Covid-19 crisis', available online: https://li.com/wp-content/uploads/2020/11/Legatum-Institute-briefing-on-poverty-during-the-Covid-crisis.pdf (accessed 17 March 2022).

Legrand, T. (2019), 'Sovereignty Renewed: Transnational Policy Networks and the Global-Local Dilemma', in D. Stone and K. Maloney (eds), *The Oxford Handbook of Global Policy and Administration*, 200–219, Oxford: Oxford University Press.

Lenin, V.I. (1917), *Imperialism: The Highest Stage of Capitalism*, Ravenio Books.

Lenin, V.I. ([1917] 1968), *The State and Revolution*, in V.I. Lenin, *Selected Works*, Moscow: Progress Publishers.

Leon, M.B. and W. Léons (1977), 'The utility of pluralism: M.G. Smith and plural theory', *American Ethnologist*, 4(3), 559–575.

Levi, M. (1989), *Of Rule and Revenue*, Berkeley: University of California Press.

Lim, S. and A. Duit (2018), 'Partisan politics, welfare states, and environmental policy outputs in the OECD countries 1975–2005', *Regulation & Governance*, 12, 220–237.

Lindblom, C.E. (1959), 'The science of muddling through', *Public Administration Review*, 19(2), 79–88.

Lindblom, C.E. (1965), *The Intelligence of Democracy: Decision Making through Mutual Adjustment*, New York: Free Press.

Lindblom, C.E. (1977), *Politics and Markets*, New York: Basic Books.

Lindblom, C.E. (1982), 'Another state of mind', *American Political Science Review*, 76(1), 9–21.

Ling, L.H.M. (2002), 'Cultural Chauvinism and the Liberal International Order: "West vs Rest"', in G. Chowdhry and S. Nair (eds), *Asia's Financial Crisis, Power in a Postcolonial World: Race, Gender and Class in International Relations*, 115–140, London: Routledge.

Linnér, B.-O. and V. Wibeck (2019), *Sustainability Transformations: Agents and Drivers across Societies*, Cambridge: Cambridge University Press.

Lipset, S.M. and S. Rokkan (1967), *Party Systems and Voter Alignments: Cross-National Perspectives*, New York: Free Press.

Lloyd, M. (2007), *Judith Butler: From Norms to Politics*, Cambridge: Polity Press.

Lloyd, M. (2013), 'Power, Politics, Domination and Oppression', in G. Waylen, K. Celis, J. Kantola and L. Weldon (eds), *The Oxford Handbook on Gender and Politics*, 111–134, New York: Oxford University Press.

Lluch, J. (2012), 'Internal variation in sub-state national movements and the moral polity of the nationalist', *European Political Science Review*, 4(3), 433–460.

Lluch, J. (2014), *Visions of Sovereignty*, Philadelphia: University of Pennsylvania Press.

Lo, K. (2015), 'How authoritarian is the environmental governance of China?' *Environmental Science & Policy*, 54, 152–159.

Lockwood, D. (1964), 'Social Integration and System Integration', in G.K. Zolschan and W. Hirsch (eds), *Explorations in Social Change*, London: Routledge & Kegan Paul.

Loorbach, D. (2010), 'Transition management for sustainable development: A prescriptive, complexity-based governance framework', *Governance*, 23(1), 161–183.

Loorbach, D. and J. Rotmans (2010), 'The practice of transition management: Examples and lessons from four distinct cases', *Futures*, 42, 237–246.

Lorde, A. (1997), 'Age, Class, Race and Sex: Women Defining Difference', in A. McClintock, A. Mufti and E. Shohat (eds), *Dangerous Liaisons: Gender, Nation and Postcolonial Perspectives*, 374–80, Minneapolis: University of Minnesota Press.

Lövbrand, E. and J. Khan (2010), 'The Deliberative Turn in Green Political Theory', in K. Bäckstrand, J. Khan, A. Kronsell and E. Lövbrand (eds), *Environmental Politics and Deliberative Democracy: Examining the Promise of New Modes of Governance*, 47–64, Cheltenham: Edward Elgar.

Lövbrand, E. and B.-O. Linnér (2015), 'Governing beyond or with the State? State Conceptions in Studies of *non*-State Climate Action', in K. Bäckstrand and A. Kronsell (eds), *Rethinking the Green State: Environmental Governance towards Climate and Sustainability Transitions*, 43–62, London: Routledge.

Lowi, T. (1969), *The End of Liberalism*, London: W.W. Norton.

Lowndes, V. (1996), 'Varieties of new institutionalism: A critical appraisal', *Public Administration*, 74, 181–197.

Lowndes, V. (2002), 'Institutionalism', in D. Marsh and G. Stoker (eds), *Theory and Methods in Political Science*, 90–108, Basingstoke: Palgrave Macmillan.

Lukes, S. (1974), *Power: A Radical View*, Basingstoke: Macmillan.

Lundqvist, L.J. (2001), 'A green fist in a velvet glove: The ecological state and sustainable development', *Environmental Values*, 10, 455–472.

MacDonagh, O. (1958), 'The nineteenth century revolution in government: A reappraisal', *Historical Journal*, 1, 52–67.

Machiavelli, N. (1988) *The Prince*, trans. Q. Skinner and R. Price, Cambridge: Cambridge University Press.

Machin, A. (2020), 'Democracy, disagreement, disruption: Agonism and the environmental state', *Environmental Politics*, 29(1), 155–172.

Machin, D.J. (2013), 'Political inequality and the "super-rich": Their money or (some of) their political rights', *Res Publica*, 19(2), 121–139.

Mackay, F., M. Kenny and L. Chappell (2010), 'New institutionalism through a gender lens: Towards a feminist institutionalism?' *International Political Science Review*, 3(5), 573–588.

MacKenzie, D.A. (2006), *An Engine, Not a Camera: How Financial Models Shape Markets*, Cambridge, MA, MIT Press.

MacKinnon, C.A. (1982), 'Feminism, Marxism, method and the state: An agenda for theory', *Signs*, 7(3), 515–544.

MacKinnon, C.A. (1983), 'Feminism, Marxism, method and the state: Toward feminist jurisprudence', *Signs*, 8(4), 645–658.

MacKinnon, C.A. (1985), *Toward a Feminist Theory of the State*. Cambridge, MA: Harvard University Press.

MacKinnon, C.A. (1987), 'Feminism, Marxism, Method and the State', in Sandra Harding (eds), *Feminism and Methodology*, Milton Keynes: Open University Press, 135–156.

MacKinnon, C.A. (1989), *Towards a Feminist Theory of the State*, London: Harvard University Press.

Madison, J. (1788), 'Letter to Thomas Jefferson', available online: https://founders.archives.gov/documents/Madison/01-11-02-0218 (accessed 17 March 2022).

Mahon, R. (1991), 'From "bringing" to "putting": The state in late twentieth-century social thought', *Canadian Journal of Sociology*, 16(2), 119–144.

Mahoney, J. and K. Thelen (2010), 'A Theory of Gradual Institutional Change', in J. Mahoney and K. Thelen (eds), *Explaining Institutional Change: Ambiguity, Agency, and Power*, 1–37, Cambridge: Cambridge University Press.

Mair, P. (2013), *Ruling the Void: The Hollowing of Western Democracy*, London: Verso.

Mamdani, M. (2020), *Neither Settler Nor Native: The Making and Unmaking of Permanent Minorities*, Cambridge, MA: Harvard University Press.

Mann, M. (1984), 'The autonomous power of the state: its origins, mechanisms and results', *European Journal of Sociology*, 25, 185–213.

Mann, M. (1988), *States, War and Capitalism*, New York: Basil Blackwell.

Mann, M. (1993), *The Sources of Social Power, Volume 2: The Rise of Classes and Nation-States, 1760–1914*, Cambridge: Cambridge University Press.

Mansbridge, J. (ed.) (1990), *Beyond Self-Interest*, Chicago, IL: University of Chicago Press.

March, J.G. and J.P. Olsen (1989), *Rediscovering Institutions: The Organizational Basis of Politics*, New York: Free Press.

Markard, J., R. Raven and B. Truffer (2012), 'Sustainability transitions: An emerging field of research and its prospects', *Research Policy*, 41(6), 955–967.

Marsh, D. (1983), 'Interest group activity and structural power: The work of Charles Lindblom', *West European Politics*, 6, 3–13.

Marsh, D. (1995), 'The Convergence Between Theories of the State', in D. Marsh and G. Stoker (eds), *Theory and Methods in Political Science*, London: Macmillan.

Marsh, D. (2002), 'Pluralism and the Study of British Politics: It is always the Happy Hour for Men with Money, Knowledge and Power', in C. Hay (ed.), *British Politics Today*, 14–37, Cambridge: Polity Press.

Marsh, D. (2009), 'Keeping ideas in their place: In praise of thin constructivism', *Australian Journal of Political Science*, 44, 679–696.

Marsh, D. (2010), 'It's Not the Economy Stupid: Or is it?' in M. Boss (ed.), *The Nation-State in Transformation: Economic Globalisation, Institutional Mediation and Political Values*, 87–109, Aarhus: Aarhus University Press.

Marsh, D. (2018), 'Meta-Theoretical Issues' in V. Lowndes, D. Marsh and G. Stoker (eds), *Theory and Methods in Political Science*, 199–218, Basingstoke, Palgrave.

Marsh, D. and C. Lewis (2014), 'The political power of big business: A response to Bell and Hindmoor', *New Political Economy*, 19, 628–633.

Marsh, D. and M. Smith (2000), 'Understanding policy networks: Towards a dialectical approach', *Political Studies*, 48, 4–21.

Marsh, D., S. Akram and H. Birkett (2015), 'The structural power of business: Taking structure, agency and ideas seriously', *Journal of Business & Politics*, 17(3), 577–601.

Marsh, D., M. Hall and P. Fawcett (2014), 'Two cheers for interpretivism: Deconstructing the British political tradition', *Australian Journal of Public Administration*, 73(3), 340–348.

Marsh, D., C. Lewis and J. Chesters (2014), 'The Australian mining tax and the political power of business', *Australian Journal of Political Science*, 49(4), 711–725.

Martí-Henneberg, J. (2017), 'The influence of the railway network on territorial integration in Europe (1870–1950)', *Journal of Transport Geography* 62, 160–171.

Martin, J. (2019), 'The postmarxist Gramsci', *Global Discourse*, 9(2), 305–321.

Martin, Lisa (2000), *Democratic Commitments*, Princeton, NJ: Princeton University Press.

Martins-Filho, P.R., B.C. Lima Araújo, K. Batista Sposato, A. Antunes de Souza Araújo, L.J. Quintans-Júnior and V. Santana Santos (2021), 'Racial disparities in COVID-19-related deaths in Brazil: Black Lives Matter?' *Journal of Epidemiology*, 31(3), 239–240.

Martinsson, L., G. Griffin and K.G. Nygren (2017), *Challenging the Myth of Gender Equality in Sweden*, Bristol: Policy Press.

Marx, K. ([1843a] 1975), 'Critique of Hegel's Doctrine of the State', in L. Colletti (ed.), *Karl Marx: Early Writings*, 57–198, London: Pelican.

Marx, K. ([1843b] 1975), 'On the Jewish Question', in L. Colletti (ed.), *Karl Marx: Early Writings*, 211–242, London: Pelican.

Marx, K. ([1844] 1975), 'Introduction to a Contribution to a Critique of Hegel's Philosophy of Law', in L. Colletti (ed.), *Karl Marx: Early Writings*, 243–258, London: Pelican.

Marx, K. ([1850 1978), *The Class Struggles in France: 1845 to 1850*, in K. Marx and F. Engels, *Collected Works, Volume 10*, 45–146, London: Lawrence & Wishart.

Marx, K. ([1852] 1979), 'The Eighteenth Brumaire of Louis Bonaparte', in K. Marx and F. Engels, *Collected Works, Volume 11*, 99–197, London: Lawrence & Wishart.

Marx, K. ([1859] 1987), 'Preface to a Contribution to a Critique of Political Economy', in K. Marx and F. Engels, *Collected* Works, *Volume 29*, 261–266, London: Lawrence & Wishart.

Marx, K. ([1871] 1986), 'The Civil War in France', in K. Marx and F. Engels, *Collected Works, Volume 22*, 435–551, London: Lawrence & Wishart.

Marx, K. ([1971] 1847), 'The Communist Manifesto', in D.J. Struik (ed.), *The Birth of the Communist Manifesto*, New York: International Publishers.

Marx, K. and F. Engels ([1845] 1987), *The German Ideology: Introduction to a Critique of Political Economy*, London: Lawrence and Wishart.

Marx, K. and F. Engels ([1845/6] 1964), *The German Ideology*, Moscow: Progress Publishers.

Marx, K. and F. Engels ([1848] 1967), *The Communist Manifesto*, London: Pelican.

Massey, D. (1994), *Space, Place and Gender*, Cambridge: Polity Press.

May, S. (2001), *Language and Minority Rights: Ethnicity, Nationalism and the Politics of Language*, London: Routledge.

Mbete, S. (2020), 'Out with the Old, in with the New?: The ANC and EFF's Battle to Represent the South African "People"', in P. Ostiguy, F. Panizza and B. Moffitt (eds), *Populism in Global Perspective: A Performative and Discursive Approach*, 240–254, New York: Routledge.

McBride, D. and A. Mazur (2010), *The Politics of State Feminism: Innovation in Comparative Research*, Philadelphia, PA: Temple University Press.

McBride Stetson, D. and A. Mazur (1995), *Comparative State Feminism*, London: SAGE.

McClure, K. (1992), 'On the Subject of Rights: Pluralism, Plurality and Political Identity', in C. Mouffe (ed.), *Dimensions of Radical Democracy: Pluralism, Citizenship, Community*, 108–127, London: Verso.

McConnell, G. (1953), *Decline of Agrarian Democracy*, Berkeley and Los Angeles: University of California Press.

McConnell, G. (1966), *Private Power & American Democracy*, New York: Knopf.

McCubbins, M.D. and T. Sullivan (eds) (1987), *Congress: Structure and Policy*, Cambridge: Cambridge University Press.

McEwen, N. (2006), *Nationalism and the State: Welfare and identity in Scotland and Québec*, Regionalism and Federalism Book Series, Brussels: Presses interuniversitaires européennes/Peter Lang.

McEwen, N. and C. Brown Swan (2021), 'Embedded Independence: Self-Government and Interdependence in the Scottish National Movement', in A. Lecours et al. (eds), *Constitutional Politics in Multinational Democracies*, 75–100, Montreal: McGill-Queen's University Press.

McIntosh, M. (1978), 'The State and the Oppression of Women' in Annette Kuhn and AnnMarie Wolpe (eds), *Feminism and Materialism: Women and Modes of Production*, London: Routledge and Kegan Paul, 254–289.

McKibben, B. (2020), 'The world after Coronavirus: The future of environmentalism', available online: https://www.youtube.com/watch?v=iE0T3i4oz0g (accessed 17 March 2022).

McKnight, D. and M. Hobbs (2013), 'Public contest through the popular media: The mining industry's advertising war against the Australian Labor government', *Australian Journal of Political Science*, 48(3), 307–319.

McLennan, G. (1995), *Pluralism*, Minneapolis: University of Minnesota Press.

McLuhan, M. (1964), *Understanding Media: The Extensions of Man*, London: Routledge & Kegan Paul.

McNamara, K.R. (2015), *The Politics of Everyday Europe: Constructing Authority in the European Union*, Oxford: Oxford University Press.

McRoberts, K. (1997), *Misconceiving Canada: The Struggle for National Unity*, Oxford: Oxford University Press.

Meadowcroft, J. (2005), 'From Welfare State to Ecostate', in J. Barry and R. Eckersley (eds), *The State and the Global Ecological Crisis*, 3–23, Cambridge, MA: MIT Press.

Meadowcroft, J. (2009), 'What about the politics? Sustainable development, transition management, and long term energy transitions', *Policy Sciences*, 42, 323–340.

Meadowcroft, J. (2011), 'Engaging with the *politics* of sustainability transitions', *Environmental Innovation and Societal Transitions*, 1(1), 70–75.

Meadowcroft, J. (2012), 'Greening the State', in P. Steinberg and S. VanDeveer (eds), *Comparative Environmental Politics: Theory, Practice and Prospects*, 63–87, Cambridge, MA: MIT Press.

Meehan, K., I.G.R. Shaw and S. Marston (2013), 'Political geographies of the object', *Political Geography*, 33, 1–10.

Mehrling, P. (2020), 'The world after Coronavirus: The future of money', available online: https://www.youtube.com/watch?v=sG9rZv_akQw (accessed 17 March 2022).

Melo-Escrihuela, C. (2015), 'Should ecological citizenship advocates praise the green state?' *Environmental Values*, 24(3), 321–344.

Mendoza, K. (2015), *Austerity: The Demolition of the Welfare State and the Rise of the Zombie Economy*, Oxford: New Internationalist Publications.

Merelman, R.M. (2003), *Pluralism at Yale: The Culture of Political Science in America*, Madison: University of Wisconsin Press.

Mernissi, F. (1992), *Islam and Democracy: Fear of the Modern World*, Reading, MA: Addison-Wesley.

Mernissi, F. (1996), 'Palace fundamentalism and liberal democracy: Oil, arms and irrationality', *Development and Change*, 27(2), 251–265.

Merriman, P. and R. Jones (2017), 'Nations, materialities and affects', *Progress in Human Geography*, 41, 600–617.

Meyer, J.W. and B. Rowan (1977), 'Institutionalized Organizations: Formal structure as myth and ceremony', *American Journal of Sociology*, 83, 340–363.

Mian, A. (2020), 'The world after Coronavirus: The future of debt', available online: https://www.youtube.com/watch?v=DW8OAj0knrI (accessed 17 March 2022).

Michels, R. ([1911] 1962), *Political Parties*, New York: Free Press.

Middlemas, K. (1979), *Politics in Industrial Society: The Experience of the British System since 1911*, London: Andre Deutsch.

Miliband, R. (1965), 'Marx and the state', *Socialist Register 1965*, 278–296.

Miliband, R. (1969), *The State in Capitalist Society: An Analysis of the Western System of Power*, London: Weidenfeld & Nicolson.

Miliband, R. (1970), 'The capitalist state – Reply to Poulantzas', *New Left Review*, 59, 53–60, reprinted in R. Blackburn (ed.) (1972), *Ideology in Social Science*, London: Fontana.

Miliband, R. (1973), 'Poulantzas and the capitalist state', *New Left Review*, 82, 83–92.

Miliband, R. (1977), *Marxism and Politics*, Oxford: Oxford University Press.

Miliband, R. (1994), *Socialism for a Sceptical Age*, London: Verso.

Miller, D. (1995), *On Nationality*, Oxford: Clarendon Press.

Millett, K. (1970), *Sexual Politics*, New York: Garden City/Doubleday.

Milliken, J. and K. Krause (2002), 'State failure, state collapse, and state reconstruction: Concepts, lessons and strategies', *Development & Change*, 33(5), 753–774.

Mills, C.W. (1956), *The Power Elite*, New York: Oxford University Press.

Mintz, B. and M. Schwartz (1985), *The Power Structure of American Business*, Chicago, IL: University of Chicago Press.

Mitchell, T. (1991), 'The limits of the state: Beyond statist approaches and their critics', *The American Political Science Review*, 85, 77–96.

Mitchell, T. (2002a), 'McJihad: Islam in the US global order', *Social Text*, 20(4), 1–18.

Mitchell, T. (2002b), *Rule of Experts: Egypt, Techno-politics, Modernity*, Berkeley: University of California Press.

Moe, T. (2003), 'Power and political institutions'. Paper read at conference on Crafting and Operating Institutions, Yale University, New Haven, CT, 11–13 April.

Moffitt, B. (2016), *The Global Rise of Populism: Performance, Political Style, and Representation*, Stanford, CA: Stanford University Press.

Moffitt, B. and S. Tormey (2014), 'Rethinking populism: Politics, mediatisation and political style', *Political Studies*, 62(2), 381–397, doi:10.1111/1467-9248.12032.

Mol, A.P.J. (2016), 'The environmental nation state in decline', *Environmental Politics*, 25(1), 48–68.

Mol, A.P.J. and G. Spaargaren (2002), 'Ecological Modernization and the Environmental State', in P. Mol and F. Buttel (eds), *The Environmental State under Pressure: Research in Social Problems and Public Policy*, 33–52, Bingley: Emerald Publishing.

Mol, A.P.J., D.A. Sonnenfeld and G. Spaargaren (2009), *The Ecological Modernisation Reader: Environmental Reform in Theory and Practice*, London: Routledge.

Moore, G. (1979), 'The structure of a national elite network', *American Sociological Review*, 44 (October), 673–692.

Moore, M. (2001), *The Ethics of Nationalism*, Oxford: Oxford University Press.

Moravcsik, A. (1998), *The Choice for Europe: Social Purpose and State Power from Messina to Maastricht*, Ithaca, NY: Cornell University Press.

Mosca, G. ([1896] 1939), *The Ruling Class*, New York: McGraw Hill.

Mouffe, C. (2000), *The Democratic Paradox*, London: Verso.

Mouffe, C. (2005), *On the Political*, London: Routledge.

Mouffe, C. (2013), *Agonistics: Thinking the World Politically*, London: Verso.

Mouffe, C. (2018), *For a Left Populism*, London: Verso.

Mountz, A., K, Coddingtin, R.T. Catania and J.M. Loyd (2012), 'Conceptualizing detention: mobility, containment, bordering and exclusion', *Progress in Human Geography*, 37, 522–541.

Mouzelis, N. (1991), *Back to Sociological Theory: The Construction of Social Orders*, London: Macmillan.

Mouzelis, N. (1995), *Sociological Theory: What Went Wrong?* London: Routledge.

Moyn, S. (2012), *The Last Utopia: Human Rights in History*, Cambridge, MA: Harvard University Press.

Mudde, C. (2004), 'The Populist Zeitgeist', *Government and Opposition*, 39(4), 542–563.

Mudde, C. (2007), *Populist Radical Right Parties in Europe*, Cambridge: Cambridge University Press.

Mudde, C. (2015), 'Populist Radical Right Parties in Europe Today', in J. Abromeit et al. (eds), *Transformations of Populism in Europe and the Americas: History and Recent Trends*, 295–307, London: Bloomsbury.

Mudde, C. (2017), 'Why nativism, not populism, should be declared word of the year', *The Guardian*, 7 December, available online: https://www.theguardian.com/commentisfree/2017/dec/07/cambridge-dictionary-nativism-populism-word-year (accessed 17 March 2022).

Mudde, C. and C.R. Kaltwasser (2017), *Populism: A Very Short Introduction*, Oxford: Oxford University Press.

Mueller, D.C. (2003), *Public Choice III*, New York: Cambridge University Press.

Müller, J.-W. (2016), *What Is Populism?* Philadelphia: University of Pennsylvania Press.

Muller, P. (1995), 'Les Politiques publiques comme construction d'un rapport au monde', in A. Faure, G. Pollet and P. Warin (eds), *La Construction du sens dans les politiques publiques: débats autour de la notion de référentiel*, Paris: L'Harmattan.

Murdoch, J. (1997), 'Towards a geography of heterogeneous associations', *Progress in Human Geography*, 21, 321–337.

Murphy, C. (1994), *International Organization and Industrial Change: Global Governance since 1850*, Cambridge: Polity Press.

Murphy, C. (2008), *The International Organization for Standardization*, London: Routledge.

Mutz, D.C., P.M. Sniderman and R.A. Brody (1996), *Political Persuasion and Attitude Change*, Ann Arbor: University of Michigan.

Nagel, J. (1998), 'Masculinity and nationalism: Gender and sexuality in the making of nations', *Ethnic and Racial Studies*, 21(2), 242–269.

Najam, A. (2021), 'What will the world look like after Coronavirus?', available online: https://greatergood.berkeley.edu/article/item/what_will_the_world_look_like_after_coronavirus (accessed 17 March 2022).

Nandy, A. (2003), *The Romance of the State: And the Fate of Dissent in the Tropics*, Oxford: Oxford University Press.

Nash, K. (2002), 'Thinking political sociology: Beyond the limits of post-Marxism', *History of the Human Sciences*, 15(4), 97–114.

Neocleous, M. (2006), 'From social to national security: On the fabrication of economic order', *Security Dialogue*, 37, 363–384.

Neocleous, M. (2008), *Critique of Security*, Montreal: McGill-Queen's University Press.

Newell, P. and M. Paterson (2010), *Climate Capitalism: Global Warming and the Transformation of the Global Economy*, Cambridge: Cambridge University Press.

Nexon, D. (2009), *The Struggle for Power in Early Modern Europe: Religious Conflict, Dynastic Empires and International Change*. Princeton, NJ: Princeton University Press.

Nicholls, D. (1974), *Three Varieties of Pluralism*, London: Macmillan.

Niskanen, W.A. (1971), *Bureaucracy and Representative Government*, Chicago, IL: Aldine-Atherton.

Niskanen, W.A. (1988), *Reaganomics: An Insider's Account of the Policies and the People*, New York: Oxford University Press.

Njagi, J.W. (2013), 'The state and sexual politics: An analysis of abortion discourses in Kenya', PhD dissertation, University of Waikato.

North, D.C. (1990), *Institutions, Institutional Change, and Economic Performance*, Cambridge: Cambridge University Press.

North, D.C. (2010), *Understanding the Process of Economic Change*, Princeton, NJ: Princeton University Press.

Ó Tuathail, G. (1996), *Critical Geopolitics: The Politics of Writing Global Space*, London: Routledge.

O'Brien, R. (1992), *Global Financial Integration: The End of Geography*, London: Pinter for Royal Institute of International Affairs.

OECD (2009), 'The global financial crisis: Causes impacts and policy responses', available online: https://www.oecd.org/finance/financial-markets/42549690.pdf (accessed 17 March 2022).

OECD (2019), *Inequality*, available online: http://www.oecd.org/social/inequality.htm (accessed 17 March 2022).

Offe, C. (1974), 'Structural Problems of the Capitalist State: Class Rule and the Political System. On the Selectiveness of Political Institutions', in K. von Beyme (ed.), *German Political Studies*, Vol. 1, 31–54, Beverley Hills: SAGE.

Offe, C. (1975), 'The Theory of the Capitalist State and the Problem of Policy Formation', in L. Lindberg et al. (eds), *Stress and Contradiction in Modern Capitalism*, 125–144, Lexington, MA: D.C. Heath.

Offe, C. (1984), *Contradictions of the Welfare State*, London: Hutchinson.

Office for National Statistics (2020a), 'Coronavirus (COVID-19) related deaths by ethnic group, England and Wales: 2 March 2020 to 10 April 2020', available online: https://www.ons.gov.uk/peoplepopulationandcommunity/birthsdeathsandmarriages/deaths/articles/coronavirusrelateddeathsbyethnicgroupenglandandwales/2march2020to10april2020 (accessed 17 March 2022).

Office for National Statistics (2020b), 'Deaths involving COVID-19 by local area and socioeconomic deprivation: Deaths occurring between 1 March and 17 April 2020', available online: https://www.ons.gov.uk/peoplepopulationandcommunity/birthsdeathsandmarriages/deaths/bulletins/deathsinvolvingcovid19bylocalareasanddeprivation/deathsoccurringbetween1marchand17april (accessed 17 March 2022).

Office for National Statistics (2020c), 'Coronavirus (COVID-19) related deaths by occupation, England and Wales: Deaths registered up to and including 20 April 2020', available online: https://www.ons.gov.uk/peoplepopulationandcommunity/healthandsocialcare/causesofdeath/bulletins/coronaviruscovid19relateddeathsbyoccupationenglandandwales/deathsregistereduptoandincluding20april2020 (accessed 17 March 2022).

Ogborn, M. (1998), 'The capacities of the state: Charles Davenant and the management of the Excise, 1683–1698', *Journal of Historical Geography*, 24, 289–312.

Ohmae, K. (1996a), *The Borderless World: Power and Strategy in the Interlinked Economy*, New York: HarperBusiness.

Ohmae, K. (1996b), *The End of the Nation State: The Rise of Regional Economics*, London: HarperCollins.

Okin, S.M. (1989), *Justice, Gender, and the Family*, New York: Basic Books.

Okin, S.M. (1999), 'Is Multiculturalism Bad for Women?' in S.M. Okin et al. (eds), *Is Multiculturalism Bad for Women?* 7–24, Princeton, NJ: Princeton University Press.

Olson, M. 1965, *The Logic of Collective Action: Public Goods and the Theory of Groups*, 2nd edn, Cambridge, MA: Harvard University Press.

Ong, A. (2007), *Neoliberalism as Exception: Mutations in Citizenship and Sovereignty*, Durham, NC and London: Duke University Press.

Ophuls, W. (1973), 'Leviathan or Oblivion?', in H. Daly (ed.), *Toward a Steady State Economy*, 214–219, San Francisco: Freeman.

Orford, A. (2011), *International Authority and the Responsibility to Protect*, Cambridge: Cambridge University Press.

Ostrom, E. (1982), 'Beyond Positivism', in E. Ostrom, 11–28, *Strategies of Political Inquiry*, Beverley Hills: SAGE.

Ostrom, E. (1990), *Governing the Commons*, New York: Cambridge University Press.

Ostrom, V. (1984), 'Why Governments Fail: An Inquiry into the Use of Instruments of Evil to Do Good', in J.M. Buchanan and R.D. Tollison (eds), *The Theory of Public Choice–II*, 422–438, Ann Arbor: University of Michigan Press.

Page, B.I. and M. Gilens (2020), *Democracy in America: What Has Gone Wrong and What We Can Do about It*? Chicago, IL: University of Chicago Press.

Painter, J. (2006), 'Prosaic geographies of stateness', *Political Geography*, 25, 752–774.

Painter, J. (2010), 'Rethinking territory', *Antipode*, 42, 1090–1117.

Pappas, T.S. (2019), *Populism and Liberal Democracy: A Comparative and Theoretical Analysis*, Oxford: Oxford University Press.

Pappas, T.S. and P. Aslanidis (2016), 'Greek Populism: A Political Drama in Five Acts', in H. Kriesi and T.S. Pappas, *European Populism in the Shadow of the Great Recession*, 181–196, Colchester: ECPR Press.

Parashar, S. (2018), 'The Postcolonial/Emotional State: Mother India's Response to Her Deviant Maoist Children', in S. Parashar, J.A. Tickner and J. True (eds), *Revisiting Gendered States: Feminist Imaginings of the State in International Relations*, 157–173, Oxford: Oxford University Press.

Parashar, S., J.A. Tickner and J. True (2018), 'Introduction: Feminist Imaginings of Twenty-First-Century Gendered States', in S. Parashar, J.A. Tickner and J. True (eds), *Revisiting Gendered States: Feminist Imaginings of the State in International Relations*, 1–15, Oxford: Oxford University Press.

Pareto, V. (1935), *The Mind and Society*, London: Cape.

Pareto, V. (1966), *Sociological Writings*, London: Pall Mall.

Parker, G. (2013), *Global Crisis: Climate Change and Catastrophe in the Seventeenth Century*, New Haven, CT: Yale University Press.

Parolin, Z., M. Curran, J. Matsudaira, J. Waldfogel and C. Wimer (2020), 'Monthly poverty rates in the United States during the COVID-19 pandemic', Poverty And Social Policy Working Paper, available online: https://static1.squarespace.com/static/5743308460b5e922a25a6dc7/t/5f 87c59e4cd0011fabd38973/1602733471158/COVID-Projecting-Poverty-Monthly-CPSP-2020.pdf (accessed 17 March 2022).

Passavant, P. and J. Dean (2001), 'Laws and Societies', *Constellations: An International Journal of Critical and Democratic Theory*, 8(3), 376–389.

Pateman, C. (1988), 'The Patriarchal Welfare State', in A. Gutman (ed.), *Democracy and the Welfare State*, 231–260, Princeton, NJ: Princeton University Press.

Paterson, M. (2007), 'Environmental politics: Sustainability and the politics of transformation', *International Political Science Review*, 28(5), 545–556.

Paterson, M. (2016), 'Political economy of greening the state', in T. Gabrielson, C. Hall, J. Meyer and D. Schlosberg (eds), *The Oxford Handbook of Environmental Political Theory*, 475–490, Oxford: Oxford University Press.

Patrick, S. (2020), 'When the system fails: COVID-19 and the costs of global dysfunction', *Foreign Affairs*, 99 (4), 40–50.

Pauwels, T. (2013), *Populism in Western Europe: Comparing Belgium, Germany and The Netherlands*, London: Routledge.

Perrott, R. (1968), *The Aristocrats*, London: Weidenfeld & Nicolson.

Peters, B.G., J. Pierre, and D.S. King (2005), 'The politics of path dependency: Political conflict in historical institutionalism', *The Journal of Politics*, 67(4), 1275–1300.

Peterson, V.S. (1992a), 'Introduction', in V.S. Peterson (ed.), *Gendered States: Feminist (Re)visions of International Relations Theory*, 1–29, Boulder, CO: Lynne Rienner.

Peterson, V.S. (1992b), 'Security and the Sovereign States: What is at Stake in Taking Feminism Seriously?', in V.S. Peterson, *Gendered States: Feminist (Re)visions of International Relations Theory*, 31–64, Boulder, CO: Lynne Rienner.

Pevehouse, J.C.W. (2020), 'The COVID-19 pandemic, international cooperation, and populism', *International Organization*, 74(S1), E191–E212, doi:10.1017/S0020818320000399.

Philo, C. and H. Parr (2000), 'Institutional geographies: Introductory remarks', *Geoforum*, 31, 513–521.

Pierce, R. (2004), 'Clemenson revisited – the rise and fall of the great English landowner?' *Policy Studies*, 25(4), 1–17.

Pierre, J. (2011), 'Stealth economy? Economic theory and the politics of administrative reform', *Administration & Society*, 43(6), 672–692.

Pierson, C. (2011), *The Modern State*, 3rd edn, London: Routledge.

Pierson, P. (1994), *Dismantling the Welfare State?* Cambridge: Cambridge University Press.

Pierson, P. (2004), *Politics in Time: History, Institutions, and Social Analysis*, Princeton, NJ: Princeton University Press.

Pierson, P. (2017), 'American hybrid: Donald Trump and the strange merger of populism and plutocracy', *British Journal of Sociology*, 68, 105–119.

Piketty, T. (2020), 'The world after Coronavirus: The future of inequality', available online: https://www.youtube.com/watch?v=220XAnjXcOI (accessed 17 March 2022).

Pletsch, C.E. (1981), 'The three worlds, or the division of social scientific labor, circa 1950–1975', *Comparative Studies in Society and History*, 23(04), 565–590.

Polanyi, C. (1944), *The Great Transformation*, New York: Farrar & Rinehart.

Pollack, M. (1997), 'Delegation, agency, and agenda setting in the European Community', *International Organization*, 51(1), 99–134.

Polsby, N.W. (1960), 'How to study community power: The pluralist alternative', *The Journal of Politics*, 22(3), 474–484.

Polsby, N.W. (1963), *Community Power and Political Theory*, New Haven, CT: Yale University Press.

Porter, M.E. and van der Linde, C. (1995), 'Green and competitive: Ending the stalemate', *Harvard Business Review* (September–October), 120–134.

Poulantzas, N. (1969), 'The problems of the capitalist state', *New Left Review*, 58, 67–78, reprinted in R. Blackburn (ed.) (1972), *Ideology in Social Science*, London: Fontana.

Poulantzas, N. (1973), *Political Power and Social Classes*, London: New Left Books.

Poulantzas, N. (1975), *Classes in Contemporary Capitalism*, London: New Left Books.

Poulantzas, N. (1976), 'The capitalist state: A reply to Miliband and Laclau', *New Left Review*, 95, 63–83.

Poulantzas, N. (1978), *State, Power, Socialism*, London: New Left Books.

Povitkina, M. (2018), 'The limits of democracy in tackling climate change', *Environmental Politics*, 27(3), 411–432.

Powell, B. and E.P. Stringham (2009), 'Public choice and the economic analysis of anarchy: A survey', *Public Choice*, 140(3/4), 503–538.

Pramudya, E.P., O. Hospes and C.J.A.M. Termeer (2018), 'The disciplining of illegal palm oil plantations in Sumatra', *Third World Quarterly*, 39(5), 920–940.

Pringle, R. and S. Watson (1990), 'Fathers, Brothers, Mates: The Fraternal State in Australia', in S. Watson (ed.), *Playing the State*, 229–243, London: Verso.

Pringle, R. and S. Watson (1992), '"Women's Interests" and the Post-Structuralist State', in M. Barrett and A. Phillips (eds), *Destabilizing Theory*, 53–73, Cambridge: Polity Press.

Prügl, E. (2010), 'Feminism and the postmodern state: Gender mainstreaming in European rural development', *Signs*, 35(2), 447–475.

Prügl, E. (2011), 'Diversity management and gender mainstreaming as technologies of government', *Politics and Gender*, 7(1), 71–89.

Przeworski, A. (1991), *Democracy and the Market*, Cambridge: Cambridge University Press.

Puar, J.K. (2007), *Terrorist Assemblages: Homonationalism in Queer Times*, Durham, NC: Duke University Press.

Putnam, R. (1993), 'The prosperous community: Social capital and public life', *The American Prospect*, 13, 35–42.

Raab, C. (2001), 'Understanding policy networks: A comment on Marsh and Smith', *Political Studies*, 49, 551–556.

Rai, S. and G. Lievesley (eds) (1996), *Women and the State: International Perspectives*, London: Taylor & Francis.

Ratner, S. and J. Altman (1964), *John Dewey and Arthur Bentley: A Philosophical Correspondence*, New Brunswick, NJ: Rutgers University Press.

Raworth, K. (2012), 'A safe and just operating space for humanity: Can we live within the doughnut?' *Oxfam Policy and Practice: Climate Change and Resilience*, 8(1), 1–26.

Razieh, C., F. Zaccardi, N. Islam, C.L. Gillies, Y.V. Chudasama, A. Rowlands, D.E. Kloecker, M.J. Davies, K. Khunti and T. Yates (2021), 'Ethnic minorities and COVID-19: Examining whether excess risk is mediated through deprivation', *European Journal of Public Health*, 31(3), 630–634, doi:10.1093/eurpub/ckab041.

Rein, M. and D.A. Schön (1991), 'Frame-Reflective Policy Discourse', in P. Wagner et al. (eds), *Social Sciences, Modern States, National Experiences, and Theoretical Crossroads*, 262–289, Cambridge: Cambridge University Press.

Requejo, F. (2005), *Multinational Federalism and Value Pluralism: The Spanish Case*, London: Routledge.

Reuters (2020), 'Sudan signs peace deal with key rebel groups', available online: https://af.reuters.com/article/commoditiesNews/idAFL8N2FW0KP (accessed 31 August 2020).

Rhodes, R.A.W. (1994), 'The hollowing out of the state: The changing nature of the public service in Britain', *The Political Quarterly*, 65(2), 138–151.

Richardson, J. and A. Jordan (1979), *Governing under Pressure*, London: Martin Robertson.

Riker, W. (1980), 'Implications from the disequilibrium of majority rule for the study of institutions', *American Political Science Review*, 75, 432–447.

Ripley, R.B. and G.A. Franklin (1987), *Congress, the Bureaucracy, and Public Policy*, Chicago, IL: Dorsey Press.

Risse, T. (2001), 'A European Identity? Europeanization and the Evolution of Nation-State Identities', in M.G.Cowles, J. Caporaso and T. Risse (eds), *Europeanization and Domestic Change*, 198–216, Ithaca, NY: Cornell University Press.

Rodrik, D. (2014), 'When ideas Trump interests: Preferences, worldviews, and policy innovations', *Journal of Economic Perspectives*, 28(1), 189–208.

Roe, E. (1994), *Narrative Policy Analysis*, Durham, NC: Duke University Press.

Rooduijn, M. (2013), 'The nucleus of populism: In search of the lowest common denominator', *Government and Opposition*, 49(4), 573–599.

Rooduijn, M. (2014), 'The mesmerising message: The diffusion of populism in public debates in Western European media', *Political Studies*, 62(4), 726–744.

Rooduijn, M. (2019), 'State of the field: How to study populism and adjacent topics? A plea for both more and less focus', *European Journal of Political Research*, 58(1), 362–372, doi:10.1111/1475-6765.12314.

Rose, N. (1999), *Powers of Freedom*, Cambridge: Cambridge University Press.

Rose, N. and P. Miller (1992), 'Political power beyond the state: Problematics of government', *British Journal of Sociology*, 43(2), 172–205.

Rosenau, J.N. (1990), *Turbulence in World Politics: A Theory of Change and Continuity*, Princeton, NJ: Princeton University Press.

Rothstein, B. (2005), *Social Traps and the Problem of Trust*, Cambridge: Cambridge University Press.

Rotmans, J., R. Kemp and M. van Asselt (2001), 'More evolution than revolution: Transition management in public policy', *Foresight*, 3(1), 15–31.

Rovinskiy, K. (2019), 'Artificial intelligence as a final verdict on old national elites', *Towards Data Science*, 23 April 2019, available online: https://towardsdatascience.com/artificial-intelligence-as-a-final-verdict-on-old-national-elites-58a6cb6575c2 (accessed 12 September 2020).

Rovira Kaltwasser, C. and P. Taggart (2016), 'Dealing with populists in government: A framework for analysis', *Democratization*, 23(2), 201–220.

Rudolph, J. and R. Thompson (1985), 'Ethnoterritorial movements and the policy process: Accommodating nationalist demands in the developed world', *Comparative Politics*, 17, 291–311.

Ruggie, John (1998), 'What makes the world hang together? Neo-utilitarianism and the social constructivist challenge', *International Organization*, 52(4), 855–885.

Rydgren, Jens (2018), 'The Radical Right: An Introduction', in J. Rydgren (ed.), *The Oxford Handbook of the Radical Right*, 1–14, Oxford: Oxford University Press.

Saari, M., J. Kantola and P.K. Sandberg (2021), 'Implementing equal pay policy: Clash between gender equality and corporatism', *Social Politics*, 28(2), 265–289.

Sabatier, P. and H.C. Jenkins-Smith (eds) (1993), *Policy Change and Learning: An Advocacy Coalition Approach*, Boulder, CO: Westview.

Sack, R. (1986), *Human Territoriality: Its Theory and History*, Cambridge: Cambridge University Press.

Sahlins, M. (1974), *Stone Age Economics*, New York: de Gruyter.

Said, E.W. (1975), *Beginnings: Intention and Method*, New York: Basic Books.

Said, E.W. (1993), *Culture and Imperialism*, New York: Knopf.

Sampson, A. (1962), *The Anatomy of Britain*, London: Hodder & Stoughton.

Sampson, A. (1982), *The Changing Anatomy of Britain*, London: Hodder & Stoughton).

Sanderson, J. (1963), 'Marx and Engels on the state', *The Western Political Quarterly*, 16(4), 946–955.

Sankey, K. (2018), 'Extractive capital, imperialism, and the Colombian state', *Latin American Perspectives*, 45(5), 52–70.

Saran, S. (2015), 'Paris climate talks: Developed countries must do more than reduce emissions', *The Guardian*, available online: https://www.theguardian.com/environment/2015/nov/23/paris-climate-talks-developed-countries-must-do-more-than-reduce-emissions (accessed 17 March 2022).

Sargent, L. (1981), 'New Left Women and Men: The Honeymoon is Over', in L. Sargent (ed.), *Women and Revolution: The Unhappy Marriage of Marxism and Feminism*, xi–xxxii, London: Pluto Press.

Sartori, G. (1970), 'Concept misformation in comparative politics', *American Political Science Review*, 64(4), 1033–1053, doi:10.2307/1958356.

Sass, J., *Remaking Monsanto: Commodification as Corporate Strategy*, New Haven; Yale University Press, forthcoming.

Sassen, S. (2006), *Territory, Authority, Rights: From Medieval to Global Assemblages*, Princeton, NJ: Princeton University Press.

Saurugger, S. (2010), 'The social construction of the participatory turn: The emergence of a norm in the European Union', *European Journal of Political Research*, 49(4), 471–495.

Scharpf, F.W. (1997), *Games Real Actors Play: Actor-Centered Institutionalism in Policy Research*, Boulder, CO: Westview Press.

Scharpf, Fritz W. (1999), *Governing in Europe,* Oxford: Oxford University Press.

Schelling, T.C. (1978), *Micromotives and Macrobehavior*, New York: Norton & Company.

Schlosberg, D. and C. Craven (2019), *Sustainable Materialism: Environmental Practice and the Politics of Everyday Life*, Oxford: Oxford University Press.

Schlosberg, D., K. Bäckstrand and J. Pickering (2019), 'Reconciling ecological and democratic values', *Environmental Values*, 28, 1–8.

Schmidt, V.A. (2000), 'Values and Discourse in the Politics of Adjustment', in F.W. Scharpf and V.A. Schmidt (eds), *Welfare and Work in the Open Economy*, Volume 1: *From Vulnerability to Competitiveness*, 229–310, Oxford: Oxford University Press.

Schmidt, V.A. (2002), *The Futures of European Capitalism*, Oxford: Oxford University Press.

Schmidt, V.A. (2006), *Democracy in Europe: The EU and National Polities*, Oxford: Oxford University Press.

Schmidt, V.A. (2008), 'Discursive institutionalism: The explanatory power of ideas *and* discourse', *Annual Review of Political Science*, 11, 303–326.

Schmidt, V.A. (2010), 'Taking ideas *and* discourse seriously: Explaining change through discursive institutionalism as the fourth new institutionalism', *European Political Science Review*, 2(1), 1–25.

Schmitter, P. (1985), 'Neo-Corporatism and the State', in W. Grant (ed.), *The Political Economy of Corporatism*, 32–62, London: Macmillan.

Schot, J. and F. Geels (2008), 'Strategic niche management and sustainable innovation journeys: Theory, findings, research agenda, and policy', *Technology Analysis & Strategic Management*, 20(5), 537–554.

Scoones, I., M. Leach and P. Newell (eds) (2015), *The Politics of Green Transformations*, London: Routledge.

Scotland Office (2015), *Scotland's Islands Areas: Guidelines for UK Government Departments*, Edinburgh: Scotland Office.

Scott, J. (1991), *Who Rules Britain?* Cambridge: Polity Press.

Scott, J.C. (1998), *Seeing Like a State: How Certain Schemes to Improve the Human Condition Have Failed*, New Haven, CT: Yale University Press.

Seabrooke, L. and D. Wigan (2016), 'Powering ideas through expertise: Professionals in global tax battles', *Journal of European Public Policy*, 23(3), 357–374.

Self, P. (1993), *Government by the Market? The Politics of Public Choice*, London: Macmillan.

Shennan, J.H. (1974), *The Origins of the Modern European State, 1450–1725*, London: Hutchinson.

Shepherd, L.J. (2007), '"Victims, perpetrators and actors" revisited: Exploring the potential for a feminist reconceptualisation of (international) security and (gender) violence', *The British Journal of Politics and International Relations*, 9(2), 239–256.

Shepherd, L.J. and J. Weldes (2008), 'Security: The State (of) Being Free from Danger?' in H.G. Brauch, Ú.O. Spring, C. Mesjasz et al. (eds), *Globalization and Environmental Challenges: Reconceptualizing Security in the 21st Century*, 529–536, Berlin; Heidelberg: Springer.

Shepsle, K. A. (1986), 'Institutional Equilibrium and Equilibrium Institutions', in H.F. Weisburg (ed.), *Political Science: The Science of Politics*, 51–81, New York: Agathon.

Shepsle, K. A. (2008), 'Rational Choice Institutionalism', in S.A. Binder, R.A.W. Rhodes and B.A. Rockman (eds), *The Oxford Handbook of Political Institutions*, 23–38, Oxford: Oxford University Press.

Shilliam, R. (2021, *Decolonizing Politics: An Introduction*, Oxford: Polity Press.

Siemiatycki, M. (2005), 'Beyond moving people: Excavating the motivations for investing in urban public transit infrastructure in Bilbao Spain', *European Planning Studies*, 13, 23–44.

Siim, B. (1988), 'Towards a Feminist Rethinking of the Welfare State', in K. Jones and A. Jónasdóttir (eds), *The Political Interests of Gender*, 160–186, Oxford: SAGE Publications.

Simmons, R.T. (2011), *Beyond Politics: The Roots of Government Failure*, Oakland, CA: Independent Institute.

Simms, B. and D. Trim (eds) (2011), *Humanitarian Intervention: A History*, Cambridge: Cambridge University Press.

Skinner, Q. (1978), *The Foundations of Modern Political Thought. Volume 1: The Renaissance*, Cambridge: Cambridge University Press.

Skinner, Q. (1989), 'The State', in T. Ball et al. (eds), *Political Innovation and Conceptual Change*, 90–131, Cambridge: Cambridge University Press.

Skinner, Q. (2008), *Hobbes and Republican Liberty*, Cambridge: Cambridge University Press.

Skocpol, T. (1979), *States and Social Revolutions*, Cambridge: Cambridge University Press.

Skocpol, T. (1985), 'Bringing the State Back In: Strategies of Analysis in Current Research', in P. Evans, D. Rueschemeyer and T. Skocpol (eds), *Bringing the State Back In*, 3–37, New York: Cambridge University Press.

Skogstad, G. (2019) 'Global Public Policy and the Constitution of Political Authority', in D. Stone and K. Maloney (eds), *The Oxford Handbook of Global Policy and Administration*, 23–40, Oxford: Oxford University Press.

Skowronek, S. (1982), *Building a New American State: The Expansion of National Administrative Capacities 1877–1920*, Cambridge: Cambridge University Press.

Smith, A. (1776), *An Inquiry into the Nature and Causes of the Wealth of Nations*, Oxford: Clarendon Press.

Smith, A. and F. Kern (2009), 'The transitions storyline in Dutch environmental policy', *Environmental Politics*, 18(1), 78–98.

Smith, A. and A. Stirling (2010), 'The politics of social-ecological resilience and sustainable socio-technical transitions', *Ecology and Society*, 15(1), 11, available online: http://www.ecologyandsociety.org/vol15/iss1/art11/ (accessed 17 March 2022).

Smith, A., J.-P. Voss and J. Grin (2010), 'Innovation studies and sustainability transitions: The allure of the multi-level perspective and its challenges', *Research Policy*, 39, 435–448.

Smith, A.D. (1986), *The Ethnic Origins of Nations*, Oxford: Blackwell.

Smith, A.D. (1991), *National Identity*, London: Penguin.

Smith, A.D. (1998), *Nationalism and Modernism: A Critical Survey of Recent Theories of Nations and Nationalism*: London; New York: Routledge.

Smith, A.D. (2000), *The Nation in History: Historiographical Debates about Ethnicity and Nationalism*, Cambridge: Polity Press.

Smith, A.D. (2002), 'When is a nation?' *Geopolitics*, 7(2), 5–32.

Smith, C. (2006), *Adam Smith's Political Philosophy: The Invisible Hand and Spontaneous Order*, London: Routledge.

Smith, M. J. (2015), 'From consensus to conflict: Thatcher and the transformation of politics', *British Politics*, 10(1), 64–78.

Solomon, S.G. (1983), *Pluralism in the Soviet Union*, New York: Springer.

Sommerer, T. and S. Lim (2016), 'The environmental state as a model for the world? An analysis of policy repertoires in 37 countries', *Environmental Politics*, 25(1), 92–115.

Sorens, J. (2008), 'Regionalists against secession: The political economy of territory in advanced democracies', *Nationalism and Ethnic Politics*, 14(3), 325–360.

Soysal, Y. (1994), *Limits of Citizenship*, Chicago, IL: University of Chicago Press.

Spaargaren, G. and A.P.J. Mol (2010), 'Sociology, Environment, and Modernity: Ecological Modernisation as a Theory of Social Change', in A. Mol, D. Sonnenfeld and G. Spaargaren (eds), *The Ecological Modernisation Reader*, 56–79, London: Routledge.

Stanley, B. (2008), 'The thin ideology of populism', *Journal of Political Ideologies*, 13(1), 95–110, doi:10.1080/13569310701822289.

Steffen, W., K. Richardson, J. Rockström, S.E. Cornell, I. Fetzer, E.M. Bennett and C. Folke (2015), 'Planetary boundaries: Guiding human development on a changing planet', *Science*, 347(6223), 1259855.

Steinmo, S., K. Thelen and F. Longstreth (eds) (1992), *Structuring Politics: Historical Institutionalism in Comparative Analysis*, Cambridge: Cambridge University Press.

Stoker, G. and M. Evans (2014), 'The democracy-politics paradox: The dynamics of political alienation', *Democracy Theory*, 1(2), 26–36.

Stoker, G. and C. Hay (2016), 'Understanding and challenging populist negativity towards politics: The perspectives of British citizens', *Political Studies*, 65(1), 4–23.

Stone, D.A. (1988), *Policy Paradox and Political Reason*, Glenview, IL: Scot Foresman.

Stone, D. (2004), 'Transfer agents and global networks in the "transnationalization" of policy', *European Journal of Public Policy*, 11(3), 545–566.

Stone, D. (2012), 'Transfer and translation of policy', *Policy Studies*, 33(6), 483–499.

Stone, D. and S. Ladi (2015) 'Global public policy and transnational administration', *Public Administration*, 93(4), 839–855.

Stone, D. and K. Maloney (eds) (2019a), *The Oxford Handbook of Global Policy and Administration*, Oxford: Oxford University Press.

Stone, D. and K. Maloney (2019b), 'The Rise of Global Policy and Transnational Administration', in D. Stone and K. Maloney (eds), *The Oxford Handbook of Global Policy and Administration*, 3–22, Oxford: Oxford University Press.

Streeck, W. (2014), *Buying Time: The Delayed Crisis of Democratic Capitalism*, London: Verso.

Streeck, W. and K. Thelen (2005), 'Introduction: Institutional Change in Advanced Political Economies', in W. Streeck and K. Thelen (eds), *Beyond Continuity*, 1–39, Oxford: Oxford University Press.

Stringham, E. (2005), *Anarchy, State and Public Choice*, Cheltenham: Edward Elgar.

Stripple, J. and H. Bulkeley (2013), *Governing the Climate: New Approaches to Rationality, Power and Politics*, Cambridge: Cambridge University Press.

Sweezy, P. (1942), *The Theory of Capitalist Development*, New York: Monthly Review Press.

Swyngedouw, E. (2015), *Liquid Power: Contested Hydro-Modernities in Twentieth-Century Spain*, Cambridge, MA: MIT Press.

Sylvester, C. (1994), *Feminist Theory and International Relations in a Postmodern Era*, Cambridge: Cambridge University Press.

Taggart, P. (2000), *Populism*, Buckingham: Open University Press.

Taggart, P. (2002), 'Populism and the Pathology of Representative Politics', in Y. Mény and Y. Surel (eds), *Democracies and the Populist Challenge*, 62–80, London: Palgrave Macmillan.

Taggart, P. (2004), 'Populism and representative politics in contemporary Europe', *Journal of Political Ideologies*, 9(3), 269–288, doi:10.1080/13569310 42000263528.

Tamir, Y. (1993), *Liberal Nationalism*, Princeton, NJ: Princeton University Press.

Tamir, Y. (2019), *Why Nationalism*, Princeton, NJ and Oxford: Princeton University Press.

Tarrow, S.G. (1998), *Power in Movement: Social Movements and Contentious Politics*, Cambridge: Cambridge University Press.

Tarrow, S.G. (2011), *Power in Movement: Social Movements and Contentious Politics*, 3rd edn, Cambridge Studies in Comparative Politics, Cambridge: Cambridge University Press.

Taylor, C. (1993), *Reconciling the Solitudes: Essays on Canadian Federalism and Nationalism*, Montreal and Kingston: McGill-Queen's University Press.

Taylor, C. (1996), 'Nationalism and Modernity', in J.A. Hall (ed.), *The State of the Nation*, 191–218, Cambridge: Cambridge University Press.

Taylor-Gooby, P. (ed.) (2004), *New Risks, New Welfare: The Transformation of the European Welfare State*, Oxford: Oxford University Press.

Teichman, J. (2007), 'Multilateral lending institutions and transnational policy networks in Mexico and Chile', *Global Governance*, 13, 557–573.

Teo, T.-A. and E. Wynne-Hughes (eds) (2020), *Postcolonial Governmentalities: Rationalities, Violences and Contestations*, London: Rowman & Littlefield International.

Teräväinen-Litardo, T. (2015) 'Negotiating green growth as a pathway towards sustainable transitions in Finland', in K. Bäckstrand and A. Kronsell (eds), *Rethinking the Green State: Environmental Governance towards Climate and Sustainability Transitions*, 174–190, London: Routledge.

Teschke, B. (2009) *The Myth of 1648: Class, Geopolitics and the Making of Modern International Relations*, London: Verso.

Teson, F. and van der Vossen, B. (2017) *Debating Humanitarian Intervention: Should We Try To Save Strangers?* Oxford: Oxford University Press.

Thelen, K. (1999), 'Historical Institutionalism in Comparative Politics', in *The Annual Review of Political Science*, Vol. 2, 369–404, Palo Alto, CA: Annual Reviews, Inc.

Thelen, K. (2004), *How Institutions Evolve: The Political Economy of Skills in Germany, Britain, the United States, and Japan*, New York: Cambridge University Press.

Thelen, K. and J. Conran (2016), 'Institutional Change', in O. Fioretos, T.G. Falleti and A. Sheingate (eds), *Oxford Handbook of Historical Institutionalism*, 51–70, Oxford: Oxford University Press.

Thomas, C. (1987), *In Search of Security: The Third World in International Relations*, Boulder, CO: Lynne Rienner.

Thomas, M.W. (1948), *The Early Factory Legislation: A Study in Legislative and Administrative Evolution*, Leigh-on-Sea: Thames Bank Publishing Company.

Thompson, M. (2012), 'Foucault, fields of governability and the population-family-economy nexus in China', *History and Theory*, 51, 42–62.

Thrift, N. (2000), 'Introduction: Dead or Alive?', in I. Cook, D. Crouch, S. Naylor and J.R. Ryan (eds), *Cultural Turns/Geographical Turns: Perspectives on Cultural Geography*, 1–6, Harlow: Prentice Hall.

Thrift, N. (2004), 'Intensities of feeling: Towards a spatial politics of affect', *Geografiska Annaler Series B: Human Geography*, 86, 57–78.

Thrift, N. and S. French (2002), 'The automatic production of space', *Transactions of the Institute of British Geographers*, 27, 309–335.

Tickner, J.A. (1995), 'Re-visioning Security', in K. Booth and S. Smith (eds), *International Relations Theory Today*, 175–197, Oxford: Polity.

Tickner, J.A. (1997), 'You just don't understand: Troubled engagements between feminists and IR theorists', *International Studies Quarterly*, 41(4), 611–632.

Tilly, C. (ed.) (1975), *The Formation of National States in Western Europe*, Princeton, NJ: Princeton University Press.

Tims, H. and H. Heimans (2018), *New Power: Why Outsiders are Winning, Institutions are Failing, and How the Rest of Us Can Keep Up in the Age of Mass Participation*, London: Pan Macmillan.

Tobin, P. (2015), 'Blue and Yellow Makes Green? Ecological Modernization in Swedish Climate Policy', in K. Bäckstrand and A. Kronsell (eds), *Rethinking the Green State: Environmental Governance towards Climate and Sustainability Transitions*, 141–155, London: Routledge.

Tobin, P. (2017), 'Leaders and laggards: Climate policy ambition in developed states', *Global Environmental Politics*, 17(4), 28–47.

Tol, G. and A. Alemdaroglu (2020), 'Turkey's Generation Z turns against Erdogan', *Foreign Policy*, 15 July 2020, available online: https://foreignpolicy.com/2020/07/15/turkey-youth-education-erdogan/ (accessed 13 September 2020).

Tonder, L. and L. Thomassen (eds) (2014), *Radical Democracy: Between Abundance and Lack*, Manchester: Manchester University Press.

Tooze, A. (2018), *Crashed: How a Decade of Financial Crises Changed the World*, London: Allen Lane.

Torfing, J. (1991), 'A Hegemony Approach to Capitalist Regulation', in R.B. Bertramsen, J.P.F. Thomsen and J. Torfing (eds), *State, Economy and Society*, 35–93, London: Unwin Hyman.

Tripp, Aili Mari (2001), 'The politics of autonomy and cooptation in Africa: The case of the Ugandan women's movement', *Journal of Modern African Studies*, 39(1), 101–128.

Truman, D.B. (1951), *The Governmental Process*, New York: Alfred A. Knopf.

Tsebelis, G. (2002), *Veto Players: How Political Institutions Work*, Princeton, NJ: Princeton University Press.

Tuck, R. (1979), *Natural Rights Theories: Their Origins and Development*, Cambridge: Cambridge University Press.

Tuck, R. (2016), *The Sleeping Sovereign*, Cambridge: Cambridge University Press.

Tullock, G. (1965), *The Politics of Bureaucracy*, Washington, DC: Public Affairs Press.

Tullock, G. (1967), 'The welfare costs of tariffs, monopolies, and theft', *Economic Inquiry*, 5(3), 224–232.

Tullock, G. (1989), *The Economics of Special Privilege and Rent Seeking*, Boston, MA: Kluwer.

Tullock, G., A. Seldon and G.L. Brady (2002), *Government Failure: A Primer in Public Choice*, Washington, DC: Cato Institute.

Turnbull, N. (2013), 'The questioning theory of policy practice: Outline of an integrated analytical framework', *Critical Policy Studies*, 7, 115–131.

United Nations (UN) (1976), *International Covenant on Civil and Political Rights*. Adopted and opened for signature, ratification and accession by General Assembly resolution 2200A (XXI) of 16 December 1966, entry into force 23 March 1976, in accordance with Article 49. Available online: http://www.ohchr.org/EN/ProfessionalInterest/Pages/CCPR.aspx (accessed 17 March 2022).

UN (2020), 'Secretary-General highlights "essential" failure of international cooperation', in Address to Security Council Meeting on Post-Coronavirus Global Governance', available online: https://www.un.org/press/en/2020/sc14312.doc.htm (accessed 17 March 2022).

UNEP (2012), *UNEP Global Environmental Alert Service: Taking the Pulse of the Planet, Connecting Science with Policy*, available online: http://na.unep.net/geas/archive/pdfs/GEAS_Jun_12_Carrying_Capacity.pdf (accessed 17 March 2022).

Usher, M. (2018), 'Conduct of conduits: Engineering, desire and government through the enclosure and exposure of urban water', *International Journal of Urban and Regional Research*, 42(2), 315–333.

van den Berg, A. (1988), *The Immanent Utopia: From Marxism on the State to the State of Marxism*, Princeton, NJ: Princeton University Press.

van den Bergh, J.C.J.M. (2011), 'Environment vs. growth: A criticism of "degrowth" and a plea for "a-growth"', *Ecological Economics*, 70(5), 881–890.

Van den Berghe, P. (1994), 'A Socio-Biological Perspective', in A.D. Smith and J. Hutchinson (eds), *Nationalism*, 96–102, Oxford: Oxford Readers.

Vaughan-Williams, N. (2009), *Border Politics: The Limits of Sovereign Power*, Edinburgh: Edinburgh University Press.

Verloo, Mieke (ed.) (2018), *Varieties of Opposition to Gender Equality in Europe*, London: Routledge.

Victor, P.A. (2008), *Managing without Growth: Slower by Design, Not Disaster*, Cheltenham: Edward Elgar.

Viroli, M. (1992), *From Politics to Reason of State: The Acquisition and Transformation of the Language of Politics 1250–1600*, Cambridge: Cambridge University Press.

Visvanathan, N., L. Duggan, L. Nisonoff and N. Wiegersma (eds) (1997), *The Women, Gender and Development Reader*, London: Zed Books.

Vogel, D. (1987), 'Political science and the study of corporate power: A dissent from the new conventional wisdom', *British Political Science*, 17, 385–408.

Vogel, D. (1989), *Fluctuating Fortunes: The Political Power of Business in America*, New York: Basic Books.

Vogel, D. (2005), *The Market for Virtue: The Potential and Limits of Corporate Social Responsibility*, Washington, DC: Brookings Institution Press.

Voss, J-P. and B. Bornemann (2011), 'The politics of reflexive governance: Challenges for designing adaptive management and transition management', *Ecology and Society*, 16(2), 9, available online: http://www.ecologyandsociety.org/vol16/iss2/art9/ (accessed 17 March 2022).

Wagner, R.E. and J.D. Gwartney (1988), 'Public Choice and Constitutional Order', in J.D. Gwartney and R.E. Wagner (eds), *Public Choice and Constitutional Economics*, 29–56, New York: JAI Press.

Wahlke, J.C. (1979), 'Pre-behavioralism in political science', *American Political Science Review*, 73(1), 9–31.

Wainwright, H. (1994), *Arguments for a New left*, 291–311, Oxford: Blackwell.

Walker, R.B.J. (1993), *Inside/Outside: International Relations as Political Theory* Cambridge: Cambridge University Press.

Walker, R.B.J. (1997), 'The Subject of Security', in K. Krause and M.C. Williams (eds), *Critical Security Studies: Concepts and Cases*, 61–81, Minneapolis: University of Minnesota Press.

Waltz, K. ([1959] 2018), *Man, the State, and War*, New York: Columbia University Press.

Waltz, K. (1979), *Theory of International Politics*, Reading, MA: Addison-Wesley.

Walzer, M. (2002), 'Nation-States and Immigrant Societies', in W. Kymlicka and M. Opalski (eds), *Can Liberal Pluralism be Exported?*, 150–153, Oxford: Oxford University Press.

Ward, H. (1987), Structural power – A contradiction in terms? *Political Studies*, 35(4), 593–610.

Washington Post (2020), 'COVID-19 infecting, killing black Americans at alarmingly high rate, analysis shows', 7 April, available online: https://www.washingtonpost.com/nation/2020/04/07/coronavirus-is-infecting-killing-black-americans-an-alarmingly-high-rate-post-analysis-shows/ (accessed 17 March 2022).

Weale, A. (2018), *The Will of the People: A Modern Myth*, Cambridge: Polity Press.

Weber, M. (1946), 'Politics as a Vocation', in H.H. Gerth and C.W. Mills (eds),*From Max Weber: Essays in Sociology*, 77–128, New York: Oxford University Press.

Weber, M. (1978), *Economy and Society: An Outline of Interpretative Sociology*, Berkeley: University of California Press.

Weiss, T.G. (2016), *Humanitarian Intervention*, 3rd edn, Cambridge: Polity Press.

Weldes, J. (1999), *Constructing National Interests: The United States and the Cuban Missile Crisis*, Minneapolis: University of Minnesota Press.

Wendt, A. (1987), 'The agent-structure problem in international relations theory', *International Organization*, 41(3), 335–370.

Wendt, A. (1999), *Social Theory of International Relations Theory*, Cambridge: Cambridge University Press.

Weyland, K. (2013), 'The threat from the populist left', *Journal of Democracy*, 24(3), 18–32, doi:10.1353/jod.2013.0045.

Wheeler, N.J. (2000), *Saving Strangers*, Oxford: Oxford University Press.

White, D. (2019), 'Ecological democracy, just transitions and a political ecology of design', *Environmental Values*, 28(1), 31–53.

Whitehead, M., B. Barr and B. Taylor-Robinson (2020), 'Covid-19: We are not "all in it together" – less privileged in society are suffering the brunt of the damage', BMJ Opinion, available online: https://blogs.bmj.com/bmj/2020/05/22/covid-19-we-are-not-all-in-it-together-less-privileged-in-society-are-suffering-the-brunt-of-the-damage/ (accessed 17 March 2022).

Widmaier, W.W. (2016), *Economic Ideas in Political Time: The Construction, Conversion and Crisis of Economic Orders from the Progressive Era to the Global Financial Crisis*, Cambridge: Cambridge University Press.

Wieringa, S. (2002), *Sexual Politics in Indonesia*, London; New York: Palgrave Macmillan.

Wilkinson, R. and K. Pickett (2010), *The Spirit Level: Why Equality is Better for Everyone*, London: Penguin.

Williams, C. and A. Smith (1983), 'The national construction of social space', *Progress in Human Geography*, 7, 502–518.

Winchester, S. (1981), *Their Noble Lordships*, London: Faber & Faber.

Wittgenstein, L. (1958), *Philosophical Investigations*, Oxford: Blackwell.

Wolfe, A. (1974), 'New directions in the Marxist theory of politics', *Politics and Society*, 4(2), 131–160.

Wolfe, A. (1977), *The Limits of Legitimacy: Political Contradictions of Late Capitalism*, New York: Free Press.

Wolfe, J. and A. DeVeaux (2020), 'How fast is the economy recovering?' *FiveThirtyEight*, available online: https://projects.fivethirtyeight.com/us-economy-coronavirus/ (accessed 17 March 2022).

Woll, C. (2008), *Firm Interests: How Governments Shape Business Lobbying on Global Trade*, Ithaca, NY: Cornell University Press.

Wood, M. (2015), 'Depoliticisation, resilience and the herceptin post-code lottery crisis: Holding back the tide', *The British Journal of Politics and International Relations*, 17(4), 644–664.

Woods, E.T., R. Schertzer, L. Greenfeld, C. Hughes and C. Miller-Idriss (2020), 'COVID-19, nationalism, and the politics of crisis: A scholarly exchange', *Nations and Nationalism*, 26, (4): 807–825.

Wurzel, R. and J. Connelly (eds) (2011) *The European Union as a Leader in International Climate Change Politics*, London: Routledge.

Yack, B. (2012), *Nationalism and the Moral Psychology of Community*, Chicago, IL: University of Chicago Press.

Yuval-Davis, N. (1997), *Gender and Nation*, London: SAGE.

Žižek, S. (2021), 'Is barbarism with a human face our fate?' *Critical Enquiry*, 47(S2), s4–s8.

Zunes, S. (2005), 'Hurricane Katrina and the war in Iraq', *Foreign Policy in Focus*, available online: https://fpif.org/hurricane_katrina_and_the_war_in_iraq/ (accessed 17 March 2022).

Zysman, J. (1994), 'How institutions create historically rooted trajectories of growth', *Industrial and Corporate Change*, 3(1), 243–283.

Index